COLLEGE STUDENT PERSONNEL DEVELOPMENT, ADMINISTRATION, AND COUNSELING
Second Edition

John Eddy
Joseph D. Dameron
David T. Borland

University Press of America™

Library of Congress Catalog Card Number: 80-5761

Table of Contents

COLLEGE STUDENT PERSONNEL
DEVELOPMENT, ADMINISTRATION AND COUNSELING
(Second Edition)

i

ii

iii

A second edition of any book in the area of college student personnel development, administration and counseling is
undertaken only when the original text has found wide acceptance among professionals. In a field as broad and diverse
as college student personnel, published books that have not
made major contributions to the literature are soon relegated
to a slot on the bookshelf, to be utilized only as an occa-
sional reference. Fortunately, the first edition of this
book did indeed make a major contribution, and since all
knowledge must be placed in the context of a dynamic and everchanging profession, a second edition is both welcome and
essential.

While the editors are accurate in reflecting the Carnegie
Council's view that the next two decades will be "golden ones"
for students, the years ahead may not have the same luster
for college student personnel professionals. Declining
enrollments, public criticism of higher education, decreased
Federal support, and a "Proposition 13" mentality among the
legislators who control our financial destiny are ominous
signs that we face a new and entirely different set of problems and concerns. The activism of the 1960s and early 1970s,
precipitated in part by the Vietnam war, no longer occupies
the minds and dictates the actions of young men and women.
In place of riots and protests, one now finds a calm (some
may even call it apathy) among college students. While students are still concerned with such issues as nuclear power
and minority rights, much of their behavior has shifted from
group activities and values to a more idiosyncratic style
that stresses individual goals and accomplishments. The
college personnel professionals, therefore, who were the vanguard in dealing with campus unrest, must now be able to deal
with less volatile, if no less demanding, tasks.

The second edition of this book is designed to help professionals meet those new challenges. While the focus and
theme of these writings is still one of aiding the professional development of present and future staff members, the
theoretical concerns of the earlier book have been skillfully
blended with the pragmatic problems of modern institutions of

higher education. Present concerns such as academic achievement, minority rights, residence hall counseling centers, leadership, administration, evaluation, research, and student retention are given ample space in this revision. To reflect the changing times, twenty new contributions, drawn from the national talent pool, have added comprehensive and insightful material to further expand and enhance the concepts advanced in the original edition.

The editors of this text are individuals with extensive background and experience in the field of college student personnel. Each has "grown up" with the profession, and all have been actively involved as teachers, writers, and working professionals since the late 1950s. Dr. Joe Dameron has long been a counselor-educator who has had extensive community and senior college experience. Dr. Dave Borland has been a college personnel administrator who currently serves as President of the American College Personnel Association. Dr. John Eddy is an acknowledged expert on career education who has a wealth of experience in grantsmanship and an active involvement in the American Personnel and Guidance Association. Their training and experience enables them to identify and bring together in a single volume the works of some of our most respected writers. Through their efforts, the reader will be led through the historical and professional developments of the field as well as through the development of the academic discipline. In addition, students and personnel workers will be able to review occupational, career, legal, in-service, organizational, evaluational, and research developments. The final section of the book provides material for conclusions and future directions.

In summary, this is a concise, yet meaningful work. It is well written, well documented, and it provides a focus for the critical issues that face the profession. It is a book that deserves the study and attention of all who dedicate themselves to the advancement of student personnel work.

James J. Muro
Dean, College of Education
North Texas State University
Denton, Texas
June, 1980

CONTRIBUTORS AND THEIR WRITINGS

ACKNOWLEDGEMENTS

Appreciation is expressed to the following authors or periodical and book editors for their contributions to this volume. Their copyrights and academic knowledgements are fully recognized and cited here from the following publications. The rights of these publications are fully protected by their copyrights.

Carolyn T. Augren, Counselor, Richland Community College, Dallas, Texas. Co-author with Joseph D. Dameron and John C. Wolfe, "Role Specification in Selection and Training of the Resident Assistant."

Jay Barnes, Dean of Students, Messiah College, Grantham, Pennsylvania. Co-author with John Eddy and Steve Murphy, "Values Education and the College Student Development Administrator."

Edward C. Bonk, Professor of Counselor Education, North Texas State University, Denton, Texas, "Affirmation."

David T. Borland, Associate Professor of Higher Education and Student Affairs Administration, North Texas State University, Denton, Texas, "Organizational Facilitation of Student Affairs," "Leadership and Management in Student Affairs," and co-author with John Eddy, "Student Affairs Administration: A Synthesis of Human Development, Institutional Development, and Management.

Betty J. Bosdell, Professor of Counselor Education, Northern Illinois University, Dekalb, Illinois, co-author with David V. Tiedeman, Walter Wernick, and John Eddy, "Career Education--Refocusing Education for Career Development," in Career Education Primer for Educators, Dekalb, Illinois. ERIC Clearinghouse for Career Education at Northern Illinois University, 1975.

CONTRIBUTORS AND THEIR WRITINGS - ACKNOWLEDGEMENTS

William A. Bryan, Vice President for Student Affairs, University of North Dakota, Grand Forks, North Dakota, co-author with John Eddy and Audrey L. Rentz, "Evaluation of College Student Affairs Divisions and Services."

Peter Cimbolic, Associate Professor of Psychology, North Texas State University, Denton, Texas, "A Model of Counseling Supervision," and co-author with John Eddy, Sheldon Siegel, and Joseph D. Dameron, "The Use of Counseling Theories in College Student Personnel Work."

Judity A. Cochran, Assistant Professor of Secondary Education, North Texas State University, Denton, Texas, co-author with John Eddy and Charles Haney, "College Student Retention Studies and Strategies."

Ina A. Couthen, Associate Professor of Education, Texas A&M University, College Station, Texas, co-author with Robert R. Reilly, "The Literature of College Student Personnel--A Sample," Journal of College Student Personnel, September, 1976.

Burns B. Crookston (deceased), Professor of Education, University of Connecticut, Storrs, Connecticut. "Student Personnel--All Hail and Farewell," Journal of Personnel and Guidance, September, 1976.

Joseph D. Dameron, Professor of Counselor Education and Student Services Administration, North Texas State University, Denton, Texas, co-author with Carolyn T. Aguren and John C. Wolf, "Role Specification in Selection and Training of the Resident Assistant."

Josiah Dilley, Professor of Counseling, University of Wisconsin, Madison, Wisconsin, "Case Studies and Decision Making," Higher Education: Participants Confronted, Dubuque, William Brown Press, 1970.

ix

John Eddy, Professor of Counselor Education and Student Services Administration, Denton, Texas, co-author with William D. Peterson and Griff D. Pitts, "Historical Perspectives of College Student Personnel Work;" co-author with Sheldon Siegel, "Status of the College Student Personnel Field: Defining the Profession;" co-author with Peter Cimbolic, Sheldon Siegel, and Joseph D. Dameron, "The Use of Counseling Theories in College Student Personnel Work;" co-author with James R. Jacobson, "Models for Personal Growth and Development," "The Future of College Student Personnel in Professional Careers," "Obtaining Employment in College Student Personnel;" co-author with Jay Barnes and Steve Murphy, "Values Education and the College Student Development Administrator," "Carl Rogers' New Insight," "Some Legal Aspects of College Student Personnel Work;" co-author with David T. Borland, "Student Affairs Administration;" co-author with William A. Bryan and Audrey L. Rentz, "Evaluation of College Student Affairs Divisions and Services," "Minority Person Contributions to College Student Personnel;" co-author with Mark Sohn, "College Student Directed Campus Programs," "Myth of the Problem Free Practicum," "Effective Practicum Communication is Essential," "Competency Based Program for College Student Personnel Development;" co-author with Sheldon Siegel, "Practicum Action Communication (PAC)," "Systems Approach to Practicum Placement," "A Guide for Educational Administrators, Counselors, and Teachers," "Human Behavior Values, Professional Experience and Life Development," "Look Ahead and Behind--A Mirror Approach;" co-author with Judith Cochran and Charles Haney, "College Student Retention Studies and Strategies;" and co-author with C. Alan Siebenthall and Jackson Eng, "An Example of Handling Student Crisis Situations."

Jackson Eng, Counselor and Associate Professor of Psychology, South Campus, Tarrant County Junior College District, Fort Worth, Texas, co-author with John Eddy and C. Alan Siebenthall, "An Example of Handling Student Crisis Situations."

CONTRIBUTORS AND THEIR WRITINGS - ACKNOWLEDGEMENTS

Barbara Gawinski, Program Director, Girl Scouts of America, Denton, Texas, co-author with Donald Martin, "Developing Leadership Skills in Student Development Staff."

Elizabeth A. Greenleaf (deceased), Professor of Education, Indiana University, Bloomington, Indiana, "Assessment of Practical Experiences for Student Personnel Development."

Charles Haney, Research Associate, Department of Counselor Education, North Texas State University, Denton, Texas, co-author with John Eddy and Judith Cochran, "College Student Retention Studies and Strategies."

Richard Harpel, Assistant Vice Chancellor for Academic Affairs, University of Colorado at Boulder, Boulder, Colorado, "Planning, Budgeting, and Evaluation in Student Affairs Programs," NASPA Journal, Summer, 1976.

Edwin L. Herr, Professor of Counseling, Penn State University, University Park, Pennsylvania, "Research in Guidance and Counseling," Phi Delta Kappa Research Issue, Summer, 1977.

Paul G. Hill, Professor of Psychology and Counseling, Governors State University, Park Forest, Illinois, "Humanized Student Personnel Services."

James R. Jacobson, Minister, First United Methodist Church, Indio, California, co-author with John Eddy, "Models for Personnel Development" from "Models for Child Development," How to Grow Today's Children, James R. Jacobson, New York, Exposition Press, 1975.

Ernest Jaski, Professor of Education and Business Administration, Richard Daley College, Chicago, Illinois, co-author with John Eddy, "A Student Information System," Journal of College Student Personnel, November, 1976; co-author with John Eddy, "Example of Career Counseling Project."

xi

CONTRIBUTORS AND THEIR WRITINGS - ACKNOWLEDGEMENTS

Joyse S. Kennedy, Distinguished Professor of Psychology and Counseling, Governors State University, Park Forest, Illinois, "Creative Career Counseling: Perspectives on Personnel Services for Minority Students."

Virginia Kirkbride, Former Chairperson of Committee on Professional Development of NAWDC, "Practicum Experience in the Masters Degree Program for Personnel Work," NADWC Journal, Winter, 1971.

Robert K. Luther, Dean for Student Development, Henderson State College, Arkadelphia, Arkansas, co-author with Virginia M. Smith, "A Functional Model for Career Development," NASPA Journal, Spring, 1974.

Harold R. Marquardt, Professor of College Student Personnel, Bowling Green State University, Bowling Green, Ohio, co-author with Gerald L. Saddlemire, "Practicums and Internships."

Donald Martin, Director of Kerr Residence Hall, North Texas State University, Denton, Texas, co-author with Barbara Gawinski, "Developing Leadership Skills in Student Development Staff."

James J. Muro, Dean of the College of Education, North Texas State University, Denton, Texas, "Foreword."

William D. Peterson, Vice President for Student Development, Whitworth College, Spokane, Washington, co-author with John Eddy and Griff D. Pitts, "Historical Perspectives of College Student Personnel."

Griff D. Pitts, Counselor, Northeastern Illinois University, Chicago, Illinois, co-author with William D. Peterson and John Eddy, "Historical Perspectives of College Student Personnel."

Robert R. Reilly, Associate Professor of Education, Texas A&M University, College Station, Texas, co-author with Ira A. Couthen, "The Literature of College Student Personnel-- A Sample." Journal of College Student Personnel, September, 1976.

CONTRIBUTORS AND THEIR WRITINGS - ACKNOWLEDGEMENTS

Audrey L. Rentz, Associate Professor of College Student Personnel, Bowling Green State University, Bowling Green, Ohio, co-author with William A. Bryan and John Eddy, "Evaluation of College Student Affairs Divisions and Services."

George P. Robb, Professor of Counselor Education, North Texas State University, Denton, Texas, "Research in College Student Personnel Services."

Donald W. Robinson, Dean of the College of Education, Oklahoma State University, Stillwater, Oklahoma, "The Student Personnel Function in American Higher Education," American Journal of Pharmaceutical Education, Winter, 1963.

Gerald L. Saddlemire, Professor of College Student Personnel, Bowling Green State University, Bowling Green, Ohio, "Training Students for Practicums."

C. Alan Siebenthall, Counselor and Professor of Psychology, South Campus, Tarrant County Junior College District, Fort Worth Texas, co-author with John Eddy and Jackson Eng, "An Example of Handling Student Crisis Situations."

Sheldon Siegel, Dean of Students, Illinois College of Optometry, Chicago, Illinois, co-author with John Eddy, "Practicum Checklist for Students" and "Status of the College Student Personnel Field."

Virginia M. Smith, Assistant Dean for Student Development, Henderson State College, Arkadelphia, Arkansas, co-author with Robert K. Luther, "A Functional Model for Career Development," NASPA Journal, Spring, 1974.

Mark Sohn, Assistant Professor of Education, Morehead State University, Morehead, Kentucky, co-author with John Eddy, "College Student Directed Campus Programs: Example in Drug Education."

xiii

CONTRIBUTORS AND THEIR WRITINGS - ACKNOWLEDGEMENTS

David V. Tiedeman, Professor of Education, Northern Illinois
University, Dekalb, Illinois, co-author with Betty J.
Bosdell, Walter Wernick, and John Eddy, "Career Educa-
tion--Refocusing Education for Career Development,"
Career Education Primer for Educators, Dekalb, ERIC
Clearinghouse for Career Education at Northern Illinois
University, 1975.

Walter Wernick, Professor of Education, Northern Illinois
University, Dekalb, Illinois, co-author with David V.
Tiedeman, Betty J. Bosdell, and John Eddy, "Career
Education--Refocusing Education for Career Development,"
Career Education Primer for Educators, Dekalb, ERIC
Clearinghouse for Career Education at Northern Illinois
University, 1975.

John C. Wolf, Counseling Psychologist, Vererans Administration, Lubbock, Texas, co-author with Joseph D. Dameron
and Carolyn T. Aguren, "Role Specification in Selection
and Training of the Resident Assistant."

AUTHORS' ACKNOWLEDGEMENTS

Appreciation is expressed to all contributors that are listed in the Contributors Section and to the journal and book editors and/or publishers who released the following materials that the authors had previously published in these journals and books:

Dameron, Joseph D., and Wolf, John C. "Academic Advisement in Higher Education: A New Model." Journal of College Student Personnel, November, 1974.

Eddy, J., and Jaski, E. "A Student Information System." Journal of College Student Personnel, November, 1976.

Eddy, J., and Jaski, E. "Career Counseling and Job Placement: Colleges and Businesses Work Together." Journal of College Student Personnel, July, 1978.

Eddy, J. Campus Religious Affairs. New York: Simon and Schuster, 1969.

Eddy, J., Wernick, W., Tiedeman, D. V., and Bosdell, B. J. "Career Education--Refocusing Education for Career Development," in book Career Education Primer for Educators, by same authors above. Washington, D.C.: National Vocational Guidance Association of American Personnel and Guidance Association, 1977.

Eddy, J. "College Student Decision Making." Phi Kappa Phi Journal, Spring, 1975.

Eddy, J., and Sohn, M. "Common Elements of College Drug Programs," Journal of National Association of Student Personnel Administrators, July, 1973, in book, Health Education, Drugs, and Alcohol: An Annotated Bibliography. Washington, D.C.: National Education Association, 1975.

Eddy, J. "Developing a Positive Belief in Yourself and Other Persons," in book Life and Management by Responsibility, by John Eddy and Gary Durst. Albuquerque: The Training Company, 1976.

Acknowledgements

Eddy, J. "Handling Stress: A Common Problem of Persons," in book Life and Management by Responsibility, by John Eddy and Gary Durst. Albuquerque: The Training Company, 1976.

Eddy, J. "Measurable Modes for College Student Services: Benefits and Output Delivery Systems," Journal of Illinois Guidance and Personnel Association Quarterly, Spring, 1974.

Eddy, J. (Editor) Principles of Marketing. Chicago: McMillan and Collier Publishing Company, 1972.

Eddy, John (co-author) and Associates. UNISTAR (User Network for Information Storage, Transfer, and Acquisition and Retrieval, Huntsville, Alabama: National Aeronautics and Space Administration and U. S. Government Printing Office, 1971.

Eddy, J. Religious Affairs at Church-Related Colleges, La Miranda, California: Center for Christianity and Higher Education, 1971.

Eddy, J. "Religious Personnel at Church-Related Colleges," in book, Handbook of College and University Administration by Asa S. Knowles (Editor), New York: McGraw-Hill Publishing Company, 1970.

Eddy. J. "Role Discovery and Role Recovery," Journal of College Student Personnel, July, 1977.

Eddy, J. "Students and Scholars Examine some Ethical Issues," in book, Education and Ethical Inquiry, by John Eddy. Johnson, Vermont: Johnson State College, 1969.

Eddy, J. "The Teacher and the Drug Scene," Bloomington, Indiana: The Phi Kappa Foundation, 1973, in book, American Education: The Task and the Teacher, second edition, by John H. Johansen, Harold W. Collins, and James A. Johnson. Dubuque, Iowa: William C. Brown Company Publishers, 1975.

Acknowledgements

Eddy, J. "The American College and Some Legal Aspects of
     In Loco Parentis," Journal of National Association of
     College Admissions Counselors, November, 1968, and
     Journal of College Student Personnel Abstracts, July,
     1969.

Wolf, John C., and Dameron, Joseph D. "Counseling Center
     Function in Two-Year and Four-Year Colleges." Journal
     of College Student Personnel, November, 1975.

INTRODUCTION

The authors believe the second edition of this book is an improved volume that will be beneficial to the profession as well as a contribution to student affairs literature. The first edition took Eddy ten years to complete; this second edition has been in the making since the first edition was published in 1977.

The major reason for this new edition at this time relates to the evolving nature of the student affairs profession. The recently published Carnegie Council's report on higher education for the next two decades has identified this twenty-year period as "the golden age of students." Anyone involved in our profession during the 1970s recognizes the significant changes that have evolved. The Council's report indicates another significant shift in the environment of higher education--a shift that might provide the basis from which the long held professional goal for the comprehensive development of college students finally can be accomplished successfully and completely.

Basic changes in this second edition, which attempt to address the professional factors and behaviors necessary to facilitate the "golden age," include adding and improving chapters. These revisions include academic advisement in Chapter 7, counseling theories in Chapter 8, career counseling in Chapter 14, values education and the college student development administrator in Chapter 15, humanized student personnel services in Chapter 18, selection and training of residence hall assistants in Chapter 19, counseling centers in two- and four-year colleges in Chapter 20, developing leadership skills in Chapter 28, organizational facilitation of student affairs in Chapter 29, leadership and management in student affairs in Chapter 30, evaluation of college student affairs divisions and services in Chapter 32, research in college student personnel services in Chapter 36, and a model of counseling supervision in Chapter 41. New appendices have also been added on such subjects as college student retention and campus crisis strategies.

In this second edition, the authors also have attempted
to give greater attention to the theoretical, personal, organizational, and professional development of present and future
staff members. Moreover, the authors have added new material
that stresses the importance of student services in the
"golden age," such as counseling centers, academic advisement,
residence hall leadership, and total staff leadership growth--
keys to college student retention in the most crucial and
critical areas facing the very survival of student services
in private and public institutions.

The second edition of this book contains other significant changes. Twenty new contributors have added their perspectives. A deliberate effort was made to include more
women and minorities as contributors. We have included
specialists in important developing areas of the profession
that often are absent in texts for student affairs professionals. We have also located successful new professionals
whose efforts and contributions often are not recognized in
the professional literature. The authors also have given
attention in this edition to obtaining vigorous viewpoints
from practitioners who continue to be at the forefront of
the profession through their involved professional activities.

The foreword of this book has been written by Dr. James
J. Muro, a national Division President of the American Personnel and Guidance Association, who is our colleague at
North Texas State University. Dr. Muro currently is President of the Association for Counselor Education and Supervision, as well as Dean of the College of Education at NTSU.
His contribution to this book is appreciated and provides an
example for the blending of counseling techniques and ther-
apies with administrative knowledge and skills--the fabric of
our profession.

The authors of this book have been involved actively in
the leadership of our profession. Joe Dameron has been a
Senator of the American Personnel and Guidance Association;
John Eddy currently serves in that same Senatorial capacity,
representing the American College Personnel Association
(ACPA). Dave Borland has been Chair of Commission I and Vice
President for Commissions in ACPA; he will serve as ACPA's
President in 1981-82. Through these and other opportunities

for professional service, we have learned how important it is
to obtain a total and holistic perspective on the field of
student development, rather than a limited geographic or conceptual viewpoint. It is in this spirit that we introduce
this new edition--one that provides a developmental approach
to the field, which, at differing times, has been called
college student personnel, student affairs, student services,
and student development. Each new title has been an attempt
by our colleagues to describe an evolving, facilitative,
creative, and caring profession that works with and for
college students. We believe these feelings are reflected
throughout this edition.

Denton, Texas   J.E.
June, 1980   J.D.D.
                                                     D.T.B.

CHAPTER 1

HISTORICAL PERSPECTIVES OF COLLEGE STUDENT PERSONNEL WORK

William D. Peterson and John Eddy
and Griff D. Pitts

. . .I try through history to improve my understanding of the present and to prepare - if
preparation be possible - for the future.

W. H. Cowley

. . .one may claim for personnel work either a
very long and honorable history or a very brief
and troubled one.

Kate Mueller

The authors are not professional historians. Like Professor
Cowley, however, we have a great respect for the assistance history can provide us in gaining an understanding of the present
and in preparing for the future. It is our position that if
student personnel workers were better students of history, the
field as a whole would be in a much better position to be proactive rather than reactive. We do believe that one mark of a
professional is an understanding of the historical conditions and
antecedents that have influenced and contributed to the development of one's chosen profession.

In this chapter, we will present an overview of the factors
that led to the development and formalization of the field known
as college student personnel. Since this is an overview, no
attempt will be made to be exhaustive. Our readers, thus, are
encouraged to refer to the primary sources which will be referenced, as well as sources such as Leonard (1) where they will
find a more extensive treatment of the historical development of
this field. Thorough reading of historical documents, some of
which have been included in the bibliography in this book, is
also encouraged.

As Mueller has pointed out in the quote cited above, anyone
writing about the history of student personnel has a choice of
claiming for the field either a very brief and troubled history
or a long and honorable one. (1) If one considers student personnel as synonymous with the personnel point of view and its
emphasis on the development of the whole student, then it is

possible to go back to the earliest centuries and find examples
of educational approaches which focused upon the total development
of the individual. For example, Cowley's research led him to conclude:

> ...that personnel work (under different names and
> unaided by research) had been going on for centuries,
> that what might be called Alma Maternal ministrations
> to students had characterized the universities of
> the Middle Ages and had been the most notable element
> in American higher education up to the time of the
> Civil War. (2)

If, on the other hand, one is to take a more restricted view
of the field and date its origins from the time when official
titles began to be applied to specialists in student personnel,
when formal statements of purpose began to be written and issued
to the public, when practicioners started to come together in
national associations, and when the first pamphlets, journals,
and textbooks were published, then one would date the start of
the field in the late 19th and early 20th century. (1)

Esther Lloyd-Jones is one example of a knowledgeable and
respected student personnel eductaor who considers the origins to
have been more recent. She writes, "Student personnel work, as
represented in most books on the subject, started in Boston about
1908 with Frank Parsons and the vocational guidance movement. It
continued on in greater force as psychological testing developed
rapidly after 1910." (3) Lloyd-Jones also considered the mental hygiene movement to be another significant contributor to
the student personnel movement. (3)

The authors' perspective is that it is useful to go back beyond the early 1900's to trace the development of student personnel movements, but not necessary to go back to the early centuries.
It is our perspective that a combination of factors which were in
existence even prior to the 20th century, influenced the development of the student personnel services as we know them today.
These include: (a) the impact of the English educational system
on the Colonies; (b) the virtually totally religious orientation of the Colonial colleges followed by extensive secularization in the 1800's; (c) the inclusion of women in institutions
of higher learning; (d) the increase in student populations;
and (e) the reaction to the intellectualistic imperialism imported by American Ph. D.'s trained in Germany.* In the remainder of this chapter we will elaborate on these influences, as
well as focus on 20th century influence.

---

* Cowley's research led him to consider factors (b), (d), and (e)
as antecedent to the impact of psychological research. We have
added factors (a) and (c).

2

The English Influence

It is a common conception on the part of many Americans that the early colonists came to this land to escape the English way of life. Nothing could be further from the truth in the case of those settlers who established the first colleges in the New World. These Cambridge and Oxford educated men desired to recreate a bit of Old England and, as a result, to create colleges that as closely resembled the English residential universities as was physically possible. The extent of English influence is reflected in the following exerpt from Rudolph.

> Not only was the curriculum brought from abroad. The concept of effective religious control was patterned on the kind of control which made Emanuel College at Cambridge a Puritan see. The residential pattern which made every American college a home away from home was of English origin. The idea of the College as essentially autocratic in clientele and purpose reflected English experience. The names of the four college classes - freshman, sophomore, junior sophister, senior sophister - came from England. The emphasis on teaching rather than study; on students rather than scholars; on order and discipline, rather than learning - all this arrived from patterns which had been emerging in the residential colleges of the English universities. (4)

From this description of the Colonial college, and the English influence on that college, we can see many factors which have contributed not only to the development of the American college as we know it today, but also to the development of the student personnel services in American higher education. In fact, what Rudolph labelled "effective religious control," Professor Cowley called "personnel work." Indeed, Cowley came to the conclusion that these early American cleric/educators "spent more time in personnel activities than they did in teaching and scholarship." (1) This was a result of their religious convictions, convictions which led them to be more concerned with saving and protecting the souls of their charges than with developing their intellect.

This extreme concern with everything that a student did dissipated somewhat with the increased secularization of institutions of higher education in the late 1800's. Another factor contributing to its demise was the increase in student populations. It is our perception, however, that much of the concern which colleges and universities, and, indeed, student personnel workers evidence today regarding the total life and life space of the student can be traced to this Puritan concern with the soul and, hence, with the total life of the individual.

3

The Residential Focus

A second major contribution of the English to the American
way of higher education as we know it, was the emphasis on housing
and boarding the students. The provision of on-campus housing
was usually one of the first priorities of newly formed colleges.
This need for housing was partly a matter of necessity and partly
a matter of philosophy. The necessity arose because there seldom were sufficient dwellings or boarding houses in the college
town where the students could stay. The philosophical position
of these early college founders was that, even if room and board
could be obtained off-campus, it was better that all students be
housed where their lives could be more closely monitored, and
where they would be less tempted to indulge in the sins of the
day such as drinking or gambling.

It should also be pointed out that the age of the youth
attending the Colonial academies, colleges and seminaries was such
that provision for their welfare was essential. Children were
often sent to schools and colleges at a very early age. According to Leonard:

> Many elementary schools took children to board at six
> years of age. In the Moravian seminaries at Bethle-
> hem children from eight to twelve years of age were
> received. The average age of Harvard students was
> from fifteen to seventeen years, and it was not un-
> common for a precocious child to be entered in the
> college at eleven. (1)

In addition to the young age of the college attenders, the separation from their families was virtually complete.

> This separation of the children from their families
> was intensified by the lack of roads and other means
> of communication between home and school or college.
> On the best roads of the Colonial period, a day's
> journey consisted of not more than twenty to twenty-
> five miles in good weather and during the winter
> months even these roads were impassable much of the
> time. (1)

Thus, the age of the students, coupled with the lack of means to
communicate with their parents, made it almost essential for the
colleges to provide room and board and to assume other parental
functions. The formal term for this type of relationship between
the college and the student is known as in loco parentis, which
literally means "in place of the Parents."

Provision of residence facilities for students has waxed

4

and waned through the 200 years of American higher education. Residence halls have been considered both as blessing and bane, as they have been the focal points and breeding places for both riots and revivals. The fact remains, however, that they provide the largest single source of employment for student personnel professionals as well as papaprofessionals, and that they have been the focus of more research and writing and student development activity than any other single student service.

Personnel Officers

In the Colonial colleges we do not find specialized personnel officers. Rather, everyone in the institution played a role in carrying out the various welfare and discipline functions. This included trustees, presidents, teaching fellows, tutors, ushers and masters, stewards, and student monitors. (1) The trustees were very active in both the administration of the college and in handling discipline. "In all colleges the president was the chief personnel officer as well as the administrative head of the institution." (1) While there were no financial aids officers per se in the early colleges, provisions were made to assist needy students. In most cases the poorer students were permitted to work for the college in return for room and board. Such work might take the form of waiting tables or working on the college's farms. In other cases, the college set aside funds for tuition scholarships. Once again, it was the task of the president to disburse such funds.

Health and Recreation

There is ample evidence that the presidents and trustees of the early colleges, particularly in the 1800's, were concerned with the health of the students. Some of the physical activities in which the students were engaged were directly related to the daily maintenance and physical improvement of the college. Tasks such as chopping and carrying wood, or damming streams, or landscaping the grounds are examples of this. The students also engaged in recreational activities, however, such as cricket, quoits, baseball, boating, swimming, skating, hiking and fishing. In the women's colleges there were also many recreational activities.

As the expanded athletic activities of the students suggest, there was a new emphasis placed upon health and a corresponding growth in the personnel services related to it. The colleges not only built gymnasiums, bath and field houses, and other facilities for the new physical education activities, but they planned and carried out programs of balanced living, gave health lectures, introduced physicians as regular members of

5

the staff, and built or set aside rooms for infirmaries.
(1)

Health lectures were included as a part of the required curriculum at many colleges, these lectures being given by the president or his wife, by members of the faculty, or by a physician.

The Influence of Women Students

The introduction of women into higher education had a great
impact on the development of the student services. In fact, the
admission of female students may have precipitated the appointment
of the first student personnel "specialists." As coeducation
became more prevalent (Oberlin was the first college to open its
doors equally to men and women, and this occured in 1837), it was
felt that steps were needed to counteract the strong possibility
of social misbehavior between men and women. The steps which
were taken came in the form of the appointment of lady principals,
matrons, wardens, and later, deans of women. It was their assignment to maintain a certain decorum and to educate the women students in the ways they should behave. Records from the period
suggest that they were quite effective in carrying out this
assignment. Women students were also the subject of some of the
earliest examples of research on students. This research, conducted by the Association of Collegaite Alumnae, was begun almost
immediately after the organization of this group in 1882.

> The research was directed toward answering several
> contemporary questions: Were women physically able
> to endure the rigors of college life? Did college
> education unfit women for homemaking? Were women
> intellectually capable of mastering college curricula?
> These surveys indicated the direction in which person-
> nel work with women should proceed. (1)

The lady principals, wardens, and matrons were the forerunner
of the deans of women. The deans of women affiliated themselves
in 1916 as the National Association of Deans of Women, and this
is the earliest example of a formal student personnel organization.

Increase in Students

It should be clear from the material which has preceded, that
personnel functions were being formed in the early American institutions of higher education, even if there were not separately
designated officers carrying out these functions. The trustees,
the presidents, the faculty, were indeed our first student personnel officers. It was entirely possible for these individuals
to wear many hats and perform many roles when the colleges were
small, the total emphasis was on the students, and trustees,

presidents and faculty were willing to stand in loco parentis.

In the late 1800's, however, institutions of higher education began to grow in size to the point where it became impossible for the president to know each student intimately, and the philosophy of many faculty members changed to the point where they no longer felt that a concern for the welfare of students was part of their role. Two factors were influential here, one being the increasing secularization of institutions, and the second being the German influence.

Increased Secularization and the German Influence

Up until the mid-1800's most every institution of higher education that was founded in this country had a predominately religious orientation. In fact, before the Civil War, "Eleven out of twelve college presidents were clergymen. One scholar has been able to discover not more than twenty-six who were not." (4) After the Civil War there was a dramatic increase in both lay presidents and lay professors.

> These lay professors had little interest in soul-
> saving. Indeed they revolted at the thought. A
> large number of them had gone to Germany for their
> training, and they returned home with the conviction
> that American colleges and universities should follow
> the German philosophy of complete disregard for
> students outside of class. The German universities
> stood at the pinnacle of academic and intellectual
> excellence, and American academicians did their ardent
> best to translate the German point of view and German
> methods to the United States. Since no one paid
> any attention to students in German universities,
> it followed ipso facto that American higher educa-
> tion shouldn't either. (1)

With the introduction of this German influence, American higher education experienced an interesting and almost complete turn-about.

Whereas in the Colonial and early 19th century colleges the lives of the students had been totally regulated, to the point where the activities of the trustees, presidents and faculty with respect to the students could rightfully be called "snooping," colleges and universities that fell under the influence of Ger-man-trained presidents and faculty virtually ignored students and paid absolutely no attention to their welfare.

Cowley speaks of this turn-about as a beautiful illustration of the psychological principles of action and reaction.

7

Lay professors educated in Germany reacted against the
overbearing paternalism of their clerical predecessors,
and they succeeded in substituting impersonalism. But
they too went to extremes and soon reactions against
their disdain of students set in. (1)

The students reacted, not with the violence that had at times
characterized their reactions to the oppressive regulations of
earlier years, but with the development of an extensive extracurriculum. "They didn't like the instruction of their German-trained
professors any more than they liked the rote-memory teaching of
the clerical professors, but now they had outlets for their energies which had not existed before." (1) The expansion of the
extracurriculum led to the appointment of a number of personnel
officers, many of whom gave their attention to students in groups
more than to individual students. "The country's first college
dean seems to have been appointed at Harvard in 1870, but he gave
most of his attention to disciplinary problems." (1)

Far-sighted administrators also reacted to the German-imported
impersonalism, although their reactions began a little later than
the student reaction. They realized that students needed certain
forms of assistance to survive in the impersonal university, and
as a result they placed renewed emphasis on residential housing,
an epmhasis which the German philosophy had scuttled, and they
also developed systems of academic advising and personal counseling.

The interest in student counseling began even
earlier than the renewal of concern over housing, and
to Daniel Coit Gilman must go the credit for appointing
the first counselor of students. John Hopkins opened
in 1876 with the country's first system of faculty
advisors, and then in 1889 President Gilman appointed
Professor E. H. Griffen of Williams College "chief
of the advisors," or as he soon came to be called,
dean. A few years later in one of his annual reports
Gilman explained the appointment by observing that
"in every institution there should be one or more
persons specifically appointed to be counselors or
advisors of students." (1)

President William Rainey Harper of Chicago faihtfully followed Gilman's tradition, and even extended the emphasis on concern for the student. In 1899, Harper delivered a lecture at
Brown University. The title of the lecture was "The Scientific
Study of the Student," and it is of significant interest to quote
at some length.

. . .in order that the student may receive the assistance so essential to his highest success, another

8

step in the onward evolution will take place. This
step will be the scientific study of the student himself.
....In the time that is coming provision must be made,
either by the regular instructors or by those appointed
especially for the purpose, to study in detail the man
or woman to whom instruction is offered.

This study will be made (a) with special reference to
his character...to find out whether he is responsible
or careless, or shiftless, or perhaps vicious; (b) with
special reference likewise to his intellectual capacity;
(c) with reference to his special intellectual characteristics to learn whether he is independent or original;
(d) with reference to his special capacities and tastes;
(e) with reference to the social side of his nature.

This feature of twentieth century education will come
to be regarded as of greatest importance, and fifty
years hence, will prevail as widely as it is now lacking.
(5)

This is certainly a prophetic statement that spoke well for
the establishment of the field of psychological testing and of
college student personnel.

We thus see that, even though the increase in student enrollment coupled with the secularization and Germanization of higher
education appeared to spell doom for concern for the individual
student, this was only a temporary appearance. The actual outcome was the appointment of officers to provide for the needs of
students, and the establishment of counseling and advising systems
that were the predecessors of the student personnel movement.

The Field Is Formalized

Through the material that has been presented to this point,
it can be seen that a number of personnel related activities were
well under way prior to 1900. It was not until after 1900, however, that the field of college student personnel began to be
formally organized. Some of the earliest evidence of formal activity, and some key dates in the history of the field, include:

    a. The deans of women first began to meet annually
        in 1903 and affiliated themselves in 1916 as the
        National Association of Deans of Women.

    b. Seven directors of student unions met together for
        the first time at Ohio State University in 1914.

    c. The first book about the field appeared in 1915.

9

c. This was a handbook, "The Dean of Women," by Lois Matthews Rosenberry (Houghton Mifflin).

d. The first formal course in the field appears to have been a course for dean of women offered by Dr. Paul Monroe at the Columbia University Summer School in 1916.

e. Several deans of men conferred together and formed the National Association of Deans of Men in 1917.

f. College physicians, whose roots we have shown to go back to the mid-1800's, organized the American College Health Association in 1920. (6)

Lloyd-Jones has highlighted the various movements which have contributed to the development of student personnel, from 1905 on. Among these we find the vocational guidance movement, which started in Boston about 1908; the use of psychological tests for classification and assignment of men which came into its own in World War I, and which, in turn, led to the scientific management movement and the work of individuals such as Taylor Scott, Bingham, Paterson, and others. The thrust of scientific management was that "man could and should be scientifically managed for greater industrial efficiency and individual productivity." (3)

Other fields or movements which contributed to the development and acceptance of student personnel work include: the mental hygiene movement, progressive education and child development, psychoanalysis, and especially, psychology.

Student personnel work drew heavily on psychology throughout (the period of 1900-1940). In the 1940's, however, reports of research and experimentation in the area of group interaction attracted more and more attention, and student personnel workers, probably the first on the college level and then on the level of secondary education, began to recognize that the social sciences might have much to contribute to the broadening objectives of their field. This appears to many to be the next big tributary which will flow into the guidance movement to modify its concepts and contribute to its power. (3)

Lloyd-Jones wrote this in the early 1950's, and indeed, we have seen that the social and behavioral sciences have contributed significantly to the conceptual development of the field.

Formal Statements

Two statements stand out in the developmental history of student personnel as being early attempts to proclaim that which the field stands for and believes in. These statements issued in 1938 and 1949, were both published by the American Council on Education and are entitled the "student personnel point of view." (7)(8)   Three main assumptions stand out in these documents:

a. Individual differences in students are anticipated, i.e., the uniqueness of each personality does not cause surprise but is expected and planned for.

b. Each individual is conceived of and treated as a functioning whole and his development in all areas of living is treated as a unit.

c. Teaching, counseling, student activities, and other organized educational efforts of the institution start realistically from where the individual student is, not from the point of development at which the institution would like the hypothetical average student.

As has been mentioned earlier, this statement obviously speaks to more of the institution than just the student personnel services. Rather, it speaks to the perspective which the student personnel profession feels is vital if the needs of students are to be met and if the individual student's education is to have the fullest impact possible.

Since the early 1960's, the Council of Student Personnel Associations in Higher Education (COSPA), has produced several documents which have had an impact on both the preparation and practice of student personnel. COSPA's Commission on Professional Development, has had particular impact on professional preparation. In 1964, the Commission published "A Proposal for Professional Preparation in College Student Personnel Work." (9)   In this document, which was revised in 1968, the Commission set forth the purposes of the college student personnel profession, the functions of college student personnel, and minimal standards for professional preparation.

In the early 1970's, the Commission was given the task of revising the above statement. However, after beginning that task it became evident to the Commission that a thorough re-conceptualization of the field was in order. The result was a new statement "Student Development Services in Higher Education," (10) that has provided a conceptual model around which many preparation programs and student personnel/student development divisions have been developed or modified.

11

COSPA appeared to have great promise as a vehicle for providing the field with a unified voice. It served as a common ground for representatives from many specialized student services to discuss the needs of the broader field. Unfortunately, after ten years or so of useful service, COSPA has been phased out and its functions have been relegated to various of the existing organizations.

The American College Personnel Association (ACPA), has also been active of late in the publication of documents that have been influential in shaping the future of the profession. For some 14 years now ACPA has been publishing a monograph series that has included individual monographs on particular services such as housing or financial aids, on important aspects of the field such as legal aspects, on the present and future of the profession, or on specific research on students. Of particluar relevance as the profession has begun to move from a student services base to a student development base, has been Brown's monograph on student development in tomorrow's higher education. (11) This book represents Phase One of the work of an ACPA project entitled the "Tomorrow's Higher Education" or "THE Project." Phase Two has consisted of model development, and the Phase Two model has just recently been released so its impact remains to be seen.

Critics of the college stduent personnel profession have long been critical about the lack of a substantial literature in the field, as well as a lack of viable models for putting theory into action. It is hoped that some of the more recent models, as well as the attempts currently underway to implement these models, will move the profession into the forefront of innovation in higher education.

Summary

Student personnel had its origins in the concern of the Colonial college trustees, presidents and faculty for the total life of the student that has a "tradition whose roots are extricably enmeshed in American higher education." (12) Their concern with the student's salvation may have overridden their concern for other aspects of his development, but it still must be said that much of what these early educators did was of a personal nature. As institutions grew in size and became more secular in nature, concern for the soul was replaced in many institutions by concern for other aspects of development, such as vocational preparation. With increased size it became impossible for the president and faculty to know each student intimately. As a consequence, either the students tended to be ignored, as was the case in institutions that came under the German influence, or special officers were appointed to take care of the discipline and other welfare functions.

12

Some of the earliest examples of these special officers were the lady wardens or principles who were appointed whenever women were admitted to previously all-male schools. In the 1900's the field became formalized and professional organizations were formed, courses were taught, books were written, and formal statements were issued. The vocational guidance movement, psychological testing, mental hygiene, psychoanalysis, social science, and the behavioral sciences have all had an influence on the development of the field in the past 78 years. The current emphasis is on student development, and this emphasis will receive further elaboration in Chapter Six.

References

(1) Leonard, E. Origins of the Personnel Services. Minneapolis, MN: University of Minnesota Press, 1956.

(2) _____ "Some History and a Venture in Prophecy." IN: Williamson, E.G. Trends in Student Personnel Work. Minneapolis, MN: University of Minnesota Press, 1949.

(3) Lloyd-Jones, E. "Changing Concepts of Student Personnel Work." IN: Lloyd- Jones, Esther and Margaret Ruth Smith. Student Personnel Work as Deeper Teaching. New York, NY., Harper & Brothers, 1954.

(4) Rudolph, F. The American College and University: A History. New York, NY., Vintage Books, 1962.

(5) Harper, W.R. The Trend in Higher Education. Chicago, IL: University of Chicago Press, 1905.

(6) Cowley, W.H. "Reflections of a Troublesome but Hopeful Rip Van Winkle." The Journal of College Student Personnel. v. 6, no. 2, Dec., 1974.

(7) The Student Personnel Point of View: A Report of a Conference. Series I, v.1, no. 3. Washington, D.C.: American Council on Education, 1938.

(8) The Student Personnel Point of View, revised ed. Washington, D.C.: American Council on Education, 1949.

References

(9) "A Proposal for Professional Preparation in
     College Student Personnel Work." Commission
     on Professional Development, Council of
     Student Personnel Associations in Higher
     Education. Nov., 1964.

(10) "Student Development Services in Higher Education."
     Commission on Professional Development, Council
     of Student Personnel Associations in Higher
     Education. July, 1972. Revised 1973.

(11) Brown, R. Student Development in Tomorrow's
     Higher Education - A Return to the Academy.
     Washington, D.C.: American College Personnel
     Association, 1972.

CHAPTER 2

THE STUDENT PERSONNEL FUNCTION IN AMERICAN HIGHER EDUCATION

Donald W. Robinson

An Overview

It is the writer's conviction that no sector of American
higher education is as universally misunderstood as the field of
student personnel services. Criticisms and charges of "coddling,"
of "spoon feeding" students, and of being antiacademic in purpose
are frequently leveled at the field, in spite of the fact that
student personnel services are not newcomers to the American
higher education scene. I was, therefore, pleased to be invited
to prepare a paper on this topic for this Journal.

Before proceeding further, the programs and activities
generally considered to be student personnel services should be
indicated. Most qualified authorities agree that student personnel services include the following activities: selection for
admission, registration and records, counseling, student health
services, student housing and food services, student activities,
student financial assistance, job placement, and discipline.
Also included are special services such as student orientation,
veteran's advisory services, foreign student programs, religious
activities, and clinics on remedial reading, speech and hearing,
and study habits. Although this group of functions are considered
to be the components of a comprehensive student personnel program,
some institutions do not attempt to provide for all of the programs
listed. Institutions also vary in the delegation of responsibility
for those student personnel services they do provide.

The basic philosophy which still undergirds modern student
personnel work was first stated in 1937 by the American Council
on Education Committee on Student Personnel (1) and was revised
by that committee in 1949. In the latter formulation, the committee stated that:

The student personnel point of view encompasses the student
as a whole. The concept of education is broadened to include
attention to the student's well-rounded development—physically, socially, emotionally and spiritually, as well as
intellectually. The student is thought of as a responsible
participant in his own development and not as a passive
recipient of an imprinted economic, political, or religious
doctrine, or vocational skill. As a responsible participant

15

in the societal processes of our American democracy, his
full and balanced maturity is viewed as a major end-goal
of education and, as well, a necessary means to the fullest
development of his fellow citizens.

The key points inherent in this philosophy may be stated
as: a recognition of the wide variations among students and of
the uniqueness, worth, and dignity of each individual; the need
to view all aspects of the student's life, both in and out of
class, as an integral part of the educative process; and a recognition that mature growth and development cannot be achieved
without active responsible participation by the student in this
process.

The History

A detailed study of the historical roots of student personnel
work is beyond the scope of this paper. However, a brief glance
is necessary if student personnel services are to be viewed in
perspective.

Although a philosophy of student personnel work is still
evolving, student personnel services are not new on the higher
education scene. From the Colonial period as described by authorities such as Cowley, (2) Leonard, (3) and Mueller, (4) student
personnel services in some form and to some limited extent have
always been present in American institutions of higher learning.
For example, it is well documented that from Colonial days on
American colleges have been vitally concerned with the morals,
behavior, recreation, and welfare of their students. Discipline,
often severe, was a major responsibility of early American college administrators. Colonial American students, unlike their
counterparts in continental universities, were required to live
and board on campus or with faculty members.

There were, to be sure, developments in higher education
during the period from about 1800 to 1850. But from the standpoint of student personnel services the establishment of co-
educational residential institutions which occured during this
time was perhaps the only development of major consequence. However, since the 1850's student personnel services have undergone
continuous evolution. Cowley (2) cites three important factors
for this development: the rapid increase in student populations
beginning after the passage of the Land Grant College Act in
1862; the secularization of higher education; and a joint
faculty-student protest against the impersonalism and extreme
intellectualism which had been imported from the German universities. Other factors such as the elective system and the advances
in personnel research during and after World War I have also been
considered contributors to the development of the field of student
personnel work.

It was because of these elements and the belief that officials of the college should act in loco parentis that the functions that were to evolve into formal programs of student personnel services were originated. At any rate, the first system of faculty advisors was organized at Johns Hopkins at the time of the founding of that institution in 1875, and in 1889 a "chief of advisors" was appointed at the same institution. Organized student personnel programs were on their way.

The Services

Many of the functions listed earlier as student personnel services would be performed as administrative necessities regardless of the presence or absence of a formally structured student personnel program. Included in this group would be admissions, registration and records, student housing and food services at residential institutions, the disciplinary responsibility, and perhaps some form of faculty advisory program. Other functions such as counseling, formal programs of student activities, student financial assistance and employment, and the more specialized aspects such as remedial clinics are less likely to be present in the absence of a defined program of student services. In any given institution, however, the prevailing philosophy will determine the nature of the program and its effectiveness. Where a student-centered viewpoint exists the emphasis will be on the contribution of functions to the maximum development of the educational opportunity available to the individual and on the contribution that the student personnel program can make in the achievement of the basic educational objectives of the institution. The student personnel program will be considered a basic part of the educational program of the institution, complementing not conflicting with the academic, and not as an adjunct or auxilary appendage. When this point of view does not exist there is a strong tendency for these functions to be considered as administrative necessities which contribute little to the educational program of the institution. Several of the major student personnel functions will be described with the first point of view in mind.

Recruitment and Admissions

The first contact a college or university has with a student takes place at the time that he requests information from the institution concerning admission. From this point until he is formally enrolled it is the responsibility of the office of admissions to provide the student with information upon which he may judge the institution and appraise his own qualifications for admission on the basis of criteria and standards of the institution. However, from a student personnel point of view, admissions is more than this. It is, from the outset, considered to be a counseling process through which an applicant is assisted in the

17

process of selecting the institution that can best meet his needs and objectives.

Counseling and Advising

Facilities for personal counseling are basic to the student personnel program of an institution of higher education. There is, however, wide variation in the extent and emphasis of counseling assistance provided, depending upon the resources and philosophy of the institution. Many critics of American higher education believe the counseling of students has been overemphasized. This is not the case. American higher institutions are complex, the student body is heterogeneous, and the decisions to be made by students are of great importance.

The major goals of the counseling program are to assist students to appraise their potentialities, to explore their objectives, to receive help with personal problems that are endangering academic progress, and to obtain vocational counseling when necessary. It is true that the counseling facilities available at some institutions are elaborate, but the emphasis is almost always on the normal student and his needs, not on the atypical or severely disturbed student. It is not the function of the counseling service to provide long-term psychiatric care, nor do student personnel authorities advocate that it should be.

Formal counseling services as have been described are important. However, a well-organized faculty advisory program is also necessary to assist students with their curricular planning and with problems of an academic nature. Furthermore, counseling programs and faculty advisory programs are not antagonistic; rather, they complement each other by making available to the student individual assistance when and where it is needed. When a student requires advice concerning academic problems, this assistance should be provided by a faculty advisor who has a personal interest in the student and who has been provided the time to work with him. When the student needs assistance with other personal problems, trained counselors should be able to help him.

Therefore, in a well-organized counseling program communications between counselors and faculty advisors are good, and the special resources of each group will be used to strengthen the total counseling and advising program available to students.

The kinds of counseling and faculty advisory programs described constitute a large segment of such assistance provided in American institutions of higher education. However, a counseling point of view pervades almost all aspects of the student personnel program. There are even some instances in which the formal counseling program begins in the residence hall.

Residence Halls

Historically, resident student housing programs developed
out of the joint necessity of providing shelter for students
and of insuring proper social control. These dual needs still
prevail, but in recent years there has been a decided shift in
emphasis.

Today, the resident student housing program has as its major
objective the provision of adequate housing accommodations for
students in a living environment that is conducive to learning.
In addition to this basic objective the informal atmosphere of
the residence hall makes available a rich opportunity to provide
educational experiences which are supplementary to the formal
learning experiences of the classroom. Consequently, in residence
hall programming it is characteristic to place much emphasis on
student participation in the development of standards, promotion
of activities, and governance of the unit. Increasingly, the
residence halls which are being designed and built provide adequate, properly located space to facilitate the achievement of
the objectives described above. In some large universities residence facilities, particularly for lower division students, are
almost self-contained units with provisions for food service and
even extensive library materials.

The residence hall is usually a very important link in an
institution's counseling and guidance program. At large institutions the head resident is frequently trained in counseling
or group work, and his assistants often are graduate students
with related professional interests. There are indications that
general counseling services are being provided increasingly in
student living units, rather than solely through the counseling
center. In all cases, however, there is a close working relationship between residence hall advisors and personnel in the counseling center. Ideally, there is an equally close relationship
between the residence hall staff and the teaching faculty.

The focus of attention necessarily has been primarily on
resident student housing for single students. However, housing
programs for married students, a post World War II development,
should also be mentioned. The primary questions regarding these
programs are whether institutions of higher learning should provide housing for married students, and on what basis? There has
been a limited amount of research regarding needs of married
students, but to date attempts to provide specialized counseling
services for them are few and far between.

Largely because of the in loco parentis responsibility,
most institutions of higher education have also exercised relatively rigorous control over off-campus housing facilities for
single students. However, in the past little effort was made to

insure that the kinds of services and opportunities provided for residence hall students were provided on an equal basis for students living off campus. Today many institutions have established counseling facilities for off-campus students which correspond to the positions of the residence hall counselors.

Health Services

The need for student health services is not generally questioned. Indeed, student health services appeared on the scene long before many other aspects of the student personnel program were organized. However, the extent of such services made available and the manner in which these services should be financed are frequently debated.

The broad objectives of the college health service, similar to other aspects of a student personnel program, are to provide specialized services that will enhance the individual student's educational opportunities. Many of our largest institutions have student hospital facilities, and the majority of all institutions have an infirmary. In either case, the intent is usually not to provide long-term hospitalization but treatment to enable students, who otherwise might have to withdraw, to return to the classroom. In addition to medical treatment responsibilities of a student health service include health counseling, student physical examinations, advice to administrators and faculty regarding students requiring special regimens, and the coordination of the campus health education program. When available, psychiatric resources are a part of the college health services, but usually with a coordination of these and regular counseling programs.

Health services are generally better at larger institutions and particularly at institutions where adequate facilities are not available in the community. Services are generally less well developed at commuter-type institutions, although many are of the opinion that these institutions share an equal responsibility for providing adequate health services for students.

Placement Service

The placement service is primarily responsible for providing students with essential vocational guidance and for assisting them upon graduation in securing employment consonant with their abilities and aspirations. Increasingly, the placement service is being extended to alumni as well as to currently enrolled students. As a function of institutions of higher education, placement became necessary when the expanding economy of the nation, the admission of students from widely varying backgrounds, and the increasing complexity of society required that the academic program be broadened to meet the needs for new and different types of programs. As was the case with many of the student personnel functions, institutions were performing the service before a program of student services was defined.

The placement function involves a direct advisor-advisee relationship and a regular follow up of graduates once they are on the job. But in addition a keen knowledge of the programs of the institution and the maintenance of a very active liaison with business and industry are necessary.

Student Activities

Responsibility for the student activities program and for student conduct was among the first to be recognized as distinct student personnel function. Mueller (4) succinctly states that the major objectives to be achieved through student activities programs are "...a favorable continuation of the socialization process of the individual; opportunities for experiences in good group interaction and relationships; and the development of leaders--for leadership on the campus and in later life."

Valid as these objectives are, in the writer's opinion it is identification with the activities program more than any other single factor, that has led to the characterization of student personnel work as being anti-intellectual in orientation. In writing about the extracurricular and student personnel work, Williamson seems to place the issue in proper context. (5) He states: "...we do hold to an educational point of view that enthrones reason as the center of education--but reason fully integrated with a social ethic and a healthy personality."

Programs of student activities range from intramural and intercollegiate athletics, student government, special interest clubs and organizations, fraternities and sororities, and clubs serving a very direct academic purpose to organizations of a religious nature. The crux of the matter from the standpoint of student personnel is not the number and variety of activities; rather, it is how well the activities program provides experiences whcih foster group interaction, opportunities for leadership training, and positive socialization experiences. To insure the latter, current emphasis in the management of student activities is away from control and toward increased student responsibility. In recent years the techniques of group work or group dynamics have been applied successfully in many areas of student personnel work but most frequently in student activities management.

There seem to be many indications that the nature of student government organizations will change rather dramatically in the years immediately ahead. Consequently, these activities require a special note. Traditionally, student government responsibilities have been generally limited to the management of social activities, action on certain types of disciplinary cases,

21

formulation of house rules within residence halls, and occasionally representation on some faculty committees.

Students and student groups are changing, and their concepts
of student responsibility are in a rapid phase of evolution.
Students are becoming more interested in national and international
affairs and are beginning to tread in areas once reserved exclusively for faculty or administrators. Whether these developments
seem good or bad depends, in part at least, on one's outlook. But
nevertheless, the nature of student government associations is
changing, and the nature of the responsibilities and issues, both
within and without the institution, in which students think they
should share is also changing in the direction of increased involvement.

Financial Assistance

A financial problem is, in any setting, a personal problem.
STudents in financial need often require assistance in locating
and evaluating institutional and noninstitutional sources of aid
and in appraising their own financial resources. The institution
must, from its standpoint, appraise the extent of a student's
financial need in relation to that of other applicants and, in the
case of scholarships or other non-repayable grants, his relative
chances of success.

Financial assistance programs generally include both student
loan funds and part-time employment opportunities. The scholarship award program is sometimes considered to be part of the
general student financial assistance program and is administered
as such. However, it often is considered to be a basic academic
responsibility managed by colleges or departments (as the case
may be). Often this matter is dependent upon the philosophy of
the institution regarding financial aid and is related to the
question of whether the primary purpose of the program is to
stimulate or reward achievement or to assist students with
financial need.

Student financial assistance has always been an important
personnel service even if it has not always been administered as
part of the total student personnel program of the institution.
However, recent emphasis on various national loans and scholarship
programs, as well as on rising costs of higher education, has
centered even more attention on the financial needs of students
and on ways of meeting these needs. With this new emphasis the
locus of opinion has shifted decidedly toward the management of
the student financial assistance programs as part of the student
personnel program and away from the management of these programs
solely through the business office or academic departments. As
this shift has taken place a cornerstone of the student personnel

22

program--concern for the individual student--has become more evident in student financial assistance programming.

Organization and Administration

Historically, the student personnel program was organized
around the concept of coordinate personnel deans responsible for
men's and women's programs respectively. However, as programs
have expanded, as new specialties have been added, and as institutions of higher education have become more complex, there has
been a noticeable shift away from this organization. There are,
in fact, a few instances--not yet a trend--where the positions
of dean of men and dean of women have been abolished or completely
reconstituted.

Although titles may vary from dean of students to vice
president for student affairs, it is now usual to find a chief
student personnel official responsible for the over-all coordination of the student personnel program. This pattern is particularly true at larger institutions and those which are publicly
supported. From an administrative point of view the chief student
personnel officer should operate at a policy-making level, and it
is generally recommended that he report directly to the president
or chief internal administrative officer. In instances where
this is not the case, the program usually suffers.

In addition to diversity in top-level administrative structure there are also differences in the delegation of administrative
responsibility for the services previously described as part of
the student personnel program. For example, there are instances
where the student housing program is administered in whole or in
part by the business office, and it is not at all uncommon for
the admissions and records programs to be administered by the
chief academic officer. However, fragmentation of programs
results in duplication of effort, less effective services to students, and mounting costs.

Expenditures for student services in comparison to total
general education expenditures provide an important measure of
the relative financial support for student personnel services.
In a forthcoming study of expenditures for student services at
541 four-year institutions (208 public and 343 private), the
writer found: public institutions spent an average of 4.2 per
cent (thirty-nine dollars per student) of the total general
educational budget for student services. At the privately supported institutions the corresponding figures were 4.4 per cent
and forty-one dollars per student. This study did not include
expenditures for student housing since these facilities are
usually self-supporting.

To this writer, the above data hardly support the contention that there is an overemphasis on student personnel services.

Trends and Issues

Rapidly increasing enrollments, estimated to reach 12,000,000 by 1980, will cause change in all sectors of higher education, including student personnel work. In all likelihood the student population will also become more heterogeneous, society more complex, the need for scientists and technicians of all types more intense, and the economy more competitive.

All of these factors, or a combination of them, could increase the need for the kinds of assistance available to students through the various facets of the student personnel program. It is also possible that the characteristics of programs will be altered if rising student costs, as well as increased enrollments, force changes in the traditional structure of American higher education. For example, there seems to be clear evidence that there will be a continued increase in the number of community junior colleges and municipal universities. At these institutions there is often a greater need for educational and vocational counseling and a more dynamic approach to student activities than at institutions with large resident student populations. On the other hand, community and municipal institutions generally do not house students, so that problems relating to housing are not present.

In the past student personnel workers have come from a wide variety of academic backgrounds. Some, perhaps the majority, have been trained in psychology, sociology, counseling, guidance, or related fields. Others however, have come from academic backgrounds that are hard to relate to student personnel work. The breadth of programs makes it difficult to identify student personnel work as a profession. However, there are clear signs of a move in this direction, such as a growing body of literature and research and the establishment of college student personnel curricula in departments of higher education. As a corollary to the latter, student personnel workers seem to be identifying more directly with higher education than with guidance and counseling per se.

Still another current trend is a revaluation of student rights and responsibilities in light of the increasing student desire to be heard on vital and sometimes controversial issues. Consequently, student personnel workers are beginning to question the extent to which traditional concepts and approaches will be effective in a changing cultural milieu, and with a student population that appears to be maturing faster. In a letter to the writer, Dean Robert Shaffer of Indiana University cites two outcomes of these related trends which are already visible: an

24

increase in student freedom in personal and social behavior and an increase in student demonstrations. Dean Shaffer cogently points out that the latter has a negative aspect, because action often replaces thought.

With both stimulus and model being provided by research of behavioral scientists on student characteristics and campus climates, there is an emerging trend toward research and experimentation in student personnel programming.

In the past student personnel programming has been directed almost entirely toward the needs and characteristics of the undergraduate student population. Although not yet a trend, questions are now being asked concerning the unique needs of graduate students for personnel services, appropriate means for providing these services, and the rationale for student services at the graduate level.

There are also signs that, as faculty rank and status at large institutions depend more and more on research and writing, some faculty members are less willing to take time away from these activities to work with individual students. One possible implication of this pattern, if it continues, is that student personnel workers will be required to provide for an even larger flow of students seeking information and advice that once was provided by the teaching faculty.

There are, to be sure, other trends and emerging developments that could be noted. However, the above seem sufficient to illustrate that college student personnel work is a dynamic, if still developing, partner in the higher education enterprise.

Some of the issues presently being discussed and facing student personnel work in the years ahead are:

In what ways can the student personnel program be identified more closely with the academic, and in what ways can the faculty resources be better utilized?

In a period of rising costs and enrollments, how can the student personnel program be maintained at a high level of efficiency when funds and trained staff members may become relatively scarce?

To what extent should students be allowed additional independence--or, phrased another way, to what extent does the concept of in loco parentis need to be liberalized or redefined?

Related to the above, to what extent should students be allowed or encouraged to participate in controversial

25

issues? What should be the role of the student personnel administrator in this matter--defender of student freedom or protector of institutional image? Again, phrased slightly differently, to what extent should student personnel work represent the student and his point of view, and to what extent should it represent the administration or faculty point of view?

To what extent might criticisms of student personnel work as earlier mentioned be valid? How much could be due to poor communication, a need for more clearly defined objectives, and research evidence supporting these objectives?

Summing Up

The counseling and guidance function in American higher education is performed through the student personnel program. The focus of attention in student personnel work is on the many facets of the student's out-of-class life and the ways in which these activities contribute to his education, but the primacy of the intellectual is clearly recognized.

The key student services and the ways in which these services contribute to the objectives outlined were discussed, as were current trends and issues yet to be decided. It was suggested that the changing educational scene may require an increasing emphasis on student service, and that there was little to support the contention that these services are being overemphasized.

References

(1) Williamson, E.G. The Student Personnel Point of View, XIII, 1 (1949).

(2) Williamson, E.G. Trends in Student Personnel Work. Minneapolis, MN: University of Minnesota Press, 1949, pp. 17-18.

(3) Leonard, E.A. Origins of Personnel Services in American Higher Education. Minneapolis, MN: University of Minnesota, 1956, p. 132.

(4) Mueller, K.M. Student Personnel Work in Higher Education. Cambridge, MA: The Riverside Press, 1961, p. 253.

(5) Williamson, E.G. Student Personnel Services in Colleges and Universities. New York, N.Y.: Mc-Graw-Hill Book Company, Inc., 1961, p. 427.

CHAPTER 3

STUDENT PERSONNEL--ALL HAIL AND FAREWELL!

Burns Crookston

In the recent literature, the following terms have been used
concurrently and at times interchangeably: student personnel,
student affairs, personnel work, student development, and human
development. The assumption that these terms refer to the same
thing is symptomatic of the confusion that has been rampant in
our field for many years, particularly the past decade. An
examination of the literature and convention programs over the
past several years suggests three schools of thought on the subject of terminology: (a) those who cling to the old student
personnel point of view will argue that all the above terms are
descriptive of student personnel work, the more glamorous terms
of student development and human development being at best merely
stylish window dressing and at worst a passing fad; (b) those
who insist there are important differences, that the terms have
distinct, if not separate meanings, and that to continue glossing
over them will only compound the confusion that exists not only
among the professionals in the field but also within the public
they serve; and (c) those who insist what we call ourselves is
irrelevant, that there is a need for what we do and the proof of
the pudding is how well we do our job, regardless of what it is
called.

My position supports the second view: There are important
distinctions that must be made, not only for our own peace of
mind but also for the benefit of faculty, administrators, parents,
students, and public. The major premises to be developed here
are (a) that student personnel work as historically defined is no
longer a viable concept; (b) that student affairs should be used
to describe an area, sector, or administrative subdivision; (c)
that student development should be used to describe the underlying philosophy of the field and the operating concepts therein,
and (d) that the nomenclature of the campus has already made the
above a reality; therefore, the professional literature and professional associations should adjust in usage and nomenclature
respectively.

Student Personnel Work

For more than a half century we have lived with the term
student personnel work, a descriptive anomaly that has seldom
been clearly understood by faculty, administrators, alumni,

27

parents, or even students. The word personnel, a military term
borrowed from the French which refers to manpower, as distinguished
from material, which refers to equipment, was first used at Northwestern in 1919 by a former World War I army officer, Clarence S.
Yoakum, to describe a newly organized placement bureau (Cowley
1936). The rapid expansion of vocational guidance, testing, and
placement activities in colleges and universities that took place
in the decade of the twenties was accompanied by the parallel
establishment of personnel offices or personnel bureaus to describe not only the place on campus in which these functions were
exercised but also the functions themselves. By the end of a
decade the term student personnel work had been expanded to describe a new "extra class domain" (Cowley 1936; Lloyd-Jones 1929,
1934) that included virtually all noninstructional activities of
the college. Thus we had taken a bureaucratic term quite properly
used initially to describe placement, testing, and vocational
guidance functions and made it a generic term for all activities,
programs and services outside the classroom, laboratory, and
library that were in any way connected with developing the student.
We then added to this conglomeration an educational philosophy
undergirding what we called the "student personnel point of view"
and said we were "educating" the students. There is little evidence that very many people outside the field have become be-
lievers.

   An educational philosophy? During a time when existentialism had yet to make its impact on higher education, Taylor (1952)
had delineated three generally accepted philosophies: rationalism, neo-humanism, and instrumentalism. To the rationalist, the
sole aim of education is the development of intellect and reason.
Neo-humanism, while recognizing the primacy of cultivating the
mind, assumes a dualism of mind and body, reason and emotion,
thought and action. Instrumentalism emphasizes the full and
creative development of the whole person.

   In relating educational philosophies to student personnel
work, Lloyd-Jones (1952) observed that under rationalism there
was little use for student personnel work save discipline and
remedial services. It was at the neo-humanist institutions where
student personnel work showed its greatest growth. Even Cowley,
who has been given credit for coining the term holism to describe
education of the whole person, while espousing instrumentalism,
actually practiced neo-humanism. He was careful to define student
personnel work as extracurricular. The faculty, assured that
student personnel workers had no intention of invading the sacred
groves of academe, allowed or encouraged student personnel people
to proceed with the development of often elaborate programs,
services, and activities to develop the student outside the classroom. It appears no mere coincidence, therefore, that the philosophical statements of student personnel work during that growth
period, the most notable being the Student Personnel Point of View

28

(Report of a Conference on the Philosophy and Development of
Student Personal Work 1937), were clearly neo-humanist, thus
giving free rein to the establishment of a separate administrative subdivision with a line to the president often coordinate
to the academic sector advocated by Lloyd-Jones (1934) and Cowley
(1936).

Under instrumentalism, espoused by Clothier and others as
early as 1931, student personnel work would serve as an integral
component of the total educational effort of the institution.
And here we come to the crux of the matter. Although writers in
the student personnel field during the late forties, fifties, and
early sixties extolled the virtues of instrumentalism as a concept, like Cowley twenty years earlier, they were, with few
exceptions, content to develop the student outside the classroom.
Not only was the practice of neo-humanism less threatening to the
student personnel worker, in reality there was little choice.
Rationalism prevailed at most institutions. Those who were concerned with the matters of the mind held the power, which they
were reluctant to share with student personnel workers. From
the standpoint of the student personnel worker, implementation of
instrumentalism might also signify the end of a laboriously
gained separate administrative domain.

Attempts at bridge building. As the separatist student personnel programs and services grew, sometimes into large, complex
bureacracies, serious communication problems developed within, as
well as with other sectors in the college. The thrust of the
movement that had gained strength outside the instructional program now sought stronger ties with the academy. Attempts to
build bridges between student personnel and the academy, particularly around strengthening general education (Blaesser 1949;
Brouwer 1949; Hardee 1955), led to a broader definition in the
literature of that period. Student personnel work now included
those processes and functions that helped build curricula, improve
methods of instruction, and develop leadership programs (Arbuckle
1953; Barry & Wolf 1957; Blaesser & Crookston 1960; Wrenn 1951).
Student personnel work no longer merely supplemented the academic
program, it was complementary to it. The student personnel worker had become an "educator" collaborating with the classroom
teacher toward the development of the student as a whole person
(Lloyd-Jones 1953; Williamson 1961), holistic in ideal, yet still
dualistic in practice. Williamson (1961, 1963), having endured
three decades of frustration with faculty rejection of student
personnel work, during which the latter had moved from "ancillary"
to "supplementary" to "complementary" but never central to the
educational enterprise, insisted his holistic out-of-the-classroom
student personnel worker was now an "educator" concerned with
matters intellectual as well as social, civic, and emotional. The
emergence of the concept of student development in the sixties
came out of the recognition that such out-of-class education would

never be fully effective until it became incorporated into the total philosophical and educational fabric of the institution.

Student Affairs

For a half century we have tried to convince both ourselves and our public, within and without education, that personnel work meant what we wanted it to mean, rather than what the dictionary said and the public understood. (Unfortunately, it has never found its way into any language save our own private jargon.) And now there has even been a decrease in the use of the term personnel in the nomenclature of our own sector of the campus. There is evidence that such titles as student affairs, student relations, student life, and student services emerged as expressions of a need to find more descriptive terms (Crookston 1974). In a recent study (Crookston & Atkyns 1974) of a stratified, representative national sample of 627 four-year colleges and universities, only 12.1 percent used student personnel in the generic title of the area and only 2.8 percent of the principal officers used personnel in their own title. Conversely, the legitimation of the term student affairs to describe a major administrative subdivision or sector had become clearly predominant. In the same study, 52.3 percent of the institutions called the sector the division, department, or office of student affairs. The most commonly used title for the principal officer was vice president, dean, director, or coordinator of student, college, or university affairs.

The Crookston-Atkyns study also confirms the establishment of student affairs as a major administrative subdivision on the same level, in relation to the president, as academic affairs, business affairs, and other principal areas such as development or public affairs at 86 percent of the institutions. Not only has the student affairs sector as a major subdivision increased nationally when compared with a study conducted in 1962 (Ayers, Tripp & Russel 1966) but its scope has been greatly expanded. Out of a list of 81 functions known to exist in the student affairs sector at one place or another, the present study showed there are 37 functions that are the responsibility of student affairs at over half the institutions. These include management functions and academically related programs and services as well as all those programs, functions, and services usually included in the old student personnel list.

An operating definition. Regardless of its merit as a descriptive term, student affairs is now firmly established as a major administrative subdivision in American higher education. But let us not lead ourselves into another nomenclature dilemma. Student affairs is not a philosophy, theory, or concept; it is an area, sector, or administrative subdivision within which there are people, programs, functions, and services, many, if not all, of which contribute to the development of students as whole

30

persons. Within this definition of student affairs, the following functions are identified: (a) all teaching, counseling, consulting, evaluation, and research functions related to or labelled as student development that are either institutionally assigned to student affairs or that function in collaboration with the academic sector; (b) all administrative or para-academic functions assigned to student affairs, such as discipline, scholastic standards, admissions, registration, orientation, records, and student leaves of absence; (c) all other programs and services provided for students by professional or paraprofessional staff that fit into the conventional historic definition of the functions of student personnel work; (d) all activities, programs, and functions generated by, run by, or controlled by students, or run by students under the control of the institution (even when there is no direct administrative control, there is an implicit coordinate or consultative responsibility in student affairs); and (e) all management functions assigned, including housing, college unions, food services, bookstore, and other auxiliary services. Also emerging is milieu management, the marshalling of all forces in the educational environment toward the creation of conditions most propitious for student development (Miller, et al. 1974).

Student Development

Space does not permit a delineation of the dramatic parade of interlocking and interacting events and circumstances of the past decade that gave rise to the insurgence of student development in the terminology of the field. As already intimated, student development is not a new concept; it is a return to holism reinforced with the unerring vision of hindsight. Freed at last from the necessity of exercising the benevolent control of the parent and from adherence to the remedial model of counseling, professionals in our field, within a time-frame of only a few years, have found themselves free to relate to students not on the basis of status, but competency; not reactively, but proactively.

Behind the clamor of demonstrations and disruptions, along with changes in student affairs, some rather dramatic changes were also taking place within many classrooms. Existentialism, the focusing inward on the self, the belief that existence precedes one's essence, and that the individual must take responsibility for one's life, has had great impact. As the examining of one's life becomes academically legitimate, the pedagogical focus must necessarily turn from the subject to the student.

As the new legally defined adult students assume increased initiative and responsibility for their learning, the teacher must acquire more versatility on role responses. The result has been new developmentally oriented courses using teaching approaches that focus on the students' application of knowledge to their own

31

growth and development as persons able to cope in a world of accelerating change. This means classroom teachers, like the student development professionals, must be capable of working effectively within a developmental frame; facilitating, collaborating, consulting (Crookston 1973). Thus, the chasm that has so long separated "teaching" in the classroom and "educating" outside appears to have narrowed to bridgeable proportions on a number of campuses. Such teachers and staff members are both talking the language and using the methodology of student development. Could this mean the dawn of a new era of holism in practice as well as in theory? Certainly the increased viability of student affairs as coordinate to academic affairs in the policy-making arena of the college can strengthen the odds. But time alone can tell.

Definitions. Student development has been defined as the application of the philosophy and principles of human development in the educational setting (Crookston 1972a; Miller and others 1974). Human development refers to the knowledge, conditions, and processes that contribute both to the growth, development, and fulfillment of the individual throughout life as a realized person and effective, productive citizen, and to the growth and development of society. Education for human development is the creation of a humane learning environment within which learners, teachers, and social systems interact and utilize developmental tasks for personal growth and societal betterment. The teaching of human development includes any experience in which a teacher interacts with learners as individuals or in groups that contributes to individual, group, or community growth and development and that can be evaluated (Crookston 1972a, 1972b, 1973).

While the above definitions argue that human development is the generic descriptive term for the field, for our purpose there is the difficulty that human development is too encompassing. It includes those processes that affect the development of persons in the whole of life--in any setting, be it school, work, family, group, community, or society at large, and at any age in any circumstance. On the other hand, student development by definition must imply a developmental process limited to an educational setting; it is, therefore, the more preferable term to describe our particular field. While student development suggests that only students are to be developed, this difficulty can be surmounted by the suggestion that all those in the educational setting by definition are "students" at one time or another, depending on the nature of the task and the type and quality of the interaction or transaction involved.

Proposes Nomenclature

Our analysis leads to the following conclusions and proposals: (a) Student personnel work should be given its due and retired into

32

history. Efforts should be made in the professional literature and
in other communications not to use the term to describe contemporary programs, services, or concepts. Although it is legitimate
to use the term in its proper definition to refer to specific
functions such as placement, it is recommended that a ten-year
moratorium be placed on any such public use of the term, after
which presumably there should be no mistake as to its proper
meaning and usage. (b) Student affairs should be used to describe
the sector or administrative subdivision on campus within which
there are people, programs, functions, and services, many, if not
all, of which contribute to student development. (c) Student
development should be used to describe the concept, philosophy,
underlying theories, and methodologies utilized in the many
settings in which student development occurs. (d) Professional
associations should change their names accordingly. The following
are recommended: (a) Change American Personnel and Guidance
Association to Association of Human Development Professions. This
adds one word (professions) to a proposal already made by Ivey
(1970). The recent addition of the Public Offender Counselor
Association highlights the character of the present APGA that
reflects the wide spectrum of concern that extends beyond the
educational institution into the whole of life. An association of
professions concerned with many aspects of human development is
both apt and appealing. (b) Changing American College Personnel
Association to the Association for College Student Development is
under current consideration and should be supported. Most other
organizations within APGA now appear functionally descriptive.
The long controversy around the use of the term guidance is recognized but cannot be dealt with here. (c) Change the names of
Personnel and Guidance Journal, Journal of College Student Personnel, and NASPA Journal to eliminate personnel and make appro-
priate rewording. The latter two come easy: Journal of College
Student Development and Journal of Student Affairs Administration.
The former requires additional consideration. Of equal importance
is editorial consistency in the use of terminology. (d) Change
National Association of Student Personnel Administrators to
National Association of Student Affairs Administrators. There are
those within NASPA who would like to change the name to National
Association of Student Development Administrators. This would be
a mistake because it would confuse a concept with a territory, the
same confusion that now exists in their present title with the
term personnel. Despite the double entendre, student affairs,
like academic affairs, has become the accepted term for our sector.
Calling the sector student development is bound to raise unnec-
essarily the territorial hackles of academicians who can rightfully
claim that student development is also their proper business, a
claim with which we should all most heartily agree.

Finally, perhaps all of the above might persuade those in our
academic colleges who are responsible for the training of professionals in our field to do something about changing their archaic

33

course titles and degrees, many of which suggest we are still
training student personnel workers to function in the 1950s.

References

Arbuckle, D.S. Student Personnel Services in Higher
Education. New York: McGraw-Hill, 1953.

Ayers, A.R.; Tripp, P.A.; & Russel, J.H. Student
Services Administration in Higher Education.
Washington, DC: U.S. Department of Health, Educa-
tion & Welfare, 1966.

Barry, R., & Wolf, B. Modern Issues In Guidance -
Personnel Work. New York: Teachers College Press,
1957.

Blaesser, W.W. The future of student personnel work
in higher education. In J.G. Fowlkes (Ed.),
Higher Education for American Society. Madison,
WI: University of Wisconsin Press, 1949.

Blaesser, W.W., & Crookston, B.B. Student personnel
work--College and university. Encyclopedia of
Educational Research (Third Edition), 1960,
pp. 1414-1427.

Brouwer, P.J. Student Personnel Services in General
Education. Washington,DC: American Council on
Education, 1949.

Clothier, R.C., et al. College personnel principles
and functions. Personnel Journal, 1931, 10, 11.

Cowley, W.H. The nature of student personnel work.
Education Record, April 1936, 3-27.

Crookston, B.B. A developmental view of academic
advising as teaching. Journal of College Student
Personnel, 1972, 13, 12-17. (a)

Crookston, B.B. An organizational model for student
development. NASPA Journal, 1972, 10, 3-13. (b)

Crookston, B.B. Education for human development. In
C.F. Warnath (Ed.), New Directions for College
Counselors. San Francisco: Jossey-Bass, 1973,
pp. 47-64.

References

Crookston, B.B. The nomenclature dilemma: Titles of principal student affairs officers at NASPA institutions. NASPA Journal, 1974, 11, 3-6.

Crookston, B.B., & Atkyns, G.C. A Study of Student Affairs: The Principal Student Affairs Officer, The Functions, The Organization at American Colleges and Universities, 1967-1972. A Preliminary Summary Report. Storrs, CT: University of Connecticut Research Foundation, 1974.

Hardee, M.E. (Ed). Counseling and Guidance in General Education. Yonders-on-Hudson, NY: World, 1955.

Ivey, A.E. The association for human development. A revitalized APGA. Personnel and Guidance Journal, 1970, 48, 527-532.

Lloyd-Jones, E. Student Personnel Work at Northwestern University. New York: Harper & Brothers, 1929.

Lloyd-Jones, E. Personnel Administration. Journal of Higher Education. March 1934, 5, 141-147.

Lloyd-Jones, E. Personnel work and general education. In N.B. Henry (Ed.), General Education (Fifty-first Yearbook, Part I). Chicago: University of Chicago, National Society for the Study of Education, 1952. pp. 214-229.

Lloyd-Jones, E. Changing concepts of student personnel work. In E. Lloyd-Jones & M.R. Smith (Eds.), Student Personnel Work as Deeper Teaching. New York: Harper, 1954. pp. 1-14.

Miller, T.K., et al. A Student Development Model For Student Affairs in Tomorrow's Higher Education. Washington, DC: American College Personnel Assoc., 1974.
Report of a Conference on the Philosophy and Development of Student Personnel Work in College and University. The Student Personnel Point of View. (American Council on Education Studies). Washington, DC: ACE, 1937.

Taylor, H. The philosophical foundation of general education. In N.B. Henry (Ed.), General Education (Fifty-first Yearbood, Part I). Chicago: University of Chicago, National Society for the Study of Education, 1952. pp. 20-45.

References

Williamson, E.G. Student Personnel Services in Colleges and Universities. New York: McGraw-Hill, 1961.

Williamson, E.G. Commentary. In E. Lloyd-Jones & E.M. Westervelt (Eds.), Behavioral Science and Guidance: Proposals and Perspectives. New York: Columbia University, Teachers College, Bureau of Publications, 1963. pp. 54-59.

Wrenn, C.G. Student Personnel Work in College. New York: Ronald Press, 1951.

36

CHAPTER 4

CONSIDER THE COLLEGE STUDENT DEVELOPMENT PROFESSION

Council of Student Personnel Associations
in Higher Education

Post-Secondary Education-- The Setting

Today, higher education faces a future unlike that of the
recent past which included burgeoning enrollments and budgets,
with the former doubling every 14 years. This profound "growth"
for post-secondary education has now leveled off. However, access
to post-secondary education continues to grow.

Post-secondary education in our democratic, pluralistic
society takes many forms to serve the very broad spectrum of persons now seeking its benefits. Most traditional of the forms is
the university, one of the most complex structures in modern
society. (The term "university," whenever it is used, includes
all 2-and 4-year colleges.) The university has three basic
missions: teaching, research, and public service. All those
associated with post-secondary education are directed toward its
most primary goal of positively influencing each student's full
development, whether the student is enrolled for one course or
many, at the age of 17 or 71.

Student Development -- Basic Assumptions

To positively influence each student's full development
(continuing education), student development makes several basic
assumptions. It assumes that all human beings express their life
goal as becoming free, liberated, self-directed, and that they
seek it through a process variously called self-actualization,
maturation, ego-integration, full-functioning, or behavioral
development. The student development specialist believes that
the potential for development and self-direction is possessed by
everyone, and education is a way of assisting the development of
this potential. The student development specialist also believes
that acceptance and understanding of persons as they are is essential; and since human potential cannot be adequately measured, the
assumption that a person possesses immeasurable potential will
best aid development. The ideal role of the student development
specialist is considered to be pro-active rather than reactive.
Programs and policies are proposed to influence student growth
positively rather than to wait for problems until they require

37

remedial and corrective action. Further, students are viewed as
collaborators with faculty, staff, and other students in the
process of their learning and growing.

Student Development Functions

To aid learning and growing, three interrelated and overlapping functions provide student development resources for each
student: consulting, administering, and instructing. A student
development specialist performs one or more of the functions in
the course of fulfilling his/her job responsibility.

The consulting function includes working with students and
other resource personnel, both inside and outside the institution,
to help provide the necessary physical, social, financial, and
intellectual resources for student development. The counseling
center is an example of a setting for consulting with students.
This function is based on the premise that the student has personal
responsibility for his/her individual development. The consultant
helps the individual focus on relationships which foster self-
growth and achievement, and which encourage increased personal
initiative, involvement, and responsibility for further progress.
Professional competence to counsel, consult, intervene, and collaborate with individuals and groups is essential. In this
function, the concept of "becoming" is an essential aspect of
personal satisfaction and fulfillment.

The administering function is based on the premise that a
systematic approach to human relationships best promotes students'
continuous growth. The Vice President for Student Personnel/
Student Development/Student Affairs functions as an administrator
a major part of the time. This function is effected through an
organization which emphasizes coordination, communication, supportive services, and policies which are established and maintained
through the professional competencies of the administrator, whose
commitment is made primarily to the educational goals of the
institution. Typical administering concerns involve clear definition of rights and responsibilities, staff development, the
means of accountability, and program development in collaboration
with other major educational divisions of the institution.
Effective and efficient achievement of these goals and the concept
of "doing" are essential to the movement toward continuous development.

The instructing function emphasizes exploration of knowledge
and integration of experience as the primary means by which the
student moves toward full development. Knowledge is gained
through investigation, research, and experience, and it is
disseminated through various forms of teaching-learning, both
inside and outside the traditional classroom. A course in personal development and career planning illustrates this function.

38

Academic competencies, including the ability to teach, to learn, and do research are elements of the instructing function which include the interdisciplinary approach and applied field of student development. In this function, "knowing" oneself and one's environment is valued as the basis for movement toward continuous development for students.

Humanizing and Personalizing Education

As colleges and universities have increased in size and complexity, as faculty and staff have faced greater demands on their time and capabilities, and as student populations have grown larger and considerably more heterogeneous, the challenge of making the college experience personally rewarding also has increased. Whether instructing, consulting, or administering, the student development specialist shares responsibility for humanizing and personalizing each student's higher education. Recognizing that students' problems are often inseparable from institutional problems, he/she may take "risks," as an advocate, to help change the students' institutional environment; or to initiate or collaborate with others in bringing necessary change, whenever the environment impedes growth and learning.

To help individualize each student's experience, the student development specialist applies caring qualities together with his/her special competencies in a multi-process of: assessing each student's needs and status; reassessing a student's status and evaluating the prescribed programs. The student is involved collaboratively to the greatest possible extent in this multi-process. The student development specialist is a partner with the teaching specialist in seeking ways to achieve the goals of the institution.

Qualifications

What does it take to become a student development practitioner? There is not one single and complete answer to that question, but six basic requirements are listed below:

1. Maintain a high level of self-development.
2. Identify, understand, make commitment to, and apply the purposes and assumptions underlying student development.
3. Acquire, hold, and enrich values, attitudes, knowledge, and skills to effectively collaborate with others, in their self-development and in the growth and maintenance of a worthwhile community.
4. Know the major elements of the three student development functions and have skills and attitudes to implement one or more of them.

5. Build student development competencies in the categories of assessment, goal-setting, and change-processes.
6. Have the motivation to work with individuals, groups,
   and organizations with application of high-level competencies.

Development of the Profession

Some aspects of the college student development field are as
old as post-secondary education itself. Various influences have
contributed to its comparatively recent evolvement as a distinctly
integral part of the educational process. The emergence of psychological testing, the mental health movement, the development
of the concepts of career planning and counseling, along with
various contemporary societal pressures, all serve to expand and
strengthen the evolving concept of this field.

Contemporary events have influenced the more than 40,000
people currently engaged in full or part-time student development
work in post-secondary education. It would appear that job opportunities in the field will stabilize during the late 1970's, with
the exception of increased opportunities in two-year colleges,
proprietary schools, and community service agencies. For a field
that included only a few deans and registrars in 1900, the
increased number of positions has been phenomenal. Today, those
who wish to prepare for a career in the student development field
can choose from widely diversified educational preparation programs at both the master's and doctoral levels. Institutions with
such preparation programs are located throughout the country.
Scholarships and fellowships are usually available in varying
amounts at the institutions concerned.

The emphasis given here on the student development field
should not in any way imply that teaching faculty are not also
engaged in many facets of student development activity. In fact,
bridging the gaps between student development specialists and
teaching specialists is a primary concern and effort.

Compensation

Salaries vary considerably from institution to institution.
Student development specialists are usually paid on a 10- or 12-
month basis and participate in the retirement, group insurance,
sabbatical, and other benefits accorded the staff of the institution. Some may have faculty rank and may elect to do part-time
classroom teaching. Entering-level positions in 1978 paid about
$12,000, which includes all benefits, and up for ten months,
while a number of top-level administrators with the title Vice
President or Dean were in the $30,000 to $44,000 salary range for
12 months with all benefits. Many positions in housing provide
additional compensation in the form of room and board. Compen-

sation grows with the assumption of increasing responsibility.

How One Advances

Student development specialists may enter the profession in
a variety of ways. Opportunities exist for residence hall
counselors and assistants in student activities, vocational/or
career counseling and placement, student financial aid, admissions,
minority affairs, and in central administrative offices. Advancement generally comes by assuming increasing responsibilities in a
specialized area or by accepting broader responsibilities for the
administration of several areas. More rapid advancement is
achieved by those who, in addition to gaining professional experience, qualify themselves by further graduate study. Chief administrative posts are increasingly offered to those who hold advanced
degrees and have had considerable post-secondary experience.

Kinds of Positions

Larger colleges and universities divide student development
functions into highly specialized assignments and build staffs in
each specific area. In many smaller two-year and four-year
colleges, however, a few people may be responsible for the entire
student development program. New functions develop as institutions
increase in size and change in nature. For example, external
degree programs, universities without walls, and continuing education contribute to the number and variety of positions available.

The areas of professional specialization described on the
following pages are some of those in which qualified persons are
placed. It is assumed that the master's degree will be required
for an entry-level position unless exceptions are noted in the
text.

Administrators of student development. The chief administrator of an institution's student development program is most
commonly known as the vice president for student affairs or the
dean of students. Major administrative functions include providing creative leadership to the student development area and
coordinating the programs described on the preceding pages.
Included in the leadership role is the responsibility for frequent
evaluation of the total impact of the student development program
to ensure that it is in keeping with the changing needs of the
students and with the institution's objectives. In addition, he/
she assists the president and other key officials in developing
institutional policies and goals, and has responsibility for staff
selection and training for fiscal projection and planning.

Responsibility is also taken for the development of proposals for funding new and creative programs designed to enhance
student life. Data are made available on student and institutional

41

characteristics for purposes of long-term policy decisions and program development.

The chief student development officer is usually assisted by associate deans responsible for specific student programs. Although these deans have a number of administrative duties, most of their time is spent working directly with students, individually or in groups. Depending on the type of campus, they may have responsibility for student activities, including student organizations, student conduct, student life in residence halls, commuter students, and minority affairs.

Preparation for these positions usually includes one or more advanced degrees and prior experience in a student development specialty. In an increasing number of colleges and universities the doctorate is required.

Admissions and records. The functions performed by officers of admissions and records are varied and numerous. Some institutions have a single office of admissions and records, while some have separate offices. Titles vary from Admissions Officer, Registrar, Director of Admissions and Records, and Dean of Admissions and Records, to a title such as Vice President for Admissions and Records.

Presently in institutions ranging from the community two-year college to the multiversity, the role of the registrar and admissions officer is expanding. The major responsibilities of the office include: (a) aiding prospective students in matching their educational needs, interests, and qualifications with the offerings, opportunities, and standards of the college; (b) maintaining the academic records of these students; and (c) providing timely and accurate data for communication, both within the college and between the college and its constituency. Sometimes the Office of Admissions and Records has responsibility for such things as student financial aid, class scheduling, publishing the catalogue, and institutional research.

The registrar and admissions officer today is usually active in top-level decision-making in administrative and educational policy areas, such as long-range planning, academic standards, enrollment projections, and student recruitment.

In order to carry out the usual duties, the registrar and admissions officer needs to be a specialist in or familiar with data processing, personnel and office management, counseling and guidance, comparative education, institutional research, public relations, budgeting, accreditation standards, space utilization, curriculum content and planning, and state and federal data requirements. The requirement for employment as a registrar and/ or chief admissions officer is usually a master's degree, at the minimum.

Career planning and placement. The role of career planning and placement has gained great importance and attention, with the professional placement counselor playing an important part in the total education process. The placement counselor offers students and alumni guidance and information so that each individual may evaluate strengths and weaknesses and select the area of career interest which best provides for personal growth and self-realization. The individual in this role is a counselor, personnel specialist, administrator, and consultant. Since the emphasis is on career planning, the bringing together of student and employer in the interview room is merely one of the final steps in the process. He/she must be a good administrator with ability and knowledge to work harmoniously with students, faculty, administrators, and employers. The career planning and placement officer must keep abreast of changes in both education and the world of work, because of the dynamic and developmental nature of the populations served.

Many of the curricular offerings in occupational guidance, personnel psychology, testing, marketing, market research, and career education are relevant to career planning and placement. Experience in a business, industrial, or college setting also enriches preparation for positions in career planning and placement.

College student housing. With the rapid growth of college populations also came a striking growth in colleges' physical facilities, including student housing on and off the campus. Generally the very existence of housing on a campus rests on educational bases—academic residential colleges, living-learning centers and environments, and intentional student development centers are terms that may be used to describe such housing. Ordinarily student housing facilities, organizations, staff, and programs are designed to bring together the academic with the student's out-of-class, community living-learning experiences. Usually, student housing takes many different forms to accommodate student differences, allowing for much student choice and access to many different kinds of groups and experiences.

With student development as a primary underlying purpose, college student housing involves four basic, overlapping work areas: business, education, food, and physical plant. Within a large and complex organization there might be a business manager, educational programs coordinator, food manager, and physical plant director. A smaller and less complex system is likely to have these functions blended together into one or more work roles.

To educationally prepare for the above work areas it is necessary to focus on five basic "knowledge" areas: administration, business, food, human behavior, and physical environment. The successful chief housing officer will be knowledgeable and experienced in all the areas.

For persons with a career commitment and appropriate preparation, college student housing does offer significant career opportunities. Importantly, it offers a relatively large number of entry-level work opportunities to prepare for such a career. It is very common for student development leaders to receive their first full-time work experiences while living and working in college student housing. At the entry level, the primary work area is education with some involvement in the business work area; and, at most colleges, these experiences are a compliment to the graduate student experience at the master's or doctoral degree level.

Counseling. Counseling and testing centers maintained by many colleges and universities afford educational, vocational/ career, and personal counseling on a voluntary basis to help the student acquire self-understanding, relate effectively to the environment, make personal decisions, and take responsibility for individual actions. Counseling may be provided on an individual basis and in group settings. A confidential relationship is maintained between the counselor and counselee. A counseling and testing center is open to all students who seek its services--those who request aid in accomplishing their development tasks and those who seek remedial help. Counselors frequently make referrals to and work cooperatively with a variety of agencies, both within the institution and in the community.

A counseling and testing center usually maintains a library of educational, occupational, and other informational materials, and provides testing as an aid to the counseling process. The center may assist with admissions, selection, and academic placement. Counseling and testing staff members may teach in the area of their academic specialty, serve as consultants, and engage in research. Many centers provide supervised experience for counselors in training and in-service education for other staff persons and student assistants. Counselors may be involved in meeting the changing needs of students. In recent years many have participated in marriage counseling, sex and drug education, and in other special programs. Counselors often give input to administrative deliberations about the environment of the institution and actively promote an atmosphere of positive mental health and human development.

A master's degree in counseling and guidance, personnel, psychology, or social work is required for positions in professional counseling or psychometry. Persons planning to do therapeutic work or aspiring to top administrative positions in counseling should have their doctorate.

Student activities. The student development educator in
student activities has responsibility for working with leaders and
members of proposed and established student organizations, particularly with student government. He/she is a resource for student
groups to use in planning, implementing, and evaluating their
activities. Frequent contact is made with students, faculty, and
other staff members of the institution as well as with alumni and
community organization representatives. Communication and cooperation is encouraged and facilitated among these groups to effect
coordination in student programs. Other typical functions of a
student activities staff include leadership education, training
workshops, consultation with students in the area of institutional
policies and procedures, research pertinent to student life, and
involvement in new student orientation. A new emphasis on administering service projects in the community is emerging. The
administrative component is becoming a particularly significant
part of student activities work.

The student activities staff member should have a broad
knowledge of the social and behavioral sciences and specialized
graduate education in student development work. Also, it is useful to have participated in campus activities as a student.

Student financial aid. A financial aid staff member assists
students with problems in financing their higher education. A
staff member must know the increasing variety and amounts of available aid in order to counsel students and parents on finances. He/
she works closely with student development deans, with admissions,
placement, counseling, academic and business administration offices.
In addition, he/she relates to faculty and alumni and to groups and
agencies offering scholarships, loans, grants, and student employment.

A financial aid administrator's training and experience should
enable him/her to understand students' fiscal management and principles of student development. Such specific skills as interviewing
and the analysis of students' financial resources are essential in
order to determine the amount and kinds of financial aid required.
In addition, he/she must keep abreast of the changing provisions
and requirements to federal, state, and local programs and be able
to prepare the required applications and reports for various offices
and agencies which provide funds. A master's degree in business or
college student personnel is suggested for a staff member in Student
Financial Aid.

Student unions. The college union is usually conceived as the
campus community center which provides not only the facilities and
services needed for living on campus but also cultural, social, and
recreational programs which enhance the educational experience of
students. The college union field is one of the fastest growing

45

professions in higher education. More than 900 colleges and universities in Canada and the United States now have unions.

College union staff members consult and work with students to provide a comprehensive program to develop student leadership. The program may embrace the areas of art, music, literature, films, recreation, social events, leadership development, lectures and discussions on current issues, and group interaction opportunities.

College union staff members also direct the operation of the physical facilities of the union building. Employee supervision and development, fiscal planning, building maintenance, campus-community relations, and facility planning are typical management functions. Part of the work of some union administrators is direction of such operations as food services, recreations areas, the bookstore, guest rooms, conference facilities, theaters, and craft shops.

Liberal arts, business administration, recreation, education, and/or food and institutional management provide good background for a person desiring college union work. A graduate degree in student personnel, business, social science, or recreation is desirable preparation for a union career. Several master's degree programs are now being offered in college union work.

Special programs. The following programs and offices are often related and/or responsible to the student development officer:

Affirmative Action--Advise college community in regard to hiring and promotion of women and minorities. Represent the institution to appropriate outside agencies.

Community relations (field experience)--Plan cooperative programs with external organizations and agencies. Organize practicum opportunities related to the student's major field. Assist in evaluating life experiences for purpose of awarding college credit.

Crisis Intervention--Arrange for resource and walk-in centers to provide information and/or assistance to students about sex, alcohol, and drugs.

Women's Programs--Provide individual and group life-planning and career counseling for all women. Act as liaison between the institution and women who seek to take advantage of learning opportunities.

Educational Opportunity Programs--Bring together academic assistance through the use of tutors, peer counselors, and special academic courses designed for students who have

46

inadequate educational backgrounds.

Religious Program Coordinator--Serve as channel of communication between the college and the religious groups. Assist
the efforts of the responsible religious groups as they
seek to minister to students and faculty.

Volunteer Program Services--Coordinate the efforts on the
part of the student and faculty to respond to various needs
in larger community, e.g., work with prisoners, assist in
poverty areas, send task forces to disaster areas.

Orientation--Plan and administer events which introduce new
students to the college community. Organize summer orientation for the older student.

Minority Student Affairs--Identify campus resources that can
be used to assist students of culturally different backgrounds. Provide leadership for a campus to recognize
appropriately the contributions of minority groups.

Foreign Student Advisement--The foreign student advisor ad-
ministers and coordinates many of the services which are
crucial in insuring a successful academic and social experience for students from other countries. The foreign student
advisor usually assists with foreign student admissions,
placement, orientation, financial aid, housing, program of
English as a second language, academic advising, personal
counseling, student-community relationships, alumni relations, and pre-departure orientation. The international
dimension of student development/student personnel work is
advanced by serving as an advisor to student organizations,
including international associations and nationality groups,
and to American students interested in study, educational
travel, work, or service projects abroad. The field of
foreign student advising offers unique opportunities to
provide leadership in cross-cultural learning experiences
involving both American and foreign students. The FSA usually is the institutional liaison to major educational exchange
agencies, national and international government offices, and,
in the interests of furthering international education, is
called upon to serve as an international officer of the
college or university.

Some of these areas have been part of the student development
division for several years and others are recent additions. En-
trants into these areas of responsibility have no single pattern.
Many people related to these special program functions have years
of training and a great deal of experience in one or more of the
special fields, while others have generalized student-development
training and experience.

Some of the functions described above have professional associations, conferences, and meetings. Opportunities in these special program areas differ widely and, more often than not, depend on the interest of the administrators as well as the training of personnel already available at the institution.

Preparation Programs--In-Service and Pre-Service

This brochure's intention is to give an overview of the various career possibilities in the student development profession. The members of the profession on each campus are a primary resource for additional information. They will be able to discuss, in detail, academic preparation programs and employment opportunities.

The diversity of preparation programs and span of functions makes it possible for a wide variety of personalities to be accommodated in this profession.

The American College Personnel Association periodically issues a directory of preparation programs. Information about this directory is available from the President of ACPA or the Chairman of Commission XII--Professional Education of Student Personnel Workers in Higher Education. The names and addresses of these persons are available in the Journal of College Student Personnel. This directory provides information about curricular emphases in the various programs throughout the country as well as about financial assistance, which varies from institution to institution. A direct contact should be made with one or more of the institutions providing professional training three to six months before you are planning to enroll.

Future questions about inter-associational activities may be directed to:

Commission on Professional Education of Student
    Personnel Workers in Higher Education
c/o APGA Headquarters
1607 New Hampshire Ave., N.W.
Washington, D.C. 20009

The first edition of this brochure, published in 1969, was prepared under the direction of the Commission on Professional Development of COSPA, Ivan Putman, Jr., Chairman. This was revised by Patricia Thrash, Robert Page, and Raymond Stockard, with Warren Kauffman serving as editor. The current edition was revised by the 1973-74 Commission on Professional Development of COSPA, Gerald Saddlemire, Chairman.

ACPA Monographs discuss several of the student personnel functions. For a complete listing of titles and information

48

about ordering, write to APGA Publications Sales, 1607 New Hampshire Avenue, N.W., Washington, DC 20009.

The COSPA Commission on Professional Development statement, Student Development Services in Higher Education, is useful for those who seek information about the philosophy of the profession and suggested curriculum for preparation programs for those who enter the profession.

COSPA--The Organization

Concurrent with authorizing a revision of this booklet, COSPA is planning a change in its structure whereby it will continue as an informal mechanism for communication but with few, if any, standing committees and commissions. The background of COSPA is best explained by the following material taken from the preceding edition of this careers booklet:

What is COSPA? "The Council of Student Personnel Associations in Higher Education is a council of national professional student personnel associations in higher education which share common objectives in the area of college student personnel work.

What are COSPA's purposes? "The purposes of COSPA are to bring together professional associations concerned with student personnel work in order to identify their common objectives, to work cooperatively in the areas of their common concerns, to clarify the role of student personnel work in higher education, and to communicate and interpret its significance to all who are interested in students and their education.

"The principal aims of COSPA are to provide a means by which member associations may exchange information and ideas for their mutual benefit; to develop and encourage study commissions pertinent to the interest of the member associations; to provide a means for promoting the professional development of the members of student personnel associations; to promote and actively support sound policies in student personnel administration; and to represent the member associations to the appropriate educational organizations, governmental agencies, and elsewhere when such representation may be useful."

49

CHAPTER 5

STUDENT DEVELOPMENT SERVICES IN POST SECONDARY EDUCATION

Commission on Professional Development of Council
of Student Personnel Associations in Higher Education

PREFACE

Gerald L. Saddlemire

This document describes the ideal roles for the student
development specialist. While the committee admits to a gap
between practice and theory, they are very conscious of practitioners whose behavior now models some of the basic concepts.
The philosophy in this document is operational in a significant
number of institutions. It then becomes appropriate to set
forth lofty though obtainable goals for staffs to move toward
with varying speeds and degrees of success.

It should be further noted that the Phase II, "A Student
Development Model for Student Affairs in Tomorrow's Higher
Education," makes assumptions about roles and urges competency
development in terminology similar to this document. This
instance of mutual reinforcement should be a matter of satisfaction and encouragement to the committees responsible for
each statement.

INTRODUCTION

Alva C. Cooper

The Commission on Professional Development of the Council
of Student Personnel Associations in Higher Education (COSPA)
was given the task of revising "A Proposal for Professional
Preparation in College Student Personnel Work." However, after
reading the statement, it became apparent that the basic formulation of an operational philosophy (The Student Personnel
Point of View) would have to be reviewed before any attempt could
be made at a statement on professional preparation.

The Commission, after reviewing the Student Personnel Point
of View documents of 1937 and 1949, began a free-floating, brainstorming, discussion from which consensus began to emerge.

Certain points of view emerged as keystones for our thinking:

1. The orientation to Student Personnel is developmental.

2. Self-direction of the student is the goal of the student and is facilitated by the Student Development Specialist.

3. Students are viewed as collaborators with the faculty and administration in the process of learning and growing.

4. It is recognized that many theoretical approaches to human development have credence, and a thorough understanding of such approaches is important to the Student Development Specialist.

5. The Student Development Specialist prefers a proactive position in policy formulation and decision making so that a positive impact is made on the change process.

The Commission then prepared a working paper on philosophy and, subsequently, on professional preparation. This was submitted to the COSPA Council and distributed to its constituent groups for reactions. It was also presented at a program session at the American College Personnel Association Convention in Chicago in the spring of 1972.

The present paper reflects reactions, criticisms, and suggestions received. The title, "Student Development Services in Higher Education," should be viewed as an inclusive term for the many areas usually included in student personnel programs. Harold Grant (ACPA), George Jones (ACURA), and Gerald Saddlemire (ACPA), drafted statements which became the basis for this document. King Bradow (ACURA), Alva Cooper (CPC), Virginia Kirkbride (NAWDC), Jack Nelson (ACUHO), Robert Page (ACUHO, former chairman of the commission), and Harold Riker (ACUHO), contributed to the development of the paper from its inception to its final form.

The Commission hopes that this document will be used for the profession as a point of departure for assessment, innovation, and development. Revisions were made in 1973-74 by the Professional Development Commission of COSPA and by members of ACPA Comm. XII, Professional Education of Student Personnel Workers in Higher Education.

51

STUDENT DEVELOPMENT SERVICES IN HIGHER EDUCATION

The purpose of student development services in higher education is to provide both affective and cognitive expertise in the processes involved in education. The specialists providing these services function in a cooperative-integrative role with the student who seeks development toward self-direction and interact with the faculty members concerned with the academic content to be acquired in this development. The student development specialist bears a responsibility toward the broad spectrum of persons who can profit from post secondary education.

Collectively, we use an educational institution to structure behavioral development so that it occurs in the most effective and efficient manner. Education includes the content of behavior (what is to be developed by a person) and the process of development (how and when it is to be acquired). Educators include experts in content and process. In general, faculty tend to emphasize content and student development specialists tend to emphasize process.

Assumptions of Student Development Specialists

Human beings express their life-goal as becoming free, liberated, self-directed, and seek it through a process variously called self-actualization, individuation, ego integration, full functioning, and behavioral development.

The Student Development Specialist believes the potential for development and self-direction is possessed by everyone. Education is a way of assisting in developing these potentials.

The student development specialist believes that acceptance and understanding of persons as they are is essential. Since human potential cannot adequately be measured, a person's possession of unlimited potential may be assumed.

Clientele

The student development specialist deals with human relationships among individuals, groups, and organizations. To do so, the specialist should be familiar with the dynamics of social structure and should be able to utilize this knowledge in facilitating student growth.

The individual. The student development specialist will draw from various conceptual models available from philosophy, psychology, theology, physiology, and other disciplines in dealing with individuals. It is further recognized that an individual's behavior is affected by involvement with other people.

52

The expression of behavior by an individual, however, may be public or private.

The group. Groups may provide a powerful learning environment to promote individual development. Involvement or participation in a group contributes to individual growth. Groups also provide a structural unit for facilitating and promoting collective experiences and normative behavior.

The organization. Organizations comprise varied components of groups and individuals. As social systems of differing sizes and relationships, they enable individuals to strengthen and/or learn additional coping behaviors such as cross cultural understanding, methods of conflict management, skills in problem solving, decision-making, and other leadership approaches.

The educational institution is composed of individuals, groups, and organizations which may provide a complete and balanced environment for human development.

Competencies

The student development specialist provides expertise in the following:

1. Assist in establishing goals for development based upon an appreciation of the unlimited potential of human beings. The goals are not only ultimate, but also intermediate, leading sequentially toward completeness.

2. Assist in the assessment procedures necessary for any individual, group, or organization to progress toward defined goals.

3. Use of various methods of change such as organizational development, systems theory, intervention theory, futures intervention to facilitate behavioral development within the individuals, the groups, the organizations, and the institution.

The competencies of each student development specialist are used in functions categorized as administrative, instructive, and consultative. These functions are integrated according to the particular responsibilities that are assumed. One may be primarily an administrator in the morning, use instructor competencies later in the day, and then participate in an evening event requiring consultant competencies. The likelihood of having a role exclusively as administrator, instructor or consultant is minimal.

Administrative responsibility. Titles applicable to this responsibility are: Vice-President, Deans, and Director with staff members as Associates or Assistants.

Instructor responsibility. When this responsibility is
emphasized, the student development specialist usually carries
the title of dean or professor, with staff members having the
rank of Associate or Assistant. The staff is organized into
schools or departments emphasizing staff relationships rather
than the line relationships of the administrator role. As a
result, evaluations and participations among colleagues in
decision-making are more highly valued.

Consultant responsibility. Major titles are counselor and
consultant with the staff associated with the Counseling Center
serving the entire institution.

Administrative function. This function is based on the
premise that a systematic approach to human relationships helps
to achieve continuous growth. This is gained through organization emphasizing coordination, communication, supportive services,
rules, and regulations which are established and maintained
through the personal competency of the leader, whose commitment is
primarily to the educational goals of the institution. Typical
administrative concerns are for clear definitions of rights and
responsibilities, for means of accountability, and program development.

In this function, achieving goals effeciently and effectively
and the concept of "DOING" are valued as the bases for movement
toward continuous growth.

Instructor function. This function emphasizes exploration
of knowledge and integration of experience as the primary means
by which the student moves toward "FULL" development. Knowledge
is gained through investigation, research and experience, and is
disseminated through various forms of teaching. Academic competencies, including the ability to teach and to do research, are
elements of the instructor function both inside and outside the
traditional classroom. The interdisciplinary and applied field
of student development is paramount.

In this function, "KNOWING" oneself and one's environment is
valued as the basis for movement toward continuous growth.

Consultant function. This function is based on the premise
that the student has personal responsibility for individual
development. The consultant helps the individual focus on
relationships which foster self-achievement and which encourage
personal initiative, involvement, and responsibility for further
progress. Professional competence to counsel, consult, intervene,
and collaborate with individuals and groups is basic to the consultant function. The consultant works with other educators to

help provide the necessary physical, social, financial, and intellectual resources for student development.

In this function, the concept of "BECOMING" is an essential source of personal satisfaction and fulfillment.

Chart I summarizes the major elements of the three functions. A change in any of the items affects and changes each of the other aspects because of the interrelatedness of functions and the various elements of functions.

The elements of the three functions are listed in separate columns but the functions must come together in various combinations for each practitioner.

CHART I

Major Elements of the Three Functions

	Administering	Instructing	Consulting
Approach	Structure Objectives	Knowledge	Personal Responsibility
Process	Organization	Teaching & Research	Counseling & Collaboration
Staff Qualifications	Leadership/ Management Objectives	Scholarship Leadership	Facilitation
Context	Primary Commitment to the Institution	Primary Commitment to the Discipline	Primary Commitment to the Students
Titles	Vice-President or Director	Dean Professor	Counselor Advisor Consultant
Structure	Division	Dept. or School	Counseling Center
Modes	Doing	Knowing	Becoming

For example, the Vice-President for Student Affairs will spend a substantial amount of time administering, but the Vice-President would also be instructing and consulting to the extent appropriate for the particular task to be performed.

The ultimate goal of all three functions is to contribute to continuous, positive self-development. Major attention is thus given to relationships which respect existing self-direction and encourage initiative, involvement, and responsibility for further development.

In all three functions, research plays an integral part.

Implementation

The organization of Student Development Services may vary, depending on the unique purposes, functions and changing aspects of a particular institution. It may also be influenced by the performance and integration of respective functions. The staff could be organized around functions with relationships to clientele and use of competencies contained in each area, or around competencies or clientele. At present, no single structure appears superior, as seen in Diagram I below.

DIAGRAM I

CLIENTELE	COMPETENCIES	FUNCTION
Institutions	Tasks	Positions
Individual	Goal Setting	Consultant
Groups	Assessment Procedures	Instructor
Organization	Change Implementation	Administrator

Professional Preparation

Strong grounding in, and commitment to student development purposes and assumptions, development of the competencies required, practicing and performing the respective functions, and consideration of various approaches to organization should be included in any preparation program. The emphases, sequences, and methods of instruction could vary from program to program, and yet each could prepare professionals of excellence.

Program of Studies. Curricular innovation is necessary in graduate programs preparing persons for student development services during the last quarter of the Twentieth Century. A critical need exists for professionals who give assertive leadership regardless of changing job titles, excised organizations, declining budgets, diversifying student bodies, and often hostile public opinion. At the same time these professionals must be open, warm, optimistic human beings. Comfortable conformity to guidelines based on traditional patterns of graduate education will not suffice. The following recommendations are general approaches to professional preparation consistent with the purposes and practices recommended in preceding sections.

Since student development is seen to be the process by which individuals gain increasing mastery of their own self-direction and fulfillment, this process should be the basic means of professional education for the student development specialist. The goal of a professional program should be the preparation of persons who, in addition to having attained a high level of self-development, have skills to collaborate with others in their self-development. They must be able to use competencies of assessment, goal setting, and change processes as appropriate in implementing the roles of consultant, administrator, and instructor in relationships with individuals, groups, and organizations.

General goals should be translated into specific objectives of the competencies needed for functioning in the professional role of the student development specialist in the processes involved in education. These objectives should be stated in terms of measurable criteria in order that performance criteria can be developed for evaluation. The following is an example of a listing of such objectives:

Program Objectives

Objectives are categorized according to three competencies: (1) Helping students move toward goals; (2) Assessing status, abilities, and progress; (3) Using strategies of change to facilitate human development. Within each category of competency, objectives are listed which illustrate the three possible functions of the student development specialist: Administering, Instructing, Consulting.

The essential features of these functions are: (1) Administrative--organize, coordinate, communicate, support, write and enforce rules and regulations, be accountable, assume and protect rights and responsibilities, emphasize staff relationships in departments. (2) Instructional--know individuals, groups, and organizations through investigational research, in order to teach. (3) Consultative--be available for student and faculty member collaboration for policy determination and problem solving that relates to improvement of student learning and environment modification.

The student development specialist is expected to master the following behavioral objectives:

I. Helping Clientele Move Toward Goals. (These behaviors are necessary professional competencies to help students with their goals.)

    A. Be able to apply various aspects of personnel management.

        1. Write job descriptions.
        2. Administer salary schedule.
        3. Recruit professional staff.
        4. Evaluate staff.
        5. Administer in-service training.

    B. Draw up and justify a budget showing fiscal management that follows planning, programming, and budgeting principles.

    C. Be able to apply legal decisions and legal processes to the collegiate institution and to all of its constituents--faculty, students, administration, and non-professional staff.

    D. Identify and assist undergraduate students who are underprepared for higher education learning experiences.

        Describe elements of an academic-assistance program.

    E. Identify the characteristics of critical thinking and problem solving so they may be applied to improved self-understanding.

    F. Demonstrate how to assist students in developing comprehensive career planning and implementation.

58

G. Demonstrate the ability to establish a productive counseling relationship with individuals and with groups.

II. Assessing Status, Abilities and Progress

A. Write a report describing the emerging style of governance on the campus and describe the political and social matrix: student, faculty, and administration.

B. List and describe the opportunities for learning in the external community so that student development may take advantage of the complete resources of a region.

C. Construct and apply a model for measurement of the effectiveness of the student development program.

Identify quantifiable outcomes of such functions as counseling, financial aids, residence halls, academic assistance, student activities.

D. Be able to state the purposes, values, competencies, and roles of a student development specialist.

E. Assess behavior of the college population using clinical and objective methods.

1. Write a comparison of life styles and cultural differences of student sub-groups.
2. State the principles of growth and development patterns of the student.

F. List the general characteristics of American higher education institutions and compare these with the specific characteristics of the local institution.

III. Using Principles and Techniques for Change To Facilitate Human Development

A. Act in accordance with the list of values (based on professional assumptions) in dealing with students from diverse backgrounds.

B. List strategies of conflict resolution on campus.

Demonstrate conflict strategies of management

59

in the power models and the collaborative
models of administration.

C. Conduct personal growth seminars and discussion
groups for improvement of self-understanding.

D. Write out a program of requirements for use by
architects.

Describe student needs to the designer of
specific educational facilities.

E. Seek solutions to student-related problems, using
fact-finding and analysis, given an attitude of
serving as defender and interpreter for student
concerns.

F. Critique human behavior research studies in order
to describe the application of the findings to
the campus population.

G. Complete a research project which tests a hypothesis related to student behaviro or institutional
characteristics.

The general terminal objective for a preparation program is:
Given a real or simulated situation where the student development
specialist will emphasize one of the three roles--administrative,
instructional, or consultative--the specialist will demonstrate
specific competencies in three areas: goal setting, assessment,
and the process of change applied to the individual, group and
organization.

The criteria for the list of objectives are derived from
the concept that the student development specialist performs so
that clientele are able to:

1. Achieve goals.
2. Manage conflict.
3. Become more self-directed and self-fulfilled.

The STudent Development Specialist should be able to be
perceived as a resource of personal satisfaction and fulfillment.
Students should be involved in an on-going process of self-
assessment, goal setting, utilization of resources, and behavioral
change. Professors of student development, student development
specialist, and graduate students should continually relate as
full collaborators. Internships and other supervised practice
should be available as needed in pursuance of particular objectives. Graduate students should be adequately compensated
for the professional services they provide during their program
of professional preparation.

The administrative organization for the program should clearly identify the student development program as a graduate program in its own right. Representatives of related departments should be consulted regularly to insure an adequate multi-disciplinary base for the curriculum. To continually improve the program, feedback should be obtained from the field on the performance of graduates.

A master's degree program should be directed toward the preparation of a beginning professional who holds basic humanistic values and evidences potential for facilitating student development. Specialist or sixth-year programs should provide resources for acquiring more sophisticated levels of competencies and functions in specific settings for student development. Programs at the doctoral level should be given particular attention to values, competencies, and functions needed for leadership in higher education. Programs at this level require a commitment to scholarship and human development.

Admission, Evaluation, and Professional Endorsement

Students seeking admission to programs of professional preparation should be assessed on the bases of values, competencies, and functions they will be required to perform as a student development specialist.

Continuing evaluation during the professional preparation program would be based on the same criteria. Those endorsed by the graduate program for admission to professional practice would thus exhibit behaviors most consistent with the professional purposes, values, competencies, and functions stated in this document.

CHAPTER 6

STATUS OF THE COLLEGE STUDENT PERSONNEL FIELD:
DEFINING THE PROFESSION

John Eddy and Sheldon Siegel

The field of College Student Personnel Work is a pre-
paradigmatic science, which means it has a number of models
utilized by its personnel, such as the In Loco Parentis Model,
the Medical Model, the Services Model and the Student Development Model. In other previous chapters, these models will be
given fuller attention. For example, by contrast, a field
that has paradigmatic science is physics.

Method of Identification

Some of the characteristics of the College Student Personnel
field are:

1. It is more rational than empirical; for example, the
area of decision making relies more on pragmatic solutions to
problem solving which comes from a personal on-the-job frame of
reference based on previous career experiences and training.

2. It is mainly prescriptive rather than predictive in its
nature. For example, case studies are used as a prescriptive
approach to problem solving. However, it is also predictive in
some areas such as financial aids and admissions whereby certain
established criteria are applied to specific student populations.

3. It is an immature science like the fields of counseling,
social work, anthropology, and other like type professions.
Each of the previously mentioned professions have no one agreed
model which is universally accepted by those who are professionals.
By contrast, the "hard sciences" such as the physical sciences
tend to be more mature since more common agreements in terms of
approaches and practices are accepted by their respective professionals.

4. It is descriptive in essence rather than "cause-effect"
that follows the scientific method. However, the professionals
in this field still find the use of the scientific method a useful tool in formulating problem solutions.

5. It is observed that within the field it ranges from
structuralist types of services such as specialists in financial

aids and records to functionalist types such as deans of students and counselors who are macro-oriented rather than micro-oriented and are generalists. The whole field has a neo-evolutionist process since the Student Development Model was accepted by the Council on Student Personnel Associations in 1972.

6. It is more ethnographic and anthropological than experimental in its practice. The reason being that the profession itself has ethical guidelines such as the American Personnel and Guidance Association Ethical Code that prohibits humans from being involved in purely scientific experiments such as done in some behavioral modification psychology projects as Masters and Johnson.

7. It applies inductive (from specific to general); deductive (from general to specific); and abductive (from a no hypothesis basis) in its rational process.

8. It is informal theoretical by contrast to formal theoretical because it relies on all forms of structured and non-structured inquiry, including serendipity or accidental discovery.

9. It is a field which is characterized by more applied research based on problems and populations that have existed or do exist as opposed to basic research akin to what the physicist does in the laboratory.

10. It is more philosophically associated to instrumentalism which asserts that ideas are plans for action. Instrumentalism would be multi-faceted in its theories and practices with a pragmatic goal of implementation and application.

Method of Observation

The field lends itself to at least four different types of observation:

1. Naturalistic observation--an example would be to observe the behavior of students in a residential living unit;

2. Psychometric--an example would be using the MMPI in assessing students' psychological status;

3. Experimental analysis--an example would be to analyze the problem that students aren't receiving proper information on financial aid; certain hypotheses would be formulated and an experimental design would be set up to test the hypotheses; and,

4. Ex Post Facto--an example review the past standardized test scores (ACT and/or SAT) of students as contrasted with a new student test group to be tested.

63

Method of Research

The following methods of research are commonly used in the field. They are not all that have been used nor are they all that might in the future be deployed.

1. Field Experiment--is a social study of particular human variables which are identified, such as student dissent, measured by observations such as picketing before a college office;

2. Field Study--is a questionnaire type of survey and it is ex post facto in nature to determine the status of a particular population or project selected;

3. Survey of Research--is a review of primary and secondary literature and it employs historical documentary research;

4. Interview Research--is a defined method of asking persons a series of structured and agreed upon questions about their or others beliefs, attitudes, opinion, behavior and so forth;

5. Pre-test and Post-test Research--is a method of using a standardized or normed instrument on a specific population of persons to determine if any change of their knowledge, attitude or actions has occurred between periods of testing (a "control group or groups" are used to compare with a "treatment group or groups" their differences, if any); and,

6. Model Testing and Building Research--is a method of testing a particular model by stimulation and other procedures by gaining strategies to build a specific model to be used for educational purposes.

Methods and Models

It is important that College Student Personnel Work Models are covered. The authors would prefer a Neo-Student Development Model based on a developmental stage theory (Parker, 1975), but would not judge other models as not being useful or practical to apply under certain conditions and in specific situations. Some of the models used by College Student Personnel Workers are:

1. The Medical Model--runs the service, area, and/or division like a medical clinic or hospital with the underlying presupposition that the doctor, nurse, or staff is always right. Students claim under this model that they are often treated more for their illness or special need rather than treated as a whole person. The efficiency of operation is often placed before the student's total development.

2. The In Loco Parentis Model--uses the Latin phrase here, which means "in place of parents," and it is run so personnel literally treat students like parents would deal with children. Again, the paternalistic staff member would be like a foster father or substitute mother with the student.

3. The Reaction and Service Station Model--is run like a gas station in responding to emergencies and needs of students. This model reacts to a student's need, be it for financial aids or for whatever help is requested.

4. The Student Development Model--is described by the 1975 document entitled, "Student Development Services in Post Secondary Education" that is published by the Commission on Professional Education of Student Personnel Workers in Higher Education of the American College Personnel Association. This is covered thoroughly in Chapter 5 of this book.

5. The Combination Model--is simply a combination of one or more of the models previously described. Personnel, within a Student Affairs Division, may use such an eclectic approach in their work.

6. The Neo-Student Development Model--is that model which the authors endorse and essentially it puts the counseling theories via Guntrip, Erickson, Glasser, Harris, Maslow, and Chickering together with the administrative theories via Drucker and Lahti using the COSPA Model of 1975--which sets forth the ten functions, roles, and goals of the work--and it emphasizes a proactive rather than a reactive approach to College Student Personnel Work. The skills and practices of Carkhoff in the Art of Helping III put the "Neo-Student Development Model" together for counseling and administrative approaches in human relations. This approach, by using these meaningful modes, will not be by its nature rigid in its stance or scope. A flexible viewpoint and application is needed in order to incorporate all areas, solidify basic purposes, and to stand the tests of changing times. Using PBE--see Chapter 29--and MBO--see Chapter 30--with the disciplines demonstrated in Life and Management by Responsibility --see Chapters 26 and 27--the College Student Personnel Staff member has some concrete approaches to use every day in his or her work. This provides the practitioner with a workable philosophy and practice. Of course, any system is entirely dependent upon dedicated and competent personnel who are sincerely interested in the welfare of the student and excellence in all of higher education. This Model offers the best opportunity for change agents, ombudspersons, and value centered personnel to do their job in serving students.

Conclusions

Chapter One describes the 1938 and 1949 statements by the American Council on Education which was entitled the "Student Personnel Point of View." However, the actual implementations of these views' implications has come in separate and supplementary college programs. "Student personnel services and instructional services together form the educational program of the institution" as Wrenn (1951) put it. Cowley (1964) describes the unique function of College Student Affairs Personnel as this--"You serve students in various noncurricular ways." However, to update the present practices of College Student Personnel Work, Miller and Prince (1977) point out professionals and paraprofessionals in Student Affairs "are being asked to handle many complex functions --goal setting, assessment, evaluation, instruction, consultation, and milieu management..." Thus, the student development approach includes both the extra-curriculum and the curriculum with credit courses being offered in human potential motivation, drug and alcohol abuse, human sexuality, occupational options, value clarification, transactional analysis applications, and other topics taught by Student Affairs staff. Thus, creative programs in the curriculum are offered on and off the campus (O'Bannion and Thurston, 1972).

References

Bachrach, A.J. Psychological Research: An Introduction. New York: Random House, 1972.

Brown, R.D. Student Development in Tomorrow's Higher Education: A Return to the Academy. Student Personnel Series No. 16. Washington: American College Personnel Association, 1972.

Cowley, W.H. "Reflections of a Troublesome but Hopeful Rip Van Winkle." Journal of College Student Personnel, 1964, 6, 66-73.

Kerlinger,F.N. Foundations Behavioral Research. New York: Holt, Rinehart & Winston, Inc., 1973.

Miller, T.K., and Prince, J.S. The Future of Student Affairs. San Francisco: Jossey-Bass Publishers, 1977.

Mueller, K.H. Student Personnel Services in Colleges and Universities. Boston: Houghton Mifflin Co., 1961.

References

O'Bannion, T. and Thurston, A. Student Development Programs in the Community Junior College. Englewood Cliffs, NJ: Prentice-Hall, 1972.

Parker, C.A. "Student Development: What Does It Mean?" Journal of College Student Personnel, July 1974.

Williamson, E.G. (Chairman) Committee on Student Personnel Work. The Student Personnel Point of View. Revised ed. American Council on Educational Studies, Series VI, No. 13. Washington: American Council on Education, 1949.

Wrenn, C.G. Student Personnel Work in College. New York: Ronald Press, 1951.

CHAPTER 7

ACADEMIC ADVISEMENT IN HIGHER EDUCATION:
A NEW MODEL

Joseph D. Dameron and John C. Wolf

Introduction

The need for constructive change in counseling functions
is being documented in counseling and student personnel journals; and traditional models for counseling centers and services such as those described by Oetting (1970) and O'Banion
(1970) no longer seem sufficient to meet student needs. Questions have been raised concerning the need for change in
counselor orientation and function. Counselor accountability,
stressed by Pulvino and Sanborn (1972) and Warnath (1972) as
becoming a major concern for the counseling profession, is
achieved by making the most efficient use of guidance worker
time, effort, and training. This is accomplished by differentiated staffing, according to training and level of professional sophistication, and then assigning staff members to those
stages of the advisement process for which they are best qualified.

A team approach, including professional counselors, guidance workers, and student assistants, is proposed, with the
emphasis at all points in the process model on individual student
responsibility for decision making. A central hypothesis in
this article is that separation of academic advisement duties
into two major divisions provides more efficient facilitation
of the advisement process. One area of responsibility is
assumed by the counseling center and the other by some other
campus agency.

Academic Advisement

The O'Banion (1972) concept of academic advisement as a
developmental process is used in our proposal. He stresses
that academic advisement is a central part of the college's
attempt to provide students with professional aid in resolving

68

the question, "How do I want to live my life?" Academic advisement is viewed by O'Banion (1972, p. 64) as the following five step, sequential process:

Step 1. Exploration of life goals, which is facilitated by the professional counselor.

Step 2. Exploration of vocational goals, facilitated by the professional counselor.

Step 3. Selection of program, facilitated by faculty advisement.

Step 4. Selection of courses, facilitated by faculty advisement.

Step 5. Scheduling of courses, facilitated by faculty and/or student assistants as available.

The emphasis upon sequential development of academic advisement as described by O'Banion is incorporated into the proposed model, but the developmental implementation outlined in this article is a major point of divergency.

Advisement Facilitation: Counselor and Faculty

The role of the counselor in the academic advisement process is far from clear. A review of student services literature, including Embree (1950), Albert (1968), Nugent and Pareis (1968), and Clark (1966), indicates counselors are becoming much more interested in the personal and social concerns of students. This research suggests that personal-social-emotional counseling is quite important to both counselor and student, and there also appear to be strong administrative implications for professional counselors who wish to become more involved in the total development process.

If the college counselor is developing a role and attitude that focuses on the increasing importance of personal adjustment counseling, individually and in groups, then who is to provide the greater part of the services in the area of academic advisement and vocational-educational guidance? Will it be the faculty member? O'Banion (1972, p. 66) has pointed out that, "Who does the advising is probably not as important as the philosophy of the institution...and the commitment and understanding with which

the counselor or instructor approaches the process." This point
is well-taken, but nonetheless it does seem to make a difference
who does the academic advising for the following reasons:

1. It is felt that there is no substitute for training,
   experience, and commitment. These are credentials
   mentioned by O'Banion, and we believe that trained
   guidance personnel possess them to a greater degree,
   in relation to developmental student academic advising,
   than do faculty members whose career choice has set
   their primary commitment and background in instructional areas.

2. Economically, the cost of using faculty members for
   implementing program choice, course choice, and, in
   some cases, course scheduling appears to be considerable
   if instructional staff members are given released
   time for such activities. The consequences of faculty-
   facilitated advisement without released time seem even
   more formidable.

3. Faculty knowledge of current trends in the competitive
   employment market may be limited by individual subject
   field interest and concentration, whereas guidance
   Personnel, trained and motivated to maintain current
   and comprehensive knowledge of these trends as a primary
   part of their job, should be more knowledgeable in this
   area.

4. Due in part to the lack of an administrative structure
   to provide such coordination, overall coordination of
   academic advisement efforts is usually lacking in
   faculty-facilitated programs.

A Developmental Academic Advisement Model

In many respects the model proposed here is similar to that
described by O'Banion (1972) in emphasizing the developmental
process of academic advisement, but the method of implementation
of this process differs significantly. The difference lies
primarily in the use of personnel for facilitating academic advisement. The call by Berdie (1972) for new methods of professional guidance worker preparation has produced a plan for the
training and use of personnel in the counseling and guidance
field built on a professional career ladder. This career-ladder
approach, described by Dameron (1972), delineates three basic

divisions: the below baccalaureate degree level paraprofessional worker, the baccalaureate degree level preprofessional worker,
and the graduate degree level professional worker. These workers
are termed the guidance assistant, the guidance associate, and
the professional counselor, respectively. This program produces
persons, trained at the below-baccalaureate and baccalaureate
degree levels, whose interest and commitment can lead to training for implementation of the third, fourth, and fifth steps of
the advisement process. If the program is to be successful, it
is essential that personnel at all levels be trained for and
committed to the job they are to do.

In the exploration of life and vocational goals, steps 1
and 2 are facilitated by the professional counselor in the
counseling center, if centralized, or in subcounseling centers
which can be distributed throughout the campus in a decentralized arrangement. These two stages in the advisement process
might be considered as those related not only to educational
and occupational development but to personal and social development as well. This portion of the advisement process can be
facilitated, at least partially, in groups to reach as many
students as possible.

However, the facilitation of program choice and course
selection, steps 3 and 4 of the model, are handled not by the
as in the O'Banion model, but by personnel whose training and
primary commitment lie in the area of vocational guidance and
program and course choice, including working knowledge of all
program offerings and related curriculums of the campus on
which they work. The baccalaureate degree trained guidance
associate, in his facilitation of steps 3 and 4, would be
administratively responsible to whatever agency assumes responsibility for implementation of steps 3, 4, and 5 of the
advisement process. He can also be assigned to work in conjunction with instructional units or departments if desired.

Therefore, the preprofessional guidance associate, rather
than the professional counselor or the faculty member, has the
responsibility for implementing most of the academic advisement process. Students see the professional counselor for
one session or a short series of sessions, possibly in a group
setting, to work through the initial clarification of life and
vocational goals. Since this clarification may take longer
for some students than for others, a provision for recycling
from steps 3 and 4 back through steps 1 and 2 is possible if
necessary. In addition, overlap between step 2, exploration

70a

of vocational goals, and step 3, program choice, would most
certainly occur, so that both the professional counselor and
the preprofessional guidance associate or advisement specialist
must work closely with one another in terms of coordination.
The recycling provision can be used should such problems as
poor academic progress, probation-suspension, or dissatisfaction
occur or if there is any other indication that the student
might need or wish to re-examine his life and vocational goals.

Step 5, scheduling of courses, is facilitated by paraprofessional assistants supervised by the guidance associate to
handle the clerical and scheduling tasks. These assistants
can but need not be students. Here much of the actual ongoing
contact with students in the advisement process is usually
found, although the recycling provision, extending back as far
through the process as necessary, is still functional. Administratively, the guidance assistant, as he is termed in the
career-ladder approach terminology, would be under the supervision of the guidance associate and would be ultimately under
the administration of the agency having supervisory responsibility for the guidance associate. Personnel active in the
facilitation of steps 3, 4, and 5 therefore maintain ongoing
contacts with the student throughout his academic program,
although the professional counselor is of ourse available on
a referral basis for problems in the process.

Student Service Agencies

Although the first two steps of the advisement process,
exploration of life and vocational goals, can best be facilitated by the professional counselor in the counseling center
or subcounseling centers throughout the campus, it is felt
that steps 3, 4, and 5 of the advisement process should be
handled by a decentralized campus agency functionally and
administratively separate from the counseling center; this
would emphasize student convenience and accessibility as
primary concerns. This agency might be called the Advisement
Center, thus creating a new student services division; or
some other unit presently operating might assume the administrative duties.

Kirk (1971) discusses the possibility of using the concept
of the career development center for the implementation of
program and course choice. He considers the career development center a merger of the services of the counseling center
and the placement center, and perhaps such an agency might

prove satisfactory for carrying out the latter three steps
of the proposed developmental advisement model. The arrangement of student service functions on a given campus would
probably determine how this question is resolved by each
institution.

Advantages of the Model

The following is a list of advantages of the model:

1. The model has a theroretical base from which to
    operate and thus can be evaluated, critiqued, and
    modified as needed. This base has been developed
    a priori rather than post hoc as is all to frequent-
    ly noted in the counseling field.

2. At all stages of the advisement process the student
    is working with personnel trained for and committed
    to the portion of the process which they are to
    facilitate.

3. Counselors are free to do what they do best, which
    results in more efficient use of time, training,
    and talent. The counselor may perform personal ad-
    justment counseling as a primary function but may
    still be involved in the academic advisement process
    to the best use of his training and experience.

4. The proposed model for academic advisement is well
    integrated with the career-ladder concept of training,
    particularly in terms of responsibility. A complete
    description of this competency-based training program
    for para-, pre-, and professional personnel in the
    guidance and counseling field may be found in the
    1973 ACES Monograph, Preparation of Guidance Associates
    and Professional Counselors within the Framework of a
    Competency-Based Program.

5. The model and its implementation allow counseling and
    guidance personnel to account for their functions in
    accordance with their training. The use of professional
    counselors in the model is especially important since
    the counselor is never a clerk, course scheduler, or
    participator in any activity that could be efficiently
    facilitated by a person of less-sophisticated training.

70c

6. This model is viewed as economical in terms of personnel as well as monetary expenditures. Administrative overhead is held to a minimum, yet adequate supervision is provided. Student assistants are used when possible, and preprofessional rather than faculty and instructional personnel are used for the majority of advising contacts.

7. Only two campus agencies are necessary for implementation of the advisement process in the model, so that the student does not get lost in the shuffle in the attempt to participate in academic advisement. Unless problems suggest recycling after the initial movement through the steps 1 and 2 of exploration of life and vocational goals, only one agency is involved.

References

Albert, G. "A Survey of College Counseling Facilities". Personnel and Guidance Journal, 1968, 46 (6), 540-543.

Berdie, R. F. "The 1980 Counselor: Applied Behavioral Scientist". Personnel and Guidance Journal, 1972, 50 (6), 451-456.

Clark, D. D. "Characteristics of Counseling Centers in Large Universities". Texas Personnel and Guidance Journal, 1966, 44 (8), 817-823.

Dameron, J. D. "Futuristic Guidance Programs: Texas in the 1980's". Personnel and Guidance Journal, 1972, 1 (1), 45-53.

Dameron, J. D. (Editor). "Preparation of Guidance Associates and Professional Counselors Within the Framework of a Competency-Based Program". Washington, D. C.: American Personnel and Guidance Association, 1973, ACES Monograph.

Embree, R. B. "Developments in Counseling Bureaus and Clinics". Educational and Psychological Measurement, 1950, 10 (3), 465-475.

Kirk, H. P. "Bringing Counseling and Placement Together". Journal of College Placement, 1971, 31 (4), 44-48.

Nugent, F. A., & Pareis, E. N. "Survey of Present Policies and Practices in College Counseling Centers in the U.S.". Journal of Counseling Psychology, 1968, 15 (1), 94-97.

References

O'Banion, T. "An Academic Advising Model". Junior College Journal, 1972, 42 (6), 62-69.

O'Banion, T.; Thurston, A.; & Gulden, J. "Student Personnel Work: An Emerging Model". Junior College Journal, 1970, 41 (3), 6-14.

Oetting, E. R.; Ivey, A. E.; & Weigel, R. C. "The College and University Counseling Center". Washington, D. C.: American Personnel and Guidance Association, 1970, ACPA Monograph, No. 11.

Pulvino, C. J. & Sanborn, M. P. "Feedback and Accountability". Personnel and Guidance Journal, 1972, 51 (1), 15-20.

Warnath, C. "College Counseling: Between the Rock and the Hard Place". Personnel and Guidance Journal, 1972, 51 (4), 229-235.

CHAPTER 8

THE USE OF COUNSELING THEORIES
IN COLLEGE STUDENT PERSONNEL WORK

Peter Cimbolic, John Eddy, Sheldon Siegel, and
Joseph D. Dameron

The College Student Personnel field includes a wide variety
of areas such as admissions, counseling veterans affairs,
health services, and a host of other student-related services
(Fitzgerald, Johnson, Norris, 1970). In spite of the broad
range of areas, there are practical and usable counseling
theories that can be used in all areas with valuable contributions to students. Many of the work activities of student
personnel professionals can not be based upon a single theory.
However, many of their functions may be based upon theoretical foundations.

The State of Theory in the Profession

There have been many attempts to define what a profession
is (Hickson and Thomas, 1969; Humphries, 1977). McGully (1966)
in his attempt to define a "helping profession" states, among
other things, that a profession is based upon specialized
knowledge. Most definitions make some reference to specialized
knowledge. The student personnel profession does indeed possess specialized knowledge, but the theoretical underpinnings
for much of this knowledge is adapted from various types of
developmental, organizational, and counseling theories.

While Student Personnel work may borrow some of its
theoretical base from counseling, it is not based on counseling along. Instead, Student Personnel workers may use counseling theory in a unique way. Student Personnel work differs
from full-time counseling in setting, clientele, and the
problems encountered. Therefore, the Student Personnel worker's
use of counseling theory must be adapted to take these differences into consideration.

The Need for Theory

Student Personnel workers are practitioners. However, most actions, although certainly not all, that are taken by professionals are predicated upon some theoretical formulation whether it be explicit or implicit. The Student Personnel professionals must make the theoretical foundations of his of her interventions and programs explicit.

Further, if programs and services are articulated within a theoretical context, then there is a basis for evaluation, a step sometimes overlooked in the student personnel profession. Every theory provides a basis for prediction of outcome. That is, if one conceptualizes a problem in a given theoretical context and treats the problem in that context, the theory will predict an outcome. If an intervention has been shown to be effective, then there is a responsibility to share the new information through scholarly activities in professional journals.

In summary, theory allows one to conceptualize, treat, predict, and evaluate. It is the authors' contention that if professionals are more conscious of the role of theory in their activities, professionalism will be enhanced.

The Use of Theory

"What treatment, by whom, is most effective for this individual, with that specific problem, under what set of circumstances, and how does it come about?" This question was asked by Paul (1969), but the authors suspect it is asked every day, by each student personnel worker in reference to each individual to whom services are expected to be rendered. Antecedent to this question, however, is the establishment of the goals of any possible interventions. The goals will be determined largely by the theory through which the problem is conceptualized (Stefflre, 1972). Therefore, the determination of the theoretical system is a critical choice.

The goals of an intervention must, of course, reflect student input. Once the goals are explicit, the Student Personnel professional can determine which theoretical approach

72

would have the highest probability of success. In making
this decision, the individuality of the professional, student,
and type of problem must be considered. Student Personnel
workers must choose a theoretical system which is consistent
with their personality, hopefully, one in which they have had
successful past experience with similar types of student
problems. The theory would also have to be appropriate for
the environmental context in which the problem occurs. As
can be surmised from what has already been stated, it is
doubtful that any one theory would be appropriate for the
professional to deal with all individuals, with all types of
problems, and in all contexts. Eclectism becomes a responsibility, not a choice.

An Eclectic Approach: One Model

     There are special counseling theories that tend to lend
themselves more to the field of College Student Personnel work
in all types of institutions of higher education, from small
colleges to large universities and professional schools.
Obviously, the older Freudian models, particularly psychotherapeutic approaches (Warnath, 1971), are neither effective
nor practical in terms of time. In some cases, Student Personnel
Counseling needs to be more direct and existentialist. After
all, the student personnel worker, more than anyone in the
educative process, seems to deal with the "here and now" on
a day-to-day basis. His or her focus must be on the student's
most immediate experience (May, 1961).

     It is not a weakness for a Student Development Counselor
to admit that they have an eclectic philosophy of counseling.
Selected counseling theories supporting the COSPA Student
Personnel Model which the authors have integrated into their
teaching and practice of College Student Personnel and the
"here and now" approach include the following (Eddy, 1977):

     1. Client-centered therapy of Carl Rogers: Rogers
         maintains that the counselor is represented by his
         attitude of self-respect for the individual and for
         the individual's capacity and right to self-direction
         (Rogers, 1951);

73

2. Network of student personnel services of E. G. Williamson:
   Williamson states that it is the responsibility of
   the educational institution to serve the needs of the
   student and that this can best be accomplished by a
   "network" of student services, all integrated to promote
   student welfare (Williamson, 1961);

3. Non-technical approaches to the small group processes of
   Rodney Napier and Matti Gershenfeld: integrating
   theory and research, Napier and Gershenfeld provide
   real life examples in expressing group problem solving
   and decision making (Napier and Gershenfeld, 1973); and,

4. Humanistic approach of Terry O'Banion: students have
   the freedom to choose their own direction for learning
   and are responsible for their choices (O'Banion and
   Thurston, 1972).

Of course, there are many other approaches that might be
mentioned that have partial applications for personal guidance
and career counseling in College Student Personnel work. For
example, applications from transactional analysis (T.A.) to
reality therapy (R.T.) have been used successfully in certain
situations as the need rises. It is time some helping professionals recognize that a myriad of counseling approaches and/or
a combination of any of them may be the suitable mode -- to
provide students the opportunity they need to grow and to develop.

The Excuse of Eclectism

Eclectism is a very popular position in Counseling and
Student Personnel work today (Garfield, 1977). To be a competent
eclectic, professionals must have total familiarity with a
number of theoretical systems which have proven to be effective
for them. If Student Personnel professionals subscribe to
eclectism, they have to be prepared to consistently articulate
the "why's and how's" of their interventions to Student Affairs
personnel and academic colleagues.

The Choice of Theory

The factors to be considered in the selection of a theoretical

74

approach must take into consideration helper variables
(personality characteristics, age, education, experience,
etc.), client variables (the nature of the problem personality,
age, educational background, etc.), and contextual variables
(office function, time available, physical setting, etc.)
(Carkhuff and Berenson, 1967). Further, the interventionist
has to consider the possible interactions of these variables
in theory selection (Carkhuff, 1963).

Selected Counseling Theories Literature Reviewed

In the counseling theories literature (Hansen, Stevic,
Warner, 1977), (Corey, 1977), (Pietrofessa, Hoffman, Spete,
and Pinto, 1978), (Patterson, 1980) are examples of authors
who cover some valuable materials which College Student
Personnel workers should read and understand before they start
formulating their own counseling theory for the profession.
It is important to accomplish this kind of self scholarship
in order to select and integrate the most useful counseling
theories into an individual counseling approach.

Helper Variables in the Choice of Theory

Each theory of counseling was written by a practitioner
as an explanation of a theoretical system that, when behaviorally
translated into practice, was effective for that particular
practitioner. However, many of the points and assumptions
of these theories were mutually exclusive. In a sense, each
counseling theory is a personal theory shared with others in
the hopes that they may come to benefit from the theorist's
experience. Each of these theories, however, are "perfect"
only for the person who originally proposed the theory. It
is "perfect" since it is the out-growth of the author's
perception of people and their problems. It is perfect in that
it implies treatment techniques which are consistent with that
theorist's unique personality.

However, when counselors choose a theoretical frame of
reference, they must be prepared to accept the fact that some
elements of a theoretical approach will be consistent with how
they know themselves while others will not. For example,
if helpers are assertive and directive, it would be difficult
for them to assume a non-directive approach in dealing with

75

students and their problems.

Just as counselors must know themselves, so must the student personnel worker. For beginning student personnel workers, it will require a "try on" of many theoretical approaches. They should retain those theoretical approaches, or their elements, which are consistent with their self-image and discard those approaches which are not.

Client and Context Variables in Theory Selection

Student personnel professionals are as much problem solvers as they are people helpers. Implicit in this statement is that although two students may present the same problem, they may experience the problem differentially as a function of their uniqueness. Additionally, the same problem may stem from various causes. Therefore, the theoretical basis through which these problems will be addressed may be different. Consequently, student personnel workers, in a sense, should become skilled diagnosticians. They must take into account the nature of the individual and the problem. Then they can attempt to determine the causes and choose a course of intervention that is theoretically consistent with all of these factors.

A contextual variable that student personnel workers must take into consideration in theory choice is the function of their agency. The function of the office may place constraints on the choice of theory. For example, a head resident in a residence hall who receives frequent complaints about a resident whose room has an offensive odor does not have the luxury of time to attempt a client centered approach in order that the student can come to better understand himself. He will eventually come to the realization that people don't like him because of his body odor. A more appropriate theoretical intervention may be a reality therapy approach which forces the individual to evaluate the consequences of his behavior on himself or others. An equally conceivable approach might be behavioral, in which some reinforcement contingencies are mutually established between the head resident and the student.

Another example involves a student brought to the dean of students' office for an alleged offense to the code of

student conduct.   Deans of students are often delegated the
role of disciplinarian.   They cannot usually avoid this function.
There is nothing to prevent them from acting as "helpers",
however.   There are many theoretical approaches that may be
available to deans in dealing with students, in order that the
encounter may be a beneficial one in the students' development.
Depending upon the type of offense, and the individuals
committing the offense, professionals may choose to intervene
in the problem with a behavioral model, a reality therapy model,
or perhaps even a client centered therapy model.

Student Development Model Advocated

    Student Development is reviewed by Parker (1974) from the
different uses of humanism, complexity and developmental stage
theory with the latter being deemed the most fruitful for
college student personnel work.   Parker concludes that "to
change the language of student personnel work into what may
be a more respectable language of student development may be
a mirage and a subterfuge for it -- what Sprinthall (1972)
has called a new bag of virtues rather than a new theory of
what should and does happen to students in the collegiate
environment...".   Nevertheless, Parker advocates that "Future
work in the student personnel field should concentrate on
the creation and testing of socio-psychological theories that
can be applied to higher education for the development of
student development" (Parker, 1975).

Summary

    This chapter conveys the need for Student Personnel workers
to be theoretically explicit but it does not attempt to delineate
all of the possible theoretical systems that may be appropriate.
Student Affairs professionals are encouraged to familiarize
themselves with counseling, developmental, and organizational
behavior theory.   In this manner, they may develop a personalized
theoretical model that is appropriate to themselves as individuals,
one that is consistent with their job function, and one that
addresses the needs of students and their problems.

    Finally, the use of explicit theory for intervention allows
professionals to conceptualize problems, imply treatment

interventions, predict the likelihood of success, and also
to provide a means for the evaluation of outcomes. The latter
point is the foundation for programmatic research, evaluating
the efficacy of helper efforts, and ultimately allowing
Student Development workers to share this information with
professional peers through publications and professional
presentations.

REFERENCES

Burks, H. M. and Stefflre, B. Theories of Counseling. (3rd Ed.) New York: McGraw-Hill Book Company, 1979.

Carkhuff, R. R. On the necessary conditions of therapeutic personality change. Discussion paper, Wisconsin Psychiatric Institute, University of Wisconsin, 1963, 1-7.

Carkhuff, R. R. and Berenson, B. G. Beyond Counseling and Therapy. New York: Holt, Rinehart and Winston, 1967.

Corey, G. Manual for Theory and Practice of Counseling and Psychotherapy. Monterey, California: Brooks/Cole Publishing Co., 1977.

Corey, G. Theory and Practice of Counseling and Psychotherapy. Monterey, California: Brooks/Cole Publishing Company, 1977.

Eddy, J. College counselors reach out. Journal of College Student Personnel. November, 1974.

Eddy, J. Carl Roger's new insight. Peace Progress, 3 (3), 1976.

Eddy, J. College Student Personnel Development, Administration, and Counseling. Washington, D. C.: University Press of America, 1977.

Fitzgerald, L. E., Johnson, W. F. and Norris, W. College Student Personnel. Boston: Houghton Mifflin, 1970.

Fullmer, D. W. and Bernard, H. W. Counseling Content and Process. Chicago: Science Research Associates, Inc., 1964.

Garfield, S. L. Research on the training of professional psychotherapists. In Gurman, A. S. and Razin, A. M. (Eds.): Effective Psychotherapy A Handbook of Research. New York: Pergamon Press, 1977.

Hansen, J. C., Stevic, R. R. and Warner, R. W. Jr. Counseling Theory and Process. Boston: Allyn and Bacon, Inc., 1977.

Hickson, D. J. and Thomas, M. W. Professionalization in Britain: a preliminary measurement. Sociology, 1969, 3, 37-53.

Humphries, J. W. Student personnel professions: is there a future? Educational Record, Winter, 1977.

May, R. Existential Psychology. New York: Random House, 1961.

McCully, C. H. Conceptions of man and the helping professions. Personnel and Guidance Journal, 1966, 44, 911-918.

McMillan, M. R. and Cerra, P. Student knowledge about a college counseling center, NASPA Journal, 10, (2), October, 1972, 138-141.

Napier, R. and Gershenfeld, M. Groups: Theory and Experience. Boston: Houghton Mifflin, 1973.

O'Banion, T. and Thurston, A. Student Development Programs in the Community Junior College. Englewood Cliffs, N. J.: Prentice-Hall, 1972.

Parker, C. A. Student development: what does it mean? Journal of College Student Personnel, July, 1974.

Patterson, C. H. Theories of Counseling and Psychotherapy, (3rd Ed.) New York: Harper and Row Publishers, 1980.

Paul, G. L. Behavior modification research: design and tactics. In Franks, C. S. (Ed.) Behavior Therapy: Appraisal and Status. New York: McGraw-Hill, 1969.

Peterson, D. R. Is psychology a profession? American Psychologist, 1976, 31 (8), 572-581.

Pietrofessa, J. J., Hoffman, A., and Splete, H. H., and Pinto, D. U. Counseling: Theory, Practice and Research. Chicago: Rand McNally College Publishing Company, 1978.

Rogers, C. Client-Centered Therapy. Boston: Houghton Mifflin, 1951.

Spirnthall, N. S. Humanism: A new bag of virtues for guidance? Personnel and Guidance Journal, September, 1972.

Stefflre, B. Function of theory in counseling. In Stefflre, B. and Grant, W. H. (Eds.) Theories of Counseling. New York: McGraw-Hill, 1972.

77c

Warnath, C. New Myths and Old Realities: College Counseling in Transition. San Francisco: Jossey-Bass, 1971.

Williamson, E. G. Student Personnel Services in Colleges and Universities. New York: McGraw-Hill, 1961.

Wrenn, C. G. Student Personnel Work in College. New York: Ronald Press, 1951.

CHAPTER 9

MODELS FOR PERSONAL GROWTH AND DEVELOPMENT:
THEORIES OF GUNTRIP, ERICKSON,
GLASSER, HARRIS, MASLOW, AND CHICKERING

James R. Jacobson and John Eddy

In this chapter, we want to reexamine our own understanding
of growing persons by looking at some models of the dynamics of
interrelationships outside of the family. If the most important
thing that a parent can give a child or youth is a self-image,
or an identity, then we must look at how this identity is developed.

The need for human love for persons through families,
extended families, and other substitute types of support families
is essential for positive human development. O'Connor has written
of the work of the Jubilee Housing Community of the Church of the
Savior in Washington, D.C. as providing such nurture for children
and adults. She writes, "Behind all the programs of Jubilee is
an effort to provide such a network of caring and support that
families will evoke potentialities and give to children a rooted-
ness that will sustain and nurture the whole of their lives,
enabling them to pour forth those lives in love."

The rationale for this loving behavior comes from the
Judeo-Christian "love thy neighbor as thyself." Consequences
of a lack of love for children is a serious matter that effects
them throughout their lives. Harry Guntrip, a psychoanalyst who
has worked all his life with deeply troubled persons, has written:

"If human infants are not surrounded by genuine love from
birth, radiating outward into a truly caring family and social
environment, then we pay for our failure toward the next generation by having to live in a world torn with fear and hate, full
of grossly unhappy people who wreck marriages and friendships
and constantly swell the ranks of the deeply disturbed, from
unproductive hippies living in a flimsy fantasy world, to crimi-
nals, delinquents, and psychopaths. In between, are the all too
common fanatical adherents of scientific, political, economic,
educational, and religious ideologies crying to call or drive us
to various types of earthly paradise, and always failing to devote
their resources to the one necessary thing, achieving a recognition of the fact that the importance of security for babies and
mothers outweighs every other issue. If that is not achieved,
everything else we do merely sustains human masses to struggle on

78

from crisis to crisis, from minor to major breakdowns. Today the world may not "keep turning" in spite of our ignorance in these matters much longer. Nor, do we want hordes of would-be scientific educators teaching psychology to mothers, for the mother's ability to give her baby a secure start in life 'does not depend on knowledge, but on a feeling' that comes naturally if she herself feels secure." (Guntrip, 1971)

In our study of models, we make two basic assumptions about growth:

1. We see growth as a process which takes place through the interaction of the parents and the child in the family setting. The parents and the children engage in a complex process of experimentation, fact-finding, screening, testing, planning, using, changing, and relearning. Within this variety of interrelationships, each person develops a self-concept.

2. The goal of this interaction is change and growth of the individual person. This growth has to do not only with the size and weight of the person, or with his increased ability to do tasks in the world, but includes his internal feelings about himself in the world.

In the following pages we look at three models of interaction which may help us understand the growth process of each person.

I. Erik Erikson

Erikson expresses an interpersonal understanding of identity.[1] He has carefully outlined eight stages of development and suggested that at each stage there is a central task to be solved. His principle for development of identity can be generalized by saying that each organism (child) has a "ground plan" out of which all parts arise. This model is consistent with our understanding of the uniqueness of each individual. The full functioning of the whole depends upon the full development of each part "at the time of ascendency."

Personality is more than the organism. It is the organism, with its own "ground plan" socialized in and through the interaction of the cultural environment in which the person grows. Each child has a different "ground plan" which includes his phsyical abilities, his mental capacities and potentialities, his talents, and all the rest of what he has as an accident of the special arrangement of genes which came together at the time of conception. This unique person with all his internal and external pressures is cast and molded in the cultural milieu of his home and the culture of his day, which filters into the home

from outside contacts, including TV. The personality development will follow a pattern regulated by two forces: (1) The
child's readiness to interact with the environment; and (2) the
opportunities offered the child in the environment. The climate
in the home at the time of the birth of a child has a direct
influence on the growth of the child.

Using this principle of development as a guide for understanding personality development, we can say that a child's
growth will be determined by two basic factors. First, the
child's readiness to interact with a widening social radius
beginning with his first dim image of his mother, and then by the
richness of the stimuli which is offered the child for development through his environment. Here the elements which are inherited in each child meet the climate in which the child's
potential is developed.

Before we summarize the stages of development which Erikson
applies to personality growth, we want to make two comments about
this kind of an understanding.

First, we want to make sure that these stages of development
are not understood as being unrelated. The stages are not clearly
defined. There is a gradualness about the development of each
stage. In a sense they all are a part of every age, but there
is a time when one's task becomes the dominant theme for the
person. There comes a time when there is an urgent pull on the
individual to enter a new phase of life. There is a call to the
fulfillment of the next "life task."

Second, we think that we need to know that the healthy
development of an individual depends upon the proper development
of each stage. If this development is blocked at an early age,
the child will be permanently damaged unless somehow that lost
trust is replaced by a relationship with a trusting person.

Now, let's look at Erikson's eight stages:

1. Infancy: Trust vs. Mistrust. The first "task" of the
infant is to develop the basic foundation for a healthy personality. The first thing which is needed is a sense of trust in himself and in his surroundings. This trust comes from his feelings
about the goodness of those who care for him. The quality of
this care gives him his dim impressions of the trustworthiness
of life. The most acute danger is the inconsistencies that may
be found in this care. As the child grows in his awareness of
his separateness from his mother, he or she may develop a basic
sense of insecurity and mistrust that can last through his whole
life. We will say more about this when we discuss the "OK and
not-OK" feelings as outlined by Harris. A child's security
structure develops very early, perhaps by the age of two.

2. Early Childhood: Autonomy vs. Shame and Doubt. As the child develops his muscles, he starts to learn through experiments with holding on and letting go. This includes the time of grasping for the world and testing it through his skin, his mouth, his hands, and his feet. Here the danger is the development of a deep sense of shame and self-doubt. Here he/she may be defeated in the battle of wills with those who are bigger and stronger.

3. Play Age: Initiative vs. Guilt. In this stage, the child's imagination is greatly expanded because of his increased ability to move around freely and to talk. It is an age of intense activity, avid curiosity, and consuming fantasies which may lead to feelings of guilt and anxiety. It is the stage of the beginnings of the development of a conscience. This tendency to feel guilty is often "overburdened by all-too-eager adults." If the parent is constantly on the child of this age, he may get the feeling that he is essentially bad. He/she may believe the bad person-good person image given by the parent and will be hard-pressed later to break this image.

4. School Age: Industry vs. Inferiority. The long period of latency before puberty is the age when the child wants to learn how to do and make things with others. In learning to accept instruction and to win recognition by producing things, he opens the way for the capacity to enjoy work. The danger in this period is the development of a sense of inadequacy and inferiority in a child who does not receive recognition for his efforts in school. Glasser calls this a "failure identity." A child who is constantly called stupid can decide that he really is stupid and give up trying to learn.

5. Adolescence: Identity vs. Identity Diffusion. The physiological revolution that comes with puberty brings rapid body growth and sexual maturity. The young person questions the authorities he relied on earlier. He has to refight many of the earlier battles. The developmental task is to integrate childhood identifications learned from the parents, with the basic biological drives, native endowment, and the opportunities offered in social roles learned from others. The danger is that identity diffusion, temporarily unavoidable in this period of physical and psychological upheaval, may result in a permanent inability to "take hold." The child with a "failure identity" from school may start to believe there is no hope for him. He seeks to fulfill the school's evaluation of him. He drops out. Without an identity of his own, he/she is open to the kind of identity offered by radical and authoritative groups.

6. Young Adulthood: Intimacy vs. Isolation. Only as a young person begins to feel more secure in his identity is he able to establish intimacy with himself and with others, both in

81

friendships and eventually in a love-based, mutually satisfying sexual relationship with a person of the opposite sex. A person who cannot enter wholly into an intimate relationship because of the fear of losing his/her identity may develop a deep sense of isolation. More than half of the complaints by persons who see physicians are for nonspecific complaints rather than for a specific ailment. This isolation drives people to alcoholism, drug addiction, or loneliness.

7. Adulthood: Generativity vs. Self-Absorption. Out of the intimacies of adulthood grows generativity. This includes the mature person's interest in establishing and guiding the next generation. The person gets a job, establishes a home, and creates a life-style. Parents have and raise children.

8. Maturity or Senescence: Integrity vs. Disgust. The person who has achieved a satisfying intimacy with other human beings and who has adapted to the triumphs and disappointments of his generative activities as parent and co-worker reaches the end of life with a certain ego integrity. He accepts his own responsibility for what his life is and was. He takes his place in the flow of history. Without this "accrued ego inte-gration" there is despair, usually marked by a display of dis-pleasure and disgust.

This very brief summary is given to show how problems of inferiority, identity diffusion, and isolation arise in a child. We now wish to give a model for handling these problems when they arise. Finally, we will give a model for gaining some in-sight into ego states developed in a growing child.

II. William Glasser

In addition to trying to outline a brief summary of the various tasks that a child has to master in order to develop a full personality, we also wish to give a model for handling problems when the personality development has been blocked. We will outline the model given to us by William Glasser. This is found in his books Reality Therapy, Schools Without Failure, and The Identity Society.[2]

Glasser has worked with failing students both in correction-al institutions and public schools. Out of his work with failing students he has developed a model for helping students when their basic growth is stunted. His goal is to save the child. His stress is primarily for school-age children, but we will use his basic approach for children of all ages because we believe that these are the necessary steps for helping a child regain confi-dence and for fully developing the personality and the self concept of any child.

Reality Therapy includes these seven basic principles. We believe these principles are valid for our interaction in the family.

1. Involvement. Glasser feels that involvement is the basic need of every human being. No one can help another person until he has broken through the intense self-involvement of failure on the part of that person. Unless the helping person is warm, personal, and friendly, little help can be achieved. Being aloof, impersonal, or emotionally distant will not bring healing to the person who needs help.

Unless the person who seeks help sees the helping person as someone who cares for him, he will not even talk about his problem. There must be a mutual interest and concern if the helping person is going to give help.

The second part of the helping person's basic orientation must be that of total honesty. As long as the person comes seeking help and feels he is being manipulated by the other, there is going to be very little in the way of real help or growth.

Glasser suggests a very simple procedure for helping your own child. He suggests that you might devote one hour a week to each child. If by giving this one hour a week to the child you are able to save one hour of therapy each week, he feels that this has been a very profitable use of your time. However, as he points out, many parents are absolutely appalled and will refuse to make this seemingly simple effort for the sake of their child.

Self-help requires getting involved with someone else. It cannot be done alone. Involvement is the first principle of Reality Therapy.

2. Current Behavior. No one can work to gain a successful identity or to increase his success without being aware of what he is doing now. As long as the person denies his present behavior, there is very little chance for the behavior to change. Regardless of whether this is a parent dealing with his child or a teacher dealing with a student, unless the person being helped is aware of what he is doing now, there is little chance for help. How can a person change what he is doing, if he doesn't know what he is doing now?

All of us know that people avoid facing their present problems in many ways. Glasser emphasizes that many of the persons whom he helps try to avoid facing what they are doing by confessing how they feel. He continues to accept the feelings of patients, but concentrates on behavior. For it is his feeling that unless one can become aware of his own behavior, he cannot learn to behave more competently. He therefore concentrates on current behavior and does not let the person off the hook by listening to how bad he feels.

The second principle of Reality Therapy is thus to make the person being helped become aware of his behavior and to understand that his behavior is a self-involvement that he chooses. No one forces him to behave as he does. When the person sees that it is his own personal choice then he also sees that he has the choice of behaving differently. A person cannot change his behavior until he becomes personally responsible for his behavior.

3. <u>Evaluate Your Behavior</u>. The person must now look at his own behavior critically and judge it on the basis of whether it is his best option. If he really feels that he has a choice, then he has to decide what the best choice may be. One of the basic principles that is involved in this is the idea that no one does anything at any time unless he believes that this behavior is the very best for him. The parent cannot make the decision for the child. He cannot say, "I know better than you do what you should do with your life." As soon as one assumes the role of judge, he is no longer a helping person.

This means that parents must ask their children to make value judgments on their behavior. We must outline options, but not give solutions.

4. <u>Planning Responsible Behavior</u>. Once a person makes a value judgment, the helping person must assist him in developing a realistic plan of action in order to change. Many people can examine their behavior and decide that it is not helping them, but they have had no experience in planning for a more successful life because they have never had one. Here is where the helping person is most helpful. Parents, teachers, husbands, wives, ministers must be people who plan their lives successfully and can give this kind of help to others.

Because planning requires a knowledge of options, a parent or minister or teacher must have available some options to suggest for the person. Later on in this book we will try to outline how we give students and our own children options where they can choose their own behavior.

5. <u>Commitment</u>. After a reasonable plan has been made, it must be carried out. The person must make a commitment to the plan. The commitment may be verbal or written. However, commitment intensifies the efforts to fulfill the new behavior. Without commitment, it is unlikely that the plan will ever be implemented. One of the characteristics of persons who have a

84

failure identity is their unwillingness to make a commitment. In fact, one of the characteristics of our present society seems to be an unwillingness to make a specific commitment. Here we may simply point out that a commitment that is in writing is often stronger than simply a verbal commitment.

6. Accept No Excuses. When a person does not fulfill his commitment, the plan must be rechecked. If the plan is still valid, then we have to find out why the person did not fulfill his commitment. If the person says, "I'll no longer commit myself to it," then he is no longer responsible. Then a new plan must be drawn up. One of the strong emphases of Reality Therapy is that contrary to the practice of many parents, in Reality Therapy we rarely ask, "Why?" It is often hard, for parents especially, to refrain from asking "Why did you do it?" By asking why, we give the person an opportunity to get off the hook by giving an excuse. We simply ask, "Are you still going to try to fill the commitment?" If you say, "Yes," then we ask "When?" We will give some examples of using this later on as we attempt to deal with specific problems in child raising. However, it is important to point out here that excuses are always bad in any kind of therapy, for excuses, rationalization, and intellectualization of any situation have a tendency to destroy a successful relationship. This kind of behavior is unacceptable in Reality Therapy. If parents are going to use the approach of Reality Therapy, they must have the ability (1) not to accept excuses, (2) not to probe for fault, and (3) not to be a detective to find out why. You simply accept the reality that whatever was done didn't work, and you seek to find something that will work in the future.

7. No Punishment. Reality Therapy is based on the prin-ciple of no punishment. Eliminating punishment is very difficult for most people who are successful. For successful people know that punishment works. Glasser uses praise but not punishment. He believes that praise leads to more responsible behavior. The purpose of punishment is to change someone's behavior through fear, or pain, or loneliness. Those who are already failing already experience fear, pain, and loneliness, and punishment simply confirms their own idea of themselves which says, "I am a failure." Every teacher, every parent, and all correctional institutions know that they have seen many people who have been punished again and again throughout their lives, and it has not improved them at all. Instead, punishment reinforces their loneliness, confirming their belief that no one cares about them. It drives them to a self-image of contempt rather than a satis-factory self-concept.

More will be said about punishment later. However, when we say that we do not believe in punishment, this does not mean that reasonably agreed upon consequences for irresponsible behavior are not outlined. The parent who makes a plan with a son or a daughter has the privilege of also making acceptable and agreedupon consequences if the plan is not followed. Then the punishment, if it is considered as such, is simply the parent holding the child to the agreement. For example, one author asked his son to clean the swimming pool. He didn't want to do it, at which time the parent said, "Well, that's your choice. You don't have to clean the pool. I'll clean it myself. However, I understand that you have some friends coming in tonight, and if you don't clean the pool then your friends cannot come, and I'll invite my friends for the evening." It was more important to the son to clean the pool and have his friends, than to avoid this behavior and lose face in the sight of his friends. The parent's responsibility, had he not cleaned the pool, would simply be to hold him to the choice and the consequences, which would mean he must call up his friends and tell them they couldn't come. Perhaps, this would be called a negotiated settlement rather than punishment.

The second thing that needs to be said about punishment is that quite often the punishment is out of proportion with the offense committed. This arrangement should not be punitive; it should be a reasonable and acceptable plan. The son could have said no for most of the afternoon and then all of a sudden have decided to do the pool, and immediately the pool would have been available to him for the evening. Finally, because punishment reduces involvement and causes people who already feel that they are failures to feel it more deeply, we must learn alternatives to punishment. We must eliminate punishment as a major weapon in the home, in families, in marriage, in social organizations, in government, and in international affairs. Giving praise for a job well done instead of rejecting the person who is below expectation will motivate people to greater success.

We believe it would be valuable for every person to know how to use these principles in approaching problems of school failure, a sense of personal failure on the part of the child, and even the failures in the areas of drugs and sex. Here is a way of handling problems without reverting to the "Big Daddy" approach to problem solving. Rather than saying "Father knows best," we are saying "You know best, and I will help you fulfill what is best for you." This kind of an approach is strongly based upon the interaction of individuals within the family rather than upon a hierarchy of authority in the family. It is based upon disciplined response rather than dogmatic directions.

III. Thomas A. Harris

Now, finally, we would like to outline for you this third area, Dr. Thomas A. Harris from the book I'm OK, You're OK.[3]

86

This third model is taken from the area called "Transactional Psychology." Here we will try to give you some specific handles in understanding a basic human transaction. A basic human transaction can be thought of in terms of one stimulus and one response by another person. For example, every time we speak or act in relation to another and the other responds, this is a transaction. Even if the other doesn't respond, this is a transaction, for his response is a nonresponse.

According to Eric Berne, in his book Games People Play,[4] a series of well-defined transactions with a predictable outcome is definite as a game. Harris has expanded on Eric Berne's idea of transactional psychology and has written a very readable book entitled I'm OK, You're OK. In this book he describes the development of OK and not-OK feelings of children. Since we have emphasized again and again in this book that the most important thing that you can give your child is a self-image, or more correctly, a positive self-image, it is important for us to understand the transactions that help to build this kind of a self-image. What we will try to do here is very briefly describe a basic transaction, and then we will try to give you a little background on the various positions of the children in a transaction.

Harris outlines three feeling states of each individual. These feeling states persist throughout the whole life of a person. They are defined as parent, adult, and child. These states are found in everyone and, as we indicated earlier, at all times during a person's life. One does not progress from the child state to the adult state, but all these states coexist. These states of mind are developed from the impressions we pick up as we grow, starting with childhood. The mind is envisioned as a tape recorder which is constantly picking up impressions from the very first day of birth. There is evidence that these impressions precede birth itself.

1. The Parent. The first thing we pick up is in terms of what happens to us--not just what we think happens, but what real people and real events happen to us. The various positions are defined in terms of how we see these events. Let me define these positions for you. First, there is the parent position. The parent gives us a huge collection of recordings in the brain which come through to us as unquestioned dos and don'ts. These are the tapes of the parent or the parent substitute and authority figures that are given to us in terms of unquestioned authority. Everything a child saw his parents do and everything that he heard them say is recorded in the parent. These recordings are primarily external. The data is taken rather straight from the events that caused the recording. Since the basic position of a child is that of being not OK, and since a child sees the adult as being OK, the child recognizes this outside authority. Here

are some of the recordings that come through to the child: "How many times have I told you not to do that," or the words, "Naughty, naughty," or "Shame," or "You're so clumsy," or a pointed finger.

Also pronouncements like, "Remember, son, we Americans never lie," or "We pay our bills," or "You are judged by the company you keep," or "You're a good boy if you clean your plate," or "You are a good boy because you obey your mother or your father," or "You can never trust a woman." And words like, "The cops are out to get you," and "Do unto others as you would have them do unto you." The important thing is that these "truths" come from one source, which is usually the only source of security for the child. Parents look six feet tall to the child, and at an early age the authority of the parent to a two-foot-tall child is unquestioned.

Now we run into some problems with the recordings. Often the parents say one thing and do another. A parent may tell a child smoking is bad for the health, while he is puffing on a cigarette. They proclaim adherence to a religion and ethical stands, while they themselves do not participate in the life of the church. They request that the kids do not drink alcohol, while they themselves imbibe. Because this data causes confusion and fear, the two or the four year old cannot handle it, so he turns the record off. Then later on we wonder why our children never listen to us. Second, a lot of parent data is in terms of "how-to" data—how to make a bed, how to eat, how to rest, how to comb his hair, and you can add your own list. Part of the parent information is extremely useful to any child. However, if the instructions are accompanied by stern warnings, a child may have real trouble reexamining the usefulness of the information in later life.

2. The Child. In addition to the recording of the parent, there is another recording being made at the same time. This is the recording of the internal events. This includes the responses the little child has to what he sees and hears. It includes the feelings about what the child saw, heard, and understood. Since many of these responses are made before the child has any vocabulary, these reactions are in terms of nonverbal feelings.

In addition to the responses, the child has urges, to empty his bowels, to explore, to know, to bang, to experience, to feel, and to express his pleasant sensations. All of these urges come into direct tension with the demands of the parents in terms of restraint, limitations, admonitions, and directions. This gives the child the feeling that he is "not OK." Even a child with a kind, loving, well-meaning parent has this feeling. When a person of any age is in the grip of his feelings, we say that the child has taken over.

88

There is a bright side to the child state. The child has a vast store of positive data. He or she is creative, curious, hopeful, joyful, and filled with a desire to explore the world. He or she lives in the present since he or she has very little past. He or she takes pleasure in the immediate that is in the feel, in the softness or hardness of things. He or she is enraptured and fascinated by life. If the parents don't frighten him or her too much by telling him or her how bad the world is, he or she is basically at home in his own Garden of Eden of innocence.

3. The Adult. In addition to the parent and child information, there is a recording which is called the adult state. This recording comes about as a result of the child's ability to find out for himself what is different about life from the way it is given to him through the parent and the child. This adult state is able to gather data and process it for future use. The adult is concerned with transforming information into useful pieces, processing, and filing life as taught by the parent, and life as felt by the child. The adult contains more of life as it is figured out by the individual. If the parent directions and the child's feelings hold up under testing, the data which he collects will confirm the child's feelings about himself.

Adult information is always being updated. Checking and validating are all a part of the adult processing. However, the adult state is very fragile in the very young child, and it can easily be knocked out by commands of the parent, which have the ring of authority, and the fears of the child, which have the feelings of inadequacy.

IV. Abraham Maslow

In order for personal development to have direction, human needs should be understood. Maslow's "Hierarchy of Needs" is used here as a blueprint for personal growth and development.

The pre-conditions for basic need satisfaction are: freedom to speak, freedom to do what one wishes as long as no harm is done to others, freedom on inquiry, freedom to defend oneself, justice, honesty, fairness, and challenge or stimulation. Maslow also emphasizes that the goal of education should be an affirmative response to life--to one's self and to one's environment.

The Maslow "Hierarchy of Needs" range from the highest to the lowest in a pyramid form, as follows:

1. Self-actualization Needs: Desire to become all one is capable of becoming.

2. Esteem Needs: Desire for self-respect and respect for others.

3. Belongingness of Love Needs: Desire to be understood and to be accepted by others.

4. Safety Needs: Desire for consistency, fairness, a certain amount of routine, and freedom from harm.

5. Physiological Needs: Desire for food, liquid, shelter, sex, sleep and oxygen.

V. Arthur Chickering

Chickering postulates seven major development vectors for the college-age population for he believes that a new development period should be defined in response to the complexity of this special time. For these young adult stages, his vectors are:

1. Achieving competence means the development of one's intellectual and social abilities, as well as physical and manual skills so that self-competence is achieved when a person is able to cope with what comes.

2. Managing emotions means the development of one's personal feelings and how to recognize that they provide relevant information for future behavior and decision making.

3. Becoming autonomous means a person needs both emotional independence--freedom from continual and pressing needs for reassurance and approval--and instrumental independence--freedom from the help of others in coping with problems and in being mobile in relation to one's needs.

4. Establishing identity means reaching a confidence in one's ability to maintain inner sameness and continuity through understanding one's physical needs, characteristics, personal appearance, sexual identification, and sex-appropriate behavior.

5. Freeing interpersonal relationships means being able to express greater trust, independence, and individuality in relationships so to be less anxious and defensive, as well as more friendly, spontaneous, warm, respectful, and tolerant toward other persons.

6. Clarifying purposes means to develop purposes with priorities and plans that integrate one's career, leisure, and life-style interests.

7. <u>Developing integrity</u> means making one's values more personal and more human so to act in accordance with a valid set of beliefs that have internal consistency to provide a guide for behavior.

This is a very brief summary of the models of Guntrip, Erikson, Glasser, Harris, Maslow, and Chickering. We have given them to help you understand that the child's or person's self-concept or self-image is formed by his relationships with others. It is clear from these models that the person who feels he or she belongs, who feels he or she is a part of a family, and has a basic feeling that his or her world is all right will have the stuff out of which a positive self-concept is built. The task of the parent or parent substitute is to see that this climate is available for each person.

Discussion Questions

1. Write three things which you remember your parent doing to or with you that you hated.

2. Write three things you remember doing with your parents that you liked.

3. Ask yourself these questions:

   a. Which of these things do I do to my children?
   b. Which child brings out the worst in me? Why?
   c. Which child can win me over most of the time?

4. What are some of the parental messages which you still hear? When do you hear them? Are they negative or positive messages?

5. Write down three statements which you often make about other people.

   a. Are you critical?
   b. Are you helpful?
   c. Do you make these same statements about your children?
   d. Is your behavior similar to that of your parents? How?

6. Think of ways you try to help others.

   a. Is your help doing you more good than it does your friend?
   b. Are you responding to a need for help, or are you offering the help before you are asked?

91

IV. An Exercise in Ego States

PARENT: Make a list of words or phrases that represent the
Parent ego state. (Example: don't, should)

_____

_____

Also develop a list of gestures, voice tones, facial expressions
that represent the Parent ego state. Note that some parent expressions are positive, and some are negative. (Example:
pointed finger . . .)

_____

_____

ADULT: Make a list of words and phrases that represent the
Adult ego state. (Example: let us test that idea,
compare the cost . . .)

_____

_____

Also develop a list of gestures, voice tones, facial expressions
that represent the Adult ego state. (Example: thoughtful
look . . .)

_____

_____

CHILD: Make a list of words or phrases that represent the
Child ego state. (Example: wow, whee, mine . . .)

_____

_____

Also develop a list of gestures, voice tones, and facial expressions that represent the Child ego state. (Example:
clap hands . . .)

_____

_____

References

Chickering, A.W. Education and Identity. San Francisco: Jossey-Bass Publishers, 1969.

Erickson, E. Psychological Issues. New York: International Universities Press, 1953.

Freud, S. Civilization and Its Discontents. New York: W. W. Norton & Company, 1962.

Glasser, W. The Identity Society. New York: Harper & Row, 1972.

Guntrip, H. Psychoanalytic Theory, Therapy, and the Self. New York: Basic Books, Inc., 1971.

Harris, T.A. I'm OK, You're OK. New York: Harper & Row, 1969.

Maslow, A. Religions, Values and Peak Experiences. New York: Viking Press, 1970.

O'Connor, E. The New Community. New York: Harper & Row, 1976.

CHAPTER 10

THE FUTURE OF COLLEGE STUDENT PERSONNEL IN CAREERS
FOR PROFESSIONALS: DEFINING AND DESCRIBING THE PROFESSION

John Eddy

Introduction

The College Student Personnel Field is a profession
because it has the following characteristics:

1. A number of well organized professional associations
with thousands of members, and with the largest being the
American College Personnel Association, a division of the
American Guidance and Personnel Association.

2. These professional associations are also united in the
Council of Student Personnel Associations in Higher Education.

3. These professional associations have regular dues, con-
stitutions and by laws, national headquarters, publications
(journals and newsletters), ethical codes, standards for practice, annual national conventions, and active committees covering
professional activities; and,

4. These professional associations are constantly looking
for the development and advancement of their particular areas
within the field of College Student Personnel Work and within
the divisions of College Student Affairs in institutions of
higher education.

The College Student Personnel profession has a long history in higher education and no concrete empirical evidence
exists for a national decrease in these functions within the
total college--divisions may change where they're located. While
some areas of college student personnel regionally numerally
fluctuate in a given year, the overall staffing of divisions
within the majority of colleges continues to increase. For
example, private colleges with lower student enrollments may
reduce their staff by one or two persons whereas growing public
community colleges will add several staff members in a particular year.

A number of higher education critics such as Humphries
(1977) have raised the question: "Is there a future for the

94

Student Personnel professional in American higher education?"
This certainly is not a new question for Socrates raised such
questions about the future of educated persons in B.C. (Before
College) times and why not? On every subject and every profession this is intellectual inquiry, and this is what it means
to be an educated person. The author would also argue for more
responsible questions to be raised about college student personnel professionals. However, it is one thing to raise questions about a profession and another thing to make irresponsible
conclusions based on a lack of concrete evidence of an overall
decrease in college student personnel professionals.

Unfortunately, some higher education critics are speaking
irresponsibly about the college student personnel profession
when they use a one case college study to prove their point
that the profession is decreasing (National On Campus Report,
1977). While certain areas within a college student affairs
division in a given year may have a decrease of staff members,
another area may also have a corresponding increase of staff
members. The growth trend continues from current National
Association of Student Personnel Administrators Reports as
new areas develop, such as minority counselors (Black, Spanish,
Native Indian, and Asian) and career counselors are now being
hired. Even the student housing area is having a comeback,
when a few years ago the critics were predicting that student
residences or dormatories would go the way of dinosaurs.

In spite of the decline of the birth rate in the country,
persons are still attending colleges at a record high rate.
While some private colleges are closing, consolidating and
becoming state supported, the trend continues for more students
to attend post-secondary institutions continues. In 1970, over
7 million students attended college, and in 1980, the prediction
is for over 12 million students to attend.

All known surveys taken, including a 1977 Gallop Poll,
reveal that the majority of high school students still are
planning to attend post-secondary institutions. More adults are
going back to colleges and universities for life-long education.
The legal immigrants coming to this country, by the thousands,
are also planning to attend post-secondary institutions. Consequently, the critics need to study the facts and figures in
present and predicted data before making their uninformed and
unfounded statements.

Answering Student Affairs Critics

The Student Affairs critics use some of the following
factors for arguments in claiming that Student Affairs is a
diminishing field:

95

1. The passage of in loco parentis;

2. The end of "easy money" for colleges;

3. The stop of student unrest; and leading to,

4. The lack of replacing college student personnel administrators (National On Campus Report, 1977).

These previously mentioned factors are half-truths and used also for propaganda purposes. First, in loco parentis has not completely passed--it still applies to students under the legal age of eighteen--and the growth of Student Affairs staff positions continues in such areas as career counseling and minority student advisers. Second, the so called "easy money" or "soft money from grants" never did support many Student Affairs personnel. The public funding for minority programs at most colleges remains fairly stable, at some colleges it has increased, and at some colleges funds are available for the first time. Third, student unrest in numbers is down from the civil rights protests of the 1960's and the war protests of the late 1960's and early 1970's. However, student protests continue in 1977 from an administration building burned at Rust College in Mississippi to a building destroyed at Kent State University in Ohio--at the site of the killing of four students and wounding four students in 1970. Fourth, some college student personnel administrator positions have throughout history not been filled for a period of time. Isolated cases of these incidents is not a fair measure of what is really happening in the field.

The fact that students themselves through their associations or work-study funding have been, or will take over some aspects of student services is not a sign of the decline of Student Affairs, but rather a hopeful use of the COSPA Student Development Model over the In Loco Parentis Model. This is viewed by many professionals as progress and not a step backward.

For example, in 1977 one university president said he was not replacing two high level Student Affairs Administrators and he would "wind down" the Student Affairs Division to create more faculty positions and expand external relations. Under the COSPA Student Development Model, Student Affairs Staff are involved more in actual credit course work (adding faculty positions) and community relations (expanding external relations). Thus, this university president, who may be ignorant of the COSPA Model, could be accidently following the new Model advocated for Student Affairs today. Consequently, it is the news media reporters and others ignorant of the COSPA Model that need to be informed as to what is really happening when they report position changes in Student Affairs.

96

Study in Chicago Area

In order to confront the critics of the profession on their
assumptions of a declining and dying profession, the author and
graduate students conducted a study in 1977 of over 40 Chicago
region institutions of higher education--selected at random--to
determine the growth rate factors of these colleges in college
student personnel positions from 1974 through 1977. The following types of institutions were studied:

1. __4__ multi-universities, public

2. __4__ multi-universities, private

3. __6__ four year colleges, private

4. _16__ public community colleges

5. __4__ private two year colleges

6. __4__ private professional colleges

7. __2__ public professional colleges

The results were as follows:

1. There was no decrease of college student personnel
workers in the past three years.

2. There was a slight increase in the employment of new
positions for college student personnel workers in the past
three years, especially in career counseling and minority
student positions.

The critics of the college student profession who predict
its demise and fall fail again and again in their articles to
do the following:

1. Study all the staff positions now classified under the
college student affairs division. These new positions are often
unknown to critics--such as minority counselors and advisers.
Often these same critics write only of the traditional student
services such as housing or activities rather than the student
development areas as student growth groups and student career
counseling.

2. Review facts and figures rather than make general
sweeping generalizations, such as Humphries, who states without
documentation, "Jobs in student personnel are increasingly more
difficult to find." Of course, jobs in college student personnel
are more competitive because: (a) Unemployed doctoral graduates

97

and masters graduates, outside of the college student personnel field, have been moving into this field for jobs; (b) The growth rate of new professional positions in the field has been stabilized, on a national average, due to student enrollment statistics; and (c) The most qualified persons attempt to enter this field each year, often starting in positions well below their knowledge and skill levels in order to get into the field.

Doom Prophets Misinterpret

There are some "doom prophets" who have been writing articles predicting the decline and even the death of College Student Personnel Work. They fail to point out that this "work" may continue to go on in another college division. Every field that is dynamic must constantly change to meet the new challenges of serving persons' needs. Why should College Student Personnel be any different in adjusting to new demands? What occurs when certain organizational restructuring happens and when some services are shifted to other divisions needs to be more accurately assessed for its total effects toward serving students rather than the loss of some services to another college division.

Thus far, the "doom prophets" have not come up with any national study to justify their claims so they can only quote isolated college cases to make these sound universally true. These "doom prophets" basically misinterpret changes in the field as failure of the Student Affairs Division to retain a certain position or hold a certain service. These "doom prophets" never include in their attack on the profession any evidence-- which is now abundant--that other areas of student services and development are added or are growing from new minority counselors to new programs for career development. These "doom prophets" often misinterpret changes in the field as final and eternal, such as: (a) First, they misinterpret a trend towards decentralization of certain offices as a decline of serving students. It may be a decline of centralization on that particular campus, but not necessarily of the total positions on that campus serving students in that service. (b) Second, they misinterpret the movement of, for example, financial aids or housing to the business office or admissions or records to the academic dean's office as a decline. It is not necessarily a decline of total services to students, but a shift of student services to other divisions of the college or university. (c) Third, they misinterpret short run trends to be long term trends, such as the demand by students for drug counseling may be less this year than last year, therefore, we need less counselors. However, they neglect to discover that more time is needed for career counseling. However, the need for more career counseling is not as dramatic as the death of students from drugs so it does not get the same attention of the mass media or the college community. People forget that counseling needs change for students in a

given time period and, of course, counselors need to be trained
and retrained to meet new demands as they rise from the students.
(d) Fourth, they misinterpret the loss of a full-time position
to be a loss of services to students. For example, one full-time
student activities person leaves to take a more attractive position at another college. The decision is to not fill the
position with a full-time person but have several work-study
students split up the tasks of this position. These same work-
study students may well take up the tasks and do excellent work
at this basically paraprofessional entry level position so that
student needs are served as well as in the past. However, the
opposite may also occur so that in one year the Student Affairs
Division is faced with hiring a full-time person to handle this
position because it was so badly handled by the several work-
study students. Nevertheless, the "doom prophets" will not do
their research to discover these situations for they want only
to find fault and failure in their analysis of the Student Affairs
Division. Of course, these are what Eric Berne has called "games
people play" and these are used to gain personal or political
power in the "power struggles" that go on between the various
divisions of a college from the academic affairs to the business
affairs, there is the usual empire building going on too.

Certainly these changes mentioned here could be interpreted
as short term declines of personnel under the Student Affairs
Division but if the total picture is revealed, the total services
to students may have stayed the same with an equal number of
personnel employed or some services may even show gains in both
categories. Where these changes have happened, it is interesting
to see the chief administrators of these areas, be they academic
or business affairs, often employing graduates of College Student
Personnel programs as their top selections. Consequently, what
really has happened is that certain power struggles are won by
other divisions to gain some Student Affairs Areas.

What better way for the COSPA Student Development Model to
be implemented in all divisions of colleges and universities
from the academic to the business but by trained College Student
Personnel Workers employed by these divisions? It makes the
unity and continuity of the COSPA Student Development Model
possible and is not that before empire building in any division,
even Student Affairs?

Being A Qualified Professional

College Student Affairs Personnel should not rest on their
past degrees, experiences, or accomplishments. Updating one's
educational training is standard operating procedure (SOP) if
one wants to keep up and give the best possible service to the
college or university where one is employed. A true professional
will try to keep qualified whether it pays you personally or not,

99

and whether your institution rewards you or not. Call it the love of the profession or "going on to perfection" as John Wesley named improving one's total life throughout life.

The problem of some College Student Personnel staff is that they did not get proper training for their positions in the first place--some were professors or teachers of history before they may have become a housing official--or they fail to improve their education to qualify as professionals in the field beyond the entry level or beyond a certain level. For example, there are qualified doctoral students at colleges and universities majoring in Student Personnel Work in Higher Education have the option to be ready, after graduation, to take a State Registered Psychologist Test and a Standard School Administrators' Test by taking certain course sequences on their Ph.D. or Ed.D. Furthermore, by fulfilling certain counseling course state certificate requirements in courses they may qualify as counselors at certain levels from K-14 in some educational systems. Moreover, by taking other course sequences, they will be able to qualify themselves as college administrators (such as in educational and business administration) and college teachers (such as in certain areas of psychology and education). Within the doctoral program, the students then also have a chance to not only study the theory of the COSPA Model but to experience it in their SPW courses within the ten functions of Student Development of the COSPA Model. The present professional concern in counselor licensure comes when certain states do not offer options for such credentials for personnel in the profession. It may mean the profession in these states need to prepare themselves to take such exams or sponsor bills in their state legislatures to be passed to handle licensure situations. The College Student Personnel Profession should set standards and monitor these standards so that a license is available for those who qualify and it is maintained by meeting regular updating of educational training. Let us hope our monitoring is better than the pre·ent medical profession--often used as a standard for other professions--where many unnecessary operations are performed daily on patients.

Problems Within The Profession

The problems within the profession of College Student Personnel are not unlike other professions inspite or despite our wishes that they might be different. Some of these are persistent problems, and this is not an exhaustive list but only a selective series, such as:

1. The shortage of women at the vice-president for student affairs and/or dean of students level at many colleges and universities;

100

2. The shortage of certain minorities at the vice-president for student affairs and/or dean of students level;

3. The lack of implementing, at depth, the Student Development Model at many colleges and universities;

4. The lack of annual emphasis on values such as basic human rights and freedoms of our nation and religious traditions within many Student Affairs programs;

5. The lack of regular in-service training of new, as well as veteran staff within Student Affairs Divisions;

6. The lack of the use of certain management tools such as PBO (Planning By Objectives) and MBO (Managing By Objectives) to strengthen the case for systematic evaluation and financial support of Student Affairs Divisions;

7. The lack of release time and financial support for improving the information and skills of existing Student Affairs Staff members;

8. The lack of support for continuous and creative new programs to reach more students at depth where basic identified needs are apparent;

9. The lack of administrative flexibility to include the input of all Student Affairs Staff; and,

10. The lack of care and concern some Student Affairs Staff show for their fellow staff, students, and themselves (their own mental health).

Promise, Potential, and Programs

The College Student Personnel field offers the promise of satisfaction for those who enjoy coming in close contact with students and helping them help themselves to solve some of their problems. Potential for movement within the field exists as jobs continue to be available and even plentiful in certain parts of the nation and in specific services of the Student Affairs Division. New programs keep developing at colleges across the country, for example, for women, minorities, returning graduates, foreign students, retired and senior citizens, and unemployed youth.

As more staff members are trained in the Student Development Model and as more staff members move away from the In Loco Parentis Model and Medical Model, more staff members should have a greater opportunity for personal growth and for job satisfaction. The fact that the Student Affairs Division has so many different services and areas, as well as roles and functions, gives personnel opportunities to vary or change positions within a Division or College without changing careers.

There are many varied programs in College Student Affairs. Unlike in elementary and secondary education, higher education offers more specialization opportunities and also more generalized positions as well in the College Student Affairs Divisions compared to the presently constructed School Guidance Divisions.

For the critics who have not studied, the United States Department of Labor predicts an increase in the average annual openings for 1974-1985 in the following area alone that involves the College Student Affairs Division:

> College career planning and placement counselors have an estimated employment in 1974 of 4,100 persons and with an average annual opening of 250 per year. Occupational Outlook Quarterly (1976).

References

Ayers, A.R., Tripp, P.A., & Russel, J.H. Student Services Administration in Higher Education. Washington, D.C.: Government Printing Office, 1966.

Eddy, J.P. College Student Decision-Making. Phi Kappa Phi Journal. Spring, 1974.

Eddy, J.P. Study of Indo-Chinese refugees and their college aspirations. Unpublished paper, Felician College, 1977.

Eddy, J.P., Thiess, D.E. and Relford, R. Study of growth rate of college student personnel profession in Chicago area, 1974-77. Unpublished paper, Loyola University of Chicago, 1977.

Heirich, M. The Beginning Berkeley 1964. New York: Columbia University Press, 1970.

Humphries, J.W. Student personnel professionals: Is there a future? Educational Record. Winter, 1977.

_____ Student Affairs A Diminishing Field? National On Campus Report. Summer, 1977.

_____ Occupational Outlook Handbook in Belief. Occupational Outlook Quarterly. Spring, 1976, Vol. 20, No. 1.

CHAPTER 11

OBTAINING EMPLOYMENT IN COLLEGE STUDENT PERSONNEL WORK:
CAREER GUIDANCE APPLIED

John Eddy

Introduction

Finding a position in College Student Personnel is mentioned
by Permaul and Thomas (1973). In this chapter, the author will
mention how entry level students and other staff persons might
identify college student affairs areas, find basic job listings,
prepare resumes or vitas, get ready for job interviews, expand
their training and experiences, and discover a position in the
field. It is a good thing if the entry level graduate student
or the experienced staff member is able to take a part-time
position or reduce his or her work load in College Student Affairs
while at the same time he or she could take one, two or three
courses each academic term towards a major in College Student
Development Work on the masters, specialist, doctoral, or post-
doctoral level. Ideally, a graduate student, working in a
College Student Affairs position, is learning practically the
knowledge and skills his or her graduate work in College Student
Development covers theoretically in classes and practically in
practicums, field work, and internships.

Systems Approach

The following systems approach is provided in finding a
position in College Student Personnel work:

First, review this book, College Student Personnel Development, Counseling and Development and/or Careers In College
Student Affairs to gain a prospective on the range of positions
available and the necessary job qualifications.

Second, review: the National Association of Student
Personnel Administrators Hotline and "Regional Newsletters";
the American Personnel and Guidance Association Guidepost
"Career Placement Center"; and the Chronicle of Higher Education
"Classified Jobs--Positions Available" section to observe the
specific requirements listed for the positions open.

Third, prepare a basic resume or vita using forms provided
by the National Association of Student Personnel Administrators

or the American College Personnel Association. Study a booklet like Merchandising Your Job Talents to make a self-appraisal to prepare your resume or vita, to write a letter of application, to learn of sources of job information, planning your time, doing job interviews, taking tests, and accomplishing follow-up efforts.

Fourth, study a book like Getting and Holding A Job that covers important elements such as: studying want ads; applying directly for a job; preparing a personal data sheet (resume or vita); reviewing employment agencies; doing a job interview; learning about job fringe benefits, social security, unions, kinds and methods of payment, payroll deductions, and income tax (state and federal); and how to best hold a job.

Fifth, use a practical manual for job hunters like What Color Is Your Parachute to prepare you practically and psychologically for each step of the walk to get a job. Being aware of the content and context of efforts such as in the Principles of Marketing helps those who have business orientation.

Sixth, to gain perspective throughout your job search occassionally review the Occupational Outlook Handbook in Brief: 1976-77 Edition or the most current edition available. A review of this book will aid the job searcher to see the broad range of positions available and how positions in College Student Personnel Work also relate to similar positions available in business, industry, government, and social agencies (Eddy, 1978). This review can give more help and hope to your job search.

Seventh, those persons who hold a position in College Student Affairs who want to advance in their careers need to consider future special workshops, graduate courses, and degrees that are appropriate to the area of specialization that the person wants to climb on the career ladder. Regular attendance at such non-credit or credit courses helps expand the horizons of persons no matter how much experience, years of service, and graduate degrees one possesses. The College Student Development Model allows for life long learning and that is what it means to be a professional who cares for persons as well as one who wants to develop fully his or her talents in working with persons.

Career Examples

Chicago State University uses a brochure entitled, "Organizing A Successful Job Campaign." The contents of this brochure are shared here for practical applications.

The student or experienced alumni who is applying for a position will profit by carefully reviewing the following advice. The assistance given will help you to organize your

104

resources more profitably.

Prepare the Proper Tools

Credentials: The most important part of a successful job
campaign are your credentials. The Office of Career Planning
can provide you with the forms necessary to establish your
credentials. The credentials should be concise, accurate, typed,
neat, up-to-date and clearly reflect your interests, qualifications and pertinent background. The purpose of the credentials
are to introduce you and sell yourself to the extent of obtaining
an interview. The credentials will not get you a job offer;
offers generally are given only after a successful personal
interview.

Credentials, if complete, contain the following materials:

1. A college interview form;

2. Two or more confidential appraisals (letters of recommendation) of classroom performance or work experience;

3. A course information sheet (personal data sheet).

Letter of Application: This is a letter designed to
introduce you and your credentials to a potential employer. The
purpose of the letter is to request an interview for a specific
job.

NOTE: When answering an advertisement, cover all the
points requested in the advertisement in exactly the order asked
for, since some prospective employers make it a point of thus
testing the applicant's ability to follow instructions precisely.

Letter of Inquiry: Very similar to the letter of application, this is a letter used when you have heard that a job
opening may be available and you wish to substantiate the information as well as requesting permission to make a formal application for the job. It is also used if you wish to find out
whether or not a particular employer may have a specific job
opening now or in the near future.

-- See Sample Letters on the Next Page --

Sample Letter Of Application

Your address
City and state
Date of writing

Prospective
Employer's
Address

Dear Mr. _____:

First paragraph--Tell why you are writing, name the position for which you are applying and tell how you heard of the opening.

Second paragraph--State why you are interested in working for this employer, specify your interests in this type of work. If you have had experience, be sure to point out what particular achievements you have accomplished in this field or type of work.

Third paragraph--Refer to the attached data sheet or resume which gives a summary of your qualifications and which illustrates your training, interests, and experience.

Fourth paragraph--Pave the way for the interview by asking for an application blank, by giving your phone number, or by offering some similar suggestion for an immediate and favorable reply. Include a stamped addressed envelope, and use an appropriate closing phrase.

Very truly yours,

your signature

Your name (typed)

Enclosure

106

Your address
City and state
Date of writing

Prospective
Employer's
Address

Dear Mr. _____:

First paragraph--Tell that you have received a report
that there is a vacancy. Mention the specific job
title of the vacancy.

Example:
I have just received a report that a vacancy exists
for an Internal Auditor in the auditing division of
your company. If this information is correct, I would
like to forward an application and have my credentials
mailed to you by the Office of Career Planning of
Chicago State University.

Second paragraph--Mention why you are qualified for
the position by including in a very brief manner your
educational and employment background.

Third paragraph--State that you would appreciate a
response from them and that you have enclosed a stamped,
addressed envelope.

Sincerely yours,

Your signature

Your name (typed)

Enclosure

Locate Potential Employers

Information regarding vacancies may be secured in many
different ways, the following are the most common sources:

OFFICE OF CAREER PLANNING: The Office of Career Planning
is the starting point for nearly all college graduates. Many
employers keep the Office well aware of their needs. Listed
are some of the sources provided by the Career Planning Office
to assist graduates in identifying job openings.

On-Campus Recruiting: This is the easiest and generally
most effective way to get a job. It is free, takes relatively
little time, and is extremely informative. Methods of successful interviewing are discussed in a separate brochure, entitled
Job Interviewing Techniques.

Vacancy Bulletin: The Office of Career Planning summarizes
and publishes a list of all job openings reported by employers.
The usual procedure is for seniors and alumni to contact these
employers directly. A binder of recent job vacancies is available to you in the office.

Bulletin Boards: Job openings and graduate and professional
school information are posted by academic departments as well as
the Office of Career Planning. You should read the bulletin
boards located throughout the campus frequently.

Publications: The most common source of information on
employers is the College Placement Annual. In addition to names
and addresses, it also identifies the type of positions normally
sought. It is not a list of current openings, but still a helpful source. There are many other sources of information for
your use in the Career Planning Library.

Faculty, Friends, Acquaintances and Relatives: Do not
hesitate to discuss job possibilities in an informal manner as
many graduates have found excellent opportunities by using these
sources. For this to be effective, you must communicate with
as many individuals as possible your interests and qualifications.
Remember to keep all of your contacts up-to-date on your job
status.

ADVERTISEMENTS: Newspapers, trade journals and professional
publications all contain valuable job leads. It is a wise idea
to scan the classified section daily, or at least the Sunday
editions. Most professional journals and trade publications are
available in the library for your use.

Successful Interviewing Do's and Don'ts

DO	DON'T
Act natural	Criticize yourself
Be prompt, neat, courteous	Be late for your interview
Carry out promises	Freeze or become tense
Ask relevant questions	Present an extreme appearance
Let employer express himself	Become impatient
Read company literature	Become emotional
Examine company ratings	Talk too much or too little
Evaluate objectively	Oversell your case
Follow procedures	Draw out interview
Make yourself understood	Make elaborate promises
Listen to the other person	Come unprepared
Present informative credentials	Try to be funny
Think of your potential service to the employer	Unduly emphasize starting salary
	Linger over fringe benefits

Why Some Students Don't Get Jobs In College Personnel Work

1. Will not purchase a car: Some students will not buy, rent, or borrow a car, or enter a car pool to take a job beyond public transportation.

2. Will not use the Local University of Career Placement Center: Some students will not fill out the forms required by the University nor will they check regularly and comprehensively with the Placement Officers at the University.

3. Will not accept entry level positions: Some students will not take beginning level jobs such as in student activities, financial aids, campus housing, and like type areas because they believe something "better will turn up"--as they put it. Then, these college student personnel openings are

filled by less qualified persons than themselves and they complain that they have no opportunities.

4. **Will not take practicums in areas of college student personnel where employment will be available:** Some students want to do only one-to-one therapy type college counseling or college group counseling. These positions are now being filled by more experienced and well trained personnel-- doctoral candidates or persons with several years job experience in a college. They should do practicums in more employable areas such as financial aids, student activities, housing and so forth.

5. **Will not take two or more practicums when they are inexperienced in professional work:** Some students do not realize their lack of experience needs to be made up with experiences in practicums and also in volunteer work that is related to the area where employment is available.

6. **Will not take more than the ten or eleven required courses to give their employers more background:** Some students only take the minimum number of courses because they fail to realize that employers have standards beyond the minimum they desire for their personnel now.

7. **Will not show assertive abilities for employment:** Some students will not assert themselves enough to find available positions so they miss more chances to take jobs they never tried for.

8. **Will not join professional organizations in college student personnel:** Some students feel they can't afford to belong to such organizations yet they wonder why employers think their lack of membership in such groups seems to indicate they really aren't as committed to the field as they should be.

9. **Will not read the professional literature to look for jobs:** Some students will not read the NASPA _Hotline_, the _Chronicle of Higher Education_, the _APGA Guidepost_, and their local college placement offices job openings list.

10. **Will not prepare a suitable vita or resume:** Some students will not spend time to study a good format for their vita and then write in excellent style all their background in one and not more than two pages.

11. **Will not study and role play job interviews:** Some students will not prepare properly for their interviews so they get poor results for their lack of efforts.

110

12. Will not seek experience in job interviews: Some students avoid stress situations, such as interviews, and thus deprive themselves of valuable experiences they need to get jobs.

13. Will not attend professional meetings: Some students will not attend professional meetings often in Chicago, such as the Illinois Personnel and Guidance Association Annual Meeting in October, the North Central Association of Counselor Educators and Supervisors Annual Meeting in November, the Illinois College in Personnel Association Midwinter Workshop in February, the American Association for Higher Education Annual Meeting in April, the National Association of Student Personnel Administrators Annual Meeting in April, and others. At these essential meetings, job openings are often mentioned and by meeting future employers they hear of job leads.

14. Will not find a part-time or full-time job and go through graduate school taking two or three years to graduate: Some students want to push through and so they load up on courses to finish in the shortest possible time. Instead of finding a job in business, industry, government, or education to study part-time--they do not see the values of getting experiences in employment for personal growth and development. Moreover, they sometimes rush so hard they begin to also complain about how tired they are of taking four courses per semester with rigorous reading and writing assignments.

15. Will not interview professionals in the field to discover what type of job they want to hold: Some students claim they can't take the time to interview professionals in the field yet they plan to go into the field--this isn't logical.

16. Will not accept any of the advice (responses 1-15) given by professional counselors: Some students do not listen or do not want to hear what professional counselors are saying to them because they want other alternatives not now available or practical at their level of training, at their lack of experience, or at their inflexible attitude.

Jobs Available

For those who would be "prophets of doom" on the future of Student Affairs employment, it would be well for them to study regularly the following publications to find out that more Student Affairs positions are listed than Academic Affairs positions:

111

1. "Career Placement Center" section of Guidepost of the American Personnel and Guidance Association;

2. National Association of Student Personnel Administrators Hotline;

3. "Positions Available" section in the Chronicle of Higher Education; and,

4. Other like type periodicals.

References

Bolles, R.N. What Color Is Your Parachute? Berkeley, CA: Ten Speed Press, 1972.

Eddy, J.P. "Career Counseling and Job Placement: Colleges and Businesses Work Together" Journal of College Student Personnel, July, 1978, Vol. 19, No. 4.

Eddy, J.P. (Ed.) Principles of Marketing. Chicago: LaSalle Extension University, 1972.

Schneider, B. Getting and Holding a Job. Phoenix, NY: Frank G. Richards Publishing, 1974.

Thomas, W. and Permaul, J. Careers In College Student Affairs. Los Angeles: California Personnel and Guidance Association, 1973.

_____ "Occupational Outlook Handbook in Brief: 1976-77 Edition." Occupational Outlook Quarterly, Vol. 20, Number 1, Spring, 1976.

CHAPTER 12

CAREER EDUCATION--REFOCUSING
EDUCATION FOR CAREER DEVELOPMENT

John Eddy, Walter Wernick,
David V. Tiedeman, and Betty J. Bosdell

Career Education Rockets into
200 Years of American Education

The American educational establishment has come a long way
during this country's first 200 years. Today over 108 billion
dollars a year is invested in education, making education the
largest single business in this nation with an annual investment
of about 8 percent of the gross national product. However, in
the midst of this accomplishment the challenges of new factors
are forcing educational institutions to change. Some of these
include declining birth rates, the decrease of enrollments in
some schools and colleges, the increase of community colleges and
area vocational schools, the energy crisis, pollution problems,
dangers to ecology, the shortage of materials, equalization
practices for women and minorities in employment, inflation
and corrections to inflation, and other elements. Along with
these challenges, career education recently rocketed into this
country's challenging educational scene as an all encompassing
educational innovation.

Although the term achieved recognition only in 1971,
career education has rocketed into educational prominence in the
four short years of its existence. For instance, on August 30,
1974, President Gerald Ford solidly put the weight of the U.S.
Presidency behind career education by announcing at a commencement address at Ohio State University:

"I do want to pledge one thing to you here and now:
I will do everything in my power to bring education
and employers together in a new climate of credibility
--an atmosphere in which universities turn scholars
out and employers turn them on....The Secretaries of
Labor and Health, Education and Welfare have been asked
to report new ways to bring the world of work and the
institutions of education closer together....Skills and
intellect must harmonize so that the wheels of industry
not only hum but sing. I propose a great new partner-
ship of labor and academia....We need new jobs and new
skills..."

113

At the same time President Ford was speaking in this state capital of Ohio, across the city career education was already being promoted at the world's largest state fair. In a booth sponsored by the Ohio Guidance and Personnel Association and others, a poster read: "For career opportunities in the real world of work call toll free - 800-282-0377 for information and opportunities...." The impact of career education has come of age in the schools and society.

Birth and launching power notwithstanding the great hopes for career education will die unless every educator quickly comprehends and acts upon the essence and subtlety of career education. This chapter has been written to promote in all educators such needed understanding of career education. The conception of career education described here is elaborate and life extensive. The educator awakening to career education doesn't need to know its depth, its extensiveness, its wholenss, and its grandness. The chapter has been written to familiarize the untutored with the wholeness and individualness that is career education.

Career and Its Development

As each person lives, the decisions he or she makes about knowing and doing mark a 'bread-crumb' path or career along the halls of time. In this regard, the person's career is like the path of bread crumbs Hansel and Gretel made to mark their passage in the woods; career is the consequence of passage. The life path, or career, can be characterized in the many ways we depict education and activity, and their consequences: by play or leisure activity; by educational courses taken either as preparation for intended work activities or merely for the knowledge which each generates; or by work kinds or activities. The path or career may also be characterized by the person, as he or she marks it in the journey through the halls of time and experiences its consequences, as well as by us. For the person personally marking a career and experiencing its consequences, the career is that person's life purpose or purposes.

Specifying a person's activities sufficiently so that career incorporates work is one of the better understood current purposes of career education. But specifying the presence of the person in his or her activities, particularly his or her work activities, and the development of that comprehension are two of the less well understood needs in career education. These two conditions, therefore, need particular attention.

Quickening and strengthening the person's own presence in his or her career constitutes the most precious as well as the most elusive of career education goals. This goal incorporates a second purpose in education for career, the purpose of personal

satisfaction as well as the purpose of societal success. The
pleasing life as well as the fruitful life become simultaneous
goals in career education.

Reading the person into his or her career is a developmental
process, not an instantaneous accomplishment. The person must be
taught how to objectify his or her self in the ordinarily subjective experience of the self. The person must also be encouraged to accept responsibility for doing this during the times of
life when his or her future pathway is not fully prescribed and/
or determined beforehand. In those periods, the person must
live the uncertain future of his or her mind products which determine for that future whatever stability expectation can give
in encouraging current action.

The enlarging objectification of self in subjective self
experiences does not emerge full blown as Minerva from Jupiter's
forehead; it must develop. The developmental processes of
objectifying the subjective self are in part physical--bodily
systems must be sufficiently matured to bear the necessary
thought processes. The needed developmental processes are also
perceptual--the brain and the mind must be matured sufficiently
to sustain the effective tension of simultaneously treating the
self both as object and subject. The needed developmental
processes are also cognitive--the mind must be matured sufficiently to think while one is acting so actions can be guided somewhat
by individual purposes. The needed developmental processes are
psychological--the body, the brain, the mind, and the situation
must be sufficiently comprehended to use the physical, perceptual,
and cognitive processes involved in self and career constructionism. Finally, the needed developmental processes are educational
--the body, the brain, the mind, and the situation must be or-
chestrated so the subtle and precious personal processes of
intuition can occur and be supported in times of personal
decision in thought and activity.

All of these reasons point to the most important and least
understood process in education, the cyclic process of partial
integration, differentiation, and reintegration in perception and
cognition. In order for self and career constructionism to
develop in conjunction with education, each student's experience
must have meaning, personal meaning. This requires that education be planned and delivered so that each new increment of self
constructed understanding has harmony with the cycle necessary
for mastery and meaning; namely, partial integration of new to
old meanings, differentiation of new meanings from old meanings;
and reintegration of new with old meanings. But all procedures
in this cycle have to go on simultaneously, deliberately, and
progressively. Understanding the need for such conditions, providing them, and making them effective are the challenges for

115

career education--an education for the development of career.

Defining Career Education

Kenneth Hoyt, Director, Office of Career Education, U.S. Office of Education, provides a comprehensive definition of career education as "preparation for all meaningful and productive activity, at work or at leisure, whether paid or volunteer, as employee or employer, in private business or in the public sector, or in the family." The authors use this definition as one standard in this volume. However, the authors are aware of the criticism of Gordon Swanson, who claims, "...American views are still an elusive collection of concepts bound together by the rhetoric of advocacy, the power of governmental incentives and the traditions of a unique context." The authors use as a second criterion for defining career education in this volume, the standard of the individual, the unique, the personal in career.

In short, this chapter uses the term "career" as inclusive of all purposeful activity, but specifies "career" as occupational, vocational, or professional on the one hand and personal and self determined on the other. Both aspects are obtained neither instantaneously, nor once and for all; each must be developed integratively.

Because career education is developmental, education for career has been conceived in five interrelated phases: Phase I occurs in the elementary school during grades 1-6 and is concerned with basic self-development and attitudes as it explores questions on what occupations are, who workers are, and how workers perform their jobs. Phase II occurs in the junior high school during grades 7-9, builds upon the awareness stage, and is concerned with prevocational and exploratory experiences in employment. Phase III occurs in the high school using grade 10, continues to provide basic career information, and is concerned with student exploration in more depth in a single occupational cluster and/or beginning specialized training on one cluster area. The cluster concept is an organizational idea of offering students skills, knowledge, and attitudes for occupational entry into a family of vocations, such as public service (the cluster), educational service (subcluster or division), and elementary education (element or one cluster area). Phase IV occurs in the senior high school in grades 11-12, or in a post-secondary institution (institute or college), and is concerned with the actual preparation of the student for a position when he or she leaves that institution. For example, the Oregon State Board of Education has adopted new graduation requirements effective with the first class of 1978 that mean that each student will be able to demonstrate educational accomplishments, besides Carnegie units accumulated, and these accomplishments or skills are for

116

the most part competency-based. Many of them are experienced
in out-of-school occupational centers.

Career develops throughout life, not just in childhood,
adolescence, and young adulthood. Ideally, therefore, career
education is not limited to K-12 nor the college years. Instead,
career education is a life-long approach that labels no student
as a dropout from formal education; but does recognize that
students stopout and dropin within and without educational
institutions in repetitions of the initial preparatory cycle.
This is Phase V of career education, recycling. It is in keeping
with the trend of educational institutions to have flexible entrance and exit requirements. Thus, more persons can have educational and occupational experiences that meet their specific
needs for employment as well as for job satisfaction. The ideal
educational system allows students to pursue an individualized
year-round approach. In other words, students must be permitted
to leave and to reenter school in order to continue their education or improve their job training--as they deem necessary.

If career education is to be successful, certain career-
related services need to be available at appropriate stages in a
student's development, including: (1) provision of instruction
for general and specific career skills; (2) provision of career
information along with counseling to cover careers and data on
the job market; (3) offering certain financial and psychological
aids as needed; (4) providing credentials necessary for job entry
as well as for continuing education; and (5) offering placement
and follow-through services.

In order to provide for personal integration, career
education has to transcend the current categorization of curricula
into "vocational," "general," and "college preparatory." These
classifications draw artificial separations between instruction
and guidance. Career education cuts across the union of a
student's thought and activity as both mature in the entire spectrum of elementary, secondary, higher, and continuing education.

Unfortunately, although the ideal can be imagined by professionals and lay people, few schools and institutions of higher
and continuing education have developed the needed approach to
career education for all of life. It is currently difficult for
a person to upgrade skills, to update knowledge, and to return
for preparation for a new position throughout his or her life.
That is why this chapter must change you. Every educator must
become a new kind of career educator if career education is to
succeed.

Understanding Why Refocusing Is Needed

The Forty-Third American Assembly sponsored by Columbia

University, "The Changing World of Work," expressed such areas
of concern as:

"Despite civil rights legislation and equal employment
actions, minorities continue to experience handicaps
in both employment and advancement. Young workers are
influenced by rising levels of education and expectations. Women's lib is pressing for equal employment.
Growing demands for early retirement reveal disenchant-
ment. Turnovers, absenteeism, grievances, union unrest,
and strikes all reflect varying degrees of job dissatisfaction. How can these problems be reduced by the
introduction of change in the nature of work and working
relationships?....

We are witnessing changes in personal values that are
seen and felt not only in the United States but around
the world. In part, we are experiencing the latest
chapter in the continuing story of the quest for fulfilling American goals and aspirations: a fair and
equitable society; an opportunity for each citizen to
participate in the forces that affect his life; a confirmation that the democratic process, does, indeed,
work for all. Now that challenge is emerging at the
most basic level of work itself...Our view is pragmatic:
improving the place, the organization, and the nature
of work can lead to better work performance and a better
quality of life in the society. A crisis, though it
may not presently exist, could confront us if business,
labor, educational institutions, community leadership,
and government fail to respond...."

The challenge to our age is to develop a more nonviolent
technology that does not tend to destroy a person's mental health.
If this society could put a person on the moon by systems
approaches to science, then, we can also put our priorities into
human values to humanize our world of work in our schools and
colleges.

Career education emphasizes priorities in personally achieved
and appreciated responsibility for human action. The priority of
career education is to equip each person to guide his or her
destiny by attending to individual career development through
cyclic stages of career awareness, orientation, exploration,
and specification all through life. By refocusing educational
systems and society, with these concerns of career education, the
fruits of a more meaningful life would continue to evolve for all
persons on this planet.

118

References

Bishop, R.; Perres, A.M.; Wheeler, D.E.; and Eddy, J.P.
Careereach. Chicago: V. Mark Publishing Company,
1977.

Hesiak, T.; Deresynski, J.; Dixon, R.; Perres, A.M.;
Wheeler, D.E.; and Eddy, J.P. College Survival.
Chicago: V. Mark Publishing Company, 1977.

Nelson, R.; Perres, A.M.; Wheeler, D.E.; and Eddy, J.P.
Decision Making. Chicago: V. Mark Publishing
Company, 1977.

Bishop, R.; Perres, A.M.; Wheeler, D.E.; and Eddy, J.P.
Job Search, Seizure, Survival. Chicago: V. Mark
Publishing Company, 1977.

Franks, L.M.; Perres, A.M.; Wheeler, D.E.; and Eddy, J.P.
Learning Skills Kit. Chicago: V. Mark Publishing
Company, 1977.

Hanson, M.C. and Eddy, J.P. Pilot Project For Vocational
Counseling. Socorro, NM: Four Corners Regional
Commission of Arizona, Colorado, Utah and New Mexico,
1971.

Nelson, R.; Perres, A.M.; Wheeler, D.E.; Eddy, J.P.
Success Core. Chicago: V. Mark Publishing Company,
1976.

Wernick, W.; Tiedeman, D.V.; Eddy, J.P. and Bosdell, B.J.
A Career Education Primer for Educators. Washington,
DC: American Personnel and Guidance Association
and National Vocational Guidance Association, 1977.

CHAPTER 13

A FUNCTIONAL MODEL FOR CAREER DEVELOPMENT

Robert K. Luther and Virginia M. Smith

During the decade following World War II, most small-to-
medium-sized colleges did not focus their energies in meeting the
career development and placement concerns of their students.
Little attention was given to the concept that making a living
needed to be part of a larger endeavor, that of making a life
(Shertzer and Stone, 1966). This apparent lack of concern
resulted from several factors: (1) a commonly accepted belief
that career planning and development was the primary responsibility of secondary school personnel, (2) the abundance of job opportunities for the college-educated individual which, in the minds
of many college administrators, decreased the need for career
development counseling, (3) a restricted job market which did not
emphasize the recruitment of women and other minorities, (4) a
general unawareness that mobility and change would be an inherent
aspect of the modern-day working force, (5) an inability to
visualize the impending upheaval and turbulance of the 60's and
early 70's, and (6) an imperceptiveness of the over-supply of
college graduates in the late 1960's.

Need for Programs at the College Level

The need for colleges to adjust their programs to meet the
changing economic conditions and job emphases was pointed out by
the recent Carnegie Commission Report on Higher Education and
succinctly underscored by Gottlieb:

First, and for many students more important, is the
perceived failure of the educational process in providing
the student with opportunities in the area of job-skill
training and work-related counseling. Many students do
not believe that they are leaving college with critical
and unique job skills. Many feel they have not been
provided with the kinds of career related data which
would enable them to find the kind of work they seek.
Most have received little, if any, hard data about the
job market, avenues they might pursue given a situation
in which they were unable to find work in their fields,

Robert K. Luther is dean for student development and Virginia M.
Smith is assistant dean at Henderson State College, Arkansas.

and little information about the expectations of potential co-workers. Many students feel that they were forced to make their career choice at a time when they had little real information about the job market and career alternatives. It is also clear that many students feel they had to make career choices with long-range consequences at a time when they were still quite unclear as to their own personal needs and desires. It seems that for many students career selection is required during a time when the student is first beginning to deal with himself and to examine seriously his relationships with others and with society. (Gottlieb, 1973)

At those colleges where some focus was given to career development, it was generally classified as a student personnel function, and supervisory responsibility for it was assigned to either the Counseling Center or Placement Office. This often resulted in piecemeal efforts and fragmented programs which failed to reach the majority of students except at graduation. The need for an integrated and systematic approach to career development has been underscored by these past failures.

In concept, career development implies that the student is stimulated and assisted throughout this academic life to examine and assess his career opportunities, interests, and goals so that he might make vocationally mature decisions upon graduation. Efforts to assist the student then must be comprehensive in nature, deal with several aspects of his development, and be totally integrated into the content and process of the institution's educational endeavors.

Throughout the past year, the Department of Student Development at Henderson State College has spent considerable time in reviewing the current literature and investigating studies relevant to career development and placement at the college level. Most studies pointed out the urgency and the necessity for more direction, programs, and systems in the area of career planning and education. (Gould, 1973; Harkness, 1972; Marland, 1973; Jensen, 1972).

The research also indicated that there has been a paucity of data on career development programs relative to college students. (U.S. News and World Report, August, 1972; Simpson and Harwood, 1973)

Gaymer stressed the importance of a dynamic career development program which would prepare students for more realistic life planning:

If students are going to receive adequate instruction and assistance in the future and about the future, I

121

believe that all those who are involved with the
careers angle of counseling must extend their knowledge far beyond what types of work exist and how
to prepare for them. They must acquire a thorough
understanding of how the complicated jigsaw of the
world of work fits together; of how one type of work
leads to another . . . Career planning must be seen
to be what it really is or should be--a way of life
and the conscious acquisition of a set of mental
tools with which to cut out one's own place in life
and to reshape that niche from time to time, either
to meet contingencies or to accomodate one's own
growth and change in one's viewpoint and ambitions.
(Gaymer, 1972)

The Model

In the last few years, a number of models have been advanced
that attempt to merge the efforts of career education at the
secondary level. Few, however, are available for college-level
use. Recently the Department of Student Development proposed a
model designed especially to meet the needs of Henderson State
(See Figure I).

Upon implementation, this model will organize the numerous
career educational materials and efforts at Henderson into a
single Career Development Center coordinated by a professionally
trained career development specialist. In turn, the process for
the integration of these efforts will be founded upon a systems
approach which will allow any student to enter the process at his
present level of awareness. The Center will span objectives and
services reaching from pre-enrollment contact for prospective and
entering students to placement and career-guidance services for
alumni.

The model, pyramidal in design, is composed of nine levels,
with each level building upon the other.

Level I of the Model

Level one focuses on a number of planned activities by the
Center staff. First of all, they will organize and present units
of study appropriate to and utilizing the staff resources of each
of the Schools of the College and the School of Continuing and
Career Education. Secondly, the staff will be available to provide individual interview time, while making available the opportunity for students to interact in mini-group sessions and/or to
hear lectures and see visual presentations by community resource
persons on campus.

Level II of the Model

In the course of their personal contacts and program activities for level one, the staff will bring about an understanding of the linkage between career development awareness and the need for self assessment by students. At this point, the Center staff will make arrangements for students to take tests or inventories, will provide needed interpretation, and will assist with the setting of tentative occupational and educational goals. Where desirable, the staff will also arrange for individual conferences with faculty members so that students may ask questions and get information to help them further in their assessment of goals based on their interests, aptitudes, and values.

Level III of the Model

Occupation and Career Development will utilize the skills of the Center staff in selecting, displaying, and circulating the software of the Center. Visibility and availability will be the focus. Similar emphasis will be given to student involvement in activities such as playing simulation games and exercies with feedback from staff; to planned and relevant field trip experiences; to display of eye-catching graphic and pictorial displays showing occupational clusters, job trends, preparation requirements, salary expectations, and other illustrative information; and to develop a weekly publication about occupations and the job market.

Level IV of the Model

Level four, "Setting of Career Objectives" is the real guidance task of the Center. At this point, emphasis will be upon helping clients set realistic, yet challenging, career objectives. This will be accomplished in both groups and in one-to-one relationships; sometimes whis will be done with informal in-Center contacts, and at other times with formally scheduled interviews and counseling sessions. At this level in the pyramid, the staff will provide small teaching sessions on the decision-making processes. Such sessions will include a study of systems analysis, problem solving, setting of objectives, and the use of established decision-analysis processes such as those presented by Kepner and Tregoe (1965). In offering these sessions, consultants will be used, such as business teachers from the college or community management specialists.

Level V of the Model

It is at this level--that of "Work Experiences"--that the Center staff must work closely with a diverse population. There will be the opportunity to develop a state-wide, college-level, cooperative training program. Such a project will call upon staff expertise in stimulating the interest and getting the necessary commitments from employers to hire students for both summer and part-time jobs related to their areas of study and training. Further, by working closely with the college's financial aid officer in the work-study program, the staff should find another opportunity for providing work experiences for students related to their occupational and educational pursuits. Over all, the Center will serve the unique functions of providing assistance in understanding basic human relationships, facilitating adjustment to supervisory styles, and arranging for analysis of career learning opportunities, while the training program in schools and industry will continue to be essentially job-skilled related.

Level VI of the Model

The natural activities growing out of this level will be the following: developing and maintaining a resource file of actual and potential employers of students; arranging for group visists (field trips) to Arkansas industries, agencies, and institutions; and conducting ongoing surveys of market needs. These activities will demand full use of the planning, public relations, and management skills of the staff in promoting mutual benefits for both the potential employer and employee.

Level VII of the Model

"Preparation for the World of Work" as an independent, yet closely related, level will require both individual and group training sessions. Emphasis will be placed on providing desirable and necessary learning experiences. These experiences will include, but not be limited to, the following:

a. An examination of work roles to include information about line and staff relationships, opportunities for minorities, routine and innovative roles, etc.

b. An examination of benefits other than wages or salary.

c. An examination of use and misuse of credit.

d. A study of income taxes.

e. An assessment of relocating considerations such as housing, climate, transportation, cost of living differential.

f. An analysis of skills and techniques of job hunting to include preparing resumes and letters of applications; securing references; utilizing private and public employment agencies; examining the advantages of listing; selecting and using publications about the job market; using telephone calls effectively; and preparing for and presenting oneself for an interview.

124

A particular function of the Center will be to plan and promote the adoption of a credit course for seniors, which would incorporate the above learning experiences.

Level VIII of the Model

Placement represents a capstone activity for the student entering the "real" world of work. It is, therefore, a logical extension of the lower levels of the model and an important step in the culmination of the career development process.

In assisting with the placement of the student, the activities of the Center will include the following:

a. Gathering, cataloging, and storing information about specific careers and employers.

b. Arranging for interviews to meet with faculty members and classes.

c. Gathering necessary information on the student's background for the confidential file.

d. Registering senior students.

e. Helping with planning and revision of the college curriculum.

f. Obtaining information from alumni and employers concerning training requirements, academic preparation, and expectations of the labor market.

g. Communicating employment opportunities or job vacancies through the use of educational technology.

h. Providing guidance in completing employment applications.

i. Conducting follow-up studies on graduates.

Level IX of the Model

The continuing service of career guidance (re-entry into the steps of the Model as necessary) will be available to the alumni. The staff will promote and encourage graduates to re-register with the Center, not only for new job placement but also to participate in workshops, mini-courses, and special programs. The focus will be on the "re-entry" concept as differentiated from the "placement-only" pattern often followed.

Summary

In summary, the necessity for revamping college programs to meet the contemporary occupational needs of the society is paramount, and vital to any comprehensive program of career development for college students is a systemwide approach, such as the model advanced. Career development must be seen as more than mere information giving; it must incorporate all facets of the institution's endeavoers from the classroom to the actual decision-making processes of the individual. Only in this way can colleges move forward in providing relevant assistance in shaping vocationally mature individuals.

References

Gaymer, R. Career counseling-- teaching the art of career planning. Vocational Guidance Quarterly, 21, September, 1972.

Gottlieb, D., et al. Institute for the study of human Development. Study Report: Youth and the meaning of work. CYSSP Report No. 3. A report prepared by Pennsylvania State University: College of Human Development. University Park, PA. February 1973, pp. 227-228.

Gould, S.B. "Toward a society of lifelong learners." Report of the commission on non-traditional study: "Diversity by design." AAUW Journal, April, 1973.

Harkness, C.A. College education-key to jobs. Vocational Guidance Quarterly, 1972, 21, 43-46.

Jensen, V.H. A model for extending career concepts. Vocational Guidance Quarterly. 1972, 21, 115-119.

Kepner, C.H. & Tregoe, B. The Rational Manager. New York: McGraw-Hill, 1965, 1973-206.

Marland, S.P., Jr. The school's role in career development. Educational Leadership. December 1972, 203-205.

Shertzer, B. & Stone, S.C. Fundamentals of Guidance. Boston: Houghton, Mifflin, 1966, 317.

Simpson, L.A. & Harkwood, R.K. Placement: From employment bureau to career development center. NASPA Journal, 1973, 225-230.

126

References

_____. After graduation--then what? <u>U.S.</u>
<u>and World Report</u>. August 28, 1972, pp. 33-35.

MODEL FOR CAREER DEVELOPMENT

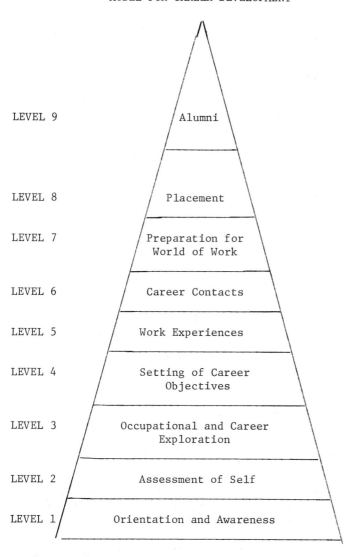

LEVEL 9   Alumni

LEVEL 8   Placement

LEVEL 7   Preparation for World of Work

LEVEL 6   Career Contacts

LEVEL 5   Work Experiences

LEVEL 4   Setting of Career Objectives

LEVEL 3   Occupational and Career Exploration

LEVEL 2   Assessment of Self

LEVEL 1   Orientation and Awareness

128

CHAPTER 14

CREATIVE CAREER COUNSELING: PERSPECTIVES
ON PERSONNEL SERVICES FOR MINORITY STUDENTS

Joyce S. Kennedy

The "roots" of creative career counseling can be found in
vocational guidance. Since pioneering efforts have been made
in widely scattered times and places, it is not possible to
point to any one work or place as the cradle of vocational
guidance or career counseling.

Pietrofesa and Splete (1975) support the premise that job
satisfaction is prerequisite to self-fulfillment and happiness.
It follows, therefore, that the idiosyncratic career counseling
needs of minority students must be important personnel considerations along with societal barriers to chosen careers. Career
development of minority students over the life span is greatly
influenced by the social environment, affecting their self-concepts
and need patterning. Osipow (1973) supports the notion that social
class circumstances beyond the control of individuals contribute
significantly to their career choices, and that a principal task
confronting youth is the development of techniques to cope with
social environment.

Precursors of creative career counseling perspectives have
come from a variety of professional fields, but have possessed a
common desire to assist students in wiser career choices and the
development of more rewarding life styles. Through continuing
efforts, the career counseling movement has matured in recent years
with a dauntless and perservering sense of mission. Creative
career counseling for minority students is a continuous and life-
long developmental process leading to educational, employment, and
leisure choices which are feasible, constructive, and rewarding.

Creative career counseling suggests an interdisciplinary
approach, and the avoidance of a narrow, rigid concept. In a very
literal sense, student personnel professionals are psycho-social
learning facilitators who must not be regarded as having all of
the career answers for others. Rather, career decisions must
always lay with the individual. It is important to understand the
impossibility of mystically looking into the future time dimension,
determining what minority students should be, and then specifically
preparing them for those ultimate careers.

Creative career counseling organizes targeted learning activities
to implement the objectives of career counseling. Career counseling

129

objectives encompass the following:

1. Gaining self-understanding and acceptance

2. Discovering personal interests and aptitudes

3. Increasing human relations skills

4. Surveying the world of work

5. Making guided educational, career, and leisure choices

According to Miller and Prince (1976), goal setting in career counseling may contribute to student development by:

1. Providing direction for professionals

2. Guiding the selection of activities (experiences)

3. Providing a framework for assessing progress

When minority students determine their own goals, they make needed positive movement toward a sense of worth and power and taking responsibility for themselves and their destiny. Self-selected, attainable goals are excellent motivators, and the process learning which accompanies goal establishment provides direction and destination.

Williamson and Biggs (1975) reveal that current student personnel professionals must aid students in change agentry in reaction to new variables. Some students may well require new and different techniques of career counseling. Career choice questions for minority students may have to be formulated, such as the following:

1. Does the career satisfy your preference of working with people, ideas, or things?

2. Do you have the personality and aptitude which are appropriate to the career?

3. Will you be able to handle the pressure and pace of the career?

4. Does the career offer acceptable standards of salary, personal satisfaction, advancement opportunities, and social relevance?

5. Does the career offer sufficient freedom and challenge?

6. Does the career involve potential discrimination in educational, training, and placement opportunities?

Answers to these questions and others can be explored with minority students individually and in groups. Crites (1971) found in reviewing research that both individual and group career counseling are efficacious in the facilitation and maturation of vocational attitudes.

As career awareness receives more national attention and resources, and as more of these activities find their locus of operation within student personnel settings, it will be necessary to scrutinize most, if not all, career approaches for relevance and adaptability to minority students. Student personnel professionals, as active participants in and close observers of work trends, will need to continually seek to interpret the meaning of work in contemporary terms, and adjust their mission accordingly if their services are to be realistic and relevant.

Employment and personnel services are seen by Lederer (1974) as generally ranging from job services to counseling services. These special services, which are usually available without cost, seek to match students to jobs which suit their aptitudes and interests. Five basic services may be provided: 1) career information; 2) career counseling; 3) referral to job training; 4) job placement; and 5) follow-up services. Lederer observes that there is a great deal of career information in public and college libraries - not all of it good. Materials may differ in authenticity and quality. Career information which was once accurate may become hopelessly out-of-date and misleading. Minority students and others may need special professional assistance if they are to avoid the pitfalls of obsolete job availability figures and preparation criteria.

Present and past social conditions have placed decided constraints on the career goals of various cultural, racial, and ethnic minorities. As a result, a high proportion of today's minority work force is either unemployed or underemployed. The Occupational Outlook Quarterly, (19, 1975) reported that black females in their teens comprised the largest percentage of unemployed workers in the labor market. Additionally, traditional hiring practices discriminate against women of all races, and systematically exclude them from many responsible, higher paying positions.

National economic trends have also had a definite effect
on the job market and, as a result, on career development.
The recent rise in unemployment figures and inflation makes
the process of securing satisfactory employment even more
difficult. Employment demands seem to be decreasing in areas
such as teaching and engineering, and increasing in such
fields as computer programming and computer technology (Occupational Outlook Quarterly, 17-18, 1974).

Implications for Student Personnel Services

Effective personnel counseling demands the development
of a flexible career program which is comprehensive in scope.
Minority persons, overlooked in the job market for many years,
develop a more limited perspective of career awareness. Career
counseling for minority students should provide extensive information about career opportunities.

Workers returning to the work force, such as housewives
and veterans, may also need special assistance in readjusting
to the world of work. Supportive counseling, career awareness,
and retraining may be needed to insure a smoother transition
into the labor market. More persons than ever before are starting second careers. Career awareness, as well as adjustment
counseling, are helpful tools in assisting the mature worker
towards a satisfying vocational change.

Future Roles for Student Personnel Professionals

In order to meet the challenge of these vocational needs,
personnel and employment workers must take a more assertive
role in the total process of career development. For example,
employers might be encouraged to hire female applicants for
positions which have been traditionally filled by males, and
challenged to acknowledge affirmative action policies with
regard to hiring racially or culturally different applicants.

In the future, student personnel professionals must be
willing and able to assume change agent roles in working to
alter existing systems which oppress various segments of our
population (Gunnings, 1972). Personnel services must include
participation in more job training and career awareness programs
in order to provide clients with the knowledge and skills needed

for optimal development.

Focusing on a creative and humane career development perspective provides the philosophical framework for fostering the vocational and avocational maturity of present and potential workers. This perspective provides a contemporary companion piece to the "Age of Aquarius" psychology, (Hill, 1973) and invites exploration of the dramatic relationship which can exist between the career needs of minority students and the demands of the economic and social environments. The range of responsibilities, from furnishing job-related information to dealing with realistic and relevant attitudes about job and career issues, presents a formidable challenge as we address what Eddy (1978) describes as "the hard problems facing the nation and the world".

In conclusion, college student personnel must react to the current challenge of change with healthy idealism tempered with a grasp of reality. New philosophical foundations will need to reflect new conditions and concerns. In the process of reconceptualization and looking forward to the future, the perspective of humane career development is proposed. The goal is a society that is free from racial, ethnic, sexual, and social prejudice, and based upon recognition of the creative talent and potential of all of its citizens.

References

Crites, J. "The Maturity of Vocational Attitudes in Adolescence," American Personnel and Guidance Association Inquiry Series, 1971.

Eddy, J. College Student Personnel, Development, Administration, and Counseling. Washington: University Press of America, 1978.

Gunnings, T. "Psychological, Educational and Economic Effects on Compensatory Programs on Blacks" in Black Psychology (ed.) Jones, R., Harper & Row, 1972.

Hill, P.G. "Psychology for the Age of Aquarius." Unpublished manuscript, 1973.

132a

References

Lederer, M. The Guide to Career Education. New York:
Quandrangle/N.Y. Times Book Company, 1974.

Miller, T. and Prince, J. The Future of Student Affairs.
San Francisco: Jossey-Bass, 1977.

Osipow, S. and Walsh, W. Strategies in Counseling for
Behavior Change. New York: Appleton-Century-Crofts,
1973.

Pietrofesa, J. and Splete, H. Career Development: Theory
and Research. New York: Grune and Stratton, 1975.

Rosenthal, N. and Dillon, H. "Occupational Outlook for the
Mid-1980's", Occupational Outlook Quarterly, Vol. 18,
No., 4, Winter, 1974.

Stevenson, G. "Counseling Black Teenage Girls", Occupational
Outlook Quarterly, Vol. 19, No. 2, Summer, August, 1975.

Williamson, E.G. and Biggs, D. Student Personnel Work.
New York: John Wiley & Sons, Inc., 1975.

132b

CHAPTER 15

VALUES EDUCATION AND THE COLLEGE STUDENT
DEVELOPMENT ADMINISTRATOR

Jay Barnes, John Eddy and Steve Murphy

The Need for Values Education

Almost 40 years ago, the world was stunned by the rise
to power of Adolf Hitler in Germany. Amazement was expressed
that a country with one of the most developed educational
systems in the world could be captivated by such a twisted,
destructive system. Shouldn't such educated people have
acted morally, responsibly, and humanely? Apparently education, even education based on a humanistic structure, offered
no guarantee of morality.

Some 35 years after Hitler rose to power in Germany, the
United States was shocked by the excesses that threatened the
heart of the American way of life. Somehow the "best and
brightest" products of America's educational system were able
to justify the abuse of the system they professed to serve.
The Watergate incident raised questions about the role of
educational institutions in the process of helping our citizens
to develop a suitable moral philosophy and a viable lifestyle
based on that philosophy. One need only peruse the daily
newspaper to reinforce the idea that a change is needed to
help us to overcome what appears to be an ineffective system
of values education and moral development.

The purpose of the material presented in this chapter is
to address the need for change by defining different approaches
to values education and by suggesting some guidelines and
resources for action. A particular concern is to stress the
importance of the student development professional in the
process of values education.

Some individuals have suggested that education, particularly higher education, is not the place for values education.
However, such an approach is naive at best. As Max Lerner
(1976) states in Education and Values:

133

At times a debate has raged about whether education
should be concerned with values. It is an idiot
debate in that form, on a hopelessly archaic question.
As well as whether religion should be concerned with
the problem of godhead. Every actor in the educational
drama - teacher, student, family, administrator, media,
peer group - is up to its neck in values. Like it or
not, education is values-drenched. The real question
is how well - with what awareness, with what skill and
meaning, with what responsibility and restraint - it
performs its function as a value carrier. (p.13)

It is an assumption of this paper, therefore, that all
education is "values education". It is not possible for
individuals to interact directly or indirectly in an educational setting in a value-free way. The selection of subject
matter, pedagogical approaches, educational goals, and socially
reinforced roles are all "values drenched". Those who are
involved in the process of education (or virtually any meaningful human activity) are assimilating not only cognitive content,
but also affective content; not only verbal information, but
also nonverbal information; not only views about traditional
academic disciplines, but also views about themselves as people.

If all education is values education, student development
personnel must be concerned with the values being communicated
through programs and interactions with students. To ignore
the process of value formation in the college student would be
as irresponsible as ignoring the physical, psychological, social,
or intellectual growth of the student. Professionals in student
development administration need to be at the cutting edge of
progress in this important area. We need to be supportive of
programs and classroom attitudes that encourage openness, inquiry,
wonder, and reflection. As students, faculty and administrators
we should be challenged to present defensible, informed stands
on issues; to see ourselves as valuable because of our inherent
worth as humans, rather than seeing our value in performance or
physical appearance; to wisely use our personal talents and
abilities; and to become autonomous in thought and expression.
We need to see values development both as an educational process
and as a human development process. We need to take a more
proactive stance in the area of values education if we are to
reach the optimistic assessment of Esther Lloyd-Jones that,
"Creative work in the field of values...is the next and by far
the most important contribution that guidance and personnel
work will make to education." (In Eddy, 1977, p. xii)

134

Historical Perspective on Values Education

Values education is not a new fad or fashion, for its roots go back at least as far as Confucius, Plato and Moses (Eddy, 1969). American education has, from the start, acknowledged the importance of values education and moral development. The Massachusetts School Law of 1642 stressed the importance of teaching children how to read so they could have more direct access to the Bible. The Massachusetts School Law of 1647, known as the "Old Deluder Satan Act", set up specific guidelines for the establishment of schools - again for the purpose of furthering the knowledge of religion in general and the Bible in particular. Harvard College was founded to prepare ministers, as were most of the early institutions of higher education. Through the end of the colonial period, the place of values education and moral development in the goals of educational institutions was firmly entrenched. During the period from the ratification of the Constitution to the end of the Civil War, America changed greatly. One significant change was the increased emphasis on the separation of church and state. With the rise of the common school movement and increased governmental funding of institutions of higher education, the control of the church over the educational institutions of the day was lessened. In spite of this, the importance of character and moral development remained central in the goals of educators. During the period from the end of the Civil War to the end of World War I, the importance of the school in the framework of the republic increased. The Kalamazoo Case of 1874 confirmed the position of the public high school and more closely linked the majority of the educational system to state funding and control. The role of religion continued to shrink not only at the secondary level and below, but also in higher education, as humanism became the dominant force. Man was to be the master of his fate, not the servant of God. He was to be the citizen of an earthly kingdom, not a heavenly kingdom. Thus, while character education was still relevant, its base was no longer religious, but secular. Perhaps because of this posture, parochial schools began to grow in importance. In Pierce vs. Society of Sisters, the U. S. Supreme Court affirmed the right of parochial school boards to exist. This officially allowed an option for parents who desired a more direct approach to values education than was offered in the public sector. This also established a support base for parochial institutions of higher education. Recent decisions, such as School District of Abington Tp., Pa. vs. Schempp on Bible reading, and Engel vs. Vitale on prayer, have reinforced the separation of church and

state and have caused some to question any values education
in the public schools which is approached from a religious
base. However, other decisions have left some doubt about
the exact dividing line between church and state. Thus,
the role of values education in the curriculum of public and
private institutions is still not settled. This unsettledness
is due not only to legal issues or questions of appropriateness in a pluralistic, democratic society, but also to dis-
agreements about the most effective way to promote values
education or moral development.

Even though the desire to develop "character", to incul-
cate "virtue", or to promote "good" behavior has been a goal
of most societies, it was not until the early 1900's that any
systematic research was done in an attempt to determine the
best way to accomplish these desires. The landmark studies
conducted by Hartshorne and May (1928-1930) through the
Character Education Inquiry at Columbia University in the
1920's led to rather dismal conclusions about the effectiveness of traditional approaches to character education. Their
conclusions as summarized by Kohlberg and Turiel are as follows:

1. The world cannot be divided into honest and dishonest
    people. Almost everyone cheats some of the time...

2. If a person cheats in one situation, it does not mean
    he will or will not cheat in another...

3. People's verbal moral values about honesty have nothing
    to do with how they act...

4. There is little correlation between teacher's ratings
    of experimental measures of honesty.

5. The decision to cheat or not is largely determined by
    expediency...

6. Even when honest behavior is not dictated by concern
    about punishment or detection, it is largely determined
    by immediate situational factors of group approval
    and example (as opposed to being determined by internal
    moral values)...

7. Where honesty is determined by cultural value-forces,
    these values are relative or specific to the child's
    social class or group (1971, pp. 422-423).

136

The Hartshorne and May studies were followed by the
Havighurst and Taba (1949) Study of 1942-1943 conducted through
the University of Chicago. The authors concluded that character was behavior that was learned through reward and punishment, unconscious imitation, and reflective thinking. The
Peck and Havighurst Study (1960) also done through the University of Chicago, was based on the assumption that moral values
were learned from other people. Their findings indicated that
once values were learned in childhood, they tended to persist
as the child matured.

The rise of humanistic psychology, the upheavals of the
1960's, and the acceptance of structuralism in the sciences
have led to additional research and theorizing in the areas of
values education and moral development. In addition, the
work of individuals such as Dewey, Piaget, and Kohlberg have
been vitally important in kindling interest in the area. From
an historical point of view, note must also be taken of the
work of B. F. Skinner (1948, 1953, 1971) and his followers in
behavior modification; Raths, Simon, Harmin, Kirschenbaum
(Raths, Harmin and Simon, 1966; Kirschenbaum and Simon, 1973)
and others in the values clarification movement; and William
Perry (1970) and his work on the cognitive-developmental theory
as applied to college students. Although this history is
abbreviated, a more complete review may be found in Kohlberg
(1964) and Hoffman (1970).

Approaches to Values Education and Theory

Several approaches have been taken to values education.
Hoffman (1970) suggests that the approaches may be divided
into three groups: (a) the original sin group which holds
that authoritative intervention is needed to prevent the child
from straying from the good; (b) the innate purity group which
holds that the child is basically good and is gradually corrupted
by society; and (c) the tabula rasa group which holds that
if children are to rise above simple gratification of biological
drives, proper adult intervention is needed. Another schema
is suggested by Kohlberg (1964). He also sees three basic
approaches: (a) the behavior approach which focuses on developing commonly accepted behaviors in the child; (b) the emotional
approach which sees guilt as a primary motivator; and (c) the
judgmental approach which sees the process of judgment in making
a moral decision as the primary place of focus.

The system with perhaps the most heuristic potential is

137

the one offered by Stewart (1974). Stewart focuses on two major
areas: the source of value as internal or external and the
temporal nature of value as absolute or relative. On the basis
of this focus, Stewart describes four approaches.

The first approach is the Traditional-Authoritarian
(Absolute Nomothetic) Approach. Two basic ideas characterize
this orientation and are summarized by Stewart in the following
statements:

1. Values are absolute, and apply to all people, at all
   times, under all circumstances, in all places. Truth
   exists objectively, is known, and can be transmitted.

2. The source of values is the culture of society. Values
   are nomothetic (p. 29).

The second category is the Cultural-Relativistic Approach
(Relative Nomothetic). The basic ideas that characterize this
approach according to Stewart are:

1. Values are absolute within any given culture, but they
   are relative from culture to culture, society to
   society, or group to group.

2. The source of values is the local culture, society,
   or group. Values are nomothetic (p. 32).

The third approach is the Absolute-Relativistic Approach
(Idiographic). According to Stewart, the two basic ideas that
characterize this approach are:

1. Values are absolutely relative to the individual.

2. Consequently, in spite of the influence of the
   environment, the ultimate source of values is within
   the individual (p. 41).

The fourth approach is the Organismic-Structural-Develop-
mental Approach (Universal Transactional). In Stewart's view,
this is the most viable approach and is characterized by the
following assumptions:

1. There are natural patterns or values/moral structures
   and behaviors that are universal to all human organisms.

2. These patterns occur in an invariant sequence of
   structural-developmental stages partly as a result
   of transactions with the environment (p. 48).

Methodologies of Values Education

A number of different methods to values education have
been attempted with varying degrees of success. The roots of
these methodologies can be seen in the four theoretical approaches
described by Stewart (1974). Some of the more common methods
are briefly discussed below.

Moralizing is perhaps one of the most traditional and wide-
spread approaches to values education when seen in historical
perspective. It assumes that either some absolute, universal
system of principles exists for all cultures or at least that
some system of principles exists that is absolute for one culture.
These principles are expounded, usually in an authoritative way,
and each individual is to attempt to live up to the behaviors
called for by the principles. The weakness of this approach
is that is appears to be ineffective, as evidenced by the Hartshorne
and May (1928-1930) studies, among others.

The opposite approach may be classified as a laissez-faire
or "hands off" approach. This approach has its roots in Freudian
psychology and is seen as a viable option by many modern educators. Freudian psychology holds that patterns of valuing are
learned at a very early age as a consequence of other developmental experiences. Therefore, all subsequent value education
is not only unnecessary, but also useless. The role of the
educator is to leave the individual alone in order to allow self-
actualization of unique individual values that were basically
pre-determined by early learning experiences. This diminished
role for educators is further emphasized by the preeminence
of desire rather than reason for the Freudians. The weaknesses
of this approach are many. First, the deterministic framework
is not compatible with a democratic society and it does not seem
to fit human experience. Second, the role of the parent and early
childhood experiences are overemphasized to a degree that goes
beyond empirical support. Finally, and perhaps most damagingly,
this approach also appears to have a low success rate.

The third approach, modeling, assumes that living your
values is the best educational method. The teacher should
strive for consistency between word and actions above all else.
This approach may be found alongside the moralizing approach
in many religious traditions. Research by Bandura and Walters

139

(1963), and other social learning theorists, lends support
to the importance of this approach. The weakness of this
approach is that it does not go far enough. It does not deal
directly enough with cognitive structure and the process of
change. It may be viewed as a necessary, but not a sufficient
approach in values education.

The fourth methodology is values clarification. This
very popular modern approach claims to have its roots in Dewey
(1909) and Piaget (1956). Values clarification is more concerned
with the process by which values are formed than it is with
specific content items. Concrete teaching methodologies have
been constructed and have found popular support in many educational settings. An important contribution of the values clarification method is an operational definition of value by Raths,
Harmin, and Simon (1966). A value must be freely chosen from
alternatives after careful consideration of the consequences of
each alternative. The individual must prize the value and
display this by being happy with his choice to the point of
willingly affirming the choice in public. Finally, the individual
must act on the choice as part of a pattern or life style.
This approach has been criticized by the developmentalists as
being superficial. In spite of claims to be focusing on the
process of valuing, the values clarification approach is seen as
focusing mainly on the content of specific values, while either
minimizing or overlooking the process of value formation and
the underlying cognitive, moral structure. This approach, is
also seen as coercive in that it relies heavily on peer pressure.
A more damaging criticism is that this approach displays a
moral relativism in which anything goes on the surface, but in
which a "bag of virtues" is clearly intended as a part of a
"hidden curriculum". A final criticism is that there appears
to be a lack of research support for the claims of the values
clarification practitioners.

The fifth approach or methodology is that of behavior
modification. This is related in some ways to the laissez-
faire and psychoanalytic approaches in that it is deterministic
and heavily stresses the role of the environment. Like values
clarification, the behavior modification methodology finds a
great deal of popular support in the classroom. The heart of
this method is that certain behaviors (responses) are rewarded
(stimulated), thus increasing their frequency of occurence.
The rewarding and the deciding of what behaviors to reward are
often done by some authority figure. The weaknesses of this method
are philosophical, logical, and practical. Philosophically,

140

it is difficult to see how this approach can be justified in a democratic society or within any system that holds a high view of humanity. It is basically a manipulative approach to education. Logically, the behaviorist assumes things in the environment (responsibility, freedom, personality) that he rejects in the subject whose behavior is being modified. Methodologically, if the system of rewards is removed, the modification tends to break down. Thus, evidence is lacking that anything more than superficial change is possible through behavior modification.

The sixth methodology is cognitivism. The cognitivists hold that moral reasoning can be successfully taught and is perhaps the most legitimate aim of education. The cognitivists acknowledge the role of the affect, but the contention is put forth that affect follows from a sound cognitive base and must be subsequent to cognitive development. The cognitive curriculum includes knowledge of the facts, arguments, and positions involved in moral issues; exercise in the skills of moral reasoning; and investigation of the nature, origin and foundation of ethics (Scriven, 1976). The weakness of this approach is its lack of balance in dealing with the affect and with the developmental process. It also displays a lack of research support.

A final methodology is that of structural (cognitive) developmentalism. The developmentalists see the structure of moral reasoning to be the key ingredient in values education or moral development. Man is viewed as an integrated whole who transacts with the environment in a way that sets up conflict or disequilibrium. The process of conflict resolution, or equilibration, allows a process of development. This developmental process is orderly, unidirectional, irreversible, qualitative, hierarchically integrated, progressively differentiated, increasingly articulated, actively created, and functionally superior to learning (Stewart, 1974, p. 258). A key ingredient in the developmental approach is the identification of the current stage of moral reasoning in an individual and exposing the individual to the next higher stage of moral reasoning. There are weaknesses in this method as well in terms of research support. An additional weakness of the developmentalist view from the cognitive perspective is that to say that higher stages are better is not provable. Thus, "the activity of moral 'uplife' is, in any case, unjustified on the basis of the developmentalists' own assumptions" (Scriven, 1975). The developmentalists may also have an overly optimistic view of man in terms of his basic

141

tendency to develop.

Concerns

It would appear that each position has its flaws; however, that should not lead us to a position of despair but to a position of action. As was suggested at the beginning of this chapter, we are dealing with values in what we do whether we like it or not. Certainly dealing with the issues in a thoughtful way is better than dealing with them in an unthinking way. As Scriven aptly says, "the cognitivist reserves the last dregs of scorn for the inactivists, who see that the ship is sinking but feel that it may make things worse if people try to find the lifeboats. Being conservative is one thing; insisting on group suicide is another" (Scriven, in Purpel and Ryan, 1976, p. 317). The first area of action should be that of research. Kohlberg and his associates have done an admirable job, but research in this area is difficult. Their findings do not justify the certainty claimed by some of their followers. It is essential that researchers from other points of view begin to rigorously investigate the area of moral development, too.

As research is conducted, it must focus on four areas. We may go so far as to say that any theory of moral development or values education which does not consider these four areas provides an inadequate model. Research must be concerned first with the structure of moral reasoning. Hard questions must be asked about the existence, generality, and invariability of Kohlberg's stages of moral development and about Piaget's model of intelligence upon which Kohlberg's theory is based. Second, research must be concerned with the process of change in holding specific values, patterns, or beliefs, and the most productive way to promote change in both structure and content. The third area of research should involve the specific content of values education. In many ways this is more an area for philosophical investigation than empirical investigation. Nevertheless, careful thinking must be done in the areas of ethics, ethical applications in value theory, and metaphysics. The nature of the society in which the education is to take place must also be considered in dealing with specific content issues. Finally, research must deal with the context in which this process of education must take place. It would seem that as a minimum, there must be a commitment to reasoned discussion, vulnerability, and honesty among all individuals involved in the process. The nature of what society is or should be and the nature of the institution are both important factors in the context. It would appear that certain approaches and positions might be more relevant than others in a democratic, pluralistic, western society. It would also seem that certain types of institutions could model for the society the types of attitudes and behaviors most productive to moral development. This will not be an easy task, but it is one which must be done--and college student development administrators must be among those leading the way.

References

Bandura, A. and Walters, R. Social Learning and Personality Development. New York: Holt, Rinehart & Winston, 1963.

Dewey, J. Moral Principles in Education. Boston: Houghton-Mifflin Co., 1909.

Eddy, J. College Student Personnel Development, Administration, and Counseling. Washington, D. C.: University Press of America, 1977.

Eddy, J. Education and Ethical Inquiry. Johnson, Vt.: Johnson State College, 1969.

Hartshorne, H. and May, M. Studies in the Nature of Character. New York: Macmillan, 1928 - 1930.

Havighurst, R. and Taba, H. Adolescent Character and Personality. New York: Wiley, 1949.

Hoffman, M. L. Moral Development. In P. Mussen (ed.), Carmichael's Manual of Child Psychology (3rd ed.). New York: Wiley, 1970.

Kirschenbaum, H. and Simon, S. (eds.). Readings in Values Clarification. Minneapolis: Winston Press, 1973.

Kohlberg, L. Development of Moral Character and Ideology. In M. L. and L. W. Hoffman (eds.), Review of Child Development Research. Vol. 1. pp. 383-427. New York: Russell Sage Foundation, 1964.

Kohlberg, L. and Turiel, E. Moral Development and Moral Education. In G. Lesser (ed.), Psychology and Educational Practice. Chicago: Scott Foresman, 1971, pp. 410-465.

Lerner, M. Education and Values. Bloomington, Indiana: Phi
Delta Kappa, 1976.

Lloyd-Jones, Esther. Dedication. In J. Eddy, College Student
Personnel Development, Administration, and Counseling.
Washington, D. C.: University Press of America, 1977.

Peck, R. and Havighurst, R. The Psychology of Character
Development. New York: Wiley, 1960.

Perry, W. Forms of Intellectual and Ethical Development in the
College Years: A Scheme. New York: Holt, Rinehart and
Winston, 1970.

Piaget, J. The Origins of Intelligence in Children (McCook,
trans.) New York: International Universities Press,
1956.

Raths, L, Harmin, M., and Simon, S. Values and Teaching.
Columbus, Ohio: Charles E. Merrit, 1966.

Scriven, M. Cognitive Moral Education. In D. Purpel and K.
Ryan (eds.), Moral Education...It Comes With the Territory.
Berkeley: McCutchen, 1976.

Skinner, B. Beyond Freedom and Dignity. New York: Bantam
Books, 1971.

Skinner, B. Science and Human Behavior. New York: Macmillan,
1953.

Skinner, B. Walden Two. New York: Macmillan, 1948.

Stewart, J. Toward a Theory for Values Development Education.
(Doctoral dissertation, Michigan State University, 1974).
(University Microfilms No. 74-27, 491).

CHAPTER 16

STUDENTS AND SCHOLARS EXAMINE SOME ETHICAL ISSUES

John Eddy

Reviewing the scholars of ancient times to the atomic age on ethical questions, is the usual approach of ethical texts. However, this book adds a new dimension by including statements of students wrestling with some ethical issues. Students have a way of bringing fresh approaches and unmasking the false. We live in an age of unprecedented ethical confusion in regard to what is right or wrong and to the meaning of human life. Man's oldest and most sacred values have come under assault by the technological conditions of life and by visions of reality being provided by the sciences. Today's interpreter of philosophy may have little effect unless he takes these matters into account.

In describing values in society and the role of ethics, A. Dudley Ward has written:

Ethics is people in action. Ethics is making and implementing decisions. As such, ethics involves the use of a mild form of coercion to the mammoth institutional power of a great nation.... These assertions are validated empirically in individual and corporate experience. Any sentient person knows that his values are the basis for his decision and action. It is essential to recognize that decisions, from the most casual to the most complex, are made ultimately by a reaction of the total self to the influences that are both implicit and explicit in the situation demanding decision.[1]

The author was fortunate to have students who dared to tackle some of the problems of mankind through their writing in a philosophical approach to ethics. Some of the edited statements of these students are presented in this chapter ranging from personal to social concerns. These statements represent some of the contemporary challenges to the day as well as the age old dilemmas facing mankind. The students in some cases have attempted to identify an ethical problem, to show the ethical implications of a problem and to illustrate a mode of attacking an ethical problem. In other cases, students have merely expressed their general opinions on certain issues. This leads to problem solving by people. As Robert Theobald has said,

"Some of us had better choose to define ourselves as world problem-solvers if world problems are going to be solved."[2]

I. The Search for Peace

One of the most important moral issues of the ages has to do with the peaceful relationship of nations to one another. The development of quick and mass death dealing devices has accelerated the public opinion against human conflict and student reactions to this issue are the following:

    A. "...War is immoral...for I believe in the Christian ethic 'Thou shalt not kill.' I cannot see the difference between one person killing another and an army killing another army. Mass slaughter is merely an augmentation of one man killing another."

    B. "Concerning the ethical position that I have in regards to matters in my own life, I feel that the problem of strife between nations is the one that is most serious to me...."

    C. "War is a barbaric waste of human life and man's creative energies. War destroys civilization, and mankind through the ages has been trying to build civilization...."

Allan Parrent has written on the need for working for peace on this planet. He writes, "While government has an obligation to foster the development of peace and actively to seek reconciliation among nations to the degree that this is possible in the context of existing international relationships....If the deeper realism which understands with Pope Paul that 'development is peace' is ever to be manifested in action, it is clear that peace must be given priority in deed as well as in word and that this must be reflected in some fashion by the way our government organizes and implements its efforts in this direction."[3]

II. The Search for Acceptance

Prejudice is another of the important moral issues of this planet. Prejudice is of many types such as racial discrimination, class bias, religious bigotry, social snobbery, rabid nationalism, and so forth. The propensity to prejudice is seen in man's self-love, self-interest and self-centeredness. When a man puts himself in the center of the universe and holds his own interests before others, the case for prejudice has been made. Student reactions to this issue are the following:

"My opinion before taking this course was actually phony because I thought the best and smartest thing to do was

146

to remain aloof and not take a personal interest in
any one's problems but my own. After a little reflection on this point, I have come to the conclusion that
my first opinion was not only immoral, but also un-
healthy for me as an individual...for I am my own
world and no one else fits in."

Martin Luther King has written on the social crisis of our
day and its stupefying complexity. He writes:

"White America must recognize that justice for black
people cannot be achieved without radical changes in
our society....The black revolution is much more than
a struggle for the rights of Negroes. It is forcing
America to face all its interrelated flaws--racism,
poverty, militarism and materialism....It reveals systematic rather than superficial flaws....White America
does not refer to skin color, but to an attitude. We
have found that there are many white people who clearly
perceive the justice of the Negro struggle for human
dignity. Many of them joined our struggle and displayed
heroism no less inspiring than that of black people....
Today's dissenters tell the complacent majority that the
time has come when further evasion of social responsibility will court disaster and death....Jesus had only
the poor and despised as his disciples, but changed the
course of mankind. Naive and unsophisticated though we
may be, the poor and despised of the 20th Century will
revolutionize this era. In our arrogance, lawlessness
and ingratitude we will fight for human justice, brotherhood, secure peace and abundance for all....When we have
won these--in a spirit of unshakable non-violence--then,
in luminous splendor, the Christian era will truly
begin."[4]

III. The Search for a Concerned Government

The problem of a concerned government is another moral
issue. How a nation cares for its people will be determined by
the justice implied in its laws, the approach of its welfare
agencies, the quality of its public services, the enforcement
of its statutes, the efficiencies of its public protectors. The
public morality may be judged by the priority the people of a
nation place upon its values on the life of a single person or
a group of people with regards to physical survival, social
acceptance, educational opportunity, job preference, housing
units, personal income, social status, etc.

Edmund Burke wrote in 1791 the following with regard to
controlling one's drives and ambitions:

Men are qualified for civil liberty in exact proportion
to their dispostion to put moral chains upon their own
appetites. Society cannot exist unless a controlling
power upon will and appetite be placed somewhere, and
the less of it there is within, the more there must be
without. It is ordained in the external constitution
of things that men of intemporate minds cannot be free.
Their passions forge their fetters.[5]

Several student reactions to this issue are the following:

A. "I feel that poverty is one of the biggest problems
    in the world today. If right and wrong can be applied
    here, then I would say that poverty is wrong....I am
    convinced that poverty exists through the selfishness
    of man. There are no excuses for its existence....
    The loss of many human lives because of extreme
    poverty is immoral, especially when technology could
    stamp out poverty. If people could only stop talking
    and start acting, many of our problems would dissolve
    gradually--including this one."

B. "I am part of society, and I must play my role....If
    I want to be recognized as an individual with rights,
    then I must regard others in that same light....I
    believe my philosophy has been strengthened by this
    course in Ethics...."

IV. The Search for a Healthful Living Environment

The pollution of the air, water and land of this planet is
serious for the survival of human species. Man's technology has
benefited him in many ways but also it has penalized him in
other ways. The automobile that provides a short cut to travel
also in it manufacture may cause a long time pollution of streams
and soil. Several student reactions to this issue are the
following:

A. "I believe in the basic goodness of all men but in
    reality we must realize that no one or thing is all
    good. There is some evil involved at some point in
    time or eternity. This last statement does not
    apply to God...."

B. "I must still contend that the person who fails to
    fight for the issues he believes in--not merely
    discussing them--is not, whatever his title or his
    gains, a man. It is, indeed unfortunate that more
    people are not willing to take a similar stand."

148

C. "During the course, I have seen that my philosophy could not stand by itself. I had a feeling of a utopian world....My world was a perfect world. This never could come true. I have arrived at this opinion from our readings and discussions."

V. The Search for a Faith or Values to Live By

Religion gives the framework for moral standards and ethical ideals. A person's associations to God or life have often been transferred to one's relationships to others. Many of the religious leaders have been persons who attempted to reform both religious practices and human relationships.

Religion tries to give meaning to life and to strengthen the morale of people by giving security and harmony found in believing in a deity that has essence. Ethical religion would tend to be less centered on doctrine and dogma that divide mankind. Theological beliefs and religious practices that would promote war or prejudice, for instance, would contradict ethical religion that would strive for peace and brotherhood. Several student reactions are the following:

A. "I feel that many people of today are putting too much emphasis on material things. They are becoming so involved with making money that they neglect the matters of real importance and their own happiness.... People may have pleasures, but the pleasure does not last nor is it necessarily right....Money cannot buy happiness. The man with the least amount of money, but who has love in his life for his fellowmen will be the happiest in the end."

B. "Religion, I thought, had to be figured out scientifically. It took time to realize, but I feel I have developed a sincere belief, and discovered that religion isn't something scientific....Ethics, as a subject, has helped me formulate my thinking, and helped me to understand myself better."

C. "Throughout the course, we came across religion in our readings and discussions....Everyone needs something to believe in, be it God or even oneself. This is the moral implication of religion....I feel religion is the basis of everything and to let it crumble would be like taking the link out of a chain--it will fall apart."

VI. The Search for Physical and Mental Health

The search for physical and mental health has been a
struggle in which mankind has always been involved. Good
health is essential for the function of personal happiness and
community welfare. While there have been many people who have
overcome poor health and physical disability to achieve marve-
lous things, it is the unusual person who accomplishes things
with such handicaps. Many outstanding people have gone to an
early grave because of a habit that cut life off, be it over-
eating, drinking, smoking, drug consumption, exercising, worrying
or exposure to the elements. Several student reactions to this
issue are the following:

A. "I feel that I have taken a good look at myself
because of this course. The people around me seem more
real to me and closer. I can understand their views
better and can try to rationalize them....Before I
felt funny or mixed-up on a lot of subjects but now I
can see why I must change my attitude toward life....
I can't always hate everyone who does me injustice
because the world would be worse off from what it was.
Man must live as an individual but also as part of
society....Thank you for at least a start on finding
my lost religion....I have listened in class but
denominational religion was never really discussed.
We spoke on many things but denominational religion
was rarely mentioned. The one thing that really did
help was thinking more clearly and more deeply in
the class and outside the class...."

B. "I have strengthened my belief in optimism, perhaps,
because I have also strengthened a previously strong
idea that life is worth living. I also believe that
optimism is a propelling force that can sometimes
motivate us to achieve certain things....An optimistic
attitude toward life, also makes it more enjoyable
and more worth living."

VII. The Search for a Meaningful Marriage

The atmosphere of a family situation makes a difference in
the rearing of children and the living of parents. Thus, a
moral issue of prime importance is how a person is raised in a
family. The lack of parental discipline, attention and affection
can seriously affect the growth of a child. A parent or guardian's
example has significant effect upon a child. In situations where
parents are not available for a desirable model, it is understandable that children may develop unwanted patterns. A stealing
and lying parent will influence his child or children to do like-
wise--if he gets away with these traits. Honesty has to be taught

150

and deeds do speak louder than words. Parents who fight each
other over issue after issue may train their child or children
to be natural warriors or to hate the opposite sex because of
inadequate exposure to human beings. Student reactions to this
issue are the following:

A. "Because of the lack of family unity, there has been
a rise in crime, in the number of unwed mothers, in
the illegal use of drugs, etc....More laws and more
policemen aren't going to prevent these crimes. I
feel that it has got to come from within the family
unit. Members of a family must do more things as a
unit and must try to establish better communication
between its members....The other night, I was trying
to study for exams and my children were screaming.
I got to screaming at them. Then, I asked myself:
'Why did I do that? What could be more important
to me than them?' I feel that if I can help them to
grow up to be responsible individuals, that I will
in some small way help our society...."

VIII. The Search for a Meaningful Occupation

Ethics is concerned with what ought to be. Therefore,
ethics relates to the improvement of persons and conditions of
people. Consequently, the issue of how a person operates within
a given job is of ethical concern. For instance, what does
it mean to slum dwellers when a profit minded real estate man
takes advantage of low income people? Moreover, what does it
mean when a prejudiced guidance counselor tells a youth that it
would be better to consider another position because society
won't allow his mental ability to be used in a job because of
the pigment of one's skin? Student reactions to this issue are
the following:

A. "In September I didn't really feel as if I wanted to
go to school, but I did because it was expected of
me so I did as I was told. The money for this semester has been almost entirely wasted....I could have
learned more on any street corner in Boston and it
would have been more interesting....I think philosophy doesn't answer problems, but reference and
research in philosophy can help explain problems.
This is the way that I will use what I have learned
in this course."

B. "Wisdom and knowledge can come from many different
directions. Some of them being old age and experience
and another being formal education."

IX. The Search for Meaningful Avocations

What one does with one's leisure time can make a difference
in one's mental attitude toward all of life. Developing meaningful hobbies and activities can broaden as well as deepen a
person which, in turn, can make a more exciting self and society.
Sometimes an interest in an avocation can turn into a livelihood.
Student reactions to this issue are the following:

A. "I feel that college life away from the home environ-
    ment is one of the best things that a young person
    could experience....We develop maturity every day here
    and it definitely helps us toward our future life....
    Learning to deal with other people...and writing impor-
    tant papers using pertinent materials are also important
    things...."

X. The Search for a Meaningful Education

Education is seen today in terms of a life-long process.
It is a matter both of formal and informal training inside and
outside the classroom. The involvement of the teacher and the
student in the learning process is essential to a meaningful
educational experience. In spite of the great stress on the
wonders of computers or "thinking machines" in education and in
all of life, there are sober commentaries being made on the limits
of such devices by experts in the field itself. Rolf Landauer
of IBM has pointed out that the process of calculation reaches
basic limits. There are some problems that are soluble in
principle which no machine can do according to Landauer.[6] Student
reactions to this issue are the following:

A. "Man's greatest dilemma is the retention of his
    individuality....We are trapped by our institutions.
    Institutions which should protect us are static and
    autocratic. The ethical implications are obvious.
    No system can be right which destroys humanity."

[1]Ward, A. Dudley, "People In Action," Engage, December 15,
1968, p. 13.

[2]Schall, Joe, "Personal Letter," December 20, 1968, p. 4.

[3]Parrent, Alan M., "The Department of Peace," Tempo,
January 15, 1969, p. 9

[4]Martin Luther King, "Last Words For The Nation,"
Religious News Service, January 15, 1969.

[5]Reston, James, "Negro Moderates Begin to Fight Negro Militants," <u>Burlington Free Press</u>, January 16, 1969, p. 20.

[6]Lederberg, Joshua, "Man Can Be Called 'Machine'--But a Most Complex One," <u>Washington Post</u>, December 28, 1968, p. 3.

CHAPTER 17

"CARL ROGERS' NEW INSIGHT"
HOW SCHOOLS AND COLLEGES SHOULD EDUCATE FOR PEACE

John Eddy

Introduction

There is a cliche that goes, "Old too soon and wise too
slow." Carl Rogers, senior spokesman of counseling psychology,
admits to this old saw when it comes to speaking out against war
and other bad social conditions. At 68 years of age in 1972, he
spoke out publicly for the first time against war and the problems of cities in a lecture the author heard him give at Northwestern University. Rogers told us that he spent most of his
life speaking and writing about one to one or small group psychological approaches to persons. However, he ignored in his public
speaking and writing the larger social problems of people such
as crime in the cities and killing in wars. Rogers' honesty is
to be admired and his statements against starting war and the
decaying of cities reveal a sensitive soul trying to alert us all
to the dangers of apathy and inaction about these social problems
of humankind.

What Carl Rogers was saying is all too often the case of many
other persons. We only concentrate on the personal activities of
life where we work as counselors with one person or in small
groups of persons on their problems. What we often fail to do
is also share our values with one person or a group of persons
that might influence a person or a group of persons to act more
responsibly about such issues as war or crime by supporting new
legislation, enforcing laws, and aiding those persons caught in
the web of social problems. It is not an "either/or" situation;
we need to have both "personal" and "social" concerns.

Why cannot a counselor have a sensitive soul for social
problems as well as for self? Of course, we can't do everything
or solve all the world's ills by our actions. However, these
excuses are often heard from counselors and other helping professionals. These statements are "copouts" not "help-outs."
There are organizations we can join that collectively can act
responsively and relevantly to try to meet human needs to help
alleviate conditions that lead to crime in cities and killing in
wars.

Despair statements I have heard over the years by counselors
and others in the helping professions are: "What can one person
do?" and "I am an insignificant person in changing this society."
If everyone believed this kind of fatalism, then, we are in
deep trouble for there is no hope or help to act for new approaches
to change conditions that destroy persons in cities and in wars.
Who would educate persons for peace?

If the schools and colleges would educate for peace, then,
we must know why we do it. A number of years ago, Dr. George
Counts was a professor of mine at Southern Illinois University
and I recall him saying in one of his classes how the institutions
of education in Nazi Germany served the interests of war plans.
In illustration after illustration, Dr. Counts pointed out how
each academic discipline was used to forward the battle plans of
those war mad Nazi leaders. Dr. Counts once wrote a famous essay
that is well known in American educational history entitled,
"Dare the Schools Change the Social Order?" Paraphrasing his
message in terms of our subject, "Dare the Schools and Colleges
teach Peace Education?"

Peace Education Rationale

There are a number of identifiable elements or factors that
are enemies of peace for all peoples. In September of 1974, the
World Council for Curriculum and Instruction held its first
world conference in England with the theme, "Education for Peace."
At the conference some "seeds of conflict" were identified by
Dr. Robert Kwaku Gardiner, Executive Secretary of the United Nations
Economic Commission for Africa. Dr. Gardiner mentioned them as:

"Arms, structural economic violence, the crisis of
numbers, absolute poverty, environmental overload, and
racism provide the seeds of conflict. A peaceful world
order calls for minds which have been awakened to the
reality of interdependence and the consequential rights
and obligations of a world citizen. The task of education is to develop a global patriotism, to inspire commitment to a larger world community, and to teach behavioral skills that can imagine, analyze, and evaluate
future possibilities and probabilities, or, in short,
the strategies of survival."

Peace Education Questions

Some questions that we should deal with in students on all
levels of education are raised by Dr. Ted Rice, President of the
United States World Education Fellowship for 1975. These questions relate directly to peace education goals. They are:

155

1. Do our school students have sufficient opportunity
   to think through and organize a philosophy of life?

2. What do they believe?

3. What encouragement do they receive to develop goals?

4. Are we helping them recognize the responsibility
   each one has in the building of a society which
   serves the needs of all of us?

One Class to Remember

Using the book, The Rumor of War, on the Viet Nam war by an
American veteran for discussion and viewing the Japanese film in
the Philippines on World War II entitled, "The Fire on the Plains"
is enough to capture the horror of war. A two hour class session
on these two materials is an experience few will ever forget as
long as they live.

Peace Education Curriculum

A peace education curriculum should include: "(1) an overall vision of peace; (2) formation in the virtues and attributes
which especially promote concern for and effectiveness in working
for peace; (3) a body of concepts and an appropriate vocabulary,
plus a knowledge of any special topics which may be relevant in
a particular situation; (4) an appropriate methodology or methodologies in working for peace; and (5) a practice competence in
action...

In terms of concepts and vocabulary of program content,
peace education requires an intellectual as well as a moral
formation. Without a satisfactory intellectual as well as a
moral content, peace education can hardly hope to advance and
gain ground against the massive forces of institutionalized injustice or of those ideologies which explicitly uphold violence.

With regard to competence in working for peace through
program content, basic competence can come only through active
involvement combined with a systematic reflection on what is being
done. Competence can be built up through case-studies; participation in the work of peace action groups; undertaking projects
of various types; acquiring relevant skills such as organizing,
ability to analyze and improve structures at every level, for
example, community development groups; lobbying; building alternative structures; and using simulation games and various group
exercises to illustrate problems, develop skills, and improve
the individual's awareness of and ability to assess relatively
complex situations." (The Irish Commission for Justice and Peace,
1976)

"In terms of personal modeling for peace education, formulation for peace must attempt to internalize the self desire to be
peaceful, to act for peace, and to act peacefully toward others.
It will have to assist people to a greater self-awareness, so
they know more about themselves and their limitations...Only in
and after freeing ourselves can we help to free others. Those
persons in whom the sense of their own human worth and dignity is
lacking or is defective cannot be expected in the vanguard of a
campaign for a more peaceful world...Before constructive change
is likely to be willingly accepted, or genuine dialogue with
others begin, or alternatives be honestly examined, a certain
level of security in the inner sanctum of a person is needed."
(The Irish Commission for Justice and Peace, 1976)

Conclusion

If the schools and colleges dare to teach peace education;
they need to provide: reasons why we need peace education;
causes for war and human conflict; modes for developing peace
education; and basic questions that relate to peace education
approaches. The teachers who dare to teach peace education need
to constantly keep informed and be hopeful and helpful models
as they try new ways to make the material relevant to student
needs. Peace education is a body of knowledge and skills that
can be related to any discipline from using mathematics to
determine the numbers of persons who have died in wars to using
religion to show values.

As this poem indicates, a teacher has an important task
in peace education:

> May we teachers walk with humanity
> In shoes of compassionate empathy
> To leave footprints of peace,
> That human wars will cease.

References

Arnold, D.; Philips, D.; Howe, M. and Eddy, J.P.
Action and Careers in a New Age, Washington, D.C.:
American Personnel and Guidance Association Press,
1973.

Eddy, J.P. "Assessing Peace Education Potential: Using
A Conference Consultation Model 1972-74." Journal of
Int'l Foundations of Education Quarterly. Spring '75.

Eddy, J.P. "A Counselor's Approach to Peace and
World Events," Peace Progress, 1975

157

References

Eddy, J.P. and Jaski, E.B. "A New Model for Peace Making Through Conflict Resolution," Peace Progress, 1974.

Eddy, J.P. "A Program for Achieving World Peace," Peace Digest, August, 1976.

Eddy, J.P. "A System for Evaluating Peace Education Materials," Mutual Understanding of Peoples and Minority Group Education. Sandai, Japan: Kahoku Shinppo Newspaper Company, 1977.

Eddy, J.P. "Education and the Theory and Practice of Peace," Peace Digest, May-June, 1975.

Eddy, J.P. "Educating for World Responsibility," World Peace Through Population Education. Bangkok, Thailand: Faculty of Education, Chulalonghorn University, 1972.

Eddy, J.P. "Dr. Paul A. Schlipp's Contributions to Philosophy through the Library of Living Philosophers Series," Improvement of College and University Teaching, Fall, 1976.

Eddy, J.P. "Educating the Whole Person from Kindergarten through College," Peace Progress, 1974.

Eddy, J.P. "Ethnic Ecology: An International Friendship Garden," Peace Digest. Nov-Dec, 1976.

Eddy, J.P. and Jaski, E. "Felician College: International Peace Center" Peace Progress, 1975.

Eddy, J.P. "How to Mediate," Peace Digest, April, 1977.

Eddy, J.P. "How Schools and Colleges Should Educate for Peace," Peace Digest, Sept-Oct., 1975.

Eddy, J.P. "New Forces to Help the World," Peace Digest. Sept-Oct., 1976.

Eddy, J.P. "The Peace Ballot," Peace Digest, Nov-Dec., 1976.

Eddy, J.P. "Peace Concerns in 1976." Peace Digest, Vol. 1, No. 3., 1976.

158

References

Eddy, J.P. "Peace Education by Religious Organizations," Peace Digest. Jan-Feb., 1976.

Eddy, J.P. "Peace March Joins Former Enemies," Peace Digest. Jan-Feb., 1978.

Eddy, J.P. "Peace Memorial Park in Hiroshima and a New Peace Proposal," Peace Digest, April, 1977.

Eddy, J.P. "Peace Ship," Peace Digest, July-Aug. 1975.

Eddy, J.P. "Peace Pilgrim" Peace Digest, Nov-Dec., 1975.

Eddy, J.P. "Return Walk for Human Peace and Prayer of Confession for Peace," Peace Digest. Jan-Feb. 1978.

Eddy, J.P. "River Redeemed: A Mexican Miracle," Peace Digest, Jan-Feb. 1978.

Eddy, J.P. "Rotary International Friendship Garden," Peace Digest, Mar-April 1976.

Eddy, J.P. "The Human Personality from the Fields of Psychology, Philosophy and Theology." Peace Progress, Vol. 1, No. 3, 1976.

Eddy, J.P. "The Need for International Education and Informed Guidance Counselors on Survival Issues," Peace Progress, 1974.

Eddy, J.P. "The Real Enemies of Man: New Forces to Help the World," Peace Progress. 1974.

Eddy, J.P. "Towards an Ideal International Peace Education Conference to Actualize Selected Educational Principles," Peace Progress, 1975.

Eddy, J.P. "You Can Talk to the State Department," Jan-Feb., 1977.

Eddy, J.P. "War Or Peace: 1976, A Bicentennial Project," Peace Digest, May-June, 1976.

Eddy, J.P. and Madden, M.A. "Peace Education through an International Dimension," Peace Progress, 1975.

References

Eddy, J.P. "World Peace Exposition and International Gardens," Peace Digest, May-June, 1975.

Eddy, J.P. "World Court Works," Summer, 1977.

Eddy, J.P. "Worldmindedness Approaches Actualized," Peace Progress, 1974.

Eddy, J.P. "Women's Contribution to World Peace," Peace Education Journal, Vol. 1, No. 1, Sept. 1977.

Eddy, J.P. and Kemg, F. "Women's Contributions to World Peace," Peace Progress, Vol. 1, No. 3, 1976.

Henderson, G. Education for Peace Focus on Mankind. Washington, D.C.: Association for Supervision and Curriculum Development, 1973.

Pickus, R. and Woito, R. To End War. New York: Seabury Press, 1974.

_____. "A Framework for Peace Education and Training." Dublin, Ireland. The Irish Commission for Justice and Peace, A Commission of the Irish Catholic Hierarchy, 1976, p. 6-10.

160

CHAPTER 18

HUMANIZED STUDENT PERSONNEL SERVICES

Paul G. Hill

Introduction

Throughout the United States, colleges and universities
are undergoing profound and sometimes painful change. There
is considerable pressure to reexamine the purposes and functions of student personnel services and to introduce new
theories and processes of professional training. In this
chapter, one of the pioneers in what Corsini (1974) refers
to as "the age of aquarius movement" proposes the rationale
of humanized student personnel services to bring services
to their proper position in relation to students. Corsini
accurately recognized that this aquarius-type project is
both noble and ambitious, and cannot be achieved without
"great personal struggle." What may be termed "project
aquarius" calls for student personnel professionals to
accept responsibility for their own existence.

New Goals of Education

The ultimate purpose of student personnel services is
to assist students toward the ideal of being humane. The
content, organization, and administration of student personnel services has undergone dynamic changes in the past
decade. The changes suggest rational progression to new
goals of education and humanized student personnel services
for the attainment of the following goals:

To understand, accept, and value self;

To understand, appreciate, and value one's own ethnic
group and culture as well as the ethnic groups and
cultures of others;

To develop positive attitudes toward (1) life-long
learning, (2) academic services, and (3) supportive
human services;

To master the skills of oral and written language
communication;

161

To master the theoretical and practical use of mathematics;

To practice habitual behavior which fosters the continuing recreation of physical well-being;

To understand and appreciate the social and physical sciences and the fine and performing arts;

To attain a full grasp of career development opportunities which lead to a rewarding and productive life;

To acquire the values and habits of responsible citizenship at multiple levels, including world citizenship;

To utilize creative theory and processes for the continuing procreation of mental and emotional well-being;

To identify and alter social institutions and systems which tend to create or perpetuate disadvantagement, maladaptive behavior, and anti-human ideals;

To ultimately explore and interpret the essence of being human--the ability to envision and actualize ideal ends.

Creative-Focus Counseling

The preceding goals support the perspective of Kennedy (1978) that humanized education provides the best possible educational experience for students who represent a composite of unique attitudes, personality traits, achievements, and abilities. The essential challenge to student personnel professionals, through creative career counseling, is to assist students in the development of positive self-concepts, intellectual development, social relationships, sense of identity, values clarification, educational plans, career plans, family concerns, leisure interests, and universal human concerns.

Creative career counseling complements what Eddy (1978) describes as the personal, existential, and complex struggle in life to find meaning in work. Creative career counseling (Kennedy, 1978) expands the struggle to a lifelong effort to find meaning in life.

162

It is important to take a fresh look at human beings (Jackins, 1972) to see what they can be without assumptions from the past. This fresh look will not be easy to accomplish because of the persistence of past suggestions, but it is a clear necessity for the development of a program of humanized student personnel services. Such a program can directly lead to creative-focus counseling for the solution of human problems. Principles of creative-focus counseling services include:

1. Self-awareness of personal emotions and attitudes is prerequisite to acceptance of responsibility of caring for and about others.

2. The welfare of the clients is of primary concern.

3. The welfare of individuals is integrally related to the welfare of society.

4. Clients have common needs as well as needs which are uniquely different.

5. Clients possess reaction and construction systems, representing realities and potentialities.

6. Society is obligated to facilitate the realization of the creative potential of individuals through the provision of developmental and curative services.

7. Curative creative-focus services emphasize the wholeness of the individual.

8. Creative-focus counseling takes note of outer expression of inner feelings.

9. Creative-focus counseling considers the effect which cultural and ethnic heritage has upon individuals.

10. Creative-focus counseling involves the community, including systems and processes, social services, and resources.

11. Creative-focus counseling views all clients as creative, intelligent, worthy, and beautiful.

12. Creative-focus counseling facilitates the liberation of the creative potential of clients--organizing talents and strengths for the solution of problems.

163

Humanizing Education

Humanized student personnel services can lead to the continuous exploration of relevant goals of education and related roles and responsibilities of student personnel professionals. New attitudes toward cultural and ethnic minorities, intercultural communication, and creative cultural pluralism may also emerge as corollaries from humanized student personnel services. This ideal holds great promise for the future through the improvement of the quality of the lives of students.

Patterson (1973) concludes that humanistic learning facilitation must be concerned with the development of students having humanistic beliefs and attitudes toward others, while assisting students in the development of positive self-concepts and self-actualization. We must not tell students how to live humanely; we can show them how only be being humanistic. A logical place to emphasize humanized student personnel services is in the training of future professionals. This assumes, perhaps unrealistically, humanistic professors. And yet, the logic and ideality of the training program as a humane locus are undeniable.

As Miller and Prince (1976) state, "Change has always been a characteristic of higher education in this country." For student personnel services, the need for renewal can take the form of concern for the humane development of students. For too long, student personnel services have been considered complements or compliments to instructional services with secondary status. This secondary status precludes the maximal humane development of students by limiting the amount of attention that can be given to their personal-social, emotional, and behavioral growth. In concert with other functional services, humanized student personnel services can and should effectively improve the individual and collective quality of life of college students.

The focus on humane development illuminates the importance of collaboration, coordination, and cooperation of all the services that usually include (Siegel, 1968) counseling,

164

testing, health service, student activities, student government, student publications, admissions, discipline, records,
residence arrangements, orientation, foreign student programs,
remedial programs, and career and educational information.
No one professional or functional service can accomplish
humanization alone. Only through the involvement of all
student personnel professionals is the reality of a humane
perspective possible.

Emphasizing Research

All student personnel professionals need to be equipped
with skills in statistics, research methodology, and evaluation. As a minimum, Williamson and Biggs (1975) suggest
that they possess positive attitudes toward research. Sharp
observational skills help professionals to comprehend sub-
leties in individual and group situations, and distinguish
between observations and inferences. Research-oriented student personnel professionals are likely to deal with their
personal biases in such a manner that they will exhibit
greater caution and objectivity in making generalizations,
identifying relationships, and forming hypotheses.

Student personnel services exist in an increasingly anti-
intellectual environment where the codeword is accountability,
and there is increasing demand for demonstration of effectiveness. In such an atmosphere, it is important not to become
more concerned with justification than with students in the
process to obtain data for the improvement of program functioning. The goals of accountability and continuing program
improvement require more than focusing on input, output, and
cost-effectiveness. A systems approach must take into
account personal-social, educational, cultural and ethnic
factors, as well as their interrelatedness to new goals of
education.

Development of Thinking-Reasoning

Pronouncements which seek to state the universal goals
for education are usually declarative and not interrogative.
The goals center around the development of cognitive mental
processes and the attainment of a certain level of cognitive

skills. The development of the thinking-reasoning powers of
the human mind is central to the continuing struggle to be
free. And yet, the age of aquarius movement views this as
not enough. It would be illogical to focus only on a cognitive theme. To do so subordinates other questions that
are equally crucial.

The development of thinking-reasoning powers include
memory and imagination, classification and generalization,
comparison and differentiation, analyzation and synthesis,
exploring and interpreting. These processes are not ends,
but beginnings, and are like the spokes of a wheel of which
thinking-reasoning power is the hub. Thus, the traditional
goals of the mastery of skills of oral and written language
communication and the theoretical and practical use of mathematics continue to be essential. Other objectives are met
through the exercise of thinking-reasoning powers, among
which are mental and physical well-being, family and ethnic
group membership, career competence, multiple citizenship,
recreative leisure, and humane behavior. Students are multi-
faceted human beings with intuitive powers and aesthetic
talents which must be recognized and enhanced in the process of education. Until now the education of students has
been overweighted with cognitive emphasis and underweighted
with substantive and affective group ends. That is to say,
they have been weakened by more preoccupation with how to
develop cognitive skills than with the ends for which the
achievement of cognitive skills should be predominant.

Where in the entire educational enterprise are students
challenged and assisted to cope with the tremendous political,
economic, moral, and cultural alternatives of this Cybernetic
Age? It is quixotic to hope that they will inevitably do so.
It is said that the educational institutions can not do
everything, and this is true. Whether time and resources
will be harnessed for the ascent of humanity depends, in
part, upon tangible choices among values, commitment to
values, and the role of values in humanized student personnel
services.

Pursuing Freedom

As far as it goes, commitment to the pursuit of freedom
is an admirable value. It is also incomplete. To urge

166

counselors and student personnel professionals to achieve
commitment to this value, yet not to demonstrate the existence of such commitment by bold and positive choices of
theory and creative processes, avoids the very ethical acceptance of responsibility demanded to get the job done. In
brief, it is necessary to be willing to attempt--and to dra-
matize our attempt--to practice our own canons of thinking-
reasoning, to carry through the mandate of humanized student
personnel services.

Freedom is not necessarily a completely qualitative
value. It becomes complete only when it is firmly embodied
in the cultural meanings--in this instance, in group and
individual, public and private goals--and then spelled out
in our institutions. Thanks to thinking-reasoning powers,
some new goals of education are emerging, and unlike the
unanticipating, innocuous lists of educational commissions,
the new goals explicitly and unequivocally are commited to
new theories and creative processes. The preceding statement
raises intricate questions about the purpose of education,
the right to facilitate learning about social institutions
and values, and the iniquities of indoctrination in the educative process.

In fact, the educational system of the nation manifests,
by what it does and does not do, very strong commitment to
indoctrination in behalf of vested interest, political, and
religious groups. The point is not to condone any indoctri-
nating invasion of academic freedom, but a more fundamental
one. Education, conceived in an ethnomethodological sense,
is the pivotal transmitter of cultural heritage, the innova-
tor of cultural evolution, and the vehicle for cultural
ascent. Education is forever saturated with implicit and
explicit commitment to characteristic norm values of people
and their social institutions.

Liberating the Human Mind

The question remains as to whether the thinking-reasoning
powers of the human mind will be utilized to envision and
actualize group values and institutions appropriate to the
Cybernetic Age--values and institutions which facilitate
humane beings. For complex reasons, traditional psychology

167

does not provide a model for the ascent of humanity through the liberation of the human mind. It is hypothesized that traditional psychology, as a sensitive barometer of the dominant cultural climate, has yielded to the same pervasive moods of prejudice and complacency. There is a close correlation between the current swing of Americans toward conformity and conventionality and the equivocating tonal qualities of the pronouncements and publications of biased psychologists.

And yet, as the American culture retreats from the ideals of equality and shows increasing signs of insecurity and unwillingness to pioneer, it is reasonably certain that student personnel professionals will have no alternative but to assume leadership roles in the curing of the temporary malaise of an extinct educational volcano. The signs of our time point to the need to search for a fresh, magnetic theory with creative processes that can supersede vacillation and end the current educational dilemma.

The path to the solution of the dilemma lies, on the one hand, in envisioning that group values and commitments are always inextricably involved in education as a cultural institution. It lies, on the other hand, in the actual emergence of creative, cooperative processes of facilitating and encouraging group decisions on normative values. These processes require honest and uninhibited communication, searching exploration and interpretation of new goals, and well-thought-out and carefully planned action strategies to implement these goals. The suggested multidimensional processes reflect the hypothesis of Aquarian Psychology that students are future-oriented, dreaming, and ideal-seeking beings, who must, in order to be mentally and emotionally happy, commit themselves attitudinally and functionally to future goals and dreams in which they believe. The belief in these common group goals must be zealous enough to continually energize an attempt to achieve them.

Promoting Cross-Cultural Understanding

Among the needed new goals for education, one looms paramount about all which requires clear and direct statement. This is the goal of cultural pluralism through cross-cultural understanding. The full significance of this goal is comprehended only in its relationship to the potential of world citizenship. The alternative is eternal struggles between the peoples of our nation and the world. Cultural pluralism is more than workable; it is imperative.

Exemplary issues that surface in the exploration and interpretation of this central goal are both intricate and complex. Included are the obstacle of endemic racism, the creativity of all peoples, the crosscultural role of the arts and sciences, the uniquenesses and commonalities of human cultures, and ultimately, the structured form for implementing cultural pluralism. To the extent that these issues are neglected in educational institutions, the goal of cultural pluralism through crosscultural understanding remains elusive. And yet, there is a plenitude of good will available for harnessing and developing good will which is only waiting to be enlisted in the struggle for human dignity in our nation and in the world.

The task of student personnel professionals is, in a much greater measure, to acknowledge their innovative role of lifting the humane sights of the educational profession toward acceptance of the stirring goal of cultural pluralism. The paramount urgency of this innovative role emerges from the thrilling challenge to participate in the creative floresence of a new educational epoch.

In placing this goal before the student personnel professional, the developer of Aquarian Psychology does not expect all of the profession to embrace it. At the same time it is recognized that student personnel administrators are the humane partners in the administrative structure of the higher educational enterprise, and it is further suggested that they also possess the highest powers of thinking and reasoning that education can develop. It follows that their efforts need to be enlisted in the liberation of the minds of students from the debilitating effects of prejudice against ethnic and other minorities, and in fostering cultural pluralism through crosscultural understanding.

References

Corsini, R. Current Psychotherapies. Itasca: F. E. Peacock Publishers, Inc., 1974.

169

De Cecco, J. The Regeneration of the School. New York: Holt, Rinehart, and Winston, Inc., 1972.

Eddy, J. P. College Student Personnel Development, Counseling, and Administration. Washington: University Press of America, 1978.

Hill, Paul G. "Psychology for the Age of Aquarius." Unpublished manuscript, 1973.

Jackins, H. The Human Side of Human Beings. Seattle: Rational Island Publishers, 1972.

Kennedy, Joyce S. "Creative Teaching," in P. G. Hill and J. S. Kennedy, Focus on Creativity. Park Forest: Project Aquarius, 1978.

Leeper, R. (Ed.) Humanizing Education: The Person in the Process. Washington: Association for Supervision and Curriculum Development, NEA, 1967.

Miller, T., and Prince, J. The Future of Student Affairs. San Francisco: Jossey-Bass Publishers, 1977.

Patterson, C. H. Humanistic Education. Englewood Cliffs: Prentice-Hall, Inc., 1973.

Siegel, M. (Ed.) The Counseling of College Students. New York: The Free Press, 1968.

Williamson, E. G., and Biggs, D. Student Personnel Work. New York: John Wiley and Sons, Inc., 1975.

CHAPTER 19

ROLE SPECIFICATION IN SELECTION AND TRAINING
OF THE RESIDENT ASSISTANT

Joseph D. Dameron, John C. Wolf, and Carolyn T. Aguren

Perspective

A growing concern in recent years has been the provision
of meaningful student services to the college student. In
particular, resident hall counseling programs have been exten-
sively studied, and the increasing emphasis upon paraprofessional utilization in helping settings has resulted in a
number of studies focused specifically upon selection and
training of the college dormitory resident assistant (RA).
The area of RA selection and training has been investigated
by Bozarth, et al. (1970) who found a positive relationship
between the effectiveness of RA helping behaviors and demonstration of empathy and warmth through analysis of RA verbal
behavior, and Mitchell, et al. (1971) who demonstrated that
short-term training paradigms can produce significant gains
in the levels of empathy and warmth shown by the RA.

A recent comprehensive review of paraprofessional effectiveness by Hoffman and Warner (1976) included consideration
of a number of studies involving assessment of RA effectiveness and training efficiency. The research reviewed further
documented that significant gains in communication skills may
be produced following relatively short training periods with
RA paraprofessional helpers (Newton, 1974; Schroeder, et al.,
1973). In research reviewed which investigated RA effectiveness, Zirkle and Hudson (1975), Newton and Krauss (1973), and
Wyrick and Mitchell (1971) all found that the RA demonstrating
high levels of helping skills such as empathy and warmth proved
more effective in facilitating positive change in student
behavior and perceived RA efficiency than the RA demonstrating
lower levels of those characteristics. Significantly, each
study utilized different criteria to define RA effectiveness,
and this factor was not mentioned by Hoffman and Warner. These
studies generally dealt with the effectiveness of training the
RA who was selected prior to training and demonstrated that
increases in interpersonal skills can be obtained through the
training of such subjects. An unanswered question revolves
around how such training efficiency might have been affected
if the primary selection of RA's had emphasized characteristics correlated with RA effectiveness.

Investigation of the efficiency of RA selection based on the results of paper and pencil tests have yielded contradictory and inconclusive results. Although Van Pelt (1968) and Murphy and Ortenzi (1966) obtained moderate success in the use of standardized test results to develop RA selection procedures, Rubin (1970), Wotruba (1969), and Dameron and Wolf (1973) found that selection of effective resident assistants on the basis of test results alone yielded inconsistent and often nondiscriminatory results. Dameron and Wolf, in a report of a two-year study of RA selection and training, hypothesized that one source of potential interference in investigating the effectiveness of RA training and selection is a lack of institutional specification and communication of RA role and overall RA program objectives. They concluded that investigation of RA selection and training might be facilitated by preceding such investigation with consideration of the effects of RA role perception upon subsequent training and selection. The role of the dormitory RA has been examined by Gonyea and Warman (1962), and Mitchell (1970) observed that RA role definition must precede successful assessment of RA effectiveness. Shelton and Corazzini (1976) have directed attention to the relationship of RA role definition to RA effectiveness in the context of RA utilization of the referral process as a helping resource. The authors emphasized the necessity for resident assistants to specify their role to the student(s) whom they are referring. It should be noted that such role specification requires that the RA be clearly aware of the RA role and the institutional expectations they are to fulfill.

The RA must perform a variety of duties and difficulty in the identification of predictors of RA effectiveness is further enhanced by the resultant difficulty in defining the role. Duncan (1967) has developed an instrument for evaluation of RA effectiveness, but the utility of such an instrument based upon the use of standardized criteria is effective only to the extent to which these standardized criteria correlate with the individual institutional criteria for RA success. The conclusion of Gonyea and Warman (1962) of over a decade ago that a general lack of agreement exists with respect to definition of RA role, function, and criteria for effectiveness still appears accurate.

The review of the literature regarding RA effectiveness as related to selection and training therefore raises the issue of the relationship of RA role specification to success-

ful investigation of RA effectiveness and to RA selection
and training procedures. The present study was designed to
investigate: (a) the effects of RA role perception upon RA
selection and training procedures, and (b) the implications
of RA role perception for the selection and training of resident assistants.

THE STUDY

Method

The present study was conducted at a major public university with a large dormitory population. Ten groups of resident
assistants (RA's), 44 males and 58 females, selected prior to
the study by the Housing Division as RA's for the fall semester,
were the subjects (Ss) in the study. These Ss participated
in a thirty-hour training program designed to increase interpersonal helping skills (after Berenson, et. al., 1966). The
major component of the training program was small group interaction by the Ss in ten groups, with each group being composed
of all RA's assigned to a particular residence hall and each
group facilitated by a graduate student in counseling. The
group training format combined both task-oriented material
from a sourcebook on resident assistant training (Powell, et.
al. 1969) with Human Resource Development (HRD) Training
(Carkhuff, 1969; 1972; Egan, 1975a). HRD training was the
primary focus of the group training process. In the course of
the group training, a number of basic concerns regarding their
perceived role were voiced by the Ss. A questionnaire designed
for this study was administered at the completion of training
to all Ss. Participation by the Ss in completion of the questionnaire was voluntary, although all Ss were encouraged to
respond.

Questionnaire

The instrument designed for the study was a six-item,
open-ended questionnaire. This questionnaire contained items
examining the role perceptions of the Ss from two perspectives:
(1) the resident assistant role and function as currently implemented, and (2) the resident assistant role and function as
ideally conceived and implemented. The respondents were also
requested to include recommendations for improved utilization
of the RA and respondent-perceived barriers to such utilization in present program implementation. Each questionnaire

173

protocol was analyzed by item and responses grouped by the
major issue represented. The responses were recorded by
frequency count in each major category to facilitate ranking
of the major response categories for each questionnaire item.

RESULTS AND DISCUSSION

Of the total N of 102, 43 males and 57 females completed
the questionnaire. Eighty-six percent of the respondents felt
that their primary function was that of an "enforcer" and that
the most important functions they performed were a combination
of clerical and monitor-custodial tasks. Although 41% of the
respondents recognized some responsibility for acting as a
helping resource, this was viewed as a secondary and usually
minor role. The general role perception of the respondents was
reflected in the motivation most frequently expressed for seeking
the RA position. Of those program participants responding,
94% indicated that their major reason for being an RA was financial in nature (free room and board is provided to resident
assistants in addition to a small monthly stipend). Other
reasons such as general interest in people and a desire to help
others were manifested in the responses, but to a lesser extent.
However, 53% of the respondents indicated a desire to increase
time spent in a helping capacity if time and training for this
role were provided and this function clarified for them. Questionnaire results are summarized in Table 1.

TABLE 1

SUMMARY OF RA QUESTIONNAIRE RESPONSES

Questionnaire Item	Rank Order of Major Response Categories by Item
1. What are the primary responsibilities of the RA?	1. Policy enforcer and monitor 2. Clerk 3. Custodian 4. Helper
2. What factor(s) detract most from job perform- ance?	1. Amount of time required for clerical and monitor tasks 2. Lack of understanding of RA job (role)

174

Questionnaire Item	Rank Order of Major Response Categories by Item
3. What was your reason(s) for making application for the RA position?	1. Financial 2. Interest in people (general) 3. Desire to help others
4. What are the most important characteristic(s) of the effective RA?	1. Leadership qualities and ability to enforce rules 2. Capability to work within system 3. Interest in people (general)
5. List your suggestions for improvement of the RA program.	1. Require less time spent in clerical tasks 2. Provide more time to spend with dormitory programs 3. Provide more time and training for assistant residents
6. How would you change the RA program, if at all?	1. Provide the opportunity for input to the administrative hierarchy regarding problems in the RA program 2. Clarify the institutional goals for the RA and the RA program 3. Increase training (all types) for the job

The interdependence between conceptualization and communication of role and function of the RA and selection and training of the RA is dramatically underscored in the questionnaire responses. The concept of the resident assistant as a para-professional helper and peer counselor which the Housing Division intended to develop in the RA program had not been discussed with the program participants prior to entrance into the training program, nor had consideration been given to relevant qualifications for such a role when selected. Although the university initiated an effort to update the resident assistant program to keep pace with changing student needs, the institution had failed to include a statement of role and function of the RA which reflected that effort and which could serve as an overall

175

guide to selection and training of the RA. The resultant
confusion regarding role expectation produced by this failure
when training was initiated appears inevitable. Rather than
providing the RA with valuable training in helping skills,
the training program may have heightened confusion and minimized gains in the effectiveness of training which might otherwise have been demonstrated as a result of participation in
the training experience.

CONCLUSIONS AND RECOMMENDATIONS

"To proceed the selection and training of resident assistants
with a definitive and clearly-communicated statement of
RA role and function by the institution will increase the
effectiveness of subsequent selection and training."

The major conclusion of this study is that to proceed the
selection and training of resident assistants with a definitive
and clearly-communicated statement of RA role and function by
the institution will increase the effectiveness of subsequent
selection and training. The suggestions regarding selection
and training of the RA which follow are applicable only if this
major thesis is implemented.

Role Specification

The role of the RA must be conceptualized and defined,
preferably in functional behavioral terms, as a prerequisite
to the establishment of an effective RA Program (Mitchell,
1970). A competency-based format such as that employed by
Dameron (1973) in the role definition of guidance associates
and counselors might be utilized. The definition must then
be adequately communicated to the resident assistants and
other student services personnel involved in the program.

"The overall scope of student services must be defined
before the resident assistant program can be placed in
its proper perspective in the institutional student
services plan."

Ancillary to the need for a behavioral RA role definition
is the implicit need for identification of the student services
which are to be provided in the residence halls and the campus
in general. The overall scope of student services must be
defined before the resident assistant program can be placed in

176

its proper perspective in the institutional student services plan.

Finally, as suggested in the literature, there is a necessity for communicating the RA role specification to other institutions. One potential reason for conflicting research results in the student services literature relating to the RA is interinstitutional role variance.

Selection and Training

Suggestions regarding RA selection and training must be considered tentative at this point, but the use of paper and pencil test information combined with other indicators of interpersonal functioning directly correlated with functional behavioral program objectives appears to warrant additional investigation.

One method of selection which might be investigated is the "work sample or job tryout" technique introduced by Mitchell (1970). In the adaptation of that approach suggested here, the RA applicant would participate in an unpaid apprenticeship of one semester with an RA already demonstrating the desired competencies. In the course of such an on-the-job training (OJT) experience, the applicants are evaluated on their ability to meet the functional behavioral program objectives established by the institution. During an initial six to eight week screening period, formal psychometric evaluation is integrated in the OJT format to assist in the selection of those candidates who will continue in the program.

In the latter portion of the semester, the use of a training program similar to the small group training used in this study supplements the OJT by providing training and evaluation in intra- and interpersonal helping skills requisite to effective RA functioning. A format such as the HRD training system developed by Egan (1975b) might be utilized in the group experience. Selection and training are thus incorporated in a single process based upon the defined RA program objectives.

176a

REFERENCES

Berenson, B. G., Carkhuff, R. R., and Myrus, P. "The Interpersonal Functioning and Training of College Students."
J. of Counseling Psychology, 1966, 13, 441-446.

Bozarth, J., Rubin, S., Mitchell, K., and Pelosi, J. "Verbal
Protocol Patterns of College Dormitory Counselors."
Counselor Ed. and Supervision, 1970, 10, 23-29.

Carkhuff, R. R. Helping and Human Relations: A Primer for
Lay and Professional Helpers. Vol. 1. New York: Holt,
Rinehart, and Winston, 1969.

Carkhuff, R. R. "The Development of Systematic Human Resource
Development Models." The Counseling Psychologist, 1972,
3 (3), 4-11.

Dameron, J. D. (Editor) Preparation of Guidance Associates
and Professional Counselors Within the Framework of a
Competency-based Program. Washington, D. C.: American
Personnel and Guidance Association, 1973, ACES monograph.

Dameron, J. D. and Wolf, J. C. "Report of the Two-Year Resident
Assistant Research Program." Unpublished research report,
North Texas State University, 1976.

Duncan, J. P. "A Rating Scale for Student Evaluation of Residence
Hall Counselors." Personnel and Guidance J., 1967, 45,
452-454.

Egan, G. "The Skilled Helper: A Model for Systematic Helping
and Interpersonal Relating. Monterey, California: Brooks/
Cole, 1975. (a)

Egan, G. Exercises in Helping Skills: A Training Manual to
Accompany the Skilled Helper. Monterey, California: Brooks/
Cole, 1975. (b)

Gonyea, G. C. and Warman, R. E. "Differential Perceptions of the
Student Dormitory Counselor's Role." Personnel and Guidance J.,
1962, 41, 350-355.

Hoffman, A. M. and Warner, R. W. "Paraprofessional Effectiveness."
Personnel and Guidance J., 1976, 54, 494-497.

176b

Mitchell, K. M. "Selection of Dormitory Counselors: What Works and What Doesn't." Research and Training Center Division Grant (RT-13). Social and Rehabilitation Service, Department of Health, Education, and Welfare, Washington, D. C., 1970.

Mitchell, K. M., Rubin, S. E., Bozarth, J. D., and Wyrick, T. J. "Effects of Short-Term Training on Residence Hall Assistants." Counselor Ed. and Supervision, 1971, 10, 310-318.

Murphy, R. O. and Ortenzi, A. "Use of Standardized Measurements in the Selection of Residence Hall Staff." J. of College Student Personnel, 1966, 7, 360-363.

Newton, F. B. "The Effect of Systematic Communication Skills Training on Residence Hall Paraprofessionals." J. of College Student Personnel, 1974, 15, 366-369.

Newton, F. B. and Krauss, H. H. "The Health-Engenderingness of Residence Assistants as Related to Student Achievement and Adjustment." J. of College Student Personnel, 1973, 14, 321-325.

Powell, J. R., Plyler, S. A., Dickson, A., and McClelland, S. D. The Personnel Assistant in College Residence Halls. Boston: Houghton-Mifflin, 1969.

Rubin, S. E. "An Evaluation of the 16 PF as a Selection Device for Undergraduate Residence Hall Assistants." Paper presented at the American Personnel and Guidance Association Convention, New Orleans, 1970. Reprinted in Reconceptualizing the Work of the Dormitory Counselor, unpublished collection of papers, University of Arkansas, Fayetteville.

Schroeder, K., Hill, C. E., Gormaly, J., and Anthony, W. A. "Systematic Human Relations Training for Resident Assistants." J. of College Student Personnel, 1973, 14, 313-314.

Shelton, J. L. and Corazzini, J. G. "The Referral Process in the Community College: Some Guidelines for Residence Hall Para-professionals." J. Of NAWDAC, 1976, 39, 102-106.

Van Pelt, N. "A Study of the Edwards Personal Preference Schedule As Related to Residence Hall Counseling Success." Student Housing Research, ACUHO Research and Information Committee, December, 1968.

176c

Wotruba, R. T. "Can Residence Hall Staff Be Selected
Scientifically?" J. of NASPA, 1969, 7, 107-111.

Wyrick, T. J. and Mitchell, K. M. "Relationship Between
Resident Assistants' Empathy and Warmth and Their
Effectiveness." J. of College Student Personnel, 1971,
12, 36-40.

Zirkle, K. E. and Hudson, C. "The Effects of Residence Hall
Staff Members on Maturity Development for Male Students."
J. of College Student Personnel, 1975, 15, 30-33.

CHAPTER 20

COUNSELING CENTER FUNCTION
IN TWO-YEAR AND FOUR-YEAR COLLEGES

John C. Wolf and Joseph D. Dameron

Introduction

The function of college counseling centers and their
relationship to the overall student services program have
been previously investigated, but with the exception of a
survey by Hinko (1971), studies have centered on four-year
colleges and universities. In an early study, Embree (1950)
found that workers in the student personnel field were concerned not only with vocational guidance but also with the
personal problems of students. Clark (1966) noted in a
study of 35 four-year universities that while the most frequently listed principal service offered by counseling centers
was vocational counseling, personal-adjustment counseling
was the next most frequently listed. Other more recent surveys,
such as those of Albert (1968) and Nugent and Pareis (1968),
indicate a trend in four-year colleges toward the provision
of counseling services, including personal-adjustment, and
a general concern for the holistic view of the student.

In view of the emergence of the community college as a
major force in higher education, and considering the nature
of the multifaceted curricula of the two-year college, the
role of counseling services on the two-year campus seems
particularly relevant for current consideration. However,
information regarding counseling services at the two-year
college level is not readily available. Hinko pointed to the
lack of research describing these services, and in his survey
of 111 large community colleges with enrollments over 5,000
(which produced responses from 67), he has provided the first
in-depth investigation of two-year college counseling services.
In his study, focused mainly on adminstrative and logistical

177

concerns rather than services provided, Hinko found that
educational counseling, academic advising, and personal-
social counseling services were rather equally distributed.
This study did not include any four-year college data, nor
was there a crosssectional sampling of two-year colleges
with respect to enrollment size.

The role of institution-defined goals and purposes in
the provision of college counseling center services has been
explored by Warnath (1972). He concluded that the forces of
the academic institution and administration rather than student
needs have played an important role in the determination of
counseling services offered in a given institution. Liberal-
arts colleges and innovative junior and community colleges
tend to support his findings in that they recognize and emphasize student freedom and responsibility supported by personal-
adjustment counseling and self-exploration. Conversely, institutions stressing occupational and technical preparation as a
primary goal generally stress short-term academic advisement
and vocational counseling. Since many junior and community
colleges have technical-occupational programs as a focal point
within their curricula, emphasis on short-term vocational
counseling might therefore be expected in such settings.

Faculty expectations of counselor role have been explored
by Mozee (1972) in a study demonstrating that institutional
settings and student development functions are not the only
factors that play a role in the provision of counseling services.
Mozee found that emphasis on academic advisement and educational
concerns was a major role stressed by faculty when referring to
counselors. He also found a wide variance between faculty role
expectations and counselor expectations. The role of human
development facilitator was not seen as a counseling role by
faculty, although vocational, academic, and guidance-oriented
functions were seen as such.

What was lacking, therefore, was a study that compared
the actual role and function of counseling services at both
two-year and four-year institutions. Since conflicting views
existed regarding the priorities ascribed to and the prevalence
of services in the areas of educational, academic, vocational,

178

and personal-adjustment counseling on both levels, such a study seemed both relevant and necessary. The purpose of the present investigation was to study the nature of counseling services at both two-year and four-year institutions.

Conducting the Study

The instrument utilized in gathering the data was a questionnaire based on two surveys conducted by Oetting, Ivey, and Wiegel (1970) and revised for use in this study. In one survey, institutions were asked whether they provided counseling facilities; in the second, the counseling director was asked to report on staffing patterns, administrative issues, and functions served by the center.

Fifty two-year and four-year colleges and universities were included in the sample, with an equal number of two-year and four-year schools represented. Both types of institutions in the sample were matched as closely as possible for enrollment size, urbanization of location, and public-private affiliation in accordance with the national percentage of higher-education facilities on this variable dimension.

The questionnaire was sent to the person considered most responsible for counseling services on each campus. From the 50 schools to which the questionnaire was sent, 36 replies were received, for a 72 percent return. In the two-year sample the return was 80 percent; for senior colleges it was 62 percent. Of the two-year college respondents, 70 percent reported that the counseling center was separate from other student services agencies; 81 percent of the senior-college respondents reported this to be the case.

Analyzing the Results

Items relating to the amount of counselor time spent in various counseling functions were included in the questionnaire. From inspection of Table 1, it may be seen that two-year college counselors spend more time in academic advisement than in personal-social-emotional counseling, whereas the opposite is true of the four-year college counselor. The emphasis on personal-

179

social adjustment counseling in the four-year school is more pronounced than the emphasis on academic advisement in the two-year school, however. Statistical confirmation for the hypothesis of differing emphases upon counseling services in the two types of college settings was provided through results of t-tests for unequal N that compared differences in mean percentage of counselor time expended between junior-college and senior-college settings for both academic advisement and personal-social-emotional counseling services. The resultant t values of 4.90 and 3.89 respectively were both significant beyond the .01 level, indicating that the two-year college counselor spends a significantly greater percentage of time in academic advisement than the four-year college counselor and that the four-year college counselor spends a significantly greater percentage of time in counseling for personal problems than does the two-year college counselor. It was noted in reviewing the questionnaire results that the percentage of counselors' time spent in these activities correlated well with ratings by respondents of the importance of counseling services rendered.

The prevalence of counseling services offered by counseling centers in the sample institutions was also investigated. Table 2 illustrates these results. It may be seen that there are consistencies as well as inconsistencies in the counseling services offered in two-year and four-year schools. In junior-, community-, and senior-college counseling centers, the most prevalent services were counseling for personal problems and academic-related counseling. However, it can also be seen that counseling for course choice and load was considerably more prevalent at the two-year level, whereas both short- and long-term counseling for emotional disorders was more prevalent in four-year counseling centers. This finding was consistent with other questionnaire information that suggests an increasing concern with student problems in other than academic areas. The finding was especially notable in four-year counseling centers. The theoretical postulation of Warnath seems to gain support, and the findings of Mozee appear cogent as well.

In considering the results of this study, several factors in addition to those already discussed by Warnath and Mozee

TABLE 1

Mean Percentage of Counselor Time
Spent in Direct Services

	Type of College	
	Junior and	Senior and
	Community	Universities
Type of Service	(N=20)	(N=16)
Academic advisement	38.9	11.5
Personal-social-emotional counseling	26.3	54.0
Other services	34.8	34.5

TABLE 2

Services Offered by Counseling Centers in Sample

	Junior College	Senior College
Service	N=20	N=16
Counseling for study problems	100%	94%
Counseling for choice of major	95	94
Counseling for personal problems	100	100
Counseling for academic course choice and load	85	50
Short-term counseling: severe emotional disorders (1-4 sessions)	65	100
Long-term counseling: severe emotional disorders (5 or more sessions)	25	62
Group counseling	70	62
Disciplinary counseling	10	25
Pre-college counseling	85	38
Summer orientation	40	56
Diagnosis for other schools	35	19
Supervision of residence hall counselors	10	31
Tutoring in academic areas	40	6
Freshman testing	95	75
Advising campus student organizations	30	19
Supervision of practicum students	50	56
Research	45	62
Student loans and scholarships	35	0
Counseling with faculty	100	81
Counseling all students on academic probation	55	25

appear relevant. First, the type of student clientele served
must be considered, as well as the general physical environment of the campus. A review of recent journal issues relating
to two-year colleges illustrates quite dramatically the growth
of this type of institution. The review also indicates that
personal and emotional problems of students may be provided
for in the milieu in which the students live, since community
colleges often have small or nonexistent dormitory populations.

The needs of dormitory residents may differ from the needs
of nondormitory students, and the counseling services may to
some degree also reflect this difference. Two-year college
students, whether living in a dormitory or not, may have defined
through their election of the two-year setting some inherent
differences in background and interests, which would also be
reflected in the counseling services offered to them. The relative accessability of two-year colleges to qualified educationally
disadvantaged students could interact with other less well-
defined and as yet unspecified socioeconomic and demographic
characteristics to help determine the differences noted between
the counseling services offered at the responding two-year and
four-year institutions in this study. To mention another potential
factor, Harris (1973) has pointed out that over two-thirds of
the students at one urban community college were less than
full-time students and held regular jobs. Community-college
students also tend to be older than the usual four-year college
student.

Second, the purpose of the institution itself must be
explored. The two-year college has a dual role as both an
academic institution preparing students for transfer to a four-
year college and an institution preparing students to enter
directly into the labor market upon completion of a technical-
occupational program. It emphasizes open admission, resulting
in a higher percentage of educationally disadvantaged students.
Therefore it appears to possess a greater need for counseling
oriented toward the advisement process. The student population
and responses in the study of Harris seem to provide confirmation
for this statement.

An additional factor deserves mention. The staff expectancies and qualifications in the two types of institutional settings probably differ. Whereas the four-year college may have a staff with several doctoral-level counselors, the two-year college is usually staffed with counselors trained on the master's degree level (Hinko 1971). The nature and depth of staff training might well interact with other factors already mentioned to affect the direction of counseling programs at the two-year and four-year institutions. The point is that the type of student and the nature of the curricula may be important variables in determining the type of counselor qualifications emphasized and the duties to which the counselor is assigned. Jones (1970) has suggested that perhaps the personal-adjustment counseling process at the two-year college might be facilitated by the addition of one or more doctoral-level counselors or a counseling psychologist.

In summary, the present study serves as a documentation of Warnath's hypothesis as well as a confirmation of Mozee's earlier findings. However, factors such as those cited above may also serve, at least partially, to explain how counseling-service priorities are determined at the two-year as well as the four-year college. Perhaps one approach to the resolution of the issue of priority assignment is already being initiated: the merger of academic-advisement and personal-adjustment counseling through the growing movement toward human-development and human-resource programs in two-year colleges, as O'Banion, Thurston, and Gulden (1970) have described. The "applied behavioral scientist" of which Berdie (1972) speaks could be the interdisciplinary person who will implement future counseling functions in both two-year and four-year college settings.

References

Albert, G. "A Survey of College Counseling Facilities". Personnel and Guidance Journal, 1968, 46 (6), 540-543.

Berdie, R. F. "The 1980 Counselor: Applied Behavioral Scientist". Personnel and Guidance Journal, 1972, 50 (6), 451-456.

References

Clark, D. D. "Characteristics of Counseling Centers in Large Universities". Personnel and Guidance Journal, 1966, 44 (8), 817-823.

Embree, R. B. "Developments in Counseling Bureaus and Clinics". Educational and Psychological Measurement, 1950, 10 (3), 465-475.

Harris, M. L. "Urban Influence on Student Personnel Services". Community and Junior College Journal, 1973, 43 (5), 42-44.

Hinko, P. M. "A National Survey of Counseling Services". Junior College Journal, 1971, 42 (3), 20-24.

Jones, T. "The Counselor and His Role". Junior College Journal, 1970, 40 (7), 10-14.

Mozee, E. "Faculty Expectations for Counselors". Community and Junior College Journal, 1972, 43 (1), 24-25.

Nugent, F. A. & Pareis, E. N. "Survey of Present Policies and Practices in College Counseling Centers in the U.S.". Journal of Counseling Psychology, 1968, 15 (1), 94-97.

O'Banion, T.; Thurston, A.; & Gulden, J. "Student Personnel Work: An Emerging Model". Junior College Journal, 1970, 41 (3), 6-14.

Oetting, E. R.; Ivey, A. E.; & Wiegel, R. C. "The College and University Counseling Center". Washington, D. C.: American Personnel and Guidance Association, 1970, ACPA Monograph, No. 11, 53-56.

Warnath, C. "College Counseling: Between the Rock and the Hard Place". Personnel and Guidance Journal, 1972, 51 (4), 229-235.

CHAPTER 21

THE AMERICAN COLLEGE AND SOME LEGAL ASPECTS
OF IN LOCO PARENTIS: HISTORICAL BACKGROUND 1636-1968

John Eddy

In Loco Parentis is a Latin phrase that Black's Law
Dictionary defines as "in place of a parent; instead of a parent;
charged, factitiously with a parent's rights, duties, and responsibilities."[1] Gruny has described the legal meaning of the
term as follows:

> In loco parentis is an ancient legal doctrine,
> almost as old as the concept of the family. In almost
> every civilization the lowest level of authority en-
> forceable by law is that of the head of the family.
> In loco parentis simply means in the place of the parent,
> and is a term used to describe a person or institution
> given familial authority over a person temporarily or
> permanently without a natural parent. A legal guardian,
> for instance, may be so described quite accurately.
> The necessity for an extension of parental authority to
> the schoolroom was obvious from the beginning for formal
> education. As with almost all common law doctrines, in
> loco parentis consists of certain rights and privileges
> coupled with their commitant duties and responsibilities
> ... A teacher's right to inflict punishment is coupled
> with a duty to do so only for a proper purpose and not
> in an excessive degree. A student's right to instruc-
> tion is coupled with a duty to give his best efforts
> toward absorption of the teachings. A student's right
> to be protected by the school from other students or
> third parties is coupled with a duty to conform to
> regulations for his own restraint and protection. Con-
> versely, a school's right to regulate student conduct
> carries with it a duty to in fact enforce regulations
> where it knows or should know they are required for the
> protection of students. No more than a court will tell
> a father exactly how to run his family, will a court
> tell a person in loco parentis how to regulate its
> charges. In both cases the courts only interfere when
> parental conduct either threatens public safety or
> amounts to a clear abuse of discretion which bodes harm
> to the child.[2]

Historical Background

The concept that a teacher or administrator of a college stands in loco parentis to his students developed in English common law. Under the paternalistic regime enforced by college authorities in the 17th century, students at Oxford and Cambridge universities in England were expected to follow many restrictions.[3] Early American colleges, beginning with Harvard in 1636, accepted this same traditional responsibility for the student's total life. Leonard has said, "It was the acceptance of the responsibility for the whole life of the students--housing, boarding, recreation, general welfare, manners, morals, and religious observances, as well as intellectual development--that set the pattern for our present-day programs of personnel services."[4] Robinson confirms this by saying, "It was because of these elements (student growth from the land-grant college movement, secularization of higher education, reaction against imported German impersonalism and intellectualism, the elective system, and personnel research) and the belief that officials of the college should act in loco parentis that the functions that were to evolve into formal programs of student personnel services were originated."[5] Williamson and Cowan have commented on the power of a legally constituted college and the historical development of in loco parentis as follows:

> Members of the academic community sometimes forget the fact that a college or university is not a democracy. Legally, a university is a corporation, with authority and responsibility for administration invested in the board of trustees by state constitution or charter. The board is granted much, but not absolute, freedom to govern the institution in the ways it judges to be consistent with its educational mission. Academic freedom, then, is not an inalienable right of students, rather it is a privilege granted or withheld by the institution... In colonial and post-revolutionary America, colleges exercised authority over every aspect of student behavior in a rigid and regimented fashion. The courts sanctioned this tradition of university-student relationship by stating that the college acted in loco parentis. But, as the father's exercise of control over his children has generally become less authoritarian, so, too, has the university's control of students.[6]

Legal Implications of In Loco Parentis

While the doctrines of in loco parentis rest upon the rights, duties and responsibilities of parents, the application of this doctrine will vary according to state laws and interpretation of courts on these laws. In the majority of states the parents have jurisdiction over their children until their twenty-first birthday (the so-called age of maturity). However, in some states the parents' responsibility ends at eighteen or when their children marry.

While some would limit the application of in loco parentis to include only those students under twenty-one years of age, this is not possible "because the rules under which the colleges regulate and control their students have developed over the years until they have been accepted by the courts as a correct and proper way to operate."[8] Some of the reasons given by the courts, in their decisions, for upholding the right of the college to practice control are based upon the following: First, that the college stands in loco parentis to the student while he is attending it;[9,10,11] second, that the governing board has the right to make all rules and regulations necessary for the governance of the college;[12] third, that there is a contractual relationship between the college and the student--used especially in dismissal cases.[13]

While the legal principle of in loco parentis applies to nearly every part of the life of the college student, there are three basic areas where its application is most often applied. These three areas are housing, activities, and discipline.[14]

Student Housing

The application of in loco parentis, as used in housing, requires unmarried minors to live in college-approved housing under rules and regulations that are set up for the student's physical, moral, and mental protection.[15,16] While this is on a legal basis with minors, a question may be raised by a student over twenty-one. The college has power to place such restrictions upon all students--regardless of their age--on the legal basis that its governing board may establish rules for its governance. However, a rule based upon this principle of law which was originally intended to protect underaged youth but now is extended to control adults over twenty-one has some questionable ramifications.[17] A court case which justifies the college's rights over students is cited as follows: In Gott vs. Berea College, the court stated that "college authorities stand in loco parentis concerning the physical and moral welfare and mental training of pupils. For the purpose of this case, the school, its officers, and students are legal entity, as much so as any family, and, as a father may direct his children, those in charge of boarding schools are well within their rights and powers when they direct students what to eat, where they may get it, where they may go, and what forms of amusements are forbidden."[18]

The college also has rights to control student off-campus housing. Specifically, "A private school may suspend a student until she moves out of a rooming house which lost school approv-

al[19],[20] and a public school may require all undergraduates,
married or single, to reside in university-owned housing or religious or fraternity dormitories to the exclusion of private
rooming houses previously approved for students."[21]

Student Activities In Loco Parentis

The area of student activities covers a wide gamut of events
engaged in by students. Extra-curricular activities, for instance,
include student organizations, social affairs, standards of conduct and conformity to the rules and regulations that cover student activities. The latter are established by the college to
help protect the student's well-being, morals, and safety. This
concern is founded upon the legal principle of in loco parentis.
Examples of this concern are hours for women students, restrictions
on the use of drugs and alcohol, appropriate dress, and chaperoning
of college-sponsored events.[22] The fact that colleges have legal
authority to regulate or forbid participation in student activities
is strongly established in the courts. Illustrations of this
regulatory power are the numerous cases where fraternities or
other secret societies are forbidden to students. "In probably
the leading case, where mere membership was forbidden even though
it was not an organization of students and bore no direct relationship to the school, the Illinois Supreme Court upheld a Wheaton
College regulation"[23] in the following statement:

> But, whether the rule be judicious or not, it violated
> neither good morals nor the laws of the land and is there-
> fore clearly within the power of the college authorities
> to make and enforce. A discretionary power has been given
> them to regulate the discipline of their college in such
> manner as they deem proper; and, so long as their rules
> violate neither divine nor human law, we have no more
> authority to interfere than we have to control the domes-
> tic discipline of a father in his family. (...the right
> to join the society) is not of so high and solemn a
> character that it cannot be surrendered, and the son of
> the related did voluntarily surrender it when he became
> a student at Wheaton College... When it is said that a
> person has a legal right to do certain things, all that
> phrase means is that the law does not forbid these things
> being done. It does not mean that the law guarantees
> the right to do them at all possible times and under all
> possible circumstances. A person in his capacity as a
> citizen may have the right to do many things which a
> student at Wheaton College cannot do without incurring the
> penalty of college laws.[24]

Student Discipline

It is in the area of student discipline that in loco parentis is most often applied as a legal doctrine. Bakken says, "all the rules and regulations established for the protection of our students are tested, not in the students' conformity to them but in the students' violation of them. This violation may be in the form of individual transgressions or individual and group rebellion against them."[25]

A recent court ruling in Boulder County (Colorado) District Court had a student charging that a disciplinary factor was involved in her flunking her English course. The student sought to have a grade changed from "F" to "B" on the ground that a failing grade was given for disciplinary rather than academic reasons with the instructor claiming the student cheated on a final examination. (This charge was not sustained.) Judge William E. Buch cited several cases (including Thomas Connelly, Jr., vs. University of Vermont) in which the general rule was given that courts will not interfere in matters of scholarship requiring judgement of any kind. Judge Buch said, "This court is of the opinion that the plaintiff has not stated a claim for relief and that the court is without jurisdiction in the matter."[25]

The concept of in loco parentis as applied to disciplinary cases is described by Bakken. He says the following:

A parent, in disciplining his child, talks to the child about his deviant behavior, reasons with him and gives him guidance.... The colleges acting in place of parents have taken this same general attitude in the past.... The community in general recognizes the status of the college as a parental figure because law enforcement officials very often turn the college student over to the college to counsel, guide, or discipline when they are accused of minor violations of community laws and regulations. This is done in the same fashion as a minor may be turned over to the custody of parents for discipline at a younger age.[27]

Students are as much subject to discipline after reaching legal age or marriage. "Again, university regulations are to protect the scholarly community and not primarily to punish offenders, although correction of offenders may have a salutary side effect. Thus, even strangers to the campus community may be regulated for the good of that community."[28,29]

Powers of Public vs. Private Institutions

Penny points out that "judicial rulings of record apply very largely to state institutions, and only a few decisions offer direction, limitation, or regulation applicable to so-called private institutions of higher education. Historically, courts have seen a considerable distinction between private and publicly supported colleges; the latter have been viewed as extensions of the general state governments and hence subject to the same mandates in dealing with the citizenry: to observe canons of due process, to refrain from unwarranted searched and seizures, to refrain from undue restriction on freedom of expression, etc."[30] Moreover, Gruny states, "Regulatory powers of private schools stem from their contract of enrollment; those of public schools from the legislature. By the time courts add implied and inherent powers in both cases, charter powers of private corporations, and contract powers of public corporations, this becomes largely a distinction without a difference."[31] Some examples of the lack of any distinction between private and public institutions of higher education with regard to decisions are the following concerning unspecified misconduct detracting from scholarly atmosphere.

Stetson University suspended a girl for "offensive habits that interfere with the comforts of others" as evidenced by her disorderly conduct in a residence hall. Against the argument that she had not broken any specific regulation or violated any direct order, the court stood behind the "common law of the college," and quoted a Nebraska law holding that a teacher "stands for the time being in loco parentis to his pupils, and because of that relation he must necessarily exercise authority over them in many things concerning which the board may have remained silent."[32]

In the same kind of court ruling based on the concept of in loco parentis, the University of Maryland denied readmission to a girl who refused to answer questions about certain rumors she forwarded to the press about the university,[33] and at Brooklyn College a student was suspended for constant criticism of the college administration.[34] As Gruny points out, the superficiality of any distinction between public and private cases is seen in these similar cases based on the in loco parentis doctrine involving both types of institutions.[35]

Answering the Charge of Double Jeopardy

One of the frequent charges of students is that a violation of a law may make them liable to both college and civil punishment. However, if they steal a college car when they are working for the college, they may be fired from their job and suspended from college for the same offense. Is this not double jeopardy on the part of the college? Is this not justified by any employer? Some ask why the college should be an exception. Of course, the college is often an exception, for the philosophy of many colleges is that disciplinary action should be an educational experience and not merely a punitive action. However, car stealing is serious and not a prank to be excused. Bakken states, "...any departure from the legal principle of in loco parentis will work a hardship upon a vast number of students who may transgress but not rebel as it will take away a protection which is now built into the system."[36]

Again, Gruny reminds us of the fundamental objective in dealing with students at college. He answers those who cry double jeopardy:

The double jeopardy contention overlooks the basic principle of university disciplinary proceedings. University regulations are for the purpose of protecting the scholarly community from disruption of its proper functioning, and not primarily for punishment of transgressors for their own correction. If the act which causes a university to limit, suspend, or remove a student for this purpose happens also to be a violation of the criminal law, this is a mere coincidence and not material to any university action. The action would have been, and often is, taken in the absence of any criminal act. Whether the act beyond a reasonable doubt deserves criminal punishment does not necessarily bear on whether it is in the interests of the community of scholars to excise an apparently disturbing influence from that body. A person has a right to liberty until he is proven to have forfeited that right; a student is accorded membership in a scholarly community only so long as he maintains himself worthy of the privilege.[37]

Students at public institutions also have a constitutional right to due process of law in university disciplinary proceedings. In Illinois, to cite but one example, a student is given "an opportunity to prove his worthiness to continue as a student in preference to the next candidate for his situation; it is not incumbent on the university to prove that, beyond a reasonable doubt, all civil rights are forfeited. There are strong legal trends toward extension of the first and fourteenth amendments into wholly new areas, but while there may well arise further restrictions on procedure in administering disciplinary sanctions, it seems unlikely that such trends will very soon affect the subject matter of regulations."[38]

Possible Solutions to Conflicts Over In Loco Parentis

It may be facetious and naive to suggest it, but a possible way to eliminate most of the need for the colleges' practice of the concept of in loco parentis with their students might be to do the following: (1) Have no university-owned housing or university-approved housing policies; (2) have no student activities officially operated or related to the university; and (3) have all law infractions by students referred directly to civil authorities. However, there is no available empirical data from any American campus that supports the thesis that the majority of parents desire that the college officials should abdicate their legal authority with regard to enforcing in loco parentis when it comes to protecting students or giving the students privileges not offered by non-college situations. Rather, all the present studies are still giving contrary evidence. Until the time comes when the majority of parents will be against in loco parentis for their youth under twenty-one years, the concept of in loco parentis will probably be with us.

Nevertheless, the application of the concept of in loco parentis to college students, who have reached the legal age of their particular state, needs to be seriously considered and revised. While the college may have the legal right and legal power to control students over twenty-one, the college should not treat students who have met the legal age with the same type of regulatory practices.

Williamson and Cowan have summarized a number of cogent arguments for a different approach to college students. They state these as follows:

> Many educators argue that the parent-child analogy is inappropriate when applied to higher educational institutions, in view of increasing numbers of students and the complexity of modern university organization. Some persons would substitute the idea that a student is a consumer who buys a product from the college or contracts for a service to be rendered by the university. A few suggest that a university is like an industry whose "products" are educated students. Others propose that students and faculty ought to be viewed as partners engaged jointly in the business of learning and advancing knowledge[39]... The fact is clear that much remains to be done before many colleges provide an atmosphere in which desirable "higher learning" can occur. Each student can contribute to desirable change in his college by studying the issues in depth and by discussing these with his professors and college administrators. Thus academic freedom will become established as relevant to the college's educational mission by the exercise of "thoughtfulness" as the academic style of living.[40]

Nevertheless, even the "AAUP Statement on Academic Freedom of Students" recognizes the parental role of the institution toward students. The paternalistic idea of protection for students concerns the college's role in acting like a parent and protecting the student against the community. The AAUP statement also reads: "If students violate laws, institutional officials should apprise them of their legal rights and offer their assistance. The institution should assert its own authority only when its interests differ from those of the general community."[41]

Throughout American history, "the courts have upheld the paternalistic concept of discipline and have allowed the colleges to enforce their rules and regulations with little or no requirement for due process, for it was recognized that disciplinary action was educational in nature. However, two recent court cases have emphasized that a student cannot be dismissed from a college unless he has had a fair hearing that is equal in fairness to those of a court of law."[42,43,44] Furthermore, the recent United States Supreme Court's 8 to 1 vote on the case of the Arizona juvenile may be a determinative force on future court cases of college students. The ruling of the Supreme Court said, on May 15, 1967, that the Constitution of the United States of American is not for adults of legal age only. American Civil Liberties Union officials commented that this may be one of the most important rulings in American history--this remains to be seen in specific college cases involving under-age students.[45]

Williamson suggests ways students might become more intelligent and conversant about their rights and responsibilities at college. This approach may be summarized as modes to channel constructively the fires of youth skepticism toward all authority and work through the reform of all society including the university's concept of in loco parentis. His recommendations are: (1) Have students continuously review their rights and responsibilities so to learn that they also have an opportunity to exercise the authority of the charter of the college. (2) Have the president and dean of students work steadily behind the scenes to communicate with both students and faculty alike on various problems. (3) Have informal and regular seminars about the problems and philosophies of higher education involving students and administrators to look at all available data while remaining open to new knowledge as it appears. (4) Have coffee and conversations with troublemakers between riots. (5) Have two alternative plans ready, if all else fails, such as (a) leave the campus to give a prearranged talk on students' freedom on another campus and (b) move up graduation exercises to allow the students a chance to meet earlier the real world outside.[46]

In Loco Parentis vs. Due Process

Some colleges and universities are moving to remove the practice of in loco parentis on their campuses. At Michigan State University an article appeared in the Michigan State News

191

in early 1966 as follows:

"Farewell, In Loco Parentis, Hello Due Process."
Both sets of guidelines issued by the Faculty Committee
on Student Affairs in the last month indicate that the
death knell of In Loco Parentis will soon be sounded at
Michigan State.[47] ... Under the proposed guidelines, a
student could claim that a particular rule either con-
tradicted one of the guidelines or failed to serve the
purposes of the university. The burden of proof is
placed on the rulemaker, not on the student.[48] ...
Biggest criticism of the committee so far is that it
has offered no panacea. It is not codifying existing
rules, or setting up a system of "price list justice"
with exact, printed penalties.[49] ... It may take a
while to implement such a revolutionary concept, committee members admit.[50] ...

Clark Kerr in a June 8, 1967, hour-long television interview,
some six months after being fired as President of the University
of California, said that the right of the university involves at
least two areas: (1) An obligation to parents to offer a suitable
college education to their youth and (2) an obligation to other
students to provide an adequate study environment. Kerr supported
an enlightened in loco parentis position throughout his interview
which concerned contemporary American university affairs.

Arthur Dibden, in a class in the Philosophy of Higher Education at Southern Illinois University on May 27, 1967, stated
that faculty and administrators, as well as students, confuse
their expectations of what can be practically accomplished by
persons (students) and institutions (colleges). For instance,
Dibden stated that the doctrine of in loco parentis causes a
moral problem in that adults ask things of young adults that they
don't ask of themselves. Parents, faculty, and administrators
ask students to be pure in areas that they aren't themselves.
However, students also demand impossible rights when they ask for
citizenship in a college when the faculty and administrators
themselves aren't citizens in the college--in a political sense
of a legally constituted unit such as the city or state. By anal-
ogy, neither are management or labor citizens of General Motors,
concluded Dibden.

On the other hand, there are those who would revise the
obsolete, oldline approach of in loco parentis. Penny says
that an alternative model utilizing the concept of in loco parentis should be tried. He says:

It may be seen as derived from what many would
consider a desirable concept of parent-child relationships, but seems to be quite different from what in loco

192

parentis has been construed to mean legally and historically. The following suggest a general framework for such an alternative.[51]

1. Obligations and expectations are clearly delineated in terms of who is to do what and when, who is empowered to act in what ways, what presumably will happen if obligations are not fulfilled. (Teachers do this sort of thing very effectively in terms of formal academic procedures; as educators, student personnel workers ought to be able to do it too.)

2. Those regulations that exist are conveniently available, concisely stated, openly discussed, and readily interpreted.

3. The rule of parsimony prevails in regard to the quantity of regulation. The interest is in as little restraint or restriction as is reasonably compatible with the maintenance of an operating social order. Additionally, there will be in effect few if any regulations that will not be largely self-enforcing in the hands of men of good will. The natural consequences of failure to comply will be self-evident and thus serve as sufficiently directing in most cases.

4. Relationships are open to what, in the political realm, have been called "unlimited negotiation" but which might better be phrased as continuous dialogue in the areas of institutional and individual objectives, rights, freedom, and responsibilities.

5. Institutional initiative is directed to enhancing active discussion of mutual freedoms and intra-institutional relationships. The administrators and faculty should be alert to possibilities for action rather than pushed to the necessity for reaction. They should be continually seeking for new ways and places to teach, for they are educators whose work includes some custodial functions, rather than custodians whose assignment happens to be an educational institution.[52]

The In Loco Parentis concept would still apply in law and legal decisions for college students below the age of eighteen. The concept still is affecting higher education in some attitudes and actions of staff and students.

193

References

1. Black's Law Dictionary, Fourth Edition, West
   Publishing Company, St. Paul, 1951.

2. Gruny, C.R. In Loco Parentis. Carbondale:
   Unpublished paper, 1966, p. 1.

3. Blackwell, T.E. College and University Administration. New York: Institute for Educational
   Research, 1965, p. 65.

4. Leonard, E.A. Origins of Personnel Services.
   Minneapolis: University of Minnesota Press,
   1956, p. 21.

5. Robinson, D.W. "The Student Personnel Function
   in American Highe Education," American Journal
   of Pharmaceutical Education. Vol. 27, No. 1,
   Winter, 1963, p. 19.

6. Williamson, E.G. and Cowan, J.L. "Students and
   Academic Freedom," The Intercollegian Orientation,
   1966, p. 15.

8. Bakken, C.J. "The Legal Aspects of In Loco
   Parentis in American Colleges and Universities,"
   Washington, D.C.: Paper read at American Personnel
   and Guidance Association National Convention,
   April 4, 1966, p. 1.

9. John B. Stetson University vs. Hunt, 88 Florida
   570 (1925).

10. Gott vs. Berea College, 156 Kentucky 376 (1913).

11. Bakken, C.J. "Legal Basis for College Student Work,"
    Washington, D.C.: American College Personnel Assoc.
    Student Personnel Series, #2. American Personnel
    and Guidance Association, 1961.

12. Bveatte vs. Board of Regents of the University of
    Oklahoma, 102 F. Suppl. 407; 72 S CT 567; 342 US
    936 (1941).

13. Carr et al vs. St. John's University, 12 NY 2nd
    802-235 NYS 2nd 834, 187 N E 2nd 18 (1962) --
    17 app Div. 2nd 632, 231 NYS 2nd 410 (1962) 34
    Mis 2d 319, 231 NYS 2d 403 (1962).

References

14. Bakken, C.J. "The Legal Aspects of In Loco Parentis in American Colleges and Universities," op. cit., p. 2.

15. "Higher Education," Christian Faith and Higher Education Institute (1965).

16. Strickland, D. "In Loco Parentis--Legal Mots and Students Morals." Journal of College Student Personnel, November, 1965. 17 app Div 2nd 632, 231 NYS 2nd 410 (1962) Loco Parentis in American Colleges and Universities," op. cit., p. 2.

18. Gott vs. Berea College, 156 Kentucky 376 (1913).

19. Gruny, C.R. op. cit., p. 7-8.

20. Pyeatte vs. Board of Regents of the University of Oklahoma, 102 F Supp. 407 (1952) aff'd 342 U.S. 936, 72 S. Ct. 567, 96 E. Ed. 696 (1952).

22. Bakken, C.J. "The Legal Aspects of In Loco Parentis in American Colleges and Universities," op. cit., p. 3.

23. Gruny, C.R. op. cit., p. 3.

24. People ex rel. Pratt vs. Wheaton College, 40 Illinois, 186, (1866).

25. Bakken, C.J. op. cit., p. 3.

26. Fitzgerald, L.E. "Association News: Court Rules on Grade Controversy." Journal of College Student Personnel, Vol. 8, No. 3, May, 1967, p. 209.

27. Bakken, C.J. op. cit., p. 3.

28. Gruny, C.R. op. cit., p. 7.

29. Morris vs. Nowotny, supra note 6.

30. Penny, J.F. "Variations on a Theme: In Loco Parentis," The Journal of College Student Personnel, Vol. 8, No. 1, January 1967, p. 22.

31. Gruny, C.R. op. cit., p. 4.

References

32. John B. Stetson University vs. Hunt, 88 Florida 570 (1925).

33. Gruny, C.R. op. cit., p. 5.

34. Ibid.

35. Ibid.

36. Bakken, C.J. op. cit., p. 4.

37. Gruny, C.R. op. cit., p. 6.

38. Ibid, p. 7.

39. Williamson, E.G. and Cowan, J.L. op. cit., p. 15.

40. Ibid, p. 16.

41. Statement on Academic Freedom of Students, AAUP Bulletin, p. 447.

42. Bakken, C.J., "Student Rights as Seen by a Lawyer and Educator," Journal of College Student Personnel, March 1965.

43. Knight vs. State Board of Education 300 F Suppl. 174, (1961).

44. Dixon vs. Alabama State Board of Education 294 F 2d 150 1961 -- 186 Supp. 945 -- 1960 368 US 930, 82 S Ct 368, 7 L Ed 2d 193 (161).

45. NBS Television News, May 15, 1967.

46. Williamson, E.G. "Rights and Responsibilities of Students" in Order and Freedom on the Campus edited by Owen A. Knoor and W. John Minter. Boulder: Western Interstate Commission for Higher Education, October, 1965, pp. 35-37.

47. Mollison, A. "In Loco Parentis," Michigan State News, 1966.

48. Ibid.

49. Ibid.

References

50. *Ibid.*

51. Penny, J.F. *op. cit.*, p. 24.

52. *Ibid.*

CHAPTER 22

LEGAL ASPECTS OF COLLEGE STUDENT PERSONNEL WORK

John Eddy

The legal aspects of college student personnel work includes
the staff liability and institutional liability of personnel on
the job (Hammond). Liability is of two general types. First,
is criminal liability and an example of this when a staff person
would take the funds of a college financial aids office with the
intent of retaining it. Second, is civil liability which includes
contract liability, tort liability, fiduciory liability, and
managing liability. Each will be covered and described by way
of an example which defines its essence.

Contract law of civil liability would happen when a staff
member or a college fails to carry out a responsibility guaranteed under an official contract in order to compensate for the
loss which occured.

Tort liability of civil liability occurs when a staff member
would improperly interfer with another person so as to cause an
injury to that person. Interference is both intentional - assault
and battery - or unintentional - negligence such as failure to
officially report a fire in a college building.

Fiduciary liability of civil liability means that the staff
member acts in the best interest of their institutions and not
for themselves if a conflict of interest arises. For example,
a college staff member who has an interest and/or ownership of a
business that sells the college where he is employed goods for
profit without a bid or with special favoritism is committing a
fiduciary liability.

Managing liability is when a staff member is involved with
a matter where the staff member has both a personal interest as
well as an official interest. For example, the staff member may
head a division - as a Dean or Chairperson - and take an opportunity to recommend his or her own salary increase as administrator
over that organizational area. This involves managing liability
where a conflict of interest is apparent.

The problem with all of these liability areas is the few
cases that have been tested in court. However, enough do exist

for these laws to stand to protect staff, students, and other citizens as they involve institutions of higher education.

Student's records are protected by the popularly called Buckley Amendment which is officially known as the Family Educational Rights and Privacy Act of 1974. Personnel need to know its contents to avoid managing liability. The purpose of this Act was so there was public access to all records whose disclosure would not harm specific student interests and this Act extends to all federally-dunded educational institutions both public and private (Kodzielski). Access to personally identifiable educational records is limited to parents of students, under the age of accountability which is 18 years, or the students themselves. Exceptions of record are letters of recommendation for students written before November 30, 1974 and parent's financial statements and recommendations written under a pledge of confidentially (Public Law 93-380, as amended by Senate Joint Resoultion 40, 1974). The continuing trend of increasing legal cases through 1977 involving students suing college personnel (Eddy, 1975) indicates a changing pattern within the past ten years (Eddy, 1968) with regard to students, the law, and higher education. The doctrine of in loco parentis has also been eradicated with the extension of constitutional rights to students at eighteen years of age.

There is a need for college and university personnel to be knowledgeable of the information presented in this article as well as materials mentioned in the bibliography at the end of this article in order to properly fulfill their roles as professionals. Many states still have not enacted, by 1977, legislation to protect the confidentiality of counselors and personnel as well as students in educational institutions (Eddy, 1971 and 1972).

References

Bakken, C.J. The Legal Basis For College Student Personnel Work. Washington, DC: American College Personnel Association a division of American Personnel and Guidance Association, 1968.

Bickel, R.D. "The Role of College or University Legal Counsel," Journal of Law and Education, Vol. 3, No. 1, January, 1974.

Blackwell, T.E. College Law, A Guide For Adminis-trators. Menasha, Wisconsin: George Banta Company, Inc., 1961.

References

Bracewell, W.A. "The Dean, The Constitution, And The Courts," NASPA Journal, 1973, 6, 101-111.

Chambers, M.M. The College and the Courts; The Developing Law of the Student and the College. Danville, Illinois: Interstate Printers and Publishers, Inc., 1974.

Drake, S.C. "An Alternative to Traditional Student Handbooks; Code of Student Legal Rights." NASPA Journal, 1973, 4, 83-92.

Eddy, J. "The American College and Some Legal Aspects of In Loco Parentis." National ACAC Journal, November, 1968.

Eddy, J. "The Law and Community College Counselors." Illinois Guidance and Personnel Association Quarterly, Winter, 1975.

Eddy, J. "Confidentiality and Draft Counseling," Personnel and Guidance Journal, December, 1971.

Eddy, J. "Need For Laws To Protect Counselor and Client," Illinois Guidance and Personnel Association Quarterly, Winter, 1972.

Epstein, N.J. "The Use and Misuse of College and University Counsel," Journal of Higher Education, November, 1974, V., XLV.

Hammond, E.H. "Staff Liability In Student Affairs Administration," National Association of Student Personnel Administrators Journal, Vol. 14, No. 4, Spring, 1977.

Hanson, D.J. The Lowered Age of Majority: Its Impact On Higher Education. Washington, DC: Association of American Colleges, 1975.

Hood, A.B. and Hodges, R.T. "The Effect of a Serious Crime Upon the Attitudes Toward Residence Hall Security," Journal of College Student Personnel, 1974, 15, 352-356.

Jackson, B.L. and Richardson, R.L. "Legal Issues in Higher Education: A Look Toward the Future." Journal of College Student Personnel, November, 1975, 6, 16, 514-519.

References

Ladd, E.T. "Civil Liberties for Students At What Age?" Journal of Law and Education, Vol. 3, No. 2, April, 1974.

Kodzielski, M.A. "Privacy In 1977: The Buckley Amendment In Perspective," National Association of Student Personnel Administrators Journal, Vol. 14, No. 4, Spring, 1977.

Keller, D. and Victor, P.M. "Student Rights and Due Process," Journal of Law and Education, Vol. 3, No. 3, July, 1974.

Laudicina, R. and Tramutola, J.L. A Legal Perspective for Student Personnel Administrators. Springfield, Illinois: Charles C. Thomas, Publisher, 1974.

Leisy, R. "The Supreme Court Decision Regarding Out-of-State Tuition," Journal of College Student Personnel, January, 1974, 1, 15, 3-4.

LeRoy, R.O. "An Interrum Report on the Buckley Amendment," College and University, Fall, 1976, Vol. 52, No. 1.

Leslie, D.W. "Some Implied Restraints On Student Power," National Association of Student Personnel Administrators Journal, October, 1973.

Miller, J. "Collegiate Sports and Other Title IX Controversies," Change, Vol. 6, No. 10, Winter, 1974-75.

O'Hara, W.T. and Hill, J.G. The Student, The College, The Law. New York: Teachers College Press, 1972.

Palley, D.B. "Resolving the Non-Resident Student Problem," Journal of Higher Education, Jan./Feb., 1976. V., XLVII.

Ratiff, R.C. Constitutional Rights of College Students A Study in Case Law. Metuchen, New Jersey: The Scarecrow Press, Inc., 1972.

Reed, O.L. and Irving, J.D. "Constitutional Challenge to Dormitory Residency Requirements: End of the Tunnel." May, 1976, 3, 19.

References

Sandler, B. "Sex Discrimination, Admissions In Higher Education and the Law," College and University, Spring, 1975, Vol.50, No.3.

Sloan, I.J. Youth and the Law Rights, Privileges and Obligations. Dobbs Ferry, New York: Oceana Publications Inc., 1974.

Young, D.P. and Gehring, D.D. The College Student and the Courts. Ashville, North Carolina: College Administration Publications, Inc., 1973.

Block's Law Dictionary: Fourth Edition, St. Paul, Minnesota: West Publishing Company, 1957.

CHAPTER 23

DEVELOPING LEADERSHIP SKILLS
IN STUDENT DEVELOPMENT STAFF

Donald Martin and Barbara Gawinski

Introduction

This chapter deals with the subject "Developing Leadership
Skills in Student Development Staff" and it incorporates a
basic philosophy helpful to becoming an effective leader in
a college environment. The ideas discussed are not new, but
they represent a compilation of personal thought and applicable
theory that are especially useful to college student personnel
staff. Previously several authors (Cohen & March, 1979; Brown,
1964) have discussed leadership in academic institutions. This
chapter is designed to help you examine your role and function
as a student development leader and employer by presenting
methods in which you can increase desired skills and job competence.

The basic principles for this chapter developed from discussions with many college student development staff who felt
they were suddenly placed in employment positions without adequate leadership training. Student development professionals
not only are placed in a leadership position within their
particular division, but also serve as a role model for students.
Student development professionals need to be able to maximize
their potential for change and examine the ways in which they
effect others.

Your Personality and Leadership Style

One of the most important determinants of your leadership
style is your basic personality and the manner in which you
relate to others. (McGregor, 1960) You may find yourself
chosen for a leadership position partly because of your personality. The idea of personality variables affecting leadership
skills has been bantered about for years. Yet, little conclu-
sive evidence has been found which shows any one type of person
is a more successful leader than another. In fact, many types
of individuals are successful in motivating people. Therefore,
the decision at hand is examining yourself and seeing what it
is you do that is effective with other people in meeting desired
goals. This may be a bit more difficult than it appears.

Effective leaders work hard at examining methods of motivating themselves and those they manage. Several of these procedures include:

1. Learn to value and accept yourself as a person. Take time to examine the parts of you that are likeable and those you would like to improve. Listen to others for valuable feedback that can help you be a better leader. If you have trouble accepting yourself, then it is often difficult to find value or worth in other people.

2. Take risks and encourage creativity. Leaders are individuals who are willing to take chances and accept the consequences this involves. Change can be a very difficult and challenging process for any person or organization. It can also be threatening to others. When the late Supreme Court Justice, William Douglas, was asked why people were afraid of him, he stated, "Ideas have been the most dangerous forces in the history of mankind." Supporting ideas from those you manage increases their initiative, self-sufficiency, and creative processes.

3. Closely examine your relationship with staff and peers. Determine what type of rapport you would like to establish and work towards that goal. Be aware of the ways you approach others. For instance, are you supportive, dependable, and generally agreeable? Possibly independent, practical, and decisive? Maybe ambitious, enthusiastic, and orderly? You may exhibit many of these characteristics, depending on the situational context. In whatever you do, maximize your potential and that of others.

Your Values

Another important aspect of your leadership style is your value system. It is taken for granted that everyone possesses prejudice in some manner. However, in a leadership position, prejudices become very visable to employees. They also may be accepted and/or adopted by other personnel. Whenever decisions are made, values are involved. Being aware of your system enables you to examine and justify the consequences of your actions as a leader.

A leader needs to be cognizant of how his/her values affect everyday relationships. For example, what types of behavior

do you like or dislike in others? How do you discuss dis-
agreements in values with staff members?

Another important aspect of this concept is the relationship of your values to institutional values. This area is often
neglected or it can be a difficult problem for student development professionals. In reality, there are no institutional
values, per se. Basically people in leadership positions have
a great deal to do with determining values policy in any college
environment. However, many apparent values are passed on from
successor to successor and become established policy. It is
important for any college student development person to examine
the basic attitudes present in a college before accepting a
position. If a large discrepancy appears, then one must decide
to either attempt changing the present values or looking elsewhere for possible employment. Finding oneself constantly dis-
agreeing with established institutional policy can make daily
job functions a difficult experience.

Power and Authority

A leader with power and authority may assume greater psychological posture with his/her group. Employees may become dependent and seek security from this person or become resistant
and oppose him/her. A most difficult task for any leader is to
balance the ratio between power and authority so that maximum
growth is allowed for both the leader and the staff.

Exerting power in order to motivate individuals to increase
their job competencies is probably the least stimulating experience an employee can encounter. (Bass, 1960) If one simply
uses a position of authority in an attempt to motivate others,
then employees will often resist the tactic. Yet, this is
sometimes the easiest means for many individuals to attempt
to increase employee work output. This method results in resentment and discouragement upon the part of a staff member.

Alternatives to the above method are most time-consuming
but possibly more valuable for all involved. Individuals are
more apt to become involved or motivated if:

1. They understand the rationale of what they are being
    asked to do and how this relates to the goals of their
    staff and/or college.

2. They have a participatory function in the decisions

205

being made. If people are recognized and contribute ideas to the group, then they will likewise be more motivated.

It is necessary that leaders determine their power needs in relationships with others particularly when decisions are made concerning individuals. The major goal desired in any decision making process is to stimulate personal growth and learning for those involved.

Open Communication and Leadership

In this section we would like to describe a leadership style based on open communication. It is the authors' opinion that people grow and learn when they are able to choose activities that contribute to group goals and exhibit freedom in their personal lives. This position assumes that people often are self-motivated, creative, imaginative, concerned, and willing to contribute maximum effort to most causes.

In this situation, the most effective leader is a resource person and a consultant to the group. (Gibb, 1967) He/she encourages creativity, non conformity, diversity, and facilitates the inner growth of the staff. A good leader feels, discusses, questions, relates and acts as human as eveyone else in the group. The leader is a person, not a role. Ideally, the leader may become expendable as the group grows in strength and functioning ability. The leader is a consultant upon which the group draws knowledge.

This style basically reflects upon the self-adequacy of the leader. Persons with a great deal of self-acceptance and personal security tend to trust others, view them as responsible and communicate with them in an open and frank manner. With open trust and communication, inter-personal relationships may flourish. Staff members are given room to grow as they assess their interests and basic potentials. They learn to experiment, express their needs and try new jobs. In other words, people are responsible for their own destinies.

In this atmosphere, employees learn to make decisions, develop significant skills and explore new goals. If controls are imposed, they are decided by the group as needs are perceived. Outside rules are not imposed. Groups which set their own objectives and goals have an internal maintenance system that is fostered by open communication.

Formal rules become less necessary because people respect
the rights of others. People spend little time trying to prove
themselves because they understand they are respected and trusted.
Energy is spent defining and solving problems, creating and
accomplishing tasks.

Indeed this type of leadership is a challenge to any college
student development staff member. It creates interdependence,
reduces authority status, and relies upon self determination.
The extrinsic reward for a person is secondary compared to the
satisfaction in completing a task. This can be especially
difficult in a college environment where products are intangible
and leadership is autocratic and resistant to democratic growth.

Resolving Conflicts

Contrary to what many people believe, conflict can be a
healthy experience for many organizations and groups. From
conflict, many good decisions evolve. The problem for persons
in student development is utilizing conflict in order to create
effective change. Again, the self esteem of any leader will be
an important variable. If a leader is threatened by disagreement or confrontation, the conflict will be halted by an authoritative stroke. In such a situation, staff members will become
acutely aware that conflict is not accepted. Therefore, if
disagreement occurs it will be expressed in a subversive manner
and resentment will grow among a staff.

The key to conflict relates back to the previous concept
of open communication patterns. If a collaborative climate is
to exist in a group, people must listen to the ideas of others
and be willing to express opposing points of view. Conflict
needs to be worked through until a decision is received. The
leader in this situation needs to be open to input from various
sources and to be able to explain in what manner the conflict
can be resolved so that there is mutual understanding and respect.

In order to reduce needless conflict, certain ingredients
within the group are necessary:

1. Individual talents are utilized.

2. Goals are understandable and reachable.

3. Openness, trust and cooperation are prevalent.

4. Staff is inter-dependent upon one another.

5. There are high intrinsic rewards.

6. There is a flexible organizational structure.

Another area of conflict for many college student development persons is the dilemma of being "stuck in the middle". This refers to completing tasks of superiors that may not utilize staff to their fullest potential. These tasks may also require individuals to postpone present projects until the assignments are completed. The primary responsibility of a leader in this situation is to develop open communication channels where accurate information is given to all involved. If there is a disagreement it should develop from understanding, not from misinformation.

Problem Solving

Even though conflicts may occur in your group sporadically, a process that is of primary importance in keeping your staff functioning is problem solving.

If problems are not acknowledged within a group, its ability to make progress will be severely hampered. A good leader knows that problems exist in groups and that confronting problems is a healthy experience. Solving a problem maintains group solidarity and increases initiative and ideas. The following three topics are of primary importance in the problem solving process.

1. Steps in the problem solving process

   a. Define the problem. Does a problem exist? Can the cause be identified? Who or what is effected?

   b. Gather ideas for possible solutions.

   c. Test ideas. Consider and eliminate alternatives. Define the best solution. Determine who or what is effected by solution.

   d. Decide. Involve group members in the decision.

   e. Plan action. Who will implement the solution? When?

2. Helpful methods for steps in the process

When methods are appropriate to group needs during a
particular step in the problem solving process, they will
be helpful. Some methods are suited only to certain
steps of this process.

   a. Problem definition: Problem census; buzz grouping;
      general discussion.

   b. Getting ideas: Brainstorming; buzz grouping; silent
      periods; individual work.

   c. Testing ideas: Role playing; case methods; general
      discussion; data gathering.

   d. Deciding: Deep freeze agenda; exploration of feelings;
      segmentation of problem.

   e. Planning action: Subgrouping; reality testing; role
      playing.

3. Common blocks to the problem solving process

   a. Blocks to problem-definition: Assumption that the
      problem is clear; overabstraction of the problem;
      assumption that the problem is unimportant and hence
      does not need definition; premature testing or
      choosing; overgeneralization of the problem.

   b. Blocks to getting ideas: Mixing of idea-getting and
      idea-testing which can produce threat; polarization;
      lack of information; overgeneralization; lack of
      experience; formality.

   c. Blocks to testing ideas: Lack of data; lack of an
      appropriate method of testing; premature voting;
      polarization; "sweetness and light atmosphere";
      overprotection of ideas by members.

   d. Blocks to deciding: Inadequate testing; lack of problem
      clarity; premature voting; polarization; voting rather
      than working towards consensus; identification of ideas
      with individuals.

   e. Blocks to planning action: Failure to get consensus;

failure to adequately test action implications; assignment of planning function to a subcommittee; failure to pin down responsibility for carrying out plan.

Motivating Others

There is a great amount of literature that discusses the theoretical aspects of motivation. Maslow and Herzberg present two approaches. A major idea in much of the research is that people want to do things because of the influence of a leader. This can be accomplished in several ways:

1. A leader sets a good example for the group and is willing to participate and volunteer for new tasks.

2. Individuals are encouraged by their _effort_ and not just by their success.

3. A leader recognizes the work of each group member to all individuals in the group.

4. A leader is able to find personal development in failure as well as success.

5. A leader delegates important tasks and decisions.

Another important aspect to motivating individuals is establishing or setting appropriate goals. When setting goals, answer the following questions:

1. Is the goal achieveable and believable to you?

2. Is the goal measurable?

3. Do you want to do it?

4. Are there alternatives?

5. Is the goal motivating and does it have value to you?

If a leader wants the best efforts from any individual, there are several things he/she must consider. Persons need to feel that they belong and are welcome in the staff. This includes a share in planning group goals and understanding what is expected of them in the group. Individuals also need

to contribute to others and to have responsibilities that are
a challenge. They need to see that progress is being made
towards goals and that their role is clearly defined in order
to work confidently. Most of all, there needs to be confidence,
loyalty, and trust in the leader.

How to Get Things Done

L. E. Moody (1971) relates 25 rules in a humanistic framework for helping leaders make their organizations more effective.
These include:

1. Study your staff and determine what makes each member
    tick.

2. Be a good listener and encourage other people to talk.

3. Criticize constructively. Criticize behavior and <u>not</u>
    the person.

4. Reprove in private and praise in public.

5. Be considerate and treat every individual as an asset.

6. Delegate responsibility for details.

7. Give credit where it is due.

8. Avoid domination. Don't try to run everything.

9. Show interest in and appreciation of the other person.
    Be positive.

10. Make your wishes known by suggestions or requests.

11. If you make a request, tell the reason why. Be consistent.

12. Let the staff in on your plans and programs even if they
     are in an early stage.

13. Never forget that the leader sets the style for the group.

14. <u>Show</u> and <u>tell</u> people that you have confidence in them.

15. Ask your staff for counsel and help.

211

16. When you are wrong or make a mistake, admit it.

17. Listen to ideas from your group.

18. If an idea isn't adopted, tell the originators why.

19. Understand that people carry out best their own ideas.

20. Be careful _what_ you say and _how_ you say it.

21. Use every opportunity to give members a sense of importance to their work.

22. Give your staff goals, a sense of direction, and something to achieve.

23. Keep your staff informed on matters affecting them.

24. Give members a chance to take part in decisions.

25. Let your staff know where they stand.

Conclusion

This chapter has provided numerous ideas for college student development staff to improve their leadership skills. Included in these topics were ideas concerning leadership style, value systems, power and authority, communication, conflict resolution, motivation, and general guidelines for group effectiveness.

As educational institutions and the role of college student development continues to grow in the following decades, the leadership abilities of student development persons must continue to increase. Effective leaders contribute to a greater extent both to the college and to the community. If student development is to be enhanced as a profession, then staff members need to be more adequately cognizant of and prepared for effective leadership training.

It seems fitting in these closing remarks to enclose a leader's eulogy entitled "A Wish for Leaders" written years ago by an unknown author. It summarizes many of the principles that have been discussed throughout this chapter.

212

A WISH FOR LEADERS

...Anonymous

I sincerely wish you will have the experience of thinking up a new
idea, planning it, organizing it, and following it to completion and having it be magnificently successful. I also hope
you'll go through the same process and have something "bomb out".

I wish you could know how it feels "to run" with all your heart
and lose horribly.

I wish that you could achieve some great good for mankind, but
have nobody know about it except you.

I wish you could find something so worthwhile that you deem it
worthy of investing your life.

I hope you become frustrated and challenged enough to begin to
push back the very barriers of your own personal limitations.

I hope you make a stupid, obvious mistake and get caught red-
handed and are big enough to say those magic words, "I was wrong!"

I hope you give so much of yourself that some days you wonder if
it's worth it all.

I wish for you a magnificent obsession that will give you reason
for living and purpose and direction and life.

I wish for you the worst kind of criticism for everything you do,
because that makes you fight to achieve beyond what you
normally would.

I wish for you the experience of leadership.

REFERENCES

Bass, B. M. Leadership, Psychology and Organizational Behavior. New York: Harper and Row, Inc., 1968.

Brown, J. D. Organization and leadership in a liberal University, Graduate Journal, Fall 1964 (6), pp. 333-338.

Cohen, M. D. and March, J. G. Leadership in Ambiguity. New York: McGraw Hill Book Company, 1979.

Gibb, J. R. Current Issues in Higher Education, 1967, In Search of Leaders, Washington: American Association for Higher Education, National Education Association, p. 55.

McGregor, D. The Human Side of Enterprise. New York: McGraw Hill Book Company, 1960.

Moody, L. E. 25 Rules for getting things done through people, American Humanics Foundation Newsletter, 1971.

CHAPTER 24

CASE STUDIES AND
DECISION-MAKING FOR COLLEGE STUDENTS AND STAFF

Josiah S. Dilley

Criticism of individuals in higher education is often criticism of the decisions these people make. Critics are saying, "So and so made a bad decision. It should have been done this way instead." Usually campus decision-makers are experienced and competent. If one should have made a different decision, why didn't he? Is it possible that he thought he had made a good decision? Can a decision be both good and bad? When are criticisms of decision-makers really justified? How does one make good decisions?

The business of making good decisions is the subject of this chapter. By carefully examining the concept of "good decision," it becomes apparent that "good" is largely an illusion--a product of people rather than of decisions. Examine an eating decision. Pork, steak, and shrimp are edible foods. A decision to eat one of them is good or bad, right or wrong, depending on the person making the decision. Is he a Catholic? A Jew? A Hindu? Is he allergic to seafood?

Since the goodness of a decision is an evaluation made by people and since people differ radically in their values, it is clear that almost any position can be taken toward any decision. It is clearly impossible for a decision-maker to protect himself from all critics. He can, however, reduce the risks of criticism by understanding various decision processes and by becoming com-petent in the process of making decisions. Much of this chapter is directed toward achieving these purposes.

Evaluating Decisions

No decision is good or bad in and of itself. How it is evaluated by people gives it its value. This observation is true of a wide range of decisions--going to college, buying a house, vacationing in the wilds of Alaska, eating horsemeat, cutting out a tumor, becoming a carpenter, buying uranium stock.

"Good-bad" judgments depend on a number of situational conditions and individual values. A first fact about decisions is to recognize that any label, good or bad, right or wrong, is a projection of the one who attaches the label and may have little

215

to do with the actual decision. When a person talks about the goodness of a decison, he is saying much more about his own values and perceptions than he is about the decision. When persons disagree about the goodness of a decision, they are talking primarily about differences in their own personal values. These differences refer to specific things and events, the usefulness of various decision processes, the responsibility of man, and criteria by which a decision should be evaluated. The first of these, differences regarding specific things such as bananas, plane rides, class absence, is widely recognized, and little need be said about them. Differences regarding more complicated aspects of decision-making are worthy of further exploration, for they often are not completely understood. They account for the use of a variety of decision processes and for much of the prevailing criticism of decision-makers.

Decision Processes

It is useful to distinguish between decision process and the product of that process, the actual decision. Process refers to the decision-maker's thoughts and actions which relate to and culminate in the actual decision.

Process varies from person to person and can include gathering information by reading, exploring, consulting; interpreting dreams; reading the stars; reciting nursery rhymes such as Eeny, meeny, miny, mo...; dissecting dog livers; and an interesting variety of other methods (see Cohen, 1964). A process can be a continuous, an intermittent, or a single act, or it can be a complex sequence of events. It can be overt or covert.

Because people have different beliefs and values, they employ different decision processes. Mary Smith consults an astrology chart, but Jane Doe wants to know what her friends think. John Jones scoffs at both and says he wants facts, while Tom Tinker says it's the principle that counts and decides on that basis. Mary, Jane, John, and Tom each believes his particular kind of process is best, and each might be critical of the process used by the others.

In a given instance, there is no real way of knowing whether a person's explanation of his process accurately describes how his decision was made. He may not be aware of all the ingredients of the process he used or he may deliberately present his process in a distorted way. This could be the case if he wanted to be thought of as a "good" decision-maker by a person advocating another process. Such problems make it difficult to study decision processes used by good decision-makers.

216

<u>Seven Decision-Making Types</u>. People employ simple and com-
plex processes. Simple processes can be grouped into seven basic
types. Each can result in a decision, but whether that decision
is good or bad depends on the person evaluating the decision.
The complexity results by incorporating all or parts of two or
more simple processes into complicated chains. The seven basic
types are (1) follow an accepted rule, (2) utilize a rational
process, (3) act to gain social approval, (4) follow your intuition,
(5) leave it to fate, (6) arrange a compromise, (7) consult an
expert.

Using the "follow an accepted rule" process, a decision-
maker arrives at the appropriate decision by applying what he
considers to be a relevant rule to the decision situation. A
university has a rule that an applicant must be in the top half
of his graduating class. An application arrives stating that
the applicant is in the bottom half of his class. The admissions
director writes him that he is not admissible. A little girl
is stopped on the street by a man in a car who wants to take her
for a ride. She remembers her mama's words, "Don't ever get in
a car with strangers." She replies, "No thank you," and runs
around the corner.

Rule, in this case, covers any written or verbal statement
or thought of such statement that provides the decision-maker
with a sufficient basis for action in the situation. Such
statements stem from a variety of sources: law, philosophy,
parental edicts, moral or ethical codes, superstitions, science,
and religion. A decision-maker can apply the first rule he thinks
of, or he can refer to several and apply the one he feels is most
appropriate or most powerful. Rules can be combined into sequences
and can include "if" statements as part of a sequence. If it is
raining and you don't want to get wet, carry an umbrella. If it
is raining and you don't want to get wet and you don't have an
umbrella, wear a raincoat. One could add a provision for staying
inside during periods of high winds or lightning. Experienced
bridge players make use of complicated sequences of rules. Computers can be programmed with a number of sequences so they can
play chess or shoot rockets to the moon.

Making a decision by rule is a very common method of deciding. The method works well in situations that repeat themselves regularly. The method is quite efficient in terms of
manpower, time, money, energy, and maintaining emotional stability.
But in novel or ambiguous circumstances where conflicting rules
can be applied or in changing societies when accepted rules are
being vigorously challenged, the rule-applying process has its
limitations.

The second method, "utilize a rational process," refers to
decisions that are made as a result of considering the expected

217

consequences. There are several versions of this process. Using one variation, the decision-maker first considers the alternatives and then considers the outcomes of these alternatives. He estimates the probability of occurrence for each outcome and indicates what numerical value he places on each outcome. He multiplies the value by the probability. For each alternative he adds the products for those outcomes associated with a given alternative, giving him a number representing the expected value for each alternative. He then maximizes, that is he chooses the alternative with the highest number.

To illustrate the process, we use a condensed version of a going-home-from-work decision taken from Bross (1965). The stated alternatives are drive a car or take a bus. Bross lists outcomes of the first alternative as "arrive home early and without incident, arrive home late due to traffic delays or accident." Outcomes for the second alternative are "arrive home early and without incident, arrive home late due to missed connections." At this point the decision process looks like this:

Alternatives	Outcomes
1. Drive a car	a. Arrive home early and without incident
	b. Arrive home late due to traffic
	c. Accident
2. Take a bus	a. Arrive home early and without incident
	b. Arrive home late due to missed connections

Bross estimates the probability of (1a) as .85, (1b) as .145, (1c) as .005; (2a) as .1, and (2b) as .9. Bross views value in terms of cost and assigns cost values to the outcomes as follows: (1a) = $.0, (1b) = $1.00, (1c) = $50.00, (2a) = $.0, and (2b) = $1.00. Bross indicates costs as negative values.

The calculation for the expected value of the drive-a-car alternative is $(.85 \times .00) + (.145 \times -1.00) + (.005 \times -50.00) =$ expected value.

The calculation for the expected value of the take-bus alternative is $(.1 \times .0Q) + (.9 \times -1.00) =$ expected value.

The alternative with the highest expected value is the "best" decision using this method.

Brim, et. al. (1962) outlines a method where value is indicated in terms of scale values instead of dollar costs. Brim feels value can be indicated as +2 = strongly desire, +1 =

218

desire, 0 = don't care either way, -1 = do not desire, -2 = strongly do not desire. The reader might substitute what he feels to be appropriate desirability scale values for the cited cost values in the Bross car example and rework the calculations. Numbers, of course, will vary from decision-maker to decision-maker because of differences in values.

The rational process is not new, but it is both lesser known and more complicated than the using a rule process. Edwards (1967) has traced it back at least as far as Bernouli. It has been widely used in the economic world and has been considered the best single decision process (Edwards, 1965). Other versions are discussed in Bross (1962) relative to the going-home-from-work decison presented here.

The rational process provides techniques for and stresses the quantifying of probability and value. In practice such numbers are elusive or unreliable, and a shrewd guess may have to suffice. Numbers and techniques for combining them help make a more exact decision, but the key concept in the rational process is not number or technique; it is attempting to anticipate probable consequences of various alternatives for action and then to choose in consideration of these probable consequences.

Using the "act to gain social approval" process, the decision-maker knows or finds out what relevant people value and then decides in consideration of these values. Relevant is defined by the decision-maker. One aspect of such a process is aptly illustrated by the phrase, "keeping up with the Joneses." If my neighbors have new cars, I have to buy one too.

When stated as "keeping up with the Joneses," the process seems to have a negative connotation. The decision-maker's behavior is controlled largely by others. But when used in other ways, the process has a more positive meaning—a car manufacturer decides to survey a sample of people to get opinions about the styling of a new car before he actually markets it; or a politician lets prevailing opinion in his precinct decide a matter for him.

How useful is the social approval method? One needs friends, family, employer, and the support of the community. In many situations, making decisions to gain their support makes a lot of sense. There are times, however, when their support is neither necessary nor needed. If one always acts to please others, he becomes a sycophant and is not generally regarded as a person with character, leadership ability, or responsibility. Other processes are necessary to maintain personal identity and to decide issues of no social import or issues where social forces have conflicting values.

219

People who use the "follow your intuition" process make decisions almost without thinking. One song phrases it as "doing what comes naturally." The decision is impulsive, reactive, in consideration of the moment. Merchants know that if they display items attractively and intimate they are bargains, shoppers will buy them impulsively.

The question must be asked, Are impulses or intuitive actions really decisions? We treat them as decisions because some people do accomplish intuitively what would require a more thoughtful decision process by others. The irresponsible, carefree, and the existential approaches to life stress intuitive and spontaneous decisions. There are many mature, responsible people who can trust their intuition, but there are others who are always in trouble because of some crazy impulse. Most people can and do respond intuitively in many daily decision situations. The question is, Is this a good way to resolve major decisions of the type normally faced by participants in higher education?

The "leave it to fate" decision process includes a variety of methods. Most are viewed in western civilization as amusing, irrelevant, or illogical. Such methods include palm reading, consulting mediums, reading astrology charts, and interpreting dreams. Any process for solving problems that involves chance, luck, or accident belongs in this category. So do all processes involving an outside source which has no known or logical relationship with the real world. Fate and lady luck are common expressions for such a source.

When a decision must be made but there is no real basis for a decision and the decision-maker wants to remain neutral, fate processes are as useful a way of deciding as man has yet been able to devise. An example would be flipping a coin to determine the winner in an election where two candidates tied. Whenever possible, however, man feels that human thought can do a better job than fate.

Following the "consult an expert" process, a decision-maker lets another person recommend a decision for him. Presumably, the other person has more information, better understanding, and more experience with whatever must be decided and therefore is capable of making a better decision than the decision-maker. Consulting a lawyer about legal matters, an architect about house design, an accountant about financial matters are common examples. If a "phony" expert, who lacks real knowledge or who advises because of an ulterior motive, is consulted, the process may fail to produce useful results. The advantages of experts are recognized, but a person seeking one should be capable of sorting out pretenders. In the case of troublesome decisions in higher education, there are not many experts available who have had such experience.

"Arrange a compromise" process is self-explanatory. Bargaining with a merchant over the price of an article for sale and management bargaining with a union to reach a wage settlement are common examples. A compromise agreement is a joint decision that is beneficial to at least two parties, but perhaps not as beneficial as either had originally wanted. If one party will not compromise, a different process must be used.

There are similarities among the different processes. For instance, some rules can be stated in social approval terms, "Son, shake hands when you are introduced to an adult." A desirability value can be put on social approval and that value may be attached to particular outcomes and incorporated in the rational process. Or, one can have a rule to consult an expert or a rule to compromise. Compromise can be viewed as striving for maximum social approval, and so the similarities continue. However, differences remain if only in the thinking of the decision-makers. Recognition of these differences is implied by adjectives used to describe people: compromising, conforming, law abiding, deliberating, impulsive.

In a stable society, the majority of people have common values and consequences are predictable. A great many decisions are easily made by knowledgeable individuals—intuitively, rationally, following an accepted rule or in consideration of social approval. The decision tends to turn out as expected, and no questions about processes are asked.

In a rapidly changing society where groups of people are challenging other groups, where the young will not adopt traditional values, and where consequences of changing conditions are not easily predictable, even knowledgeable individuals using any or all processes are going to have decisions go sour. Then the process is questioned. It may be that regardless of the process or the product, some decisions will be rejected by some group. Literally, the decision-maker can't win.

Applying the Processes

Let us reexamine the Perilous Job Interview decsion as a "can't win" type of decision and see which of the seven decision-making processes would be most helpful. In this case, a university president was confronted by a group of students demanding that Company X be barred from coming on campus to recruit employees. The students said that if necessary, they would physically prevent the company's recruiting because it manufactured war material.

An intuitive decision by the president could go either way, depending on how he responded to the immediacy of the situation. He could reach into his pocket for a coin to flip if he decided

to let fate make the decision for him. He could consult experts
to advise him, but in this situation it is not obvious who the
experts are, whether they might agree or disagree among themselves. The president, then, could use any of these three
processes to help him with his decision.

If the president tried to apply the rule process, he would
have discovered that at the time of the confrontation there were
no specific rules pertaining to conditions under which interviews
should be cancelled, how students could be prevented from interfering with interviewees' right to interview, how to act in the
face of threatened disruption, possible student-initiated violence,
or how to control student mobs on campus and in buildings. The
president's authority is designated in very general terms and
does not automatically indicate what he can, or even should, do
in specific situations like this. Because there have not been
similar situations on his campus, he does not have a precedent
to follow. What might an accepted rule be?

Following the social approval process, the president would
seek out relevant groups to determine how they feel about the
situation. He calls faculty members from all disciplines and
asks what they recommend. Some tell him the interviews should
be held and police called in if necessary. Others are outraged
at the idea of bringing police onto a college campus, pointing
out that this has never been done before and would create a
dangerous precedent. Another group says that the right to dissent must be protected, and yet another wants to find a compromise position and prevent student versus student violence at all
costs. The president cannot dermine the number favoring each
solution. The alumni association tells him to follow a strict
line, but the student association directs him to follow a soft
line. The president sadly concludes he cannot gain social
approval from all parties by following any one course of action.

If he tries the compromise process, he will probably not
succeed either. The dissident students claim they can't speak
for the hundreds of students who favor disrupting the interviews.
Many faculty and alumni are not in favor of compromise because
that would be "giving in" to the students.

Using the rational process, the president thinks of alternatives: (1) hold the interviews as scheduled, (2) hold the
interviews but change time and/or place, (3) cancel the interviews, (4) talk Company X into cancelling or changing the interviews. He tries to calculate the probabilities of the consequences that might occur from each, but ends up guessing, because
in this situation there is really no way of calculating a probability. Are the students bluffing? In this case any of the
processes could result in a decision, but would it be a "good"
decision? In cases like this, does it make any difference which
process is used?

Defensible Processes

Seven decision processes have been examined and applied to a troublesome decision. In any decision situation, all or none of the processes may achieve similar results depending on chance, acts of God, amount of information available to the decision-maker, and the values of the decision-maker, plus the value of those who will evaluate it. Except for the "leave it to fate" process, all processes incorporate personal values so that different people using the identical process can make different decisions. As has been stated, whether or not a particular result is good depends on who is asked to evaluate the decision. Some evaluators would judge on the basis of how it was made, others on what happened afterwards, and some on what was actually decided.

Does this mean that it makes no difference how one makes decisions? Does this mean there is no point in trying to make good decisions since the decision-maker can't be sure of the outcome? Not at all! He may not win a particular decision situation, and he may never win according to a certain percentage of people, but he can come out ahead over a long period of time and with a majority of evaluators. How? By competently following a defensible decision-making process.

Think of the Job Interview case again and compare a decision-maker who considers alternatives, consequences, and how people might evaluate his decision and then decided to hold the interview as scheduled after flipping a coin. Society formulates ideas of what man should do. When he does what is expected, he is viewed as acting reasonably. His actions are defensible; people are less critical and more supportive. In the Job Interview case, people would say it is better to exert best judgment than to abdicate personal responsibility and let "Lady Luck" make the decision.

In situations where consequences of actions are not easily predictable, it is unreasonable to expect man to accurately predict them. However, it is reasonable to expect him to try to anticipate possible consequences and to make an effort to determine which ones are likely to occur. It is unreasonable to expect man to know in advance exactly how groups of people will react to events that have never occurred before, but it is reasonable to ask him to try to assess what the reaction might be. If he has tried to gather as much information as possible, consulted with relevant others, thought out the possible effects of various alternatives, he has done three things. He will be more likely to achieve desired results than if he had done nothing. He has followed a process that a reasonable person would be expected tofollow in order to make an important decision, and he has followed it competently. Is it reasonable to expect more?

223

What does competently mean? Decision processes are not automatic. Each contains the possibility for foolish actions, and the decision-maker is expected to obtain the maximum potential of the process. He is expected to maximize influencing factors so that they work to his advantage. In betting on a dice game, the competent decision-maker is on the lookout for loaded dice. In consulting an expert, the competent decision-maker will try to determine whether the expert has ulterior motives. In determining social approval, the competent decision-maker will try to obtain an unbiased sample.

What does defensible process mean? It is simply the series of actions that people expect other people to follow in particular kinds of situations. There is a great deal of ambiguity in that statement, and readers can find examples of decisions where people differ as to what actions are expected. But that's the way the world is, and there appears to be no immediate change in sight, especially in our changing society with the crucial decisions facing participants in higher education. The best one can do is shrug off uninformed criticism, be less critical of others caught in similar situations, and competently try to follow a reasonable decision process as consistently as possible.

CHAPTER 25

COLLEGE STUDENT DECISION-MAKING:
GOVERNANCE TO GRIT

John Eddy

Decision Making by college students reached its height in
higher education history during periods in the 1960's when student power, as a result of social protest demonstrations, was
exerted in a maximum effort. This discussion of college student
decision-making is based on an address given at Loyola University
of Chicago on April 2, 1973, before a combined group of students
and College Student Personnel Administrators in a credit course
in Student Leadership. Before progressing, it is important to
define certain terms in order to achieve maximum clarity of
expression.

College student decision-making means here: (1) the
opportunity for students to express their opinions and obtain
their needs on the major official committees and boards of the
college where administrators, faculty, and/or trustees are duly
elected and/or appointed as representatives; (2) the opportunity
for students to obtain their wants or desires through their duly
elected and/or appointed positions on the major official governing committees and boards of the college; or (3) the opportunity
for students to obtain their wishes through official college
channels without an opportunity to be heard or represented by
themselves at the major official governing committees and boards
of the college. In other words, college student decision-making
is not limited to being heard as given official representation,
but, rather, the concrete actions that come from their demands is
the key criterion measure intended in the term, "power of student
decision-making."

Higher education history means here: (1) the span of higher
education that begins in Western Europe in the Middle Ages; and
(2) the selected moments when student power seemed at a zenith.
College student decision-making may be viewed, in general, in
either one way or the other. One position is that every area of
college life should invoke representative student decision-makers
on all college committees including the hiring, rating, and firing
of college staff members (faculty, administrators, and support
workers). The other position is that student decision-making
should be limited to certain college committees such as student
government and student activities such as suggested in the book,

225

College Development Programs in the Community and Junior Colleges
by O'Banion and Thurston.

Student power means here: (1) the actual strength students have exerted to get their demands; and/or (2) the potential student strength which students have in getting their demands met.

Let us first look into the history of college student power and decision-making. During the Middle Ages, students in Italy, not far from Loyola University of Chicago's Rome Campus, had the power to hire and fire their faculty. This antiquated time in history actually marks achievement of the high point of student power in higher education history. From that mountain-top of student power, we have gone to the valleys of higher education institutions now in trouble over their tax exempt status with the federal government because of their lack of student integration practices--where nearly complete control is based over the students In Loco Parentis par excellence by its administration, faculty, and trustees.

In American higher education, the year 1964 at the University of California at Berkeley began a new era in students making demands for influence over their lives, the curriculum, the faculty, the administration, and all that makes up an institution of higher education. In the summer of 1972, the author studied in Berkeley and saw the newest People's Park ecology approach of the students who with their bare hands broke the new asphalt pavement just put in by the University for a parking lot for vehicles. Colleges and universities which have been confronted with student power since that historical milestone have given more students decision-making opportunities from token tidbits to significant symbols of authority in their institutions.

Scholars of student power claim that student decision-making has peaked now with students not applying the pressures to the extent they did in certain times in the 1960's and the early 1970's. The sociologists of higher education claim students have, for the most part, returned to their studies, extracurricular activities, and outside work to spend their energies.

Practicality

If one studies the colleges and universities with regard to student decision-making, the following seems to be evident to the author--from having studied the higher education literature and having served at both large and small institutions of higher education throughout the nation:

(1) It is easier in small institutions to exert student power--if the students are well organized, if they keep up their demands, and if they are in positions to make the officials take

226

them seriously.

(2)   Student representation on key administrative, faculty, and/or trustee committees has been disappointing--as researcher Paul Dressel has pointed out--in terms of actual numbers of students allowed, students, being responsible to use their opportunities, and students gaining respect of other committee members. The reasons are legion for students not doing their duty.   Perhaps Eric Erikson's Youth, Identity Crisis is as good an explanation as any for this phenomena.   Youth, according to Erikson, have key decisions to make on career, marriage, self-identity and on other things that involved them in time-consuming situations.

(3)   Student power may be as strong on campuses where there is no student representation on key faculty, administration, or trustee committees.   Of course, the measure of student power is always in terms of potential or actual strength.   It appears that even when only 5 percent or less of the student body are activists, they have manifested power beyond their student numbers in getting their demands.   Unfortunately, the demands have often been considered and sometimes reached faster by physical demonstrations than by rhetoric in key committee meetings.

Nitty-Gritty

The nitty-gritty of the power game played by students in decision-making is: How much power can you psychologically effect on the persons who can change the rules, policies, and regulations that an institution uses to run its operation?   Control and respect are strong middle-class values in our society. Certainly, fear is a powerful element in the persuasion of persons. The fear is often inspired in college administrators that things are out of control and that the persons who have the power to hire and fire will look on these situations unfavorably--especially if the administrator gives in to student demands.   Destruction of property or disruption of the academic process on campus by threat or example is often involved.

In the United States, those administrators who have most often felt first the greatest pressures of student demands have been those employed in college student personnel services as Deans of Students.   These persons are closest to the students in terms of responsibility for all student campus behavior.

Tragedy

The "Dean Between" might well describe the Dean of Students whose authority is often limited but whose responsibility, ironically, encompasses the whole campus.   Incidently, the author has served as a Dean of Students at two different institutions of higher learning and is working on a book to have this title--

227

"The Dean Between." This gap between authority and responsibility is one of the ambiguity problems with the position. One functions as a counselor, administrator, and even as a law enforcement officer at times when no campus police are present--this shows the role conflicts within the work.

When a student power crisis occurs, the Deans of Students are thrown into the campus fires as expendable firemen without fireproof suits. The evidence is seen in the fact that the most common hostage in American higher education has been the Dean of Students. Of course, the author does not advocate this kind of behavior or any type of pressure tactics. These in the long run will be contra-productive. To capture the Dean, and hold him or her until the other college officials give in to certain demands, has been the name of the college student power game. In 1972, some of the author's graduate students could not visit a public community college for several days because this type of action was taking place at that institution.

Fire bombing in the residence halls and classrooms has been another technique of fear used by the fanatics. The author has been a college student personnel worker on campuses where fire bombings have been deployed. In one case, by a matter of hours, the author and scores of students missed being killed or crippled. The author, in another case, nearly died with scores of students in a smokefilled dormitory fire started by an emotionally sick student who had some of the highest college entrance test scores at the college. In both cases, these incidents could be traced to persons who were using fear techniques to disrupt the college in order to get action on demands and/or attention.

Opportunity

On those campuses where the following factors are evident, some communications are improved which aid in student decision-making. Some of these factors are:

(1) Having a well-staffed and relevant college student personnel staff with a favorable staff-student ratio of 300 students or less to one staff member;

(2) Having a special staff person serve as an ombudsman for students;

(3) Having regular surveys on student concerns by college student personnel services, students in the social sciences, and others; this information is then used to improve student rapport with the staff;

(4) Having undergraduate credit courses conducted by selected members of the college student personnel staff in areas

228

that relate to students, such as student leadership, resident hall assistant leadership, and student development seminars;

(5) Having regular recognition for student leadership via the student newspaper, radio station, arts periodical, leadership banquet, letters of congratulation from college student personnel staff, certificates for service on various committees, and so forth;

(6) Having a campus ministers association that meets regularly with the college student personnel staff in sharing mutual concerns for and of students;

(7) Having each term open town meetings on campus with some college student personnel staff chairing the sessions--students, faculty, administration, and support services personnel are all invited (secretaries, maintenance workers, and others);

(8) Having open weekly sessions with students by the Deans of Students each term over a noon hour in the college cafeteria, perhaps called "Chats with the Deans";

(9) Having goals, using management by objectives, for college student personnel services set in September and announced on campus bulletin boards with specific dates for accomplishment;

(10) Having a variety of gathering places on campus that are open where students, faculty, administrators, and others can converse--student union with rathskeller or coffee house atmosphere, an artistic type room in a residence hall, and similar kinds of places;

(11) Having a more realistic approach to the In Loco Parentis concept by college staff members, such as providing apartment living arrangements; and

(12) Having a work-study program that involves nearly 100 percent of the students in meaningful and creative work throughout the area.

The phrase In Loco Parentis still has meaning on some campuses, although it appears to be dead or dying nearly everywhere. There are still times when college officials act in place of parents--as the Latin translates. Sometimes these occasions bring the college in conflict with student wishes, and at other times the student encourages the college officials to protect him or her. Acting from the position of In Loco Parentis, college officials will find that the courts in most cases will uphold them, but that the tendency today is to have students act for themselves. When the college official uses the In Loco Parentis position on a student, it reduces the student's decision-

making processes and limits student freedoms. Ideally, it
would be good if all students could live in a fraternity or a
sorority type of setting where they governed themselves, disciplined themselves, and provided for themselves.

Militancy

Since 1964, the two national student organizations that have
significantly influenced student decision-making are the National
Students Association (NSA) and the Students for a Democratic
Society (SDS). In 1973, only the NSA--historically a more moderate group--survives in a real sense as a national group having
significant influence among college students. The SDS--a recent
radical group--has had many internal conflicts has destroyed
itself by breaking up into small splinter groups; many of these
also have died or are dying. On many campuses, SDS and the
groups it has spawned have lost their credibility with students
due to their radical positions and sometimes violent behavior.
The author recalls facing SDS efforts as they moved from other
campuses into college classes and tried to take over the teaching
functions even disregarding the tuition paying students. Ken
Saurman in his dissertation study on the NSA and SDS, for his
doctorate at Loyola University of Chicago in Student Personnel
Work in Higher Education, reports some of this information.

Nevertheless, the SDS--during their height of power in the
late 1960's--radicalized other student groups such as the NSA.
The militancy characteristic of the SDS was a confrontation type
model which other student groups used in the 1960's in order to
gain more decision-making power. Their confrontation approach
often alienated staff and students whom they were trying to win
over. It was a dangerous approach that sometimes erupted into a
small-scale war on some campuses. The author recalls as a Dean
of Students calling off a recruitment conference by the military
(army, marines, air force, and navy) when SDS members threatened
to counter their efforts.

Currently many radical students have graduated, dropped out,
gone to Canada or overseas, or gone underground in their activities on the campus. The effectiveness of radical students in
increasing student decision-making has, in 1973, had a negative
influence on the vast majority of students and staff.

Some of the reasons that militancy and the confrontation
model have declined and are being rejected in the present scene
are:

(1) The end of America's ground involvement in the Vietnam
war by February, 1973, and air bombing by August, 1973;

230

(2)   The end of the military draft by June, 1973;

(3)   The fear of death and injury of students, both pro-
testers and uninvolved, as happened at Kent State, Jackson State,
and Southern State;

(4)   The threat of the destruction of campus buildings at
many colleges and the increase of campus security police;

(5)   The recognized abuse of student power by SDS and
other groups;

(6)   The changes on campuses allowed by college trustees,
administrators, and faculty have defused many students' demands;

(7)   The threat of loss of student financial aid to those
students found guilty of campus disruptions; and

(8)   The strict actions against student militancy through
law enforcement actions, warrants, and court injunctions by some
college administrators, backed by public support.

Apathy

Student compliancy has always been a problem in students
exercising their student decision-making in student government,
student activities committees, or all-college committees. This
traditional apathy of students in the affairs of the college--
even activities paid for by their activity fees--has always been
a concern of faculty and administration, as well as of active
students who do care about their events. Even in the student
highest-interest peak in campus affairs in the late 1960's, only
a small percentage of students were ever involved in all the
possible areas that were open to them to participate in decision-
making. In fact, the author recalls many cases in which students
denied themselves leadership positions because they were simply
too much work. Even the students admitted it.

Community Responsibility

The average college today has responsibilities and obligations beyond its campus. Some of these, in most states, for
different types of colleges and to various degrees of relationships, are the following:

(1)   There is the immediate surrounding community about
every college, and they have city councils that have elected
student representatives in some places; (2) There is the Junior
College Board which is responsible for the public community-
junior colleges, and in Illinois one member is now a non-voting
student member; (3) There is the Higher Education Board which

231

is over all colleges both public and private, and in Illinois one member is now a non-voting student member; (4) There is the State Legislature which sometimes provides financial aid for both public and private colleges--in the Minnesota Legislature a 21 year old college student is a member; and (5) There is the Federal Congress which provides both financial resources for both public and private colleges--students serve on some congressional staffs so they have a built-in internal lobby. The author mentions all of these units as communities of different types. Now, some students believe they should have their own representatives on all the previously mentioned levels, rather than be represented by elected representatives of all the people.

With the many types of communities, it can be confusing as to how students might relate themselves effectively beyond the campus in their decision-making. However, more students are now trying to get elected as the 18 year old voters get out to vote.

Liberty

Since 1965, a number of documents on the rights of students have been circulated and jointly sponsored by major higher education organizations. The most famous and best recognized of these statements of freedoms is entitled Statement on Government of Colleges and Universities. This document is sponsored by such distinguished groups as the American Association of University Professors, American Council on Education, Association of Governing Boards of Universities and Colleges, and others.

This document has been used by students and staffs as a bill of rights for students in many institutions of higher education. The document provides excellent guidelines in the areas influencing student decision-making. It would be well for students and staff to use this document and the Report of the American Bar Association Commission on Campus Government and Student Dissent in a workshop each year sponsored by student governments to inform students of their rights.

Other approaches in which this document might be communicated to students would be to: (1) publish parts of it in each issue of the campus newspaper each year until it is entirely covered; (2) publish a summary of it in the Student Handbook; and (3) have numerous copies available in the Student Activities Office for students to study and to share.

Responsibility

The Student Handbook and the College Catalog are basic documents of the college and/or university, providing rules, regulations, and responsibilities of a student area where he or she can exercise his or her decision-making. While studies

232

indicate that few students read either their respective Student Handbook or College Catalog, these are primary sources for students as they practice their citizenship on campus.

Responsibility is a large word covering a wide spectrum of subjects on campus. If everyone was responsible on campus, there would be no need for campus security, which continues to be the fastest-growing area of support personnel on campus due to increasing theft, vandalism, rape, and other crimes. Some graduates, dropouts, and their acquaintances sometimes return to the campus as trouble-makers. Some of these persons get involved in destroying and even stealing property on campus, at the expense of students and the college. The author remembers, when serving as a Residence Hall Director, of an alum who destroyed a fire alarm system while under the influence of drugs.

Unity

A systems approach for student decision-making on problems of the campus could aid many students in seeking solutions. The author suggests the systems approach as learned and practiced in a project with National Aeronautics and Space Administration while serving as a Fellow of that government agency.

Voluntary

During the year 1971-72, the United States Department of Health, Education, and Welfare awarded drug education funds to 20 colleges and universities in the nation, based on the condition that these volunteer programs would be totally student-administered and operated. The author was involved in investigating and reporting on this Federal program to professional educational societies those same years. This program was a historical landmark in American higher education, for the Federal government for the first time dramatically recognized student decision-making through this experimental program that set aside a total of $700,000 over a two-year period into student-run campus drug programs.

Another new trend among students in the 1970's in seeking more decision-making opportunities involves students approaching the college and university administrators through a "consumer advocate" role via the model of Ralph Nader's "raiders." This approach involves students hiring or acquiring qualified attorneys and using the courts to help them in obtaining their demands. The national growth of consumer advocate-type groups has increased the pressures for these approaches on some of the nation's campuses.

The opportunity for student decision-making is at an all-time high today on most American campuses. However, unless

233

students exercise their rights and opportunities, few wrongs will be corrected or changed. If students are not using their opportunities, no structure is appropriate for them in improving their decision-making. Students must be motivated to exercise their right to make decisions. That motivation, hopefully, will come from the students themselves, and not from the administration or other influences outside their peer group.

CHAPTER 26

DEVELOPING A POSITIVE BELIEF
IN YOURSELF AND OTHER PERSONS

John Eddy

Building Trust Relationships

The greatest challenge since the beginning of humankind has been how men, women and children can learn to live with each other. This is the basic problem humankind needs to work on and work out daily, in order to avoid psychological and physical damage from killing and war itself. Human Relations Training is the need we must stress if humankind is to survive. Human Relations Training is defined and described here as a process that helps persons learn knowledge and skills to develop and maintain good relationships with persons. It means we need programs in our families, schools, businesses, organizations and governments to build trust, to discover personal and planetary peace. As David Johnson has said:

"Little happens in a relationship until the individuals learn to trust each other. Because of this, forming a climate of trust is one of the most important tasks. In fact, the first crisis most relationships face involves the ability of two individuals to trust themselves and each other. Trust is absolutely essential for a relationship to grow and develop. In order to facilitate the development of a relationship, you must learn to create a climate of trust which reduces your own and the other person's fears of betrayal and rejection, and builds the hopes of acceptance and support."
(David Johnson, Reaching Out: Interpersonal Effectiveness and Self-Actualization. Englewood Cliffs, New Jersey: Prentice-Hall, Inc., 1972, p. 43).

Providing a Rationale for Human Relations Training

Human Relations Training provides an opportunity for persons, through structured experiences, to develop trust-building relationships. Carl Rogers has given a rationale for this approach to human relationships in a summarized fashion as follows:

"I have come to trust persons--their capacity for exploring and understanding themselves and their troubles, and their

ability to resolve those problems--in any close, continuing
relationship where I can provide a climate of real warmth
and understanding... I trust I have made it clear that over
the years I have moved a long way from some of the beliefs
with which I started: that man is essentially evil; that
professionally he is best treated as an object; that help
is based on expertise; that the expert could advise, mani-
pulate, and mold the individual to produce the desired
result... I believe that for me interpersonal relationships
best exist as a rhythm--openness and expression, and then
assimilation, flow and change, then a temporary quiet;
risk and anxiety, then temporary security. I could not
live in a continuous encounter group... It is necessary
for me to stay close to the earthiness of real experience.
I cannot live my life in abstractions. Consequently, real
relationships with persons, hands dirtied in the soil,
observing the budding of a flower, or viewing a sunset, are
necessary to my life. At least one foot must be in the soil
of reality... I challenge, with all the strength I possess,
the current American belief, evident in every phase of our
foreign policy, and especially in our insane wars, that
"might makes right." That, in my estimation, is the road
to self-destruction. I go along with Martin Buber and the
ancient Oriental sages: "He who imposes himself has the
small, manifest might; he who does not impose himself has
the great, secret might."
(Carl Rogers. Journal of Humanistic Psychology. Vol. 13,
No. 2, Spring, 1973).

The approaches of Human Relations Training mentioned in this
book emphasize human growth, development and potential approaches.
Reasons for this are given by the author as follows:

"The Thomas Harris and James D. McHolland approaches,
ideally, would aid educators and others to be more
self-aware, more open, and more able to assess their
own sensitivity, achievement, motivation, and relat-
edness to others by going through these human relations
programs."
(John Eddy, The Teacher and the Drug Scene. Bloomington,
Indiana: Phi Delta Kappa Educational Foundation, 1973,
p. 21).

Identifying Background Theories

The background theories for Human Relations Training with
regard to the philosophy of human nature used here comes from
Rogers (1957) and Maslow (1970). Rogers (1961) describes the
person who emerges from this client-centered therapy as:

"This person is more open to all the elements of his
organic experience, a person who is developing a trust
in his own organism as an instrument of sensitive
living"...
(Carl Rogers. On Becoming a Person. Boston: Houghton-
Mifflin, 1961).

Again, Maslow (1970) describes this psychologically healthy
person as follows:

"First of all the most important of all is the strong belief
that man has an essential nature of his own... Second,
there is involved the conception that full health and normal and desirable development consist in actualizing this
nature, in fulfilling these potentialities... Third, it is
now seen clearly that most psychopathology results from
the denial or the frustration of man's essential nature."
(Abraham Maslow. Motivation and Personality. 2nd ed.
New York: Harper and Row, 1970).

Selecting the Preferred Process

The Human Relations training propositions preferred by the
author are well stated by Robert Carkhuff in four statements,
such as:

"Proposition I. The core of functioning or dysfunctioning
(health or psychopathology) is interpersonal."

"Proposition II. The core of the helping process (learning
or relearning) is interpersonal."

"Proposition III. Group processes are the preferred mode
of working difficulties in interpersonal functioning."

"Proposition IV. Systematic group training in interpersonal
functioning is the preferred mode of working with difficulties in interpersonal functioning."

(Robert R. Carkhuff. Helping and Human Relations: A
Primer for Lay and Professional Helpers. Vol. 2, Practice
and Research. New York: Holt, Rinehart and Winston, Inc.,
1969, p. 130).

Self-Help Approaches Support Group Process

Dr. Victor Frankl, psychologist who advocates biblio-therapy
and meditation therapy, tested his beliefs in a prison camp in
World War II. Two books that may aid persons in the creative
reading for the understanding of self (biblio-therapy) and meditation therapy are: (1) La Hayes, Tim. How to Win Over Depres-

237

sion; (2) Gordon, J. and Melton, Dorothea. The Ways of Meditation.

Knowing Human Relations Training Values

In order to build trust between persons and in order to find
personal peace as well as planetary peace, certain values are
assumed by the author in actualizing this approach to Human Relations Training. The value approach of PEER, a project funded by
the National Institute of Mental Health, is advocated here as a
basis in dealing with persons. It is summarized here by Ardyth
Hebeisen as:

1. Both the good and the bad exist in life. We recognize
the bad, we deal with it, but, basically, we choose to
focus on and celebrate the good, the positive, the
emotions and experiences which help us transcend self-
defeating negative attitudes.

2. All people at core are acceptable.

3. The uniqueness of each person is special, worth sensing
and celebrating. It is not necessary to be like all
others to be what one "ought" to be.

4. Rejection, shame, "Not OK" feelings and communications
interfere with growth and a healthy, wholesome way of
being a person.

5. The more congruent (honest and open) a person is, the
more whole, and in the long run, the more effective
he will be in personal relationships.

6. Honesty is desirable. Masking real feeling or manipulation and exploitation of others are not desirable.

7. Empathic skill, the ability to sense and respond to
what another person is feeling, is a desirable quality.

8. It is good to understand and share meanings, perceptions and experiences between persons.

9. It is desirable to be able to make a decision to do
something and then carry it out. Goal directedness
is valued.

(Ardyth Hebeisen. Peer Program for Youth. Minneapolis,
Minnesota: Augsburg Publishing House, 1973, p. 8).

Handling Unacceptance of Persons

One of the most difficult problems facing intrapersonal relationships is handling the rejection of others. Elizabeth
O'Connor mentions this problem as follows:

"The capacity to transcend their generation's culture and
mind set is what made the discoveries of Copernicus and
Darwin and Freud more than the discoveries of genius.
All three had to overcome 'dread of the community,' for
their discoveries were to strike hard at some of man's
cherished illusions. In the realm of the spirit, their
heroism singled them out as giants among men. Fear of
losing the acceptance of those to whom we belong will
turn the most intrepid of us from the path of self-
discovery as well as discovery that might threaten the
external orders in which we live."
(Elizabeth O'Connor. Our Many Selves: A Handbook for
Self-Discovery. New York: Harper and Row, 1971, p. 19).

Structuring Experiences for Personal Development

In order to grow and develop as a person in relationship to
others, there are at least six levels of structuring experience
that may be used in Human Relations Training. They are given as
follows by David S. Abbey and Ronald H.T. Owston:

1. "Withdrawal--day dreams, fantasy;

2. Rituals--rigid set of transactions; word strokes;

3. Pastimes--chitchat; gossip discussion of sports,
   cooking, etc.

4. Activities--frequently organized with others; may
   be 'work' or hobbies;

5. Games--transactions with 'payoffs' for players;

6. Intimacy--the ultimate goal; a rare experience
   shared with another."

(David S. Abbey and Ronald H.T. Owston. Transactional
Analysis Social and Communication Training. Chicago:
Human Development Institute, 1973, Figure 1, p. 1).

Learning to Help Yourself

It is important to have a goal-oriented program if you want
to make Human Relations Training work in your life and in the
lives of others. As Robert R. Carkhuff points out, this is the

239

way to grow and go on to develop personally:

> "Every step becomes a goal in a smaller program, i.e.,
> attending (listening and observing); attending physically
> (eye contact and leaning); squaring (right should to left,
> facing, and erect);.... Every goal becomes a step in a
> large program, i.e., living skills (program development
> skills, problem-solving skills); interpersonal skills
> (initiating, personalizing, responding, and attending);
> .... A program is the first step of an efficient but
> lengthy journey to fulfillment.... Every program becomes
> a step in a larger system, i.e., international development
> skills (social planning skills, community development
> skills, management skills, working skills, learning skills,
> and living skills)."
> (Robert R. Carkhuff. How to Help Yourself: The Art of
> Program Development. Amherst, Massachusetts: Human
> Resources Development, 1974, pp. 164-166).

Help for Anxiety, Depression, and Loneliness

Dr. Alan Walker, founder-director of Life Line International
in 1963, has said that the most common human problems are anxiety,
depression, and loneliness. This conclusion is drawn from the
research analyzing millions of telephone calls received from dis-
tressed persons by LLI which is a crisis counseling service
active in 182 centers in 12 countries. (Chandler, Russell.
"Anxiety, Depression, Loneliness...Chicago Sun-Times, May 18,
1976).

Finding Meaning in Work

Human Relations Training should lead to worthy goals, such
as discovering the meaning of work and play in life. The
author relates his philosophy and practice on this subject as
follows:

The meaning of work for each person will depend on many
factors, such as: does the person enjoy the work that he or she
does to earn a living?; does this person have a basic philosophy
of life (faith beyond oneself--in God and in mankind) that includes a view of some type of work as a meaningful exercise?;
and does the person have ways to keep his life alive so some kind
of work can always have meaning now and after official retirement from a particular job?

It is impossible for me to present an objective viewpoint--
beyond speaking to myself--on this subject, "The Meaning of
Work." This presentation is certainly colored, prejudiced or
biased by my own insufficient approach to the topic. Therefore,
I humbly confess that I cannot separate my own thoughts or prac-

tices from what should be an ideal or model for another person on the meaning of work. What each person does with this subject or topic seems to me has to be done on a personal existential basis in order for meaning to occur or to be communicated. It is a personal, complex struggle in my own life to find meaning in work and I do not have a neat formula nor a set of answers-- let alone one simple solution for you.

However, I will inadequately share with you some personal opinions of how I am trying to find meaning in my work and what limited examples seem to inspire me on this lifelong effort to discover meaning for work. Of course, the lives of Jesus Christ, Saint Paul, Saint Francis, John Wesley, Martin Luther King and Helen Keller do offer me some witnesses of how to find meaning in work.

My philosophy of work is not fully developed, but I will share the following:

1. Work as an activity is often as much as play for me. I enjoy my present work as it gives meaning to others and to myself--the two can go together as we appreciate working with persons. Consequently, work has a value which should make us feel well and worthwhile in order for it to have healthful meaning for the whole of our lives.

2. Therefore, my hobbies are also work as much as they are play, recreational or avocational in nature. In fact, if I could retire now, my present interests beyond my current vocation, career or position, would keep me going with little time to spare or share. For example, I mention here my family and my work, as with the International Association of Educators for World Peace --a non-governmental agency of the United Nations. Moreover, if I had the means to retire, I would engage in such things as are related now to my family, professional and university work, human relations, and peace concerns. I like my work that much!

Some books that I recommend to persons interested in ex- panding their meaning of work and play for living vitally are:

1. The Holy Bible--it speaks of work some thirty-three times and I suggest reading such passages as Psalms 111:2 and Galatians 2:16 for meaning.

2. The Success System That Never Fails--it tells the story of Clement Stone, who turned failures in his job into meaning through prayer, hard work, faith in God and his neighbor.

3. I'm OK - You're OK--it provides an approach to find meaning in not only work but all of life, as it is related by Thomas Harris.

241

(Shirley Odegaard (ed.). <u>Old People Are Human Also</u>. Skokie, Illinois: Social Concerns Commission, Central United Methodist Church, 1974, pp. 3-4).

Giving Feedback to Persons

In Human Relations Training, it is important to use appropriate good judgement in providing feedback to persons. For example, George M. Gazda and associates state this very well:

"Important as it is to reinforce effective behaviors, it is also important that we attend to ineffective behaviors and the development of alternative ways of behaving. Through negative feedback, persons can be helped to correct their distortions and other maladaptive habits. The feedback should provide them with new intellectual or emotional experiences. Constructive negative feedback not only can help one see aspects or a situation he has missed, but it also can help him reduce the blind spots in his personality. Feedback, then, can sometimes be stressful, but when it is well timed and offered with empathy, respect, warmth and genuineness, it can be an important contribution to the helpee's growth. It is important to note that when one gives negative feedback appropriately, he is simply criticizing some aspect of another's behavior; this is not the same as rejecting him as a total person... Because of the dangers involved, we recommend that one give mainly positive feedback in the early stages of a relationship. Negative feedback is better received and used after an atmosphere of mutual trust and respect has been established. (George M. Gazda. <u>Human Relations Development: A Manual for Educators</u>. Boston: Allyn and Bacon, Inc., 1973, p. 40).

Providing Guidelines for Group Relations

In Human Relations Training, there are some guidelines that have been found to be effective in addition to the materials suggested for structured experiences. They are:

1. "Illumination" by Ray Kasten is a prayer that helps keep group participants sensitive to other persons.

2. "A Credo" by Thomas Gordon, founder of Effective Training Associates and Parent Effectiveness Training (PET), is a statement on relations with others.

Learning How to Communicate Effectively

How does one communicate effectively when one feels the

need but hesitates because of our psychological self limitations and the felt pressures of cultural conditioning? Human Relations Training, as it uses Assertive Training, can enable persons to communicate more effectively. For example, Assertive Training is elaborated by Joan Pearlman and Karen Coburn (authors with Lynn Z. Bloom of the book, The New Assertive Woman) to mean the following:

"Have you ever: Been reluctant to ask a doctor questions because you didn't want to take up his time? Been too timid to ask a mechanic exactly what was wrong with your car because you didn't want to appear stupid? Been hesitant to question an error on a restaurant bill because you were afraid of making a scene? If you have trouble bringing yourself to do these and other things you feel you have the right to do, maybe what you need is assertiveness training.

It can help anyone, but women need it more because they have been taught that being passive is part of being feminine... The technique isn't as aggressive as it sounds. A distinction is made between being assertive and being aggressive.

It's a matter of what your intent is. Assertive behavior is a direct, honest expressive of ideas, desires, and feelings. Aggressive behavior expresses the same things, but without taking into the account the rights of others. The aggressive intent is to dominate and get your own way no matter what.

The key to assertive behavior is self-confidence. Too often, they say, someone trying to decide what to do puts the issue in extreme terms: What is the worst thing that could happen if I go ahead and do what I want? But there is no reason to expect the worst. Too many other options are more likely to occur.

The idea of an assertive woman as an O.K. thing to be is new. Being feminine and being assertive used to be almost mutually exclusive.

Society is still reinforcing passive behavior in women. In a man it's called wishy-washy or milktoast, and a man who acts that way may even be called feminine. In a woman, it's called being nice and accommodating.

Learning how to be assertive is one thing, they agreed; learning when to be assertive is another. If something at work bothers you, but speaking up might cost you a job you like, you may have to suffer in silence.

243

When you do choose to assert yourself, you may not get
your request met...but you feel better about yourself.
You have the right to ask, just as the other person has
the right to turn you down."
(Coburn, Karen and Pearlman, Joan. "Mechanics of
Assertiveness: How to Demand an Answer." Chicago
Tribune, Sunday, January 4, 1976, Section I, p. 28).

Relating Self-Evaluation and Assertiveness Training

In Human Relations Training, assertiveness training is
projected by making a comparison of nonassertive, assertive, and
aggressive behavior as they occur in human relationships. The
following chart aids the reader in making these kinds of assess-
ments in various human interactions. It is often difficult to
judge the effectiveness of our behavior when faced with a conflict
of rights between ourselves and another person. Just getting
what you want may not be the best criterion, especially if your
approach has permanently antagonized your adversary or engendered
feelings of guilt within yourself. A better indication is the
way you and the other person feel about yourselves after the
conflict has been resolved. Simply, assertive behavior, as
opposed to submissive or aggressive behavior, generally makes
you feel good and gains the goodwill of your opponent; it may
even make that person your friend. The chart below may be used
to evaluate the overall effectiveness of your actions and reactions to delicate or intimidating situations, with the middle
column. Assertive Behavior, suggesting the most effective
approaches add their emotional benefits. If you find that your
actions consistently place you at the far right or left of the
behavior scale, you may be a good candidate for Assertive Training. Either way, you should learn something interesting about
yourself and the way you affect others.

Item	Nonassertive Behavior	Assertive Behavior	Aggressive Behavior
Characteristics of the behavior	Emotionally dis- honest, indirect, self-denying, inhibited	(Appropriately) emotionally honest, direct, self-enhancing expressive	(Inappropri- ately) emo- tionally hon- est, direct, self-enhancing at expense of another, expressive
Your feeling when you engage in this behavior	Hurt, anxious at the time, and possible angry later	Confident, self- respecting at the time and later	Righteous, sup- erior, depreca- tory at the time and possibly guilty later

244

Item	Nonassertive Behavior	Assertive Behavior	Aggressive Behavior
The other person's feelings about herself when you engage in this behavior	Guilty or superior	Valued, respected	Hurt, humiliated
The other person's feelings toward you when you engage in this behavior.	Irritation, pity, disgust	Generally respect	Angry, vengeful

Chart reprinted from An Introduction to Assertive Training Procedures for Women, copyright 1973, by the American Personnel and Guidance Association, reprinted with permission.

Standing Up and Accepting Yourself and Your Situation

There comes a time in life when a person who wants to grow and develop has to put behind the defense mechanisms and rationalization. Jess Lair has said it concisely and plainly:

"You've got a choice, pick up whatever tools you've got and go with them. But don't sit around crabbing and complaining and crying. I don't like the tools I've got to go to war with either sometimes, but they're the best ones I've got. I ain't much, baby--but I'm all I've got. Right? It seems to me that's all there is to it. Now, you say, 'I'm scared, frightened.' So what, so what else is new? So am I... Freud says there's two things in the world, to love and to work, so you've got to find some love and you've got to find some work that will give you dignity and self-respect. And that doesn't mean things that are mean and distasteful and hard. So you learn to love and you learn to work and the two, they help each other back and forth."
(Jess Lair. I Ain't Much, Baby But I'm All I've Got. Greenwich, Connecticut: Fawcett Publications, Inc., 1972).

Jess Lair in his book, I Ain't Much Baby, But I'm All I've Got, deals with the ideas and experiences which effected his life. A serious heart attack led him to evaluate his values, fears, and goals. This kind of career searching is happening to many other persons and it is refreshing to find an honest author handle it. Again, in Hey, God, What Should I Do Now?, Jess Lair and his wife Jacqueline Carey write of the tragedy of the heart attack and its impact on their lives so that their faith in God became a meaningful relationship they shared together as well as

with their children. Finally, in the book I Ain't Well-But I
Sure Am Better, Jess Lair explores the problem of loneliness and
provides his solution in Mutual Need Therapy (MNT) which is based
on establishing relationships with a few intimate friends we can
trust, whom we care about and who care about us. These friends
like us the way we are and are glad to see us when we appear for
they have no program for our improvement--You're Ok. What Jess
Lair has discovered is appropriate to clarify here in terms of
going beyond a program in Human Relations Training to form life-
giving relations with persons in a meaningful manner. There is
a poem that says it so well how self confidence is necessary to
life:

> If you think you are beaten, you are,
> If you think that you dare not, you don't,
> If you'd like to win, but you think you can't,
> It's almost certain you won't.
>
> If you think you'll lose, you've lost.
> For out in the world you'll find,
> Success begins with a fellow's will,
> It's all in the state of mind.
>
> If you think you are outclassed, you are,
> You've got to think high to rise,
> You've got to be sure of yourself before
> You can ever win a prize.
>
> Life's battles don't always go
> To the stronger or faster man,
> But soon or late the man who wins
> Is the man who thinks he can.

T.A. in Personal Transaction Assessments

The Human Relations Training approach here uses Transactional
Analysis (T.A.) as an intellectual tool to enable persons to
analyze and to understand the basis of behavior and feelings.
Thomas Harris in his book, I'm OK - You're OK, explains the concepts of "Parent," "Adult," and "Child" as states that have
different effects on a person's behavior in social intercourse
broken into units with each called a "transaction." J. Douglas
Hickerson explains these three states as:

"The Parent state is the activation of mental recordings
or past observations of parents and to others in similar
authority roles which unconsciously motivate authoritarian,
coercive or restrictive behavior in the present. The
Child ego state is the influence of activated recorded
sensations and experiences of childhood, these produce the
carefree, joyful behavior of the "natural child" or

246

the submissive, restrained behavior of the "adaptive
child" reacting to parental figures in the present. The
Adult state is the level of conscious reality testing
which, when effectively developed, enables the person to
recognize and maintain rational control of the parent-
oriented or child-oriented behaviors which occur in
transactions with others."
(J. Douglas Hickerson. "Transactional Analysis and the
Student Personnel Worker." NASPA Journal, Summer, 1973).

   In Human Relations Training, T.A. is used as one of the
important tools in aiding persons to assess themselves and others.
Muriel James and Louis Savary treat the subject of using T.A. in
handling religious experience. In the Preface of their book, The
Power at the Bottom of the Well, they say:

      "Although everyone has a variety of religious experi-
      ences, we discovered that few people possess a psycho-
      logical frame of reference for evaluating them. Trans-
      actional analysis has proved to be such a tool for us.
      And we'd like to share what we found. In particular, we
      showed how people's ego states--the Parent, Adult and Child
      parts of their personalities--may influence their theologi-
      cal ideas as well as their transcendent religious experi-
      ences.

      Incidentally, we've used all of our ego states in
      writing this book. From the Child in us comes our excite-
      ment, joy, enthusiasm, and a feeling of being OK with
      each other, with you, and with God. From the rational
      Adult in us comes information and techniques to use in
      self-understanding. From the nurturing Parent in us
      comes the biblical proclamation restated in contemporary
      words, 'God says you're OK.'"
      (Muriel, James and Louis Savary. The Power at the Bottom
      of the Well).

Translating T.A. Terminology in a Specific Situation

   In Human Relations Training, four categories of T.A. are
used for personality assessment. Using a combination of the
Thomas Harris book I'm OK - You're OK, and the Muriel James book,
Born to Love, the following might be used to translate the age-
old, familiar New Testament "Good Samaritan" story:

   1. Traveler: I'm not OK--You're OK! (The traveler's
       script called for getting hurt).

   2. Priest and Levite: I'm OK--You're not OK! (The
       hurt traveler was not acceptable).

247

3. Robbers: I'm not OK--You're not OK. (Here the
    robbers are feeling inferior and not trusting others).

4. Good Samaritan: I'm OK--You're OK! (He feels good
    about himself and others).

Personnel working in the helping professions (such as
counselors, teachers, administrators, and others) are using T.A.
in preparing persons for a better relationship with others.
Research on student dropouts reports that students indicate the
following reasons for their leaving colleges: (1) negative teacher attitudes toward students, (2) student conflicts with students;
and (3) lack of support for students.

Relating Career Education and Career Counseling

Relating career education and career counseling to Human
Relations Training is done by using the book, A Career Education
Primer for Educators, by Walter Wernick, David V. Tiedeman, John
Eddy and Betty J. Bosdell. See Appendix D for this material,
which also contains the most complete bibliography or identified
corpus of ERIC literature on career education.

The reading of the book, A Career Education Primer for
Educators, before participating in the three Human Relations
Training Exercises recommended here is suggested. This will help
the reader and group participant find greater meaning in these
exercises.

Learning to Work Together

An exercise that Human Relations Training uses to develop
group decision-making is an exercise called "The NASA Game."
This exercise is found in Appendix A and should be an early exercise used in trust building.

Following "The NASA Game" the next exercise used in Human
Relations Training is found in Appendix B and is called Transactional Analysis Social and Communication Training by David S.
Abbey and Ronald H.T. Owston. The author uses this exercise
through page 133 and the purpose of this exercise is to help
facilitate the development of persons in trust building.

Next, the author uses the Human Potential Seminar Participants' Workbook by James D. McHolland and it is mentioned in
Appendix C. The purpose of this exercise is to help persons
develop self-affirmation, self-determination, self-motivation
and regard for others. The skills emphasized in this exercise
are personal unfoldment, empathetic recall, action goal setting,
recall of peak experiences, formative experience association or
recalling "Mini Peaks," acknowledgement and analysis of your

248

satisfactions, achievements and successes, clarification of
personal values, acknowledging your personal strengths, long-
range goal setting, conflict identification and resolution, and
life-style; planning for meaning. The purpose of this exercise
is stated by Joseph L. Kleeman:

"The Human Potential Seminar (HPS), developed at Kendall
College and being adopted widely, is a significant contribution to the emerging model of student personnel work
(Brown, 1972), (O'Banion, Thurston, Gulden, 1972) and to
the human potential group movement (Kleeman, 1972). The
HPS is an effective contribution to the emerging model of
student personnel work because it provides a framework for
student personnel workers to focus their efforts on positive changes in the behaviors of all members of the college community, as opposed to efforts to passively provide services only for the student having academic or
emotional difficulties. The HPS is an effective contribution to the human potential group movement because it
is based on a highly positive view of the nature of man
while demonstrating the dramatic effects of immediate
interpersonal feedback and self-affirmation in the context
of intensive small group experience."
(Joseph L. Kleeman. "The Human Potential Seminar: A
Contribution to an Emerging Model of Student Personnel."
Kendall College: Unpublished paper, 1974).

The contributions of the Human Potential Seminar come from
Dr. James McHolland, then Director of Counseling at Kendall College of Evanston, Illinois. Dr. McHolland originated the concept
of positive reinforcement in cooperation with the W. Clement and
Jessie V. Stone Foundation. This Program called the Human Potential Seminar is an integral part of Kendall College's two-year-
old Academic Skills Program and it has been a part of the College's
curriculum for eight years. Hundreds of colleges and universities
throughout the nation use all or part of this HPS approach.

"Each HPS is a time-limited, supervised and positively-
oriented human development process composed of a series of
specific activities designed to help persons toward greater
self-regard for themselves and regard for others. The ultimate goals are those of self-determination, self-motivation,
and increase in self-worth, and self-confidence. Seven
phases are a part of the experience. Throughout the seminars,
participants are encouraged to bring the future into the
present by goal setting. Students are supported to constructively comment upon each other's goals in terms of
achievability, believability, desirability, and measurabil-
ity. Personal unfolding, modeled by the leader begins the
Seminar, and each participant is invited to share experiences
that have helped him or her become who he or she is now.

249

In the peak experience recall, participants are encouraged to share positive life experiences. Various patterns of motivation are exposed and each participant is enabled to think more positively about himself or herself in order to assume more responsibility for future actions. Next, each participant's values are clarified by answering and reviewing with the groups responses to prepared questions. A values auction helps persons to promote learning about personal values in stress situations that will assist the student in life career situations.

During the strength acknowledgment phase, individual strengths are shared and reinforced with the focus on areas of latent potential. Participants are encouraged to commit themselves to short-range and long-range goals of their own choosing based on what they have discovered about their behavior. No labeling is made of participants. For example, all human beings are not achieving at their highest possible levels so we are all "underachievers" in not using our fullest potentials. The point here is that persons are not put into categories that reinforce negative self-concepts. Finally, the ultimate goal is to encourage each participant to transfer what he or she can learn to a more effective and satisfying life style outside of and beyond the group. Follow-up research indicates the experience continues to provide participants helpful insights beyond the credit course." ("A Column From Kendall." Evanston Review, January 1, 1976, p. 36).

Scheduling the Training Sessions

The Human Relations Training schedule is as follows, using a 2-1/2 class session, which would be about a one semester three-credit graduate course:

First session: A discussion on small groups of the chapter, "Developing a Positive Belief in Yourself and Other Persons," will be accomplished.

Second session: "The NASA Game" will be covered and The Art of Helping by Robert Carkhoff will be used.

Third session: The exercise on T.A. will be completed.

Fourth session: A discussion on A Career Education Primer For Educators and the COSPA Student Development Document will be done.

Fifth through Sixteenth session: The exercises on the HPS will be achieved.

250

CHAPTER 27

HANDLING STRESS: A COMMON PROBLEM OF PERSONS

John Eddy

The need for emotional stamina in counseling and administrative work in higher education has not been properly addressed in the professional literature of college student personnel and college counseling. Mueller (1961) and Ball (1977) mention the importance of mental health and emotional-psychological stamina respectively in their writings. Ball's statements are specifically to the point when he says:

"The major emphasis during counselor preparation is on the client's concerns, with little if any emphasis on what happens to the counselor. If this is so, the beginning counselor has not been adequately prepared to face the disparity between theory and reality or between the emotional-psychological demands and the net result of counseling effort. Many counselors after training realize that the emotional demands are too great for the amount of return and quietly leave the profession... More emphasis on the emotional-psychological stamina and energy required of the counselor could strengthen existing training programs. For example, training programs might point out that the practitioner can expect to feel an emotional psychological energy drain.

The counselor often experiences energy drain and may not understand it or find ways of replenishing the energy loss. Ideally, the energy loss would be replenished by counselee feedback saying that the counseling efforts were effective. Unfortunately this is not often the case. It is disconcerting to the fledgling counselor to learn that expected outcomes do not equal input effort. In fact, it is the unusual counselee who makes a special effort to give the counselor direct feedback regarding the outcomes"...

In this chapter, the college student personnel worker is given many different modes to use to face the stress situations that come throughout a person's career in the field. These approaches are provided here to aid both the beginning graduate student as well as the veteran with years of experience in college student affairs. There is always some approach to learn, relearn, practice, and do again to help a person work through stress.

From the homemaker hearing crying children to the worker feeling the pressures of over demanding positions, stress is everywhere the common problem of people. Consequently, it is essential that persons learn how to deal with stress to live better, to live longer and to live in improved relationships with other persons. How to identify stress and how to cope with stress is an important survival skill for any person. Persons in the helping professions should be examples in this area. Thus, in human development training, handling stress is a key component for career productivity as well as personal peace. Executives in higher education and business have begun taking short courses in handling stress for the sake of personal health and performance. This chapter provides some practical tools to aid all persons regardless of their occupation to better handle stress in all of life.

Persons need to choose carefully among the many self-help programs that are available to aid persons in handling their problems. There are some self-help programs that use extreme encounter type approaches that have devastating effects on some persons that may cause some persons to require psychiatric hospitalization, psychiatric treatment, and counseling work.

Life-Style A Problem

The life-style of the citizens of the United States is the major cause of cancer, not chemicals found in food or in the environment, claims Dr. John Wersburger, Vice-President for Research at the Naylor Dana Institute of the American Health Association. For example, he mentioned smoking is the cause of a large portion of lung cancer while industrial chemicals may cause only one per cent or less of cancer cases. Smoking causes stress in a person's body and non-smokers also become more stressful when tobacco smoke reaches certain levels.

For those persons who are heavy drug users from alcohol to other drugs, extra stress is placed upon the normal body functions. Drug abuse adds to the increase of personal stress as much as any excessive work demands. (Thus, as Biometeorology shows, weather will have even a greater effect in increasing stress as weather produces changes in the body.)

Discover Your Stress Areas

The Menninger Foundation has suggested a list of questions for persons to take a self-inventory on their mental health. Here are some eight representative questions to assess yourself:

252

(1)   What are my goals in life and how realistic are they?

(2)   Is my use of time and energy helping me to reach these goals?

(3)   Do I have a proper sense of responsibility or do I try to do too much and fail to acknowledge my limitations?

(4)   How do I react to disappointments and losses?

(5)   How am I coping with stress and anxiety?

(6)   What is the consistency and quality of my personal relationships? Are my contacts with others superficial, meager and unrewarding?

(7)   From whom do I receive and to whom do I give emotional support? Do I avoid getting support from others for fear of appearing weak?

(8)   What is the role of love in my life? How much time do I give to listen and care for others?

Honesty in answering these questions is the first step in identifying the areas that need problem solving. Of course, these are questions that take a life-time to answer as well as to work out. In a sense, solutions are always in process with the honest person.

Dealing With Stress

Some helpful guidelines from the Christophers for persons looking for aids to handle stress are:

(1)   Look for the causes of stress such as the Menninger Foundation's Checklist previously mentioned.

(2)   Examine your relationship with other persons and how to make them more personable so to lessen the stress on other persons.

(3)   Evaluate your behavior, for example, not every argument is worth winning, for while defending your values is important, it is essential for perspective to ignore lesser issues.

(4)   Be positive by not concentrating on your failures but by recalling your past successes to develop your self-esteem.

253

(5) Seek advice and counsel by confiding in a friend or professional counselor.

(6) Do something for others for this act of service can help break the focus on self and reduce stress caused by self pity.

(7) Do one thing at a time so that you can feel you have accomplished something.

(8) Learn to pace yourself by taking a break like going for a walk, looking out a window into a park of living plants and so forth.

(9) Exercise can refreshen a person after mental work just as reading a book can relax some persons after physical action.

(10) Create a quiet place where you can meditate or pray as recent studies point to these sources of spiritual growth as helpful to keep body functions healthy even as they reduce stress.

Again, in the book Type a Behavior and Your Heart by Dr. Meyer Friedman and Dr. Roy Rosenman, they state ten ways to cut down on stress such as:

(1) Plan some idleness every day.

(2) Listen to others without interruption.

(3) Read books that demand concentration.

(4) Learn to savor food.

(5) Have a place for retreat at home.

(6) Avoid irritating, overly competitive people.

(7) Plan leisurely, less-structured vacations.

(8) Concentrate on enriching yourself.

(9) Live by the calendar, not the stop watch.

(10) Concentrate on one task at a time.

Having a Philosophy of Life

It is important for the human development educator, counselor or specialist to have a well defined philosophy of life and to set goals that support your ideals. "Slow down, you move too fast," advises a hit song by Simon and Garfunkel.

Dr. Ronald E. Barnes, former Vice-President of Student Affairs at North Dakota University and present consultant on stress, has said that many persons are spending their time and energy at jobs that do not help them get closer to their "goals in life" so this causes major stress in their lives. Value clarification of these personal discrepancies is a starting step for solution of this problem in stress.

Challenging Adult Apathy

Dr. John W. Gardner, Director of Common Cause and former Secretary of the U.S. Department of Health, Education and Welfare, has said: "The adult tends increasingly to confine himself or herself to the thing he or she does well and to avoid the things in which he or she has failed or has never tried. If you want to keep on learning, you must keep on risking failure."

Identifying the Workaholic

Workaholics are persons who regularly overwork out of compulsion and are addicted to their work. The results of workaholics addiction can lead to career problems, poor health and even early death. There is a difference between work lovers and workaholics. Dr. Carl Jung has distinguished between the workaholic and work lover by saying that the work lover works hard, and long by choice so he or she can stop without suffering from acute withdrawal pains. However, the workaholic has trouble relaxing and taking a vacation. For the work lover, his or her work is also his or her play. However, the workaholic has mixed motives from seeking status that comes from the admiration from persons because he or she doesn't approve himself or herself to allowing guilt feelings to drive his or her work activities.

Recognizing one's busyness is the first step in working with the workaholic. A classical example of identifying one's busyness as a workaholic is given by Dr. Wayne Oates, author of Confessions of a Workaholic. Dr. Oates recognized his problem when his 5-year-old son asked for an appointment to see him.

In the book, Type a Behavior and Your Heart, Dr. Meyer Friedman and Dr. Ray H. Rosenman divide workers into two categories such as: (1) high-pressure persons are labeled as type A work addicts and their characteristics are excessively ambitious, are overly competitive, and are frequently hostile as they are pressured by deadlines. (2) Low-pressure persons are classified as type B work addicts who lose themselves in dull paperwork and routine and their characteristics are to become overly dependent upon the organization they work for so they have little selfhood of their own.

Humankind: A Dangerous Species and Stess Producer. There
is a sign over a mirror in the Primates House at the Lincoln Park
Zoo in Chicago, Illinois that reads:

> "You are looking at the most dangerous animal in
> the world. It alone of all animals that ever lived can
> exterminate (and has) entire species of animals. Now
> it has achieved the power to wipe out all life on earth."

This brief statement provides a challenging thought to all
humans for Homo Sapiens have the power through super bombs to
destroy all living persons and plants in the world. Thus, it is
crucial that all citizens of all governments work to preserve the
peace to avoid fiery ashes for this planet. However, not so
dramatic personal damage and ends come prematurely to persons
daily by the misues of human power through attitudes and actions
that cause violence and destruction. Human beings are the greatest stress producers toward their fellow human beings.

Dr. C. G. Jung, psychiatrist, identifies four personality
types based upon his observations so persons tend to be thinking
types, feeling types, intuitive types, or sensuous types.
Dr. Gordon Milton in The Ways of Meditation writes, "Meditation
or prayer comes more naturally to some personality types. Part
of the maturing discipline of the prayerful life is to overcome
the typologizing and to move into an integrated personality state.
In such a state the polarities in the self would be balanced and
the forms of prayer would all be natural, using the approach
called "The Relaxation Response."

In the book, The Relaxation Response[*] by Dr. Herbert Benson
the author mentions that stress is a killer and that learning to
relax and meditate is one way to cut one's chances of high blood
pressure or a heart attack without risking adverse side effects that
come from other approaches. The approach that Dr. Benson recommends is one that can be adjusted to any religious person's view
for it does not take a particular religious language but religious
language can be added according to one's religious faith. For
example, instead of using the word "one" the religious believer
could use a word of his or her faith such as God, or Jesus, or so
forth. Millions of religious persons have used such a process
for thousands of years. Those persons who have no religious
affirmation may use the exercise just as it is formulated as it
is given below:

First Step: You find a place to sit in a comfortable position
so you can remain quiet.

[*]The Relaxation Response by Herbert Benson, M.D. New York:
William Morrow & Co., Inc., 1975.

Second Step: You close your eyes.

Third Step: You relax all your muscles by beginning with your feet and moving through your head. You keep these muscles all relaxed.

Fourth Step: You breathe through your nose. By breathing easily and naturally, you become aware of your breathing process. When you breathe out, you say the word "one" and the word "one" when you breathe in.

Fifth Step: You continue this fourth step practice for 10 to 20 minutes. You should not use an alarm but check with a watch to gauge this period of time--opening your eyes to read the time. After the 10 to 20 minute period is over using the fourth step, sit quietly for a few minutes with your eyes closed. Then, open your eyes and sit quietly but do not stand up for a few minutes.

Sexth Step: You should not worry about your achieving a deep level of relaxation. Let your body take over and let relaxation take place in its own way. If distracting thoughts occur, keep returning to the word you are using in your fourth step exercise--"one" or whatever word you use for this exercise. You should practice the technique once or twice daily but not after any meal for a two hour period as the digestive processes tend to interfere with the process.

_____

References

Arnold, D.L. "Counselor Education as Responsible Self-Development." Counselor Education and Supervision. 1961, 1, 185-192.

Ball, W.R. "Emotional Stamina--The Practitioners Dilemma" Counselor Education and Supervision, 1977, 16, 3, 230-232.

Brody, J. "Doctors Warn that EST's Self-Help Might Turn Into Sickness For Some." Chicago Tribune, May 3, 1977, Section 2, page 5.

Counselor's Handbook. Washington, D.C.: U.S. Department of Labor, U.S. Government Printing Office, 1967.

Eddy, J.P. and Durst, G.M. Life and Management by Responsibility. Albuquerque, New Mexico: The Training Company, 1976.

References

Lewis, E.C.   The Psychology of Counseling.   New York:
Holt, Rinehart & Winston, 1970.

Mueller, K.H.   Student Personnel Work in Higher Education.
Boston: Houghton Mifflin, 1961.

Shertzer, B. & Stone, S.C.   Fundamentals of Counseling.
Boston: Houghton Mifflin, 1968.

Srebalus, D.J.   "Rethinking Change in Counseling."
Personnel and Guidance Journal.   1975, 6, 415-421.

CHAPTER 28

STUDENT AFFAIRS ADMINISTRATION:
A SYNTHESIS OF HUMAN DEVELOPMENT, INSTITUTIONAL
DEVELOPMENT, AND MANAGEMENT

John Eddy and David T. Borland

Human Development in Student Affairs

Throughout the history of the student affairs profession,
emphasis has been placed on the concept of individual development. This emphasis coincided with the simultaneous development and expansion from the late nineteenth century of both
the student services function in colleges and universities
and the field of psychology. The synthesis of these two
areas resulted in a statement of the "personnel point of view"
in 1937, which focused professional attention on development
of the "whole individual" by recognizing the potential for
development within each student and accepting professional
responsibility for the facilitation of that potential.

That basic professional position was revised at various
times, but tended to rely almost exclusively on the psychological
basis of the individual. Within the institutional context,
this emphasis on human development also focused on the "extra
curriculum" as the base from which the "whole student" was to
be developed. More recent authors have advocated a wider foundation for the effective practice of the student affairs profession.

Brown (1972), for example, indicated that the total
environment of the student, including the academic arena, must
be the domain of the student development educator. He identified eight roles - diagnostician, consultant, programmer,
technologist, college professor, administrator, behavioral
scientist, and researcher - as the organizational mechanisms
by which human development for students could be facilitated
in "a return to the academy". Miller and Prince (1976) integrated the traditional emphasis on human development with the

259

need for specific implementation of this emphasis within colleges and universities. These four assumptions, as the basis for the student affairs profession, recognized (1) the potential for development within each individual, (2) the actualization for this development as an individual's own responsibility, (3) a need for systematic intervention into one's environment, and (4) that the accomplishment of development goals requires new and varied experiences.

Institutional Development in Student Affairs

Just as the early efforts in the profession of student affairs tended to focus on individual development, the more recent focus on the total environment of the student has given little emphasis to the necessity of developing the institutional skills necessary to create effectively and efficiently the environment facilitative of human development. College student affairs work may be categorized as a human service activity. As is the case with any activity that takes place in an organization, certain management functions are essential if the profession is to fulfill its roles completely. The necessity for a sound philosophy and practice of institutional development has been heightened in recent years by a stress on accountability.

Over the past few years, thirty-three states have passed legislation or joint resolutions featuring some type of accountability, and over a dozen states are considering such action. During this same period voluminous literature on accountability has appeared. While many authors have neglected a definition of accountability, educational accountability may be described briefly as an approach to maximize the most effective and efficient use of staff, financial resources, materials, facilities, and equipment, using some performance measures as assessment tools.

A variety of techniques have been developed to facilitate accountability. While many of these techniques first were applied in industrial settings, they have been applied more recently in government and education. The pressure from the public for accountability in institutions of higher education has placed internal institutional pressure on the subsystems of colleges and universities. The student affairs subsystems at many institutions are being required to account specifically for their activities and many either have been eliminated or reduced severely in scope for failure to demonstrate their effectiveness. If the goal for student affairs truly is to facilitate the human development of students, it is required now that a balance of activity be placed on the institutional dimensions of that goal.

The institutional context within which most student affairs work is accomplished is becoming increasingly complex. Knowledge about the organizational paramenters of colleges and universities in that complex environment is crucial for student affairs personnel. Not only is the knowledge of one's own institution vital, but also awareness of the potentiality of various combinations of personnel, structural, and personal factors in other institutions and in theory are required to determine the best institutional environment for human development. The creation of fluid, interdependent, and symbiotic institutional relationships toward the effective and efficient facilitation of total institutional mission must be as vital to student affairs professionals as has been their traditional commitment to students.

Management in Student Affairs

The student affairs profession includes the need for management/administrative strategies in institutions of higher education for effective and efficient institutional delivery systems that meet student needs. There are numerous administrative tools and techniques that are especially helpful for college administrators today, many of which have been used in business, industry, and public service agencies.

Traditionally, student affairs professionals have viewed management techniques with a skeptical eye. Skeptics in several types of organizations have believed that knowledge and skills of management were not applicable to their situations because (1) their personnel are not "business-oriented", (2) they need "better people" to carry out the "real functions"

of the institution, and (3) their work with human development
is so unique and intangible that efforts to measure results
or organize more efficiently certainly would reduce their
effectiveness. Also, many who have been educated in the
traditional counseling or psychology models fear obsolescence.
Borland and Thomas (1976) have indicated, however, that while
new skills and perspectives must be adopted to implement
student development goals, much can be accomplished by applying
current compentencies in new ways and with new constituencies.

The Carnegie Council's report (1980) on the future of
higher education has indicated that the period until the turn
of the century can be characterized as the "golden age of
students". Unless institutions can analyze, plan, and execute
the changes required for this "new age", the result may be
disasterous. Student affairs professionals will find themselves
with a grand opportunity to provide invaluable leadership for
their institutions, as student needs are accomodated. The
general role for student affairs becomes obvious - as mediators
of the inevitable conflicts between student needs and institutional mission. That role must be accepted professionally,
not only by "the adminstration", but by each student affairs
staff member as appropriate for their individual skills and
institutional positions.

The role of student affairs preparation programs in the
synthesis of these three areas of professional endeavor is
clear. First, the traditional reliance on the counseling model
must be balanced with the institutional and the managerial
dimensions required for the future facilitation of student
needs. Second, the integration of these three areas of
professional endeavor also must be accomplished so that the
full synergistic effects of individual effort will be realized.
Finally, the total scope of professional activities must be
analyzed and comprehended, so that traditional fears may be
eliminated.

For example, Lawrence and Lorsch (1967) identified an
interesting paradox between two organizational thrusts regarding
accountability parameters, that must be monitored carefully
by student affairs professionals in their mediation role between
institutional goals and student goals. These two major thrusts

262

in organizations as they attempt to analyze, change, and implement action in relating to everchanging environmental conditions are (1) toward greater order, systemization, routinatization, and predictability, which is generally feared in student affairs and (2) toward greater openness, sharing, creativity, and individual initiative which is traditional in student affairs.

Certain techniques, such as critical path systems, planning, cost effectiveness, and systems design, facilitate the first thrust, while other techniques, such as human potential seminars, value analysis, and brainstorming, facilitate the second thrust. The significant point here is that in contemporary and future student affairs practice, the facilitation of both thrusts must be accomplished through the synergistic energies of human development, institutional development, and management in order to meet professional goals.

REFERENCES

Borland, D. T., and Thomas, R. E. "Student Development Implementation Through Expanded Professional Skills", Journal of College Student Personnel 17: 145-149, March, 1976.

Brown, R. D. Student Development in Tomorrow's Higher Education. Washington, D. C.: APCA, 1972.

Carnegie Council on Policy Studies in Higher Education. Three Thousand Futures: The Next 20 Years for Higher Education. San Francisco: Jossey-Bass, 1980.

Lawrence, P. R., and Lorsch, J. W. Organization and Environment: Managing Differentiation and Integration. Boston: Harvard University Press, 1967.

Miller, T. K., and Prince, J. S. The Future of Student Affairs. San Francisco: Jossey-Bass, 1976.

CHAPTER 29

ORGANIZATIONAL FACILITATION OF STUDENT AFFAIRS

David T. Borland

The bulk of activity in the area of student affairs has
been within institutional contexts. The focus for this professional activity, however, has been on the development of
students as fully functioning individuals. The historical
development of the student affairs profession has neglected
to a great extent the professional responsibility for the
organizational environment in which students develop. An
understanding of basic organizational parameters can facilitate more effectively the traditional human development goals
for students, while concurrently facilitating the institutional goals necessary for student development and for current
demands for accountability.

Organizational Process

With the advent of the industrial revolution during the
19th century, mass employment of large numbers of people
necessitated a new social form -- the industrial organization.
Historically, the development of the industrial organization
has progressed through three basic theoretical phases. The
first phase viewed the organization in economic terms. The
organization was conceived as a rational decision maker,
whose primary goals was that of efficiency, as determined
by rudimentary cost analysis techniques. The organization
was an authoritarian force in the lives of all who participated
within it. People who performed the work of the organization
were perceived as machines or as parts of machines who were
interchangeable and replaceable.

The management styles facilitative of the economic theory
of organizations emphasized the formal structural aspects of
organizational process. The "universal principles of management"
school of thought, as represented by the work of such people

as Mooney and Reiley, constructed a set of rules by which the
efficient organization could be accomplished. The emphasis
of these principles was the order, discipline, and centralization of authority at the top and the duty of subordinates
to obey. These principles also viewed the egalitarian concepts
of worthy leadership, equity, initiative, and stability of
tenure as requisite parts of an efficient organization. These
principles were refined further primarily through the work of
Taylor (1911) in the concept of "scientific management".
Taylor's work emphasized the measurement of the process of
task accomplishment toward the goal of maximizing the efficient
interrelationships among the components of the task. He
measured distances, time, and the size of the components and
designed the process that brought these elements to their most
efficient levels within the workplace.

The second theoretical stage of organizational inquiry
was concerned primarily with the behavior of people in the
organization. After the social form of industrial organization
moved into the 20th century, there began to appear problems of
organizational process that were not being explained by existing
theories. The most reknowned example was the work done at the
Hawthorne plant of the Western Electric Company by Mayo (1933).
The attempts there to measure the effects of illumination for
the optimal production rate were unsuccessful. Primarily
through the work of such people as Mayo and Roethlisberger
(1941), who used the knowledge of the developing discipline
of psychology, the theories and research results of behavioral
science began to be applied to industrial organizations. Such
problems as worker isolation, fatigue, and monotony, which
could not be explained completely through "scientific management", became the focus of organizational inquiry. The study
of individual and group behavior and the informal groupings
of people within organizations led to the formation of the
"human relations" theories. Viewing organizations as people
who form everchanging coalitions of decision makers in the
resolution of organizational problems, the concepts of motivation
and leadership and the sociometric techniques of analysis
became a part of organizational knowledge and process.

The current theoretical phase is one characterized by a
synthesis of the previous two stages. While the first stage
emphasized structure and the second stage emphasized human

relationships, each almost excluding consideration of the other, this phase, often referred to as the structuralist stage, attempts to integrate the earlier formal and informal phases. This integration recognizes the inevitable strain between organizational demands and personnel needs and requires that neither factor can be ignored if maximal organizational efficiency is to be achieved. Etzioni (1964) has emphasized that the focus for this synthesized approach is the search for a rational balance between these two needs in a particular organization, rather than the continual search for the perfect organization.

The implementation of the third phase is being investigated currently and has expanded this inquiry beyond industrial organizations into virtually all social organizations. Although studies into higher education organization are rather recent, they are beginning to lead to a better understanding of higher education administration. The advent of systems theory as a descriptive tool and systems analysis as the investigatory mode have been successful. The flexibility of contingency theory of leadership, information theories of the organization, and differentiation and integration of organizations, are examples of this synthesized approach to organizational process.

Organizational Structure

Transforming desired institutional process into an organizational structure that is facilitative of student affairs goals has remained a challenge for the profession. An understanding of a systems approach and the organizational structures proposed as models for facilitating student development goals should assist in meeting that challenge effectively.

Systems theory

A system is a series of interrelated and interdependent parts (subsystems), which interact in such a manner that a change in any one subsystem affects the whole system (Huse and Bowditch 1977). In analyzing a system, study of the interrelationships among these subsystems is at least as important as is study of the subsystems themselves.

267

A system has six elements which are vital to a comprehensive understanding of the environment that could facilitate student development.

1) Complexity and Interdependence -

The existence of subsystems denotes the complex nature of a system. Rather than operating in an independent and isolated manner, these subsystems are interdependent in nature. If, for example, the standards for admission to an institution were changed, the interchange between the subsystems of students, faculty, and administrators in an institution of higher education also could change. Over time, the student body would acquire a different character, which would affect the size and style of the faculty who served these differing students. The differing faculty and student character also could require altered administrative personnel in substance and in style.

2) Openness -

Systems are open to influence by other systems. A change in the economy or in student behavior on campus, as viewed by the legislature or the general public, can provide for a differing level of financial support or differing regulations. In effect, any system is a subsystem of a larger system, theoretically to infinity, all of which can affect the original system openly.

3) Communication -

Communication is the continuous and cyclical process by which interaction among systems is communicated. The communication made in systems is characterized by (a) an input from external influence or from within the system itself, (b) the operations stage within the system which process the input, (c) the output of the operations stage which goes out to those external influences, and (d) the feedback process which uses the output to revise the system in the form of additional input.

268

4) Balance -

In any system there are two conflicting forces, one
for change and the other for maintaining the status
quo. These two forces are in dynamic interaction
as a result of the open communications processes and
continuously strive toward resolution or balance.
In an open environment new input will upset the
balance either toward change or toward a status quo
situation and there will be an effort to regain
balance. This is the process by which systems grow
in response to needs or else stabilize to consolidate
recent growth.

5) Multiplicity of Goals -

As a result of the openness and complexity of systems,
a multiplicity of goals form. Often those goals are
complementary, but when they conflict, the communications
and balance elements begin to work toward goal conflict
resolution. Since goal conflict sets these processes
in motion and since growth can be a consequence of these
processes, goal conflict itself can be a positive
process that should not necessarily be avoided; rather,
it should be analyzed and managed properly.

6) Formal and Informal -

Systems have formal aspects (rules, procedures,
organizational charts) as well as informal elements
(personal and social goals of individuals and groups).
For example, student activities directors may enjoy
their positions because of the interaction with
colleagues and students, as well as the duties and
goals of the office itself.

Institutional Models

An organization or institution, then, is a continuing system,
which is able to differentiate and integrate human activities.
These activities utilize, transform, and weld together a set

of human, material, and environmental resources into a problem solving whole (Huse and Bowditch 1977). The structural form of the institution should reflect the best possible manner in which its goals can be achieved, utilizing the processes that are consistent with organizational mission. Among the organizational models available for higher education mission are the following.

A) Collegial model -

The traditional model of organization for institutions of higher education has been the collegial model - the "community of scholars". This model of the faculty centered institution that was imported from the European continent through England became the predominant structure in the colonial colleges. The concern for students in early America was primarily academic. The traditional pastoral scene of a professor and students equally contemplating the eternal truths of the world is one that virtually has disappeared; yet, the attempt to keep or regain that structural or governance form persists.

The emphasis on the academic development of students led to the situation where faculty, who realized that other student needs had to be met, resolved the problem through the establishment of what has become the student affairs division in colleges and universities. This organizational separation has made the collegial model more difficult to establish in a comprehensive manner in contemporary higher education. Brown (1972) recommended a return to the collegial concept for student development educators, as facilitated by a total learning environment --- "a return to the academy".

B) Bureaucratic model -

In reaction to the increasing complexity of society, the demands on colleges and universities have changed its structure continuously. While the stated goal of academicians has been to maintain the collegial model,

270

the societal conditions required for the bureaucratic
structure to evolve have become dominant. Weber
(Henderson and Parsons 1947) described the following
conditions as necessary if an organization were to
be classified as a bureaucracy --- a large scale
organization with a definite social function, a
division of labor into specialized personnel, written
rules and regulations, a hierarchy of authority,
the roles of subordinates and superordinates, and
an impersonal nature which prevents discrimination
in the application of the organization's rules.

Weber presented the concept as a positive facilitator
of human activity, but the popular perception of
bureaucracies as inhibitors of human progress really
provides evidence that the pure bureaucratic concept
has been misapplied, misused, and abused. In either
case, however, the application of the principles of
bureaucracy to most contemporary institutions of
higher education provides the conclusion that they are
bureaucratic in most of their organizational operations,
notwithstanding traditional denials.

C)   Political model -

Baldridge (1971) expressed dissatisfaction with both
the collegial model and the bureaucratic model as
accurately descriptive of the organizational structure
of colleges and universities. He viewed authority in
higher education as flowing not only from faculty,
as in the collegial model, or from the upper levels
of the authority structure, as in the bureaucratic
model, but also from various constituencies both within
and from outside of the walls of academe.

In viewing higher education more from a systems perspective, then, Baldridge proposed that institutional
mission in colleges and universities could be understood
better if the political model were utilized. He saw
that these varying constituencies had differentiated
levels of influence, not only among themselves, but at
differing periods of time. These constituencies
(subsystems) tended to have more influence when they

271

were able to build coalitions with other constituencies. The more successful these coalitions were in building strong bonds with other subsystems and the more they were able to use the existing formal system, the more likely that their view of institutional mission would prevail. As examples of these shifting centers of influence and political shifts for self maintenance, one need only look at the influence of the faculty in the 1950's and 1960's, the impact of students in the 1960's, and the reestablishment of administrative authority in the 1970's in political atmosphere of accountability and its consequent reaction among other campus constituencies in the phenomenal growth of unions on campus.

D) Matrix pyramid –

Viewing the bureaucratic and collegial models as conflict-ing and generally ineffective in explaining compre-hensively the structural environment facilitative of student development and viewing the political model as being applied to higher education in a parochial manner, Borland (1977) proposed a matrix pyramid model. Higher education exists in an environment that requires consistent monitoring and change and yet has not developed the organizational structure to accommodate that change. As in most established organizations, change is viewed initially with skepticism. The mechanism of aggressive neglect is used by those in power in this age of accountability to give the appearance of aggressive action or change, while simultaneously setting in motion organizational barriers to negate the effect of such change.

The matrix pyramid attempts to violate the absolute bureaucratic lines of power, to expand the horizon of activity for collegial authority, and to provide access to political coalitions for all constituencies equally. This organizational model reduces the tall bureaucratic structures in higher education to only four levels, centralizes responsibility for institu-tional locomotion, expands authority for substantive

decisions to the lowest level of the college or
university, and provides immediate access to the
power systems of institutions, regardless of the
length of tenure of any individual or institutional
subsystem. By changing the formal structure, the
assignments of personnel, and the administrative
mechanisms by which inevitable organizational conflict
is resolved, the matrix pyramid model opens itself
to environmental influence for all of its constituencies. With the "golden age of students" predicted
by the Carnegie Council (1980), the potentialities
for student development advocates seem to be enhanced
by the matrix pyramid model.

In conclusion the facilitation of human development
objectives for students in higher education requires more than
just the knowledge and methods by which the development of
human beings is accomplished. Institutions of higher education
must be viewed as systems, just as a human being is a system,
and it is only through the symbiotic development of both
students and colleges and universities that the professional
goals of student development will be accomplished.

REFERENCES

Baldrige, J. V. Power and Conflict in the University. New York: Wiley, 1971.

Borland, D. T. "Aggressive Neglect, Matrix Organization, and Student Development Implementation," Journal of College Student Personnel 18: 452-461, November, 1977.

Brown, R. D. Student Development in Tomorrow's Higher Education. Washington: APGA, 1972.

Carnegie Council of Policy Studies in Higher Education. Three Thousand Futures: The Next 20 Years for Higher Education. San Francisco: Jossey-Bass, 1980.

Etzioni, A. Modern Organizations. Englewood Cliffs, N. J.: Prentice-Hall, 1964.

Henderson, A. M. and Parson, T. (Eds.) Max Weber: The Theory of Social and Economic Organization. New York: Free Press, 1947.

Huse, E. F. and Bowditch, J. Behavior in Organizations: A Systems Approach to Managing. Reading, Massachusetts: Addison-Wesley, 1977.

Mayo, E. The Human Problems of an Industrial Civilization. New York: Macmillan, 1933.

Roethlisberger, F. J. Management and Morale. Cambridge: Harvard University Press, 1941.

Taylor, F. W. The Principles of Scientific Management. New York: Harper, 1911.

CHAPTER 30

LEADERSHIP AND MANAGEMENT IN STUDENT AFFAIRS

David T. Borland

As inquiry into organizational processes developed, a
concomitant interest in the leadership and managerial facilitation of goals also developed. As the effects of organizational structure and process on the behavior of individuals
and groups were demonstrated, the role of influential individuals in both the formal and informal dimensions of organizational mission became evident and vital to success. Applying
this general organizational knowledge specifically to student
affairs requires that in order for student affairs goals to
be accomplished, not only is the knowledge of student development and institutional development vital, but also the administrative knowledge and skills to facilitate the interaction
between individuals and organizations is required.

Leadership and Management

On a general level often the terms "leadership" and
"management" are used synonymously. More precisely, there is
a distinction in these terms, which has particular significance
for student affairs administration. While the term "management"
has been utilized primarily in business and industry, its
synonym in education has been "administration". Management
or administration refers to the process by which institutional
goals are implemented. The primary focus is on the behavior
of those in charge of the organization to see that the specific
tasks leading to goal accomplishment for the institution are
efficiently and effectively planned, organized, performed,
monitored, and evaluated. In student affairs, for example, this
strict definition would require that effective administrators
be people who facilitate such activities as balanced budgets,
full residence halls, efficient collection of financial aid
loans, or judicial regulation of student behavior.

The term "leadership" represents a broader concept in that
it focuses on the ability to meet all goals that exist within
an organization. A leader will see that the accomplishment of

275

the goals of the variety of individuals in an institution are as significant to the welfare of the organization as is the achievement of the institution's goals. In the purest sense, the "manager/administrator" is concerned for the welfare of the institution, while the "leader" is concerned for the welfare of the people in the institution, as well as for the institution itself. The leader sees that the most efficient and effective management meets institutional goals through facilitation of the accomplishment of individual goals in a symbiotic manner. For example, a student affairs leader is one who meets the goal of full residence halls by seeing that the living and learning environment for students, and the employment environment for staff, is meeting their expectations, rather than by administrative regulations for mandatory residence.

If the model of the "leader" is to be facilitative of the professional goals of student affairs, both individual goals and institutional goals must be accomplished. Since individual needs and institutional needs inevitably conflict in any organization, the primary activity for an effective leader/administrator is conflict resolution. Many authors (Lawrence and Lorsch 1967; Baldridge 1971; Borland 1977a; Hersey and Blanchard 1977; Katz and Kahn 1978) have identified the inevitability or organizational conflict and its desirability in a thriving, growing institution, as long as its resolution is competent. The competent resolution of conflict is dependent primarily on the orientation and skills of the formal and informal leadership available in any particular institution.

Leadership Style

Leadership style or orientation has been a subject of much debate. Various leadership theories have been conceived and studied, which provide a variety of foundations for leadership behavior in organizations. A sampling of these theories would include: Argyris' immaturity-maturity theory (1969), Herzberg's motivation-hygiene theory (1966), Likert's management systems theory (1961), and McGregor's Theory X and Theory Y (1960). These and other theories of organizational functioning and leader effectiveness attempted to expand on the traditional concept of leadership as autocratic, democratic, or laissez-faire and the traits theory in which the proper combination of personality factors that a person was "born with" led to effective leadership.

As leadership theory and research continue to develop, it becomes increasingly clear that more effective leaders "are made, not born". An integration of the various work on leadership has led to the "contingency management" approach to understanding, learning, and applying a series of skills to facilitate organizational activity. These skills would vary for the leadership of differing organizations, dependent on such factors as the traditional personality characteristics of the leaders, but equally significant would be the demands of the particular role, superordinate and subordinate expectations, and variables within the specific environment in which that organization operates. Hersey and Blanchard's life cycle theory of leadership (1977) is one attempt to integrate the various leadership theories and to apply that knowledge to the management of organizations. In contemporary thought about leadership, then, there is less emphasis on one's "style" and more emphasis on one's abilities to analyze, plan, organize, implement, and evaluate the various personality, interactive, and environmental factors that impact an organization.

Organization Development

As the contingency approach to management gained greater credibility, the significance of organizational influences on human behavior became a focus for effective leadership. Contingency management requires a flexible approach in attempting to integrate the needs of the organization and the needs of individuals. In the field of student affairs, there has been more emphasis on understanding human behavior and less interest on the analysis of organizational behavior. In order to meet the changing needs of the future in higher education, however, an understanding of the process of organization development, as facilitated by the flexible orientation of contingency management, is required.

An application of the aspects of organization development has been applied to the field of student affairs (Borland 1980). A five step process was detailed for the integration of institutional, student, and professional goals in colleges and

universities. The first step of clarifying the varying·and
often conflicting goals of the various constituencies in any
institution of higher education is vital for organizational
success. These goals become the standards by which organizational, individual, and professional progress (success or
failure) must be evaluated.

The second step in meeting the needs of students in
higher education is a comprehensive and systematic assessment
of the environment in which a particular institution exists.
This assessment should consider both the formal and informal
aspects of the institution, including student characteristics,
structural components, and personnel elements, as well as
the interactive relationships among these factors. Included
in this administrative assessment should be consideration
of both the assets and liabilities provided by student development programs, as well as an evaluation of the resources and
barriers which exist within an institution that will facilitate
or impede the success of student development programs.

The final three steps of this organizational process
move the standard goals and environmental assessment to implementation. The third step is the selection of the strategy
by which these goals and environmental factors should be
implemented. This strategy, then, is reduced in the fourth
step to the planning of specific tactics by which the strategy
will be administered. The final step is the construction of
specific objectives by which progress toward the original
goals may be measured. This last step also provides the feedback requirement of systems theory, by which the continuing
organizational and administrative process is refined, corrected,
and again implemented.

Administrative Processes

The administrative implementation of the organizational
plan above requires specific knowledge and skills in a variety
of areas. The everchanging environment in which higher education
and student affairs find themselves currently requires an ever-
expanding diversity of administrative skills. These skills
in the future will require student affairs professional activity

278

from counseling to collective bargaining and from sensitivity training to cost/benefit analysis.

While the following chapter discusses the administrative areas of planning, budgeting, and evaluation of student affairs programs, this chapter will conclude with brief discussions of organization development processes, management by objectives, and collective bargaining, which will become additional activities of the future for most student affairs professionals.

Organization development processes -

There are a variety of specific skills that are utilized in understanding and implementing organization development. Among these techniques are counseling, power analysis, sensitivity training, reorganization, confrontation, consultation, cost/benefit analysis, and therapy groups. Within this brief list are skills that have been included in the traditional programs of professional preparation for student affairs personnel, but also included are new skills in which each professional must be prepared in the future. These skills in differing combinations are used in facilitating organization development, as indicated by many proponents such as Beckhard (1969), Fordyce and Weil (1971), French and Bell (1973), and Sikes, Schlesinger, and Seashore (1974).

Among the general activities in which these skills are used are: (1) third party facilitation - in which external intervention brings an objective perspective often necessary to resolve problems among those working closely together; (2) goal setting - in which the clear delineation of direction and methods for achieving that direction is specific both for the institution and its subsystems; (3) education and training - in which the application of instructional methods can lead to productive organizational activity; (4) interpersonal relations - in which an analysis is conducted into the role and personality factors in organizational interaction; and (5) team building - in which a specific subsystem's activity is analyzed and structural and interpersonal linkages are developed to increase efficiency, effectiveness, and satisfaction. There are many other activities that should be created

279

uniquely for the particular environment of any specific campus.

Management by objectives (MBO) -

Management by objectives is a specific technique, which
was introduced in the business sector, and has gained some
acceptance in higher education. The technique was introduced
by Drucker (1954); refined by others, such as Odiorne (1965);
applied to higher education by Deegan and Fritz (1975) among
others; and, applied to student affairs by Harvey (1972).

The MBO system builds upon both systems theory and on
contemporary theories of leadership/management. MBO provides
the evaluative feedback communication conduit required for a
self correcting system by specifying particular behavior and
levels of performance for both the individual and the organization. Its principles are based on the comprehensive leadership theories, which express confidence in one's subordinates,
such as McGregor's Theory Y leader, Herzberg's motivation-
seeking leader, Argyris' mature leader, and Likert's System 4
leader.

These principles as analyzed by Harvey (1972) include the
tenets that: (1) MBO cannot be imposed; (2) responsibility
and involvement must be shared by all participants; (3) those
responsible for a specific objective must be the ones to
construct it; (4) immediate institutional problems cannot be
solved by MBO; (5) a long term commitment in numbers of years
is required for success; (6) both organizational and individuals'
needs must be met; and (7) it requires the characteristics of
flexibility, discipline, perserverance, and individuality.
Harvey analyzed MBO further by indicating its advantages and
disadvantages, which on balance would seem to favor such an
administrative approach. The primary failure of most attempts
at MBO is that the principles are not followed or are misapplied
for a variety of personal and professional reasons.

Finally, the construction of the objective is vital for
success of this process. Rather than a general statement of
hopes or desires, an accurately constructed objective must
include all of the following elements: (1) identification of

the target population to be affected by the objective; (2) the
specific behavior to be performed; (3) the minimum measurable
level for that behavior; (4) the time limit in which the
behavior must be performed; and (5) the institutional commitment of resources to be directed toward achievement of the
objective. Each goal would be measured by a series of qualitative and quantitative objectives that are measurable, consistent,
ethical, and achievable. In this manner each leader, subordinate,
and superordinate, as well as the institution itself, would
exist in a symbiotic relationship that could lead most clearly
to desired results in an environment that requires specific
accountability.

Collective bargaining -

One of the most recent trends in contemporary higher
education is the movement to embrace the trade union model of
employer and employee relationships. The entire area of personnel
administration is one that student affairs personnel often
have left to "the administration". In the professional environment stressing the human development of students, student affairs
professionals often neglected the human development of institutional colleagues at both the professional and classified levels.
This was disturbing particularly because many of the basic skills
needed for effective personnel administration are an integral
part of traditional student affairs preparation programs and
an integral part of the behavior of student affairs professionals
when working with students.

At this writing approximately 20 percent of institutions
of higher education are involved with collective bargaining,
including many student affairs professionals. There are basic
principles of personnel administration that would make the
formalization of employee relations under the system of collective
bargaining unnecessary in higher education generally (Borland
1976) and in community colleges specifically (Borland 1977b).
The basis for these principles primarily is to view employee
relationships with the same concern and reverence that the
student affairs profession has viewed student relationships.
Specific actions that are recommended include becoming knowledgeable about collective bargaining, reviewing current practices

281

and procedures with employees, taking affirmative action on behalf of employees, and facilitating employee interaction in total institutional process, especially within a formal communication process. These administrative and human development behaviors may forestall the necessity of intervention by third parties through organization of labor unions.

If the facilitation of human development is a goal for the student affairs profession for employees, as well as for students, acceptance of the employees' formal decision to be represented by a collective bargaining agent must be implemented. Specific guidelines for professional action in such a situation have been provided by Borland (1979). Three specific roles for student affairs professionals described were as: (1) mediator between the various employee groups regarding the impact on students that a particular contract or clause might have; (2) negotiator as part of either the negotiating team itself or at least as part of the support teams to be sure that student interests are considered in a contract; and (3) consultant using human relations skills to facilitate acceptance of the new relationships that collective bargaining will generate.

The consequences of collective bargaining on campus could be impediments or facilitators of student development goals. If the process of formalized employment relationships and the resulting negotiations is divisive, students could be injured by such consequences as divisions between faculty and counselors or higher tuition required to meet the costs of a contract. The effects of one strike by student affairs professionals for example, were not facilitative of student development goals (Borland, MacLean, White, and Scott 1979). Conversely, if the three roles described above are performed effectively by student affairs professionals, consideration of student needs in the construction of the contract or in its administration may actually benefit both students and the student affairs profession. For example, if the student development goal of integration of student affairs and academic affairs is to be realized, inclusion of the concept in the faculty contract clause on workload would make that integration a legally enforceable condition.

In conclusion, the analysis of management and leadership here may lead student affairs professionals to see these concepts as independent activities, skills, and processes, each attempting to facilitate student development. In reality, however, the various leadership theories and administrative processes are interdependent, if success is to be achieved. The flexibility of contingency theories and the processes of organization development, MBO, and collective bargaining actually can be supportive of each other as well as of students, staff, and the institution itself.

REFERENCES

Argyris, C. Integrating the Individual and the Organization.
    New York: Wiley, 1964.

Baldridge, J. V. Power and Conflict in the University.
    New York: Wiley, 1971.

Beckhard, R. Organization Development: Strategies and Models.
    Reading, Massachusetts: Addison-Wesley, 1969.

Borland, D. T. "Employee Relations Without Collective Bargaining,"
    Journal of the College and University Personnel Association
    27: 35-39, April/May, 1976.

Borland, D. T. "Aggressive Neglect, Matrix Organization, and
    Student Development Implementation," Journal of College
    Student Personnel 18: 452-461, November, 1977a.

Borland, D. T. "Gaining the Initiative in Collective Bargaining,"
    Community College Frontiers 5: 10-15, Summer, 1977b.

Borland, D. T. Collective Bargaining and Student Affairs:
    Guidelines for Professional Action - NASPA Journal 16:
    1-42, Winter, 1979.

Borland, D. T.; MacLean, S.; White, B. C.; and Scott, J. E.
    "Student Affairs on Strike: A Descriptive Analysis,"
    Journal of College Student Personnel 20: 202-208, May, 1979.

Borland, D. T. "Organization Development: A Professional
    Imperative." D. G. Creamer (ed.), In Student Development
    in Higher Education: Theories, Practices, and Future
    Directions. Cincinnati: ACPA, 1980.

Deegan, A. X. and Fritz, R. J. MBO Goes to College. Boulder:
    University of Colorado, 1975.

Drucker, P. F. The Practice of Management. New York: Harper
    and Row, 1954.

Fordyce, J. K. and Weil, F. Managing with People: A Manager's Handbook of Organization Development Methods. Reading, Massachusetts: Addison-Wesley, 1971.

French, W. L. and Bell, C. H. Organization Development. Englewood Cliffs, N. J.: Prentice-Hall, 1973.

Hersey, P. and Blanchard, K. H. Management of Organizational Behavior: Utilizing Human Resources. Englewood Cliffs, N. J.: Prentice-Hall, 1977.

Harvey, L. J. "Administration by Objectives in Student Personnel Programs," Journal of College Student Personnel 13: 293-296, July, 1972.

Herzberg, F. Work and the Nature of Man. New York: World Publishing, 1966.

Katz, D. and Kahn, R. L. The Social Psychology of Organizations. New York: Wiley, 1978.

Likert, R. New Patterns of Management. New York: McGraw-Hill, 1961.

McGregor, D. The Human Side of Enterprise. New York: McGraw-Hill, 1960.

Odiorne, G. S. Management by Objectives. New York: Pittman, 1965.

Sikes, W. W.; Schlesinger, L. E.; and Seashore, C. N. Renewing Higher Education from Within. San Francisco: Jossey-Bass, 1974.

CHAPTER 31

PLANNING, BUDGETING, AND EVALUATION
IN STUDENT AFFAIRS PROGRAMS:

A MANUAL FOR ADMINISTRATORS

Richard L. Harpel

AN OVERVIEW OF ACCOUNTABILITY

Management involves the combining of resources and activities
in such a way as to produce a desired outcome. The simplicity of
this statement could lead one to believe that management is a
fairly straightforward process. The task of management in higher
education, however, is far from straightforward. The difficulty
of the task is a function of the complexity of the desired outcome. While it is true that scarcity of financial resources is
a major problem in higher education today, a more fundamental
problem is the lack of management skills in the profession. In
other words, while increased financial resources could solve many
problems for struggling schools and colleges, the effective use
of these resources can in no way be guaranteed given current higher
education management practices.

Student Affairs administrators are particularly vulnerable
when it comes to management skills. Student Affairs services have
long been justified more on idealistic and humanitarian grounds
than on tangible evidence of impact or outcomes. Such arguments,
while necessary, are no longer sufficient to justify a large investment of institutional resources. The Student Affairs administrator must become a skilled manager in order to compete for
these resources. Added to a sound philosophical rationale for
Student Affairs services must be planning skills, budgeting competence, and evaluation expertise -- all notably lacking in the
current training of professionals. We have entered into a new
era of accountability.

Being accountable means being a good steward. We have been
entrusted with physical and financial resources as well as a responsible role in the development of young people. It is not

This manual was developed by the Division of Research and Program
Development of the National Association of Student Personnel Administrators, 1976.

unreasonable that we should be called upon periodically to account for our stewardship. Recently, demands for accountability in higher education have become much more sepcific and systematic in nature. They have taken the form of such questions as:

a) What student needs are met by your servcies?
b) What are your goals and objectives?
c) What are the outcomes and products of your activity?
d) What are the true costs of your activity?

The purpose of this chapter is to assist student affairs administrators in becoming better managers and thus more accountable. Drawing on several management models designed to assist in decision-making, resource allocation, and evaluation, this manual provides a step-by-step ("cookbook") set of procedures which can be used as a guide for implementing an accountability system at the Student Affairs level at an institution.

The management concept upon which this chapter is based is composed of the following major elements and is illustrated in Figure 1:

--Identifying a Need or Problem
--Assessment of Environmental Constraints
    --Social
    --Economic
    --Political
    --Legal
--Stating Program Goals
--Defining Program Objectives
--Translating the Plan into a Set of Activities
--Clustering Related Activities Under Program Headings
--Allocating Resources (Budgeting) to Programs
--Evaluation of Results

While each of these elements may be operating to some extent on most campuses, they are often performed independently of one another. This chapter should assist in relating each of the elements into a meaningful system - one which is an iterative process and which allows for program growth and flexibility as conditions and needs change. It should be recognized that the development of the management system is as much an art as it is a science, and may take several months:

> One could spend many months and even years trying to develop the 'perfect' program structure before implementation, but such a perfect program structure does not exist anyway, and since it is best to try to come up with something reasonably soon, get it into operation, and then let it evolve over time. (1)

In developing this manual, the Division of Research and Program Development of the National Association of Student Personnel Administrators is aware that the application of an impersonal management model can often gloss over much of the subjective and personal nature of Student Affairs activities. The outcomes of counseling, for example, are not easily quantified and attempts to develop proxy outcome measures (such as contact hours) can be extremely artificial and inadequate. Furthermore, the Research Division recognizes that the significant cost in terms of time and effort which such a system represents can be prohibitive for many colleges. Indeed the danger exists for the accountability procedures themselves to develop into the "tail which wags the dog." And finally, it must be recognized that even though accountability procedures are rational and systematic, the environment in which we work is often irrational and highly political in nature.

In spite of the potential negative aspects associated with the accountability systems, the Research Division believes that these are outweighed by the potential benefits. In a national survey conducted in 1974 by the Research Division (Harpel, 1975), it was determined that the following benefits accrue to those institutions which had implemented accountability efforts:

a) a new sense of direction and purpose had been developed among the Student Affairs staff;
b) evaluation feedback was made available to professional staff for program development;
c) unmet needs of staff and students were identified;
d) more external recognition and visibility of Student Affairs activities were gained;
e) in many cases, increased financial support was received.

The procedures outlined here are not meant to replace student development theories, but to provide a framework in which these theories can be articulated. It must be emphasized again that accountability systems should be regarded as tools and the effective used of a tool depends greatly upon the skill of the user. The manual is simply a guide. Although it has been derived from actual institutional experiences, it is meant to apply to all types of post-secondary settings. The user should freely modify the model to best fit their own institution.

PLANNING

Identification of a Need or Problem

For Student Affairs administrators, the identification of a need can be both a theoretical and an empirical exercise. Student development theories may vary, but all agree on the point that the college years represent a critical period in the physical, emotional, and intellectual development of young people. Furthermore, there is common agreement that the college environment itself represents a set of stresses which are unrepresentative of the environments from which students come. Taking into account psychological and sociological research, Student Affairs administrators can reach general conclusions concerning student needs and can make use of general taxonomies which will assist in program planning and development. Major contributions to the understanding of human learning and development can be found in the concepts od developmental tasks (Havighurst, 1961), stages of development (Erickson, 1963), growth trends (Sanford, 1962), hierarchy of needs (Maslow, 1970), vectors of development (Chickering, 1969), and many others.

It is essential, however, that the statement of needs which is to adequately serve as a sound basis for Student Affairs programs must be stated in more specific terms than general theory. Furthermore, the statement must be free from jargon or "in house" language which fails to communicate to the general public or other members of the campus community. To avoid generalities and develop a statement of needs which relates to reality, the Student Affairs staff should focus on the population to be served both through systematic research and by observation.

> Guideline 1: Define the need to be met by a comprehensive and accurate description of the Target Population to be served.

In defining the target population, one must be careful to remember that Student Affairs professionals operate in an institution of higher learning, not a hospital or mental health clinic or employment agency. This factor will be discussed further in the next section. It cannot be emphasized too much, however, since a needs statement cannot encompass the complete range of human needs. It must focus on the student as a student - a learner in an educational environment where the instructional function is primary.

A needs statement should be short and to the point and should include the following elements:

a) description of the social and cultural uniqueness of the target population;
b) description of the academic aptitude and achievement of the target population;
c) description of the likely barriers to success in the educational environment;
d) assessment of the ability of the institution to effectively satisfy the needs of the target population.

Not until a need is identified and described can a reality-based goal statement be produced. It is the meeting of the needs of the target population which is the ultimate test of the worth of a program. It is possible to have goal statements, objectives, and even measured outcomes which bear little or no relationship to the true needs of the students. More often than not, this is true because we have started the planning process without determining what we are planning for.

A number of standardized instruments are available to assist in this needs-assessment process. They include such instruments as:

American Council on Education (ACE) and U. C. L. A. Freshman Questionnaire, Alexander Astin, Center for the Study of Evaluation, U. C. L. A.

College and University Environment Scale (CUES), Educational Testing Service, Princeton, N. J., 2nd edition.

College Student Questionnaire (CSQ), Educational Testing Service, Princeton, N. J.

Omnibus Personality Inventory (OPI), Center for Research and Development in Higher Education, University of California (now Center for Research and Development in Higher Education), Berkeley.

Higher Education Measurement and Evaluation Kit (KIT), Robert Pace, Center for the Study of Evaluation, U. C. L. A.

College Characteristics Inventory (CCI), Psychological Testing Service, Syracuse University.

Institutional Functioning Inventory (IFI), Educational Testing Service, Princeton, N. J.

Institutional Goals Inventory (IGI), Educational Testing Service, Princeton, N. J.

Institutional Self-Study, American College Testing, Iowa City, Iowa.

Outcome Measures and Procedures Manual (OMPM), National Center for Higher Education Management Systems (NCHEMS), Boulder, Colorado.

While the advantages of standardized instruments are the provision of machine scoring services and the availability of normative data, many institutions have developed their own questionnaires which are less expensive to administer and very adequate for their purposes.

The combination of student questionnaire responses with information already gathered during the administrative process (test scores, high school rank, and other demographic data) will begin to produce a profile of student needs and characteristics which will provide the basis of a needs statement.

The directors of the minority student support programs at one institution produced the following statement which might serve as an example of a description of their target population:

> Example: The target population served by the Educational Opportunity Programs (EOP) differs from the traditional University population in its socio-economic background, educational preparation, and ethnic, cultural, and linguistic heritage. As a consequence, the EOP student is faced with special barriers which impair his educational progress. The removal of these barriers has not previously been addressed by the traditional University support services. These barriers include academic skill deficiencies, financial insecurity, cultural and social isolation within the University environment, and uncertainty regarding their future.

Assessing Environmental Constraints

Student Affairs professionals enjoy a somewhat unique relationship with students within the academic community. The bulk of their student contacts are outside the classroom and are related primarily to social, emotional, and other non-academic issues. Both through their training and their campus roles, student affairs professionals are taught to view the student as a whole person.

Recent literature has focused on the issue that student development is an interactive process between the person and the environment, and that change takes place as much through the manipulation of the environment as through attempts to influence the person (Crookston, 1975, Kaiser, 1975, Banning, 1973). Nevertheless, along with this new focus on the environment has come an increased awareness by many student affairs professionals that they are in control of very few environmental factors which influence students.

A Division of Student Affairs on a college campus is just one sub-environment in a larger environment. The institution itself is just a part of the larger community, which in turn is a part of a state and national system of post-secondary education. As a Dean of Students plans programs to meet student needs, he or she must understand the relationship of these many environments. The ideal program will not always be possible given the environmental constraints surrounding it.

The more thorough and complete the job of student needs assessment, the more critical it becomes to be aware of the environment in which they are manifested. A college campus is not and never will be equipped to meet the complete range of needs which students bring with them. Too often, student affairs planning ignores this fact and expectations are created which are bound to be frustrated.

The college cannot find a job for every graduate, or a scholarship for every applicant. The college cannot promise to straighten every student's teeth, resolve every Oedipus complex, nor even graduate every student who matriculates. The college cannot fulfill all these expectations because, first of all, that is not what a college is all about. Secondly, many factors which produce student needs are beyond the control of the institution.

> Guideline 2: Planning must include a description of the environment and those social, economic, political, and legal constraints on the ways the needs of the target population can be met.

Ideally, many of the environmental constraints would be clearly identified in an institutional statement of purpose. Student Affairs administrators are painfully aware, however, that such statements are insufficient guidelines to planning, if indeed, such a statement exists at all at their institutions. In such cases, the Dean of Students is forced to define the purpose of the institution in the best way possible and proceed in good faith.

The following elements should be included in a description of environmental constraints which relate most directly to Student Affairs programs:

a) Social constraints - social standards and expectations of the students, the community and the alumni, etc.
b) Economic constraints - sources of funding for student personnel programs (general fund v. users fees), high cost of qualified professionals, financial health of the institution, etc.
c) Political constraints - institutional attitudes toward student support services and staff, national preoccupations and priorities (e.g. consumer emphasis, career emphasis), where the Student Affairs Division rests in the "pecking order," etc.
d) Legal constraints - rights of privacy (e.g. Buckley Amendment), civil rights (e.g. Title IX), governance structure (e.g. public v. private), etc.

An analysis of the environment is not necessarily a quantitative exercise, but should yield a comprehensive picture of the environment which might include supportive data or project quantitative results. A careful analysis will increase the likelihood that planning and programming will be reality-based.

Statement of Goals

Those who have labored through the development of goals statements and the writing of objectives which are "measurable" or "behavioral" will testify to the drudgery which is often associated with the task. Almost without exception, however, the evidence shows that such hard work pays off for the organization.

The task usually will start out on an enthusiastic note. People enjoy talking about philosophical issues related to their work. However, when forced to examine the assumptions upon which their goals are based and to relate their goals to those of other parts of the institution, and to specific activities being performed, the task begins to lose some of its spontaneity. Often discussion degenerates to the semantic level and digressive arguments concerning the difference between goals and objectives. Pressed toward closure, however, and the meeting of some deadline for completion most groups are able to produce statements which reflect collective approval and input. The dynamics of this process can be very healthy and open up lines of communication previously neglected.

While "purists" would champion the crucial distinctions between goals and objectives, it is urged that such distinctions not be allowed to sidetrack the process of articulating goals. For the purposes of this chapter, goals are defined as broad abstract statements describing an ideal intent, state, or condition (mager, 1972). A goal statement is a creed or a statement of mission. Objectives, on the other hand, are more specific statements which ideally describe desired behavior in measurable terms and acceptable criteria of performance.

Goal statements must be developed within the context of problem solving, as described in the first two steps (Figure 1). A clear statement of needs and environmental constraints automatically will suggest goals to be achieved. Attempts to define goals independent of this analysis of needs or a study of the target population to be served, usually results in the statements of the personal biases of the student affairs staff which may or may not relate to student or institutional needs.

No single employee within the organization operates outside of the goals or priorities of the organization. The goals of the organization should be the motivating factor for professional and support staff alike, and every activity performed by every staff member should contribute to the achievement of goals. A sense of commitment to and identification with organizational goals, however, can hardly be expected where goals are dictated from above.

While it is true that members of a student affairs staff must operate within an institution with predefined goals, they do have the opportunity to participate in the development and review of sub-goals which apply more specifically to their own activities. To the greatest possible extent, all members of the organization should be involved in this process. Secretaries, for example, sometimes have a more articulate and straightforward sense of

293

mission than many professionals. Given the opportunity, they often can clear away a great deal of the theoretical "fuzziness" and jargon which crop up in goal statements.

Writing goal statements is not an annual event, but review of existing statements can be. Goals, as defined, are long-range, idealistic statements which should hold true over time. But people forget and the annual review can serve as a re-affirmation of "why we are here." In any event, whether writing new goals or reviewing existing goals, several questions may assist in the task:

a) Does the statement assist in describing why we come to work every day?
b) Does the goal describe the ideal result of our activity?
c) Is the goal related to the needs of our target population?
d) Does the goal take into account the environmental constraints (e.g. is it consistent with the purposes of the institution)?

Guideline 3: Goal statements should be long-range, abstract statements describing ideal results, and their development and review should include as many members of the organization as possible.

Referring once more to Figure 1, it must be emphasized that goal development or review is part of a total process. Goal statements are not ends in themselves. They are just part of a more rational, systematic approach toward management - the achievement of desired outcomes. If a Dean of Students embarks on this process, he or she should be prepared to consider the entire process. This is urged for one basic reason: the law of diminishing returns. Accountability can be a threatening concept. The process of examining goals can create stress as old assumptions are challenged and new directions are suggested. A great deal of sensitivity must be exercised by the Dean of Students in this process. Too often, after the effort has overcome resistance and stimulated new enthusiasm (a very frequent by-product of the process), the goals are bound in an unattractive cover and placed on the shelf. Time goes by and the enthusiasm and expectation degenerates into cynicism. To resurrect the goals at some future time or to attempt to begin the process again is not likely to produce a great deal of commitment on the part of a disillusioned staff.

In other words , the Dean of Students or chief student affairs administrator has a responsibility for leadership. If commitment and follow-through is to be expected from the staff, the Dean must set the example.

Stating Objectives

Goals are very difficult to measure. Indeed, if they truly represent the ideal, their achievement should always be just beyond our grasp. We move toward their achievement in incremental steps. These imtermediate levels of success are defined to "operationalize" the goals. They translate goals into actual events. We then generalize from the particular. If such-and-such happens, we believe we are moving toward the achievement of our ideal. These "operational statements" or "intermediate steps" toward the goals are called objectives. If goals are long-range, general statements, then objectives are short-range, specific statements which describe outcomes which we can measure at the end of a finite period of time, say the end of an academic year.

In an ideal world, objectives are descriptive of behavior and are measurable in quantitative terms. Therein lies the rub for most people in student affairs. Many of the outcomes of services in this area are not immediately evident, nor easily measured in quantifiable terms. The recent demand for "quantified," "behavioral" objectives has alienated many student affairs professionals attempting to demonstrate their accountability by writing objectives for their work.

It should be recognized from the beginning that campus environments are not the "ideal world." Student affairs objectives are difficult to quantify. This does not mean however, that objectives cannot be measured. Measurement may have to be stated in narrative form instead of numbers, but measurement can and must take place. A description of a changed condition may be as effective a measurement of an objective as quantitative increases or decreases.

> Guideline 4: Objectives should describe some terminal condition or behavior. (How do you know when you get there?)
> Objectives should define some criterion of acceptable performance. (How much of what is enough?)

In writing objectives, a friendly caution is offered to avoid the use of at least two verbs - provide and facilitate. While those two words convey an intuitive meaning to most student affairs professionals, almost nothing is communicated about outcomes. If, for example, the objective of the Counseling Center is "to provide services for student growth and development," the mere existence of the Center meets the objective. Services are being provided, and that is all which was expected. Nothing is suggested as to the expected outcome of those services.

Similarly, the Counseling Center may describe its objective

"to facilitate student growth and development within the campus environment." Once again, almost any activity could be said to be facilitative. It would be more informative to describe the ideal outcome toward which the facilitation is directed than to suggest facilitation is an end in itself.

This is not to imply that there are perfect objective statements. However, as stated in the guidelines, we are striving as nearly as possible to describe some terminal condition or behavior. In doing so, try to use words which suggest something will get done, such as: produce, start, design, train, complete, implement.

TABLE 1: Sample Goal and Objectives for Student Affairs Programs

Target Population:
All matriculated students at out institution. At a more specific level, certain sub-populations of students with special needs such as adult students, minority students, commuters, veterans.

Needs Analysis:
Studies at our institution have produced the following catagories of needs: a) financial needs; b) physical needs; c) educational deficiencies; d) personal adjustment needs; e) career and vocational needs.

Goal Statement:
The GOAL of the Division of Student Affairs is to assist students in eliminating obstacles which interrupt their educational progress and to broaden students' opportunities for personal, social, cultural, and intellectual development within the campus environment.

Objectives:
a) To improve students' basic skills required for the selection and achievement of educational goals.
Terminal Bahavior: Overcoming of some skill deficiency and/or the selection of degree objective.
Acceptable Criteria: "X" increase in skill competency. Selection of major by the beginning of the Junior year.

b) To supplement the financial resources of students with financial need.
Terminal Condition: The elimination of financial need of all applicants who qualify.

b) Acceptable Criteria: No delay in educational progress due to financial inability to pay.

c) To assist students in their selection and pursuit of career and vocational choices.
   Terminal Behavior: Selection of a satisfying job or post-graduate option.
   Acceptable Criteria: Increased congruence between measured ability, interest, and reported satisfaction with career choice for graduates.

d) To improve students' basic skills required for personal, social, cultural growth and development.
   Terminal Conditions: Demonstrated ability to productively engage in human relationships; expressed positive self-concept; internalized set of values; demonstrated ability to manage emotions; demonstrated ability to make choices.
   Acceptable Criteria: "X" reduction in educational delays due to social or emotional stress. "X" reduction in incidents of interpersonal conflicts. "X" increase in intercultural activities and participation.

Finally, if objectives are things for which we may be held accountable, then they must describe desired outcomes over which we have control. An objective of a balanced institutional budget is not something for which the Dean of Students should be held accountable; a balanced student affairs budget is. Student affairs professionals are not soley responsible for the quality of mental health of students on campus. To look at some objectives of counselors, however, one would discover that many are willing to be held soley accountable for the outcomes in this area. Objectives must be realistic and limited to our capabilities. Table 1 is provided as an example of how the first draft of a student affairs goal statement and set of objectives might appear.

Plan of Action

Now that we know where we want to go, we must decide how we want to get there. This step can be approached either from the standpoint of developing activities which have never been done before, or the review of activities that have been done for a long time. As with goals, we are usually not starting from "scratch." We are beginning to take a new look at a broad range of activities which have grown up over time. In either case, we are examining the relationship between activities and objectives. This process can be extremely revealing. Activities may be discovered which are being duplicated across departments. Activities which are vital to the accomplishment of certain objectives may not be performed at all. Other activities which are being performed bear no relationship whatsoever to the stated goals or objectives.

The purpose of this step is to relate all activities being performed in the Division of Student Affairs to the stated objectives. Since activity represents dollars, time, and energy, any activities which do not contribute to the achievement of an objective should be discontinued. Duplication of effort is not necessarily bad; only future evaluation of outcomes can suggest whether or not consolidation of effort is wise. It is not unusual for more than one department in an organizational structure to be contributing to the same objective in unique ways.

> Guideline 5: Activities should bear a direct, logical relationship to the goals and objectives of the organization.

This arranging of activities under stated objectives is a crucial exercise leading to the next step in the management sequence described in Figure 1.

The Program Structure

The program structure is the key to the management system suggested in this chapter. It provides a new way of looking at our organization. Normally, we view ourselves through an organization chart which illustrates which departmental units report to managers, who in turn, report to offices and managers up the line. The program structure illustrates the organization from the standpoint of objectives. Since objectives refer to expected outcomes, the program structure arranges the organization in such a way as to describe resources and activities required to achieve these outcomes.

For the purpose of this manual, a "program" is described as a logical cluster of activities and resources serving a common objective. The "name" of each program is suggested by its objective. For example, the cluster of activities which are performed to achieve the objective "to supplement financial resources of students with financial need," might be named the Financial Assistance Program. In a typical Student Affairs Division, we might find that several departments within the Division contribute in part to the activities in that program, e.g. Financial Aid Office, Student Employment Office, Veterans Office. An extremely helpful resource in understanding program structure is Technical Report 27, Program Classification Structure, by Warren W. Gulks, National Center for Higher Education Management Systems, Boulder, Colorado.

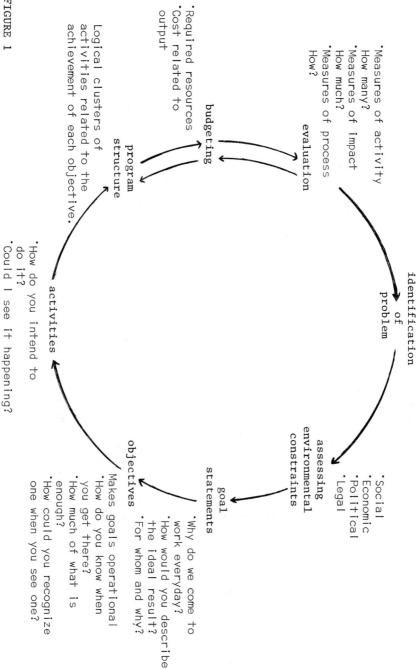

*Measures of activity
 How many?
*Measures of impact
 How much?
*Measures of process
 How?

evaluation

*Required resources
*Cost related to
 output

budgeting

Logical clusters of
activities related to the
achievement of each objective.

program
structure

*How do you intend to
 do it?
*Could I see it happening?

activities

identification
of
problem

assessing
environmental
constraints

*Social
*Economic
*Political
*Legal

goal
statements

*Why do we come to
 work everyday?
*How would you describe
 the ideal result?
*For whom and why?

objectives

Makes goals operational
*How do you know when
 you get there?
*How much of what is
 enough?
*How could you recognize
 one when you see one?

298a

FIGURE 1

To illustrate further the contrast of program structure with organization structure, refer to Figures 2 and 3.

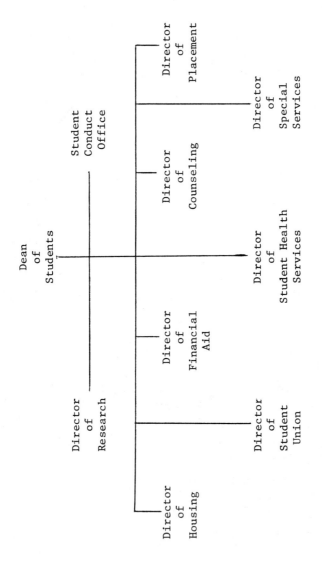

FIGURE 2 – STUDENT AFFAIRS ORGANIZATIONAL CHART (example)

298b

Student
Affairs

Educational Support Program	Financial Assistance Program	Career and Vocational Planning Program	Student Development Program
Includes activities in the offices of:	Includes activities in the offices of:	Includes activities in the offices of:	Includes activities in the offices of:
Counseling Housing Special Services	Financial Aid Special Services	Placement Counseling Housing	Counseling Student Conduct Student Health Special Services Student Union Housing

298c

FIGURE 3 - STUDENT AFFAIRS PROGRAM CHART (example)

An organization chart reflects a political and social order within the organization. Given the mix of certain personalities, the existing organizational structure is often time-tested and proven to be the best way to get things done for the time being. A program structure is a theoretical model built around desired outcomes. It is not necessary that the organizational structure match the program structure. The allocation of resources and activity can be reflected by either program or department. Table 2 illustrates the clustering of activities to form a program structure.

Table 2
STUDENT AFFAIRS PROGRAM STRUCTURE

Goal Statement: The GOAL of the Division of Student Affairs is to assist students in eliminating obstacles which interrupt their educational progress and to broaden students' opportunities for personal, social, cultural, and intellectual development within the campus environment.

Program	Activities
I. Educational Support Objective: to improve students' basic skills required for the selection and achievement of educational goals.	1. Academic Advising 2. Curriculum Development 3. Tutoring 4. Instruction (teaching) 5. Reading and Study and Skills Training
II. Financial Assistance Program Objective: to supplement the financial resources of students with financial need.	1. Application and Data Processing 2. Need Assessment & Awards 3. Federal & State Reporting 4. Emergency Loans 5. Financial Aid Info Service
III. Career and Vocational Planning Program Objective: to assist students in their selection and pursuit of career and vocational choices.	1. Career Counseling 2. Career Placement 3. Job Development 4. Vocational Research
IV. Student Development Program Objective: to improve students' basic skills required for personal, social, and cultural growth and development.	1. Personal Counseling 2. Social/Recreational Activities 3. Cultural Activities 4. New Student Orientation 5. Residential Programs 6. Interpersonal Skills Workshops

Guideline 6:   The Program Structure should describe an organi-
               zation in terms of clusters of activities performed
               to achieve stated goals, illustrating both what is
               done in the organization and why.

The list of activities in Table 2 will vary for each campus.
The list should be as complete and comprehensive as possible and
clear enough to describe to the average layman (e.g., parent,
legislator) exactly what is done. One point should be made
concerning administrative activities. It will be noted that
activities such as staff meetings, which consume so much time,
are not included in the list of activities. If the activities are
to be a description of the allocation of effort, administrative
time and effort either can be added to each program as another
activity, or prorated across the others. Either method is acceptable.

BUDGETING

Budgeting is the allocation of resources to various activities
for their accomplishment. Budgeting implies commitment and a sense
of priorities. When it comes to providing money and people, we are
placing our faith in our planning and stepping out on that faith.
Budgeting represents priorities in that there are never enough
resources to do everything we want to do. So when we finally
decide to commit resources to one activity, something else must go
unfunded. A budget is a statement of what we think is _most_ important, or _most_ likely to produce the results which we desire.

Types of Budgeting

It is not the purpose of this manual to explore theories of
budgeting in detail. It is important to note, however, that a
type of budgeting is being suggested here that differs fundament-
ally from the common approach. The current style of budgeting
generally is an incremental approach: "X" more dollars of FTE than
what we have now. Each year we seek to add on an extra position or
amount of money to do this or that new thing or lighten an increasing work burden on existing staff. The focus is on more
resources (inputs) to do more things. Rarely, if ever, are resources shifted from some other activity to devote to this new
priority. This would mean that something currently done would
have to be discontinued--a very painful decision, and generally
avoided.

Program budgeting is quite different than incremental budgeting. It is "zero based" in the sense that it assumes nothing
and builds its case. It does not start with the assumption that
last year's budget is a fixed base to which we can add more

resources. It begins with an objective, a desired outcome, and describes the resources necessary to achieve that outcome. The focus of a program budget is on outcomes rather than inputs.

An incremental budget is generally expressed in a line-item format, i.e., a line showing how many staff in the organizational unit, a line showing how many hourly staff, a line for supplies and expenses, a line for travel. A program budget combines the proportion of each of these resources (people, dollars, travel) which is devoted to each program (or objective). It describes the unique combination of each type of resource necessary to achieve each objective.

Anyone should be able to inspect a program budget and see the relationship between goals, objectives, activities, resources, and outcomes. A program budget should describe exactly how the addition of an FTE or dollars will result in increased efficiency or effectiveness. The relationship between resources (inputs) and outcomes has never been very apparent in an incremental budget.

> Guideline 7: A budget should be a plan which allocates resources, orders and gives priority to various activities, and relates resources to outcomes.

Building a Program Budget

A program budget adds up to the same number of dollars and FTE staff which our line-item budget does. It just arranges these resources in a more meaningful format. Building a program budget entails a "crossover" from the existing account structure to a program structure.

> Step 1 - The first step is to assign to each activity the proportion of staff time and operational dollars spent on that activity in a given year. This may be done in a variety of ways. Staff members may be asked to estimate what percentage of time they spend on each activity by means of an annual Staff Activity Analysis Form. Monthly statements on budget accounts can be inspected to analyze general categories of expenditures to be assigned to various activities. More systematic logs can be kept by staff members throughout the year to provide a more "empirical" estimate of time spent on various activities. Whatever the method used, the purpose of this step is to begin to reflect the costs associated with each activity. Table 3 provides a sample form which might be used by each departmental unit.

Table 3

Departmental Form for Assignment of
Percent of Staff Effort to Programs

Department: Financial Aid

Staff	FTE	Salary	Programs							
			Educational Support		Financial Assistance		Career and Vocational Planning		Student Development	
			FTE	$	FTE	$	FTE	$	FTE	$
Director	1.00	18,000			.85	15,300	.10	1,600	.15	2,700
Asst. Dir.	1.00	16,000			.90	14,400				
Counselor	1.00	11,500			1.00	11,500				
etc.										
Totals										

298g

Table 3 provides a level of detail which describes only the program breakdowns. If desired, another table could be developed for each program to describe the allocation of effort at the activity level.

Step 2 - The next step is to transfer the assigned FTE and dollars to the program structure format as illustrated in Table 4. As has been pointed out, the FTE and dollar sub-totals for each program may represent pieces of several departmental budgets identified as contributions to that particular program. The grand totals, however, should equal the total budget for the Student Affairs Division.

When completed, a program budget similar to that in Table 4 will allow for the comparison of program costs within a Division of Student Affairs or even activities within programs. For example, it takes 6.60 FTE at this sample institution to perform the function of "application processing" and total of $57,580. This process turns out to be the most expensive activity in the Financial Assistance Program. Whether or not this amount is too high or too low must be determined by evaluation, but at least the costs are identified.

Combining these costs with some measure of activity (e.g., number of applications processed) can yield a unit cost of output, or, in this case, the cost of each application processed. The resources needed to produce a certain increased output can be more accurately assessed, as well as the consequences of a budget cut.

Program Accounting

A method of simplifying the crossover to a program budget is to develop an accounting system which will more closely match programs and activities. In this way, the monthly statements of account begin to serve as program reports and hand calculations are minimized or eliminated.

For example, all offices which fall into the Educational Support Program may be assigned account numbers in 1100-1109 series. Offices in the Financial Assistance Program might then be assigned accounts in 1110-1119 series, and so on.

See Table 4 - Page 302f

Only in the case of offices which serve more than one program would there be the necessity to adjust the monthly statement of account to properly assign costs to the other programs.

Table 4

Program Budget for Division of Student Affairs

Goal Statement: The MISSION of the Division of Student Affairs is to assist students in eliminating obstacles which interrupt their educational progress and to broaden students' opportunities for personal, social, cultural, and intellectual development within the campus environment.

Programs	Activities		BUDGET			
		FTE	Staff Salaries	Hourly Wages	Supply & Expense	Totals
I. Financial Assistance Objective: to supplement the financial resources of students with financial need.	1) Application processing.	6.60	49,600	980	7,000	57,580
	2) Need assessment and awards.	2.75	32,250	250	5,200	37,700
	3) Federal and state Reporting.	.45	3,690	620	1,000	5,310
	4) Personal budget advising.	1.85	14,720	135	3,000	17,855
	5) Emergency loans	.90	5,100	75	500	5,675
	6) Financial aid information service.	1.00	5,940	420	1,700	8,000
	SUBTOTALS	13.55	111,300	2,480	18,400	132,180

EVALUATION

Operations Indicators
1) No. of applicants
2) No. of awards
3) No. of students with unmet needs

Import Indicators
1) % of qualified applicants who receive aid
2) No. of students who withdrew from University due to financial difficulties

Only in the case of offices which serve more than one program would there by the necessity to adjust the monthly statement of account to properly assign costs to the other programs.

EVALUATION

It is left to another monograph to cover more adequately the
subject of evaluation. The measurement of outcomes in higher
education is of great concern to administrators, parents, faculty,
and students alike. It is also an area which is complex and
handicapped by ambiguity and a lack of explicit measures. Yet
evaluation remains as perhaps the most critical element in the
entire management process. Outcome information is the only means
by which corrective action can be taken or by which new planning
can take place. Without information concerning outcomes, continuously "reinvent the wheel," expend resources blindly, and run the
risk of disillusioning both students and ourselves.

Evaluation can take many forms and the Dean of Students need
not be a measurement expert to obtain valuable feedback concerning
program effects. Lack of energy to make the effort is a more
common shortcoming among Deans, than a lack of technical skills.
Even random interviews with student consumers is more valuable than
no information at all.

Another major problem in evaluation besides a lack of energy is
the difficulty of evaluating an effort for which there is no clear
objective. In such a case, outcomes are either overlooked or any
outcome if found acceptable. When objectives are clearly stated
and there is a clear sense of purpose, evaluation becomes considerably easier.

For the purpose of this manual, evaluation is limited to the
simplest measures necessary to answer basic questions concerning
student services. How many students are you serving? Are students
satisfied with the services they receive? Are you achieving your
objectives? Are you achieving these objectives at the least cost?
For a fuller discussion of measuring outcomes in higher education,
an excellent reference is the Outcomes Measures and Procedures Manual
by Micek, Service, and Lee of the National Center for Higher Education Management Systems.

Types of Indicators

For purposes of the management model described in this manual,
two basic types of measures are suggested:

1) measures of activity (e.g. how many students served, how
   many applications processed.)
2) measures of impact (e.g. increased skills, reduction of
   conflict, increased occupancy.)

Unfortunately, most evaluation efforts appear to stop with the measurement of activity. Counting noses is important but does not describe a change in behavior or a new set of conditions which result from our activity. Admittedly, it is easier to measure activity than it is to measure impact. If we truly believe, however, that quality is as important as quantity in higher education, then we will continue to make every effort to improve our ability to measure impacts.

A very helpful introduction to the topic of outcomes is Technical Report 40, Sidney S. Micek, and Robert A. Walhaus, An Introduction to the Identification and Uses of Higher Education Outcome Information, National Center for Higher Education Management Systems. In their report, the authors suggest the following criteria for outcome measures (p. 26):

1) the measure must be valid
2) the measure must be reliable
3) the data must be available
4) the data should not cost too much to gather
5) the data should not take too much time to gather
6) the measure must not constitute an invasion of privacy

Both measures of activity and of impact should relate directly to the original objective. Will these measures be genuine evidence that the objective has been met? Often we may feel that certain measures may be flattering while they are unrelated to our original purpose. For example, a tutoring service may experience high frequency of use, but by students who are already high achievers and self-motivated. An evaluation might indicate that low achievers are not using the service. Mere headcount use would not reveal this.

Guideline 8: Evaluation should include both measures of activity and measures of impact which, when related to objectives and costs, will describe the effectiveness and efficiency of programs.

Methods of Evaluation

Evaluation is conducted for a variety of purposes. It can be done in support of a management model or as an in-depth study of a particular project. When measuring activities, evaluation can be rather routine. When measuring impacts, a more thorough study may be appropriate.

The Division of Student Affairs at the University of Colorado has developed a Client Contact System which makes use of a mark sense sheet. A portion of the sheet can be precoded (i.e., department

and program) and the remainder filled in by a secretary or receptionist for every student who uses the services of that particular office.
Different departments can develop their own codes for certain types
of services unique to themselves.

Client contacts are defined as the formal delivery of the preliminary service of each department. These would include those
contacts scheduled by appointment, channeled through a receptionist,
or directly requested by students. Informal, chance meetings with
students which do not actually result in a delivery of a primary
service would not be recorded.

Each semester the data from completed sheets are transferred
to punched cards through an optical scanner. This saves in key-
punching, as well as eliminates one possible source of error.

The student number provides easy access to the campus Student
Term Master File and such data elements as student major, sex, age,
residency, high school rank, test scores, G.P.A., etc. These data
are used to develop an ongoing profile of students who use the
various services.

Data are summarized each semester to show the total number of
student contacts and the number of individual students served by
department and by program. In addition, a complete profile of
student users is generated for each department.

While a client contact system such as that described above will
assist in measuring activity, a more thorough approach is required
for measuring quantitative impacts. Measures of impact may be
studied by use of either institutionally developed instruments or
standardized measures similar to those used in Part II for needs
analysis. The instruments listed there can be used on a follow-up
basis to provide measures of change. In addition, national norms
supplied by the testing agency can be used for comparative purposes.

Obviously, however, not all impacts are of a subjective nature
which must be teased out by questionnaires. An increase in the
securing of jobs by graduating seniors, or the increase in reading
speed and comprehension of students using the learning resource
center are objective measures which can be gathered from records.
The key factor is that impact indicators must be developed and not
ignored. All evidence must be considered in an evaluation, not
just that which is easily gathered. Again, just because objectives
may not be quantifiable, it does not follow that they are not
measureable. A narrative description of change can be very effective.

The management plan described by this manual is not complete without a plan for evaluation. Outcomes must be related to costs in order to measure efficiency and to objectives in order to measure effectiveness. Table 4 is a sample of a completed program plan. The plan includes goals, objectives, program structure, a budget, and measures of activity and impact.

In Conclusion

What has been presented in this manual has been an introduction to the key steps in a management system which is intended to be outcome oriented. The suggested guidelines and procedures are meant to stimulate the thinking and creativity of Student Affairs Professionals as they consider the environment on their own campuses. There is no perfect system and individual modifications to the suggestions can be made. The important thing is to begin.

The system described here is a rational system. One step follows naturally from the previous step and the process is meant to be a cycle. Information gathered through the evaluation should assist in reviewing the goals and objectives (Did we set our sights too high or too low?), the activities and programs (Are we doing the right things to produce change?), and the budget (Do we have the right combination of resources to achieve our goals?). Following corrective action in any of these areas, the cycle begins again.

To claim such a system is rational suggests that management is a science. This is true only to a certain extent. There are too many uncontrolled variables to call management a "science" as in the physical world. Management is also an art.

So we find ourselves with a rational system in an irrational environment--a political environment. As distasteful as they may sound, we all know that it is true. And Deans of Students read to develop their political "skills" as well as their management skills. It is hoped that this manual will assist those responsible for the management of student affairs programs. Improved student affairs management programs will have a positive effect upon the delivery of services, staff morale, and upon the political milieu as well.

References

Banning, J.H. "Program budgeting and classifications systems: An example of their use for counseling centers," WICHE, 1972, No. 5.

References

Banning, J.H. "The ecosystem model: Designing campus environments," WICHE Monograph of Project on Improving Mental Health on Western Campuses, 1973.

Browder, L.H., Jr. Emerging patterns of administrative accountability. Berkeley, California: McCutchan Publishing Co., 1971.

Carnegie Commission on Higher Education. Papers on Efficiency in the management of higher education. New York: McGraw-Hill, September, 1972.

Chickering, A.W. Education and Identity. Jossey-Bass, Inc. Publishers, 1971.

Crookston, B.B., "Milieu management," NASPA Journal, Vol. 13, No. 1, Summer, 1975.

Dilley, F.B. Program budgeting in the university setting, Educational Record, Fall 1966, 474-489.

Dressel, P. "Measuring the benefits of student personnel work," Journal of Higher Education, January 1972.

Crucker, P.F. The Practice of management. New York: Harper & Row, 1954.

Drucker, P.F. Management: Tasks, responsibilities, practices. New York: Harper & Row, 1974.

Erikson, E.H. Childhood and society. New York: Norton, 1963.

Farmer, J. Why planning-programming-budgeting systems for higher education? Boulder, Colorado: Western Interstate Commission for Higher Education, 1970.

Feldman, K.A. and Newcomb, T.M. The impact of college on students. Volume I and II. San Francisco: Jossey-Bass, Inc. 1969.

Fisher, G.H. The analytical bases of systems analysis, The RAND Corp., May 1966, No. 27, p. 3363.

Gulko, W. "Program classifications structure," Technical Report 27, NCHEMS, WICHE, Boulder, Colorado, January 1972.

Harpel, R.L. "Accountability: Current demands on student personnel programs," NASPA Journal, Vol. 12, No. 3, Winter 1975.

References

Hartley, H.J.   Educational planning-programming-budgeting:
A systems approach.   New Jersey: Prentice-Hall, Inc. 1968.

Havighurst, R.J.   Developmental Task and Education.   New York:
David McKay Co., 1961, 2nd ed.

Huff, R.A.   Inventory of educational outcomes and activities.
Boulder, Colorado: NCHEMS at WICHE, 1971.

Immegart and Pilecki, An Introduction to systems for the
educational administrator.   Menlo Park, California;
Addition-Wesley Publishing Co., 1973.

Kaiser, L.R.   "Designing campus environments," NASPA Journal,
Vol. 13, No. 1 Summer, 1975.

Knezevich, S.J., Program budgeting.   Berkeley, California:
McCutchan Publishing Co., 1973.

Lahti, R.E.   "Implementating the system means learning to
manage your objectives," College and University Business,
LII, 2, (February, 1972),pp. 43-46.

Lahti, R.E.   "Management by objectives," College and University
Business, LI (July, 1971), pp. 31-32.

Lahti, R.E.   Innovative college management.   San Francisco:
Jossey-Bass, Inc. 1973.

Lyden and Miller, Planning-programming-budgeting: A systems
approach to management, 2nd edition, Chicago: Markham
Publishing Co., 1972, 423 pp.

Mager, R.F.   Preparing instructional objectives.   Belmont,
California: Fearon Publishing Co., 1962, 60 pp.

Maslow, A.   Motivation and personality.   New York: Harper &
Row, 1970, 2nd edition.

Micek, S.S. and Walhaus, R.A.   An introduction to the
identification and uses of higher education outcome
information.   Technical Report 40.   National Center for
Higher Education Management Systems, at WICHE, Boulder,
Colorado, 1973.

Micek, S.S.; Service,A.L.; and Lee, Y.S.   Outcome measures
and procedures manual.   Boulder, Colorado: Western
Interstate Commission for Higher Education, 1974.

References

Micek, S.S. and Arney, W.R. The higher education outcome measures identification study: A descriptive summary. Boulder, Colorado, Western Interstate Commission for Higher Education, 1974.

Morrissey, G. Management by objectives and results. Menlo Park, California: Addition-Wesley, 1970.

Pavese, R. "Program budgeting in higher education." Educational planning-programming-bedgeting: A systems approach, by Harry J. Hartley. New Jersey: Prentice-Hall, Inc., 1968.

Peters, P.E. A planning, programming, budgeting system adapted for the student affairs and student services program at the University of Missouri-Columbia. Technical Report of Dean of Student Affairs Office, University of Missouri -- Columbia, March, 1972.

Sanford, N. The American college. 2nd edition, New York: John Wiley and Sons, Inc., 1967.

Wildavsky, A., The politics of the budgetary process, Boston: Little, Brown, 1964.

Webb, E.J.; Campbell, D.T.; Schwarts, R.D.; Sechrest, L., Unobtrusive measures. Chicago: Rand McNally, 1966.

Western Interstate Commission for Higher Education, Outputs of higher education: Their identification, measurement, and evaluation. Papers from 1970 seminar sponsored by WICHE, ACE, and CRDHE (Berkeley), WICHE, P.O. Crawer P, Boulder, Colorado, 1970, 130 pp.

Yee, A.H. Perspectives on management systems approaches in education. Educational Technology Publications, Englewood Cliffs, New Jersey, 1973, 154 pp.

CHAPTER   32

EVALUATION OF COLLEGE STUDENT AFFAIRS DIVISIONS AND SERVICES

William A. Bryan, John Eddy and Audrey L. Rentz

Introduction

"Evaluation" is a term that confuses many people and
occasionally creates fear among student affairs staff members.
Dressel (1976) sees evaluation as "...both a judgment of the
worth or impact of a program, procedure, or individual and
the process whereby that judgment is made" (p.1).   This
definition would certainly create concern on the part of
staff because of the power-laden words "judgment", and "worth".
Cronbach (1963) more simply defines evaluation as the
"collection and use of information to make decisions about an
educational program" (p. 672).   For divisions of student
affairs to be effective, it is necessary to assess student
needs, to determine a plan of action to meet these needs,
and to evaluate the effectiveness of any particular strategy.
Evaluation is an essential responsibility of any program.
Simply put, it is a process of collecting data about what
has been accomplished, about the results of the plan of
action.   The information collected would help student
affairs staff make appropriate decisions and to provide
necessary feedback to staff.

Colleges and universities will face continuing economic
pressures in the 80's, most notably projected decreases
in enrollment and a change in clientele as suggested by
Centra (1980).   With projections of increased enrollments
of adults, women, minorities, and handicapped students,
no doubt student affairs staffs will develop many new
programs to respond to the identified needs of these students.
Student affairs divisions can provide information vitally
needed by institutions of higher education regarding the
retention of students.   The importance of our work can
only be amplified as a result of our increased attention to

the effectiveness of our services. We need to continue to
ask questions such as "What are the changing needs of students
who arrive on our campus today?", "Why do students leave
our university?", "Are students aware of the numerous
resources on the campus that will enhance their personal
development?", "What effect do specially designed programs
have on the persistence of students at the university?", and
"Are services designed to meet specific outlined objectives
and to further the accomplishment of the goals endorsed by
our universities?" Evaluation can help student affairs
personnel make sound judgments about future directions and
program changes needed.

Why Evaluate?

Change is ever present in the field of education as
in society in general. Change is necessary in student
affairs work not for the sake of change but for the purpose
of meeting the shifting identified needs of the clientele
we serve. Evaluation assists us in planning for appropriate
change in new directions. Educators evaluate for any
number of reasons -- to demonstrate the viability of a
program, to build justification for a program budget, to
be accountable, to evaluate staff, to do what is felt to
be necessary, to prove a point, to maintain what is, and
hopefully, to chart directions for planned change. The
statements below are developed from Deegan and Fritz's
(1976) reasons for formal performance appraisal (pp. 233-
236).

1. Evaluate to improve performance of a program or
    activity. The key here is "improving".

2. Evaluate to determine how effective a program is
    and what should be done now.

3. Evaluate to develop people.

4. Evaluate to provide the basis for coordinating
    college, division, and department objectives and
    goals.

5. Evaluate to determine appropriate program actions.

Evaluation is practical, pragmatic, and political. It fortifies the role and/or the place of the student affairs division within the institution. As Shaffer (1973) described, it builds a realistic power base for institutional input. In addition, current issues facing post-secondary education will continue to hold our attention and form a rationale for evaluation. The student affairs practitioner knows only too well the implications of these issues for a student affairs program: decreasing enrollments, diverse student populations, budgetary constraints or reductions, increased emphasis on content acquisition by vocationally oriented students, and unionization among college and university faculties. All of these are motivation enough for the aggressive and forward looking chief student affairs practitioner to be concerned with facilitating continuous and cummulative evaluation studies each year. These studies should focus on the value of individuals, programs, program outcomes, resource utilization, and the impact of the total student affairs program on the academic community it serves. For effective evaluation, it is important that input from staff self-studies, student services, alumni questionnaires, and others are properly included in the total assessment scheme or plan. Without effective evaluation, the college student affairs division lacks the power of persuasion to promote its personnel, policies, programs, and projects designed to help students help themselves.

What Is The Process?

The approach taken in a division of student affairs to implement evaluation is extremely important. Evaluation is a term that staff may fear or misunderstand. Coan (1976) designed a study to determine the beliefs and attitudes about evaluation held by student personnel professionals. He conducted a workshop program on evaluation and determined that attitudes and beliefs can be altered as a result of an educational experience. Findings in his study suggest that an effective strategy to stimulate evaluation might be

to build staff appreciation for the worth of evaluation.
Well planned workshops might also assist staff in becoming
more secure with their role and contributions and enhance
their own professional development in the area of evaluation.
A primary step in the process of evaluation is the education
of staff to promote staff comfort and understanding and
to deal with individual misunderstandings. The evaluator's
purpose is not to mandate but to build an understanding
of the value of evaluation.

A number of questions should be asked as evaluation
begins: (1) What is our motivation to evaluate? (2) What
are the costs and benefits of the proposed evaluation?
(3) Are there significant issues surrounding the evaluation?
(4) Are there concerns for the rights of those participating
in the evaluation? (5) How will the data be analyzed?
(6) How will the results be used? Mink, Shultz, and Mink
(1979) state "evaluation is a process of asking questions
and collecting information as a basis for making decisions",
(p. 170). These authors suggest that the process of
evaluation involves:

1. Specifying goals and achievement criteria.

2. Deciding on methods of data collection.

3. Gathering data.

4. Analyzing data.

5. Interpreting data.

6. Deciding value of data.

7. Making decisions for change.

8. Taking appropriate action.

It is important in the process of evaluation to involve
staff at every level and to discuss all issues openly. It
would also be essential to us in student affairs to involve
faculty and students. The process of evaluation must be

continuous if our work is to contribute significantly to
the mission of our institution.

Criteria for Evaluation

A single question forms the foundation for any evaluation:
"How well or to what degree is a specific person, program,
or activity doing what it was assigned to do?" Or put in
another way, "Of what value is the person, program, or
activity under investigation?" This question implies the
need to ascertain three other factors: First, what was
the program designed to do; what were its original objectives?;
Second, what is happening now as a result of the program?;
Third, how do the original objective(s) compare to what
is happening now?

On the basis of responses to these three questions, a
last step involves a judgment about what modifications can
be made in the program to produce results which are more
valuable or a better fit with the program's objectives. In
addition, these three queries form the basis from which Feder
et al (1958) must have evolved the following checkpoints
for an evaluation of a program as cited in the American
Council on Education of Student Personnel Document of 1958:

1. The degree that each student service relates to
   the institutional objectives and is influenced
   by them.

2. The efficiency and effectiveness of daily operations.

3. The attitudes and comments of the college community
   towards the program.

4. The staff morale.

5. The results of the areas and services in terms of
   students reached, the depth of student contact,
   and frequency of student contacts.

303

Using Evaluation Information - Accountability

The most important aspect of evaluation is the use of
the information gained. Too often student affairs practitioners do not devote enough attention to the evaluation
"product". Collected information can be used in a variety
of ways to design needed programs or activities for
students, to build a case for increased funding of programs,
to communicate effectively the value of services to students
and faculty, to establish the value of the division's
existing services, and to gain support from boards of higher
education and legislatures for needed programs.

Once evaluation reports are completed, feedback
sessions should be planned as appropriate within the
institutional setting. Full disclosure of information is
wholesome and productive to a vital, responsive student
affairs division. Too often decisions are made without total
review of available information.

Change is the end result of evaluation. The proper
climate for change is vital to the success of proposals
that might be made. It's necessary within the institutional
climate to estimate student, faculty, and staff receptivity
to proposed changes. In proposing change as a result of
evaluation information, one must explain rationale for the
change or proposed direction, identify the results that
will occur as a result of change, invite questions and
answer the, gain input from constituencies who should be
appropriately involved, anticipate potential problems
and provide answers, and seek involvement in outlining
a plan of action for change.

Evaluation in a division of student affairs involves
looking at key results for each area, identifying problems,
determining the approach to be followed in solving these
problems, and identifying new ways to accomplish objectives.
In the planning process, student affairs staff should
identify ways to incorporate evaluation in order to monitor
the primary results expected from each department. This

involves a periodic review of the level of attainment of expected results, solving problems, and implementation of new innovations which help further develop stated objectives.

Future Directions

Student affairs staffs must pay more attention to the evaluation of services and programs on an on-going basis. A major component within each division should be research and evaluation. This component should provide assistance to total division efforts as well as consultation and development services for each department seeking to evaluate its activities. For too long, student affairs staff have not actively pursued the development of evaluation efforts, nor have they actively discussed implications of evaluation findings for divisions of student affairs or the university in general. For services and programs to continue to be vital to the campus, student affairs personnel must pay suitable attention to evaluation. The resulting effects can only be valuable to staff, division goals, and ultimately to the development of students. This information is also vital to the retention of students and to the total campus in general. Increasingly, evaluation units will be funded in divisions of student affairs resulting in better communication as to the value of its programs, the needs of students, and strategies to meet these needs. Proper evaluation is a key to the success and acceptance of the division of student affairs. Student affairs practitioners must become responsive and active in the pursuit of this endeavor.

In the 80's, student affairs divisions will be forced to place emphasis on evaluation (Hanson, 1978; Kuh, 1980) so we can make rational judgments about the value of the continuance of our programs -- be they personnel, specific activities, or resources allocated to help achieve the objectives of the division...helping students help themselves to grow.

REFERENCES

Centra, J. A. "College Enrollment in the 1980's: Projections
    and Possibilities." The Journal of Higher Education,
    January/February 1980, 51, No. 1, 18-39.

Coan, D. L. "Effects of a Workshop on Perceptions about
    Evaluation." Journal of College Student Personnel,
    May 1976, 17, No. 3, 186-189.

Cronbach, L. J. "Course Improvement Through Evaluation."
    Teachers College Record, 1963, 64, 672-683.

Deegan, A. X. and Fritz, R. J. MBO Goes to College
    (2nd ed.). Boulder, Colorado: University of Colorado,
    1976.

Dressel, P. L. The Handbook of Academic Evaluation. San
    Francisco: Jossey-Bass Publishers, 1976.

Feder, D. D. et al The Administration of Student Personnel
    Programs in American Colleges and Universities.
    Washington, D. C.: The American Council on Education,
    1958.

Hanson, G. R. Evaluating Program Effectiveness. San Francisco:
    Jossey-Bass Inc. Publishers, 1978.

Kuh, G. (ed.) Evaluation in College Student Services.
    Washington, D. C.: American College Personnel Association,
    Monograph Series, APGA Press, 1980.

Mink, O. G., Shultz, J. M. and Mink, B. P. Developing and
    Managing Open Organizations. Austin, Texas: Learning
    Concepts, 1979.

Shaffer, R. H. "An Emerging Role of Student Personnel -
    Contributing to Organizational Effectiveness."
    Journal of College Student Personnel, September 1973,
    14, No. 5, 386-391.

CHAPTER 33

MEASURABLE MODES FOR COLLEGE STUDENT SERVICES:
BENEFITS AND OUTPUT DELIVERY SYSTEMS

John Eddy

This chapter presents some possible measurable modes for College Student Services, University Student Affairs, or Campus Student Development Activities. The chapter was stimulated by an Illinois College Personnel Winter Workshop entitled, "Student Services Management by Objectives--The Quality and the Money."

The Workshop dealt with management by objectives and a taxonomy for College Student Services. However, the measurable modes for College Student Services was not mentioned in the formal lectures.

Some of the possible raw benefit factors that might be used as starters for College Student Services are:

1) Letters or notes of appreciation from students, parents and others to Services personnel;
2) Questionnaire results from students that have used various Services over the years;
3) Numbers of students using different Services per year;
4) Numbers of students contacted by Services for various program opportunities available per year;
5) Numbers of students referred by Services personnel to other college or other agencies per year;
6) Types of problems or topics handled by Service personnel per year;
7) Amounts of incoming monies to the Financial Aid Office from all sources each year;
8) Amounts of incoming monies from alumni and the positive relationship of the alumni to any Services--based on a questionnaire sent to all alumni contributors over the years;
9) Amounts of incoming monies to the Housing Office from all sources each year;
10) Numbers of students who are admitted by the Admissions Office per year;

11) Percentage of students that are retained through some terminal degree program per year;

12) Numbers of students that graduate from some academic program per year that had contacts with Services;

13) Number of students placed in jobs by the Placement Service; and,

14) Numbers of alumni favorably evaluating services and areas via surveys.

The author does not presume that the aforementioned benefit factors are all that are apparent. After identification of these selected benefit factors, comes the different problem of giving some index and scale to these benefit factors that could be based on a cost analysis and a value analysis. If the survival of the institution is based on financial income, would the monies from all Service sources weigh higher than saving students from suicides in a given year? It is a good question, for is not the saving of one life worth more than any sum of dollars--if you believe in life above possessions?

On the other hand, as McNulty discovered in this study, analyzed alumni giving has some revealing insights for supporting service benefit factors. For example, alumni giving reveals that certain services were contributing aspects to the alumni feeling positively about the college so that this is a case for the worth of the service. Furthermore, the alumni giving based on a rank order of services is revealing of their worth to these graduates.

The identification, speculation and interpretation of the benefit factors remains to be worked out in more refined terms. Experts are working on these aspects and computers are waiting for the programs. The profession of College Student Personnel may be better for this but it is still questionnable if all that is being done can be ever properly measured--it is more a problem of values than money.

Another problem with this list of benefit factors is that the author may be mixing some apples with oranges in this analysis. However, until there is a better clarification of the fruits of these Services, it will not be known what the specific fruits are.

Recommended Readings

Balderston, F.E. and Weathersby, G.B., PPBS in Higher Education Planning and Management from PPBS to Policy Analysis. Berkeley: University of

Recommended Readings

    California, May 1972.

Bowen, H.R. and Douglass, G.K. _Efficiency in Liberal Education_, New York: McGraw-Hill Book Company, 1971.

Chert, E.F. _The New Depression in Higher Education_ New York: McGraw-Hill Book Company, 1971.

Corbally, J.E. "Future Financing of Higher Education" Urbana Illinois College Personnel Association Mimeographed Paper, 1973.

Eddy, J.P. and Durst, G. _Life and Management Responsibility_. Albuquerque, New Mexico: The Training Company, 1976.

Jellema, W.W. _Efficient College Management_, San Francisco: Jossey-Bass, 1972.

Jellema, W.W. "Institutional Priorities and Management Objectives," _Liberal Education_, May 1971.

Mortimer, K.P. _Accountability in Higher Education_ Eric Cleringhouse on Higher Education, February 1972.

McNulty, J. "Alumni Giving and University Student Personnel Services" Bloomingdale, IL: Unpublished doctoral study delivered at Northern Illinois Association for Educational Research, Evaluation and Development, 1977.

Schultze, C.L. _The Politics and Economics of Public Spending_, Washington, D.C. Brooking's Institution, 1968.

Winter, R. "Accountability and Student Personnel Services," Urbana: Illinois College Personnel Association Mimeographed Paper, 1973.

The More Effective Use of Resources, Carnegie Commission of Higher Education, New York: McGraw-Hill Book Company, June, 1972.

The Output of Higher Education: Their Identification, Measurement, and Evaluation, WICHE, Boulder, July, 1970.

CHAPTER 34

A STUDENT INFORMATION SYSTEM

Ernest B. Jaski and John   Eddy

A model of a student vital statistics and delivery system
is proposed to enhance the effectiveness of student services
and institutional accountability. This model incorporates guidelines for its planning, organization, development, implementation, and evaluation. Implications for admissions, programming,
instruction, research and alumni relations are also indicated.

Student personnel services information systems are being
increasingly recognized as central to any college or university.
They provide structure and provide a justification for any
college claiming to be student-centered.

The student personnel program should touch the life of
every student, and it should be recognized as an integral part
of the total educational program. Ideally, student personnel
services should be based on clearly defined objectives and resources for the implementation of activities to help achieve
those objectives and should receive feedback to evaluate the
degree of success in meeting the goals. Services functioning
merely to expedite the operation of the institution will no
longer suffice. Considerable planning, competent leadership,
and accurate information are indispensable if the program is to
be effective and respected. Such a strategic approach can make
service to the students a more meaningful reality.

The basic goal of a student information system (SIS) is not
merely the identification or collection of the elements of the
system, but the adequate conceptualization of their interaction
and interdependence. Such a conceptualization is designed to
achieve better problem identification and more effective student-
oriented decision making. Two of the major areas of concern to
student personnel service management, according to Dressel (1973),
are (a) studies of changing student needs and problems and (b)
evaluations of the programs and assistance provided to alleviate
these needs and problems. In the process the information system
should be expected to serve the day-to-day operational needs of
students and provide an informational base suitable for research
and long-term planning related to institutional philosophy, goals,
and policies.

310

An evaluation of benefits should ascertain to whom benefits accrue most frequently, the modes and costs of delivering the benefits, and the alternatives--both in benefits and in delivery systems. This evaluation is essential to discharging the informational and therapeutic responsibilities of student personnel services. As Dressel (1973), Brown (1972), Corbally (1973), and Herron (1970) have observed, these responsibilities include such specific functions as student orientation, provision of remedial or developmental experiences for disadvantaged students, academic counseling and advising, environmental manipulation, and interpretation of student needs and the concerns of students, parents, family, community, staff, and administration.

One of the measurable outcomes that could be expected to result from the informational and therapeutic role implementation is that students' abilities, interests, and aspirations rather than arbitrary departmental and college requirements would become the basis for student programs. Improved educational goal-oriented accountability to the board of trustees, and to the public, would be a commitant advantage.

State legislatures, representing the tax-paying public, are increasingly demanding accountability for results (Sullivan & O'Hare 1971; Winters 1973; Woodington 1972). This challenge is compounded by the constantly rising level of student expectations concerning the benefits of their college attendance. Indicative of the response to the growing demand for accountability is the requirement by some states for annual reports by state-supported colleges and universities. In Illinois, as well in other states, community colleges are required by recent legislation to submit to their community college boards annual institutional research reports stating student characteristics, career program enrollments, number of students completing a program, and other information related to student profiles and development.

The American Council on Education also requests student data on questionnaires that ask for more than demographic characteristics. Therefore, more and more schools are establishing an Office of Institutional Research within their Division of Student Affairs.

Several objectives for the design of a college or university student information system have been presented by Saupe and Montgomery (1970). They are summarized as follows: What data should be collected? What are the appropriate categories and definitions? How should it be collected, stored, and retrieved? How can the different types of data be interrelated for specific purposes? For increased efficiency in the use of data, the system should be available by way of a computerized program that will be both readily accessible and easily understandable to its

311

expected users who have been delegated the decision-making responsibility.

A Taxonomy of Student Services

The taxonomy of student services listed in Figure 1 indicates the broad spectrum of student services frequently offered by large colleges and universities. The relative importance of each will vary by size of institution, academic caliber of the student body served, public versus private status, residential or commuter status, and other factors.

The taxonomy represents an organizational schema usable as a basis for the coordination and comparison of services offered. This can also help to suggest the myriad of data which a student affairs division may wish to consider using in its SIS. In the initial stages of developing an SIS structure, it would be advisable to use only some of the coded categories listed. Only when the system appears to be effectively meeting its objectives would it be feasible to expand the sources of information from which data would be collected.

This expansion would probably cover a period of at least several years, being implemented through separate stages of development. For example, stage one would entail collecting data on incoming freshmen. The second stage would collect information designed to provide a basis for the analysis of the success of students as it can be related to their incoming characteristics. The second stage would also provide an identification of dominant student needs while at college. Stage three would collect information to further review the academic success of students and would provide a correlational analysis and a statistical test of significance on student characteristics and student performance in various fields or skills. A final phase to supplement the foregoing statistics and analysis requires a follow-up study of alumni and other external subpublics identified in Figure 1 under "public environment."

Sources and Kinds of Data

For analysis it is convenient to categorize the SIS into the four groups shown in Figure 2. The second category, testing and related divisions, may not represent an administrative unit for some colleges and universities, but in institutions with at least 10,000 students it is commonly a separate office.

Research includes data that are used more in the research and planning functions of the unit. Some operational categories are included, however, such as counseling center and student activities. These areas require a minimum of operational support but include strategic information vital to research. Included in

312

student research information are demographic, psychological, and sociopsychological data facilitating multivariate analysis research. Before a school uses an instrument such as the Institutional Goals Inventory, distributed by Educational Testing Service, the SIS can supply the required background information to form the basis for collecting and interpreting the data for an institutional self-evaluation. For example, at Rockford College, Rockford, Illinois, a research-consultant team used SAT and ACT scores plus demographic characteristics and the stated major interests of students as a method of distinguishing student subcultures at the college. Identified intergroup value differences on the relative importance of the goals of liberal arts education led to the school's reexamination of the objectives of their curriculum. For Rockford College the SIS "was very useful for improving the college's marketing, accountability, and planning functions" (Giddens 1974).

Each section of the registration files should be conceived as a building block that fits within a total configuration (Mellott 1973). For example, at Illinois State University, an information system is applied to establish enrollment projections for various curricula, to conduct unit cost studies, and, as a consequence, to more equitably allocate the school's resources.

With this conception as the criterion of design, each new phase will add a module interfaced with the previous one. At times it will be necessary to consolidate modules for convenience and efficiency, but these, again, must be modular in nature. Physical file requirements should not force abandonment of the logical file concept.

Student Activities Clearinghouse

Another potential use of student data is the establishment of a student activities clearinghouse (Eddy 1974). One major objective evident in many colleges is for students to know each other better through sharing information, interests, and skills with each other. A computer bank can be set up by having students complete computer cards indicating their special skills, interests and needs. The computer can then match students by their respective needs and interests, helping to bring students together at a counselor's initiative for further exploration or development of their interests and needs.

Other Selected Data on Student Outcomes

The following data suggest the kinds of data to be considered for inclusion in the SIS, especially for a follow-up of alumni:

1. Students' values--incoming and graduating.
2. Retention rate.

313

3. Course revisions.
4. Special services used by students.
5. Special skills developed in college.
6. Student activites engaged in by student while in college.
7. Visits with a counselor.
8. Career placements—correlation to academic major.
9. Occupations of graduates.
10. Salary range of recent graduates—low, high, average.
11. Future educational plans.

Some data are closely related, such as career placements and salary range of graduates. For example, a study of graduates and their subsequent careers was conducted at Joliet Junior College (Racchini 1974) and led to a review of its career curricula.

Such discrete data as special services used by the student or admissions tests scores would have to be subcategorized or refined for utilitarian application within the SIS. For example, admissions tests scores would have to be further identified by academic fields. Other student statistics suggest a need for a longitudinal comparative study, for example, career goals or students' values in freshman and, later, in senior year. Furthermore, for an information system to be optimally effective, the user should not only receive information from the system but should be able to give feedback on how useful the system is (Havelock & Benne 1967).

Dissemination

Some common avenues of communicating the findings derived from these student statistics are periodic summary reports, newsletters, departmental or divisional meetings, and the use of other professional media. The alternatives for dissemination usually do not require large expenditures of money and can serve effectively in attracting public awareness of the ongoing student services supplied by a student affairs division. Ostensibly, such methods can also contribute to sound public relations for the college or university.

Evaluation

Both quantitative as well as qualitative, formal as well as informal, measures of evaluation can be adopted to appraise the degree of success realized in using an SIS. A structured or semistructured questionnaire can be distributed to students and faculty asking for feedback on how well the system is serving their needs; interviews with users can supply both objective and subjective information. Statistical analysis can range from simple univariate statistics, such as means and percentages, to

314

more sophisticated, heuristic, multivariate analyses, including linear regressions and possible canonical correlations or discriminant functions.

Summary

One basic model of a student information system has been presented here as a guide. Initially, the kinds of student data to be collected and the sources as well as methods of acquiring this information can be used by the counseling staff, faculty, and administrators. Also to be identified are the strategies for disseminating the findings emanating from the data and for evaluating the effectiveness of their use in order to achieve optimal benefits from the operation of this system. The SIS model furnishes a data bank that can be relevant, service-oriented, universal, and longitudinal (Smith 1970). Finally, the SIS model is adaptable to the three major decisions that have evolved from institutional research in the past three decades: operating, management, and policy (Fisher & Schoemer 1973).

The development and operation of an SIS is a demanding project. Services to be provided to meet the recognized needs and interests of students, identified by the SIS, will have to be budgeted for and actively implemented. The anticipated results in enhanced student development, however, can increase the productivity of higher education. An important role change that college student personnel workers can undergo through a scientific creative use of a student information system is from maintainer and operator of the system to a strategist and changer of structure.

References

Brown, R. Student development in tomorrow's higher education: A return to the academy. Washington, D.C.: ACPA, 1972.

Corbally, E., Jr. Address to the Illinois College Personnel Association, Champaign, Illinois, February 1973.

Dressel, P.L. Measuring the benefits of student personnel work. Journal of Higher Education. 1973, 44, 15-26.

Eddy, J. Student activities clearinghouse. Unpublished manuscript presented in Guidance 428 Course. Community-Junior College. 1974

References

Fisher, C.E. & Schoemer, J.R. What happens to the data you give to the office of institutional research? College and University, 1973, 48, 425-435.

Giddens, T.R. Remarks at annual fall Illinois Association for Institutional Research Conference. Carbondale, Illinois. September 1974. (Mimeo)

Havelock, R.G. & Benne, K.D. An exploratory study of knowledge utilization. In G. Watson (Ed.) Concepts for social change. Washington, D.C.: National Education Association. 1967, 47-70.

Herron, O.R., Jr. (Ed.) New dimensions in student personnel administration. Scranton, PA: International Textbook Company. 1970.

Mellot, R.N. Student data base construction and critique. College and University. 1973, 48, 437-443.

Racchini, A. Follow-up report of the Joliet Junior College career program graduates of 1973. Joliet, Ill.: Joliet Junior College, 1974. (Mimeo)

Saupe, J.L. & Montgomery, J.R. The nature and role of institutional research. Memo to a college or university. Monograph of the Association for Institutional Research. November 1970, 7.

Smith, H.D. Data banks--Why? How? What results to expect. College and University. 1970, 45, 569-84.

Sullivan, H.J. & O'Hare, R.W. Accountability in pupil personnel services: A process guide for the development of objectives. Belmont, CA: California Personnel and Guidance Association, 1971.

Winters, R. Accountability and student personnel services. Address to the Illinois College Personnel Association, Champaign, Illinois, February 1973.

Woodington, D.D. Accountability from the viewpoint of a state commissioner of education. Phi Delta Kappan. October 1972, 54, 95-97.

Figure 1

Student Information System*

SIS

Admissions and Related Divisions
  High school data
  Demographic data
  Health records

Testing and Related Divisions
  Admissions test scores
  Achievement test scores
  Placement and credit examination
    results
  Academic achievement expectancy
    data

Research and Related Divisions
  Student research information data
  Counseling center data
  Student activity data

Registration Division
  Master file data
  Master schedule data
  Grade report file
  Academic history file
  Graduation and degree information

Operations and Research Reports

Figure 2

Student Services Taxonomy*

1000	Academic environment	2214	Physical examinations
1100	Tutoring	2215	Laboratory services
1200	Continuing education	2216	Pharmacy
1300	Practicums and internships	2217	Environmental health and safety
1400	Remedial and supportive services	2218	Rehabilitation services
1410	Courses	2219	Speech and hearing
1420	Learning skills	2220	Mental health
1421	Reading	2221	Counseling
1422	Writing	2222	Therapy
1423	Study		
1430	Supportive materials	3000	Social environment
1500	Counseling and advising	3100	Financial aids
1510	Career/vocational	3110	Grants and scholarships
1520	Course/curricula	3111	Packaging
1600	Testing services	3112	Revisions
1700	Study abroad services	3112	Certification
1800	Non-graduation termination	3120	Loans
		3121	Short term
2000	Living environment	3122	Intermediate
2100	Housing services	3123	Long term
2110	Room assignment	3120	Student employment
2120	Enforcement of housing regulations	3131	On campus
2130	Off-campus housing info & approval	3132	Off campus
2140	Child care services	3133	Summer
2200	Health services	3200	Job placement
2210	Physical health		
2211	Emergency services		
2212	Out-patient services		* From the University of Illinois –
2213	Hospital services		Student Services Division.

318

Figure 2
Student Services Taxonomy
(Continued)

3300 Policies and regulations - law enforcement
3310 Staff assistance agencies
3320 Discipline system task - campus security
3330 Registered organizations
3400 New student orientation
3500 Counseling
3510 General-personal
3520 Disciplinary
3530 Emergency
3560 Veterans
3570 Drugs
3580 Legal
3590 Marriage and family
3600 Campus programs
3610 Entertainment
3620 Educational
3630 Recreational
3640 Skill development
3700 Campus organizations advising

4000 Public environment
4100 Parents
4200 Alumni
4300 General public
4400 Professional
4500 Governmental
4600 Prospective students

CHAPTER 35

MEASURING THE BENEFITS OF STUDENT PERSONNEL WORK

Paul L. Dressel

Of the seven words composing the title of this article,
five pose problems of definition and application. Since three
of the words form a well-known triad (student personnel work),
the task implied by the title reduces to answering a series of
questions regarding the nature of student personnel work, the
character of its benefits, the measurement of those benefits, and
the relationship of those benefits to costs. I doubt that we can
arrive at a satisfactory definition of what student personnel
work is by describing what student personnel workers do. First
of all, the tasks subsumed under the term include too many
diverse and unrelated specialties, including admissions, records,
registration, financial aids, residence halls, organizations,
governance, counseling, placement, and student unions. In fact,
it has always seemed to me that student personnel folk have
attempted to seize upon everything involving students except the
classroom and academic matters pertaining directly to it. In
addition, student personnel workers have sometimes sought to
provide or to control credit courses covering general orientation,
study habits, sex knowledge, marital problems, discussion of
current issues, etc., etc. The list of student personnel activities given by the Council of Student Personnel Association in
Higher Education, for example, includes such diverse items as:
Understanding the college student as a learner and a person;
facilitating communication between students and others in the
institution and in the community; interpreting the goals, values,
objectives, and actions of students and their institutions, one
to the other; understanding and influencing the significant
forces operating within the college community as they affect
individual students and student groups; conducting and interpreting research on psychological, social, and cultural forces
influencing student performance and behavior. The range of
activities implied by the list well displays the tendency of
student personnel workers to grab hold of everything that's not
nailed down by the faculty and even to imply that what is nailed
down is so poorly done that student personnel people ought to
tear it up and start over. Accordingly, I believe that the
future of the field depends in great part upon a more restricted
conception of what student personnel work is and a clearer statement of the benefits involved. I have no final answers to these
issues, but I propose here to develop a pattern of analysis

320

essential to defining and evaluating the benefits of student personnel work.

I should like to return to the questions suggested at the beginning of my comments.

What is student personnel work? Let us simply note that this can be defined in various ways: by its purposes, by its activities, by its clientele, and by its results or benefits. Thus, this question leads to three subsidiary questions: What are the benefits of student personnel work? To whom do the benefits accrue? How can the benefits be measured? And, because of the diversity of the field, one additional question becomes important. Into what natural subgroups do the functions and benefits of student personnel work fall?

What are the costs of student personnel work? The diversity of activities subsumed under student personnel work suggests that costs must be determined for the various subgroups of activities related to the functions and particular benefits. The problems of funding any activity in the university are complicated and never have been solved to anyone's satisfaction; but, in any case, the sheer allocation of dollars to the various functions and benefits of student personnel work is insufficient. Economists talk of opportunity costs—the benefits foregone by expenditures on a particular activity. Thus, for example, if it were demonstrated that the number of dollars assigned to a student personnel program would permit average class size to be reduced from twenty to ten students, many faculty members would argue that the benefits of the smaller class would greatly exceed those achieved by the student personnel work program.

Do the benefits of student personnel work, by activity, function, and types of clientele, justify the costs? Again, the answer to this question must not be simply in terms of the cost per student or the cost per benefit. We can answer the question only by an honest attempt to determine whether the benefits of particular parts of the program transcend benefits that might be derived from alternative patterns of expenditure of the same dollars. This view is even more pertinent now than a few years ago. Many presidents have looked upon student personnel work as an investment in maintaining control of students by keeping them occupied and contented, thereby eliminating embarrassment by attempts which would bring public disfavor. Since student personnel workers no longer provide this insurance, other acceptable justifications are needed.

Definitions of Student Personnel Work

Traditional. One approach to a definition of student personnel work places it in the context of the three major pur-

321

poses and functions of higher education. Student personnel workers do provide instruction for students, especially in the areas of affective development, maturation, leadership training, etc. The fact that these experiences are not offered through credit courses makes the instructional function less obvious and perhaps more akin to independent study than to formal classroom instruction. With the advent of external or off-campus instruction and degrees, this role of student personnel work may become less significant. Indeed, on most university campuses it is a very minor element in the student personnel picture in that it indirectly affects only a few students. Student personnel work provides some instruction for administration and faculty by interpreting the concerns and needs of students and by examining the environmental implications and interactions with the academic program.

Student personnel work also provides a vast array of services. Health services have often been included, though never really assimilated. Drug education has furnished the basis for a joint effort in recent years. Some part of student personnel work, including lectures, interest groups, and cultural events, is simply a provision of entertainment for students. Other aspects of student personnel work have been concerned with the alleviation of student concerns and problems and with the assistance and coordination of student nonacademic activities. As implied earlier, for many years student personnel work was seen as providing restraints or discipline through interpretation and enforcement of rules and regulations, but the more recent role seems to be that of interpretation and perservation of student rights. However, the students' concern about rights has frequently been as much or more directed to the academic faculty than to student personnel workers; hence, much of the negotiation and activity on defining and providing for preservation of student rights have had limited involvement by student personnel workers.

The third traditional area, research, is also fitting for student personnel work. Two major areas of reserach seem to be appropriate: (1) studies of changing student needs and problems, and (2) evaluation of programs and assistance provided to alleviate these needs and problems.

Alternatives. One might depart from this traditional trinity of purposes and define student personnel work as a composite of programs designed to facilitate the educational goals of the university by (a) providing personal and group contacts and services; (b) coordinating and directing nonacademic experiences so that they contribute to educational development; (c) mediating between students, parents, faculty, administration, and community; (d) studying, interpreting, and making recommendations regarding psychological, social, and cultural forces influencing student

322

performance and behavior. This alternative interpretation differs in two ways from the first. On one hand, it makes evident that student personnel work exists to facilitate the educational goals of the university; and, on the other, it provides some basis for analyzing the way in which this facilitation takes effect. Areas such as admissions, records, registration, financial aids, orientation, counseling, placement, services for special groups of students (foreign; adult; physically, emotionally, and educationally handicapped), involvement in residence halls and other housing units, assisting student organizations, governance, judiciary involvement, interpretation and monitoring of rules and regulations regarding morals and order, and coordination of recreational and cultural programs in this approach are all seen as activities which facilitate the major functions of the university. The management role becomes a major function in many of these, but more specifically the educational goals or the benefits of student personnel work may be seen on a more realistic basis than when student personnel work is idealistically viewed as an almost independent educational enterprise in the university. I would suggest that the benefits of student personnel work regarded in this second way as facilitating the educational goals of the university are as follows: (1) get students in and keep them in college; (2) keep students busy, happy, and healthy; (3) help students to select educational programs and courses in relationship to their own interests and capabilities and their ultimate goals as well as the needs of society; (4) encourage maturation, self-actualization, affective development, social skills, etc., indirectly by exercising influence on faculty and administration, and more directly by contacts with individual and groups of students. I recognize that these benefits are at a much more mundane level than many student personnel workers like to see themselves operating. However, I believe this is a realistic statement and that the burden of proof is on any individual who would claim that student personnel work really makes contributions far beyond these four benefits.

Areas of Responsibility (A Possible Realignment)

Administrative and Fiduciary. The functions of admissions, records, registration, and the distribution of financial aids seem to me to be primarily administrative and fiduciary functions. These are to be carried out in accordance with policies determined by the faculty and in ways which are fair to the students. These areas are essential to getting the student in college and keeping him there. They have no direct relationship to the education of the student, and the primary concern is that they be effectively performed.

Management and Coordination. A secondary responsibility involves management and coordination. This includes the role of student personnel workers in residence halls and other living units, their work with organizations and activities, and their responsibilities in the area of recreation--including perhaps entertainment, the arts, intramurals--and possibly some aspects of library services. Students should have a major role in each of these ares and the role of the student personnel worker may well become more advisory and facilitating than it has been in the past.

Informational and Therapeutic. A third area of responsibility is primarily informational and therapeutic. This includes such functions as orientation, remedial or developmental experiences for the disadvantaged (physically, educationally, emotionally, culturally), counseling and advising, environmental manipulation, and interpretation of student needs and concerns to students, parents and family, community, staff and administration. This area, it seems to me, keys in on the major responsibility of student personnel work. It is one that will need to be continued in the future for all campus institutions and some aspects will be essential even for off-campus or external degree programs.

Law and Order. A fourth area of responsibility I am, for lack of a better phrase, designating as maintenance of law and order. It includes concern and responsibility for students' rights and also for interpreting student obligations. It includes concern about morals, drugs, and other behavior which, carried to the excess, jeopardizes the educational function of the campus and the welfare of individuals and those close to them. It also involves concern about the roles and relationships of students in university governance and to federal, state, and local government. My own predilection would be to interpret this area of responsibility as one in which the task is that of interpreting to external agencies the character of an educational institution while neither expecting nor requesting special treatment for students with regard to the laws of the community or the state. This may involve student personnel workers in interpreting to students the fact that a college is not a sanctuary and that the student on campus is fully responsible for his behavior. I believe this fourth area of responsibility needs to be interpreted somewhat differently than it has been in the past, and I believe that it needs more development as a field of activity of student personnel workers. I would also suggest that perhaps the informational, the therapeutic, and the law and order areas of responsibility are the primary ones which justify the field of student personnel work. The administrative and fiduciary responsibilities are closely interrelated with the academic functions and can (perhaps should) be assigned to academic or management personnel.

Problems in Evaluating or Measuring Benefits

The fact that we do so little significant evaluation in education indicates that there are very serious problems in evaluating or measuring its benefits and of criteria that are acceptable indices of these benefits. But a prior and a very pervasive problem is the extent of bias and emotion that is involved. At times it seems almost impossible to carry on discussions of evaluation without seriously disturbing some segment of those who are involved. One is reminded of the lad who attended a Sunday school picnic and afterward reported to his mother that they had sung a new song after eating. The song, as he recalled it, was: "We can sing though full we be," an understandable misinterpretation under the circumstances of the phrase, "weak and sinful though we be." I'm not suggesting that student personnel workers are weak and sinful, but rather that our attempts to evaluate them may seem to them to say this.

If my observations are reasonably accurate, student personnel workers, as a group, have never been held in high respect as colleagues by the faculty. In part, this is because student personnel workers have often (and with good reason) been critical of the faculty, especially in comments to students. In part, it is because student personnel work competes for funds. And it is, in part, because student personnel work, from the point of view of many faculty members, over-emphasizes personal and social development at the cost of an intellectual emphasis. Thus, any attempt to evaluate personnel work is likely to be greeted by a segment of the faculty as an opportunity to recapture some funds better used for other purposes. Since many of the activities and goals of student personnel workers are not shared by segments of the faculty, open discussion of the field will certainly evoke displays of bias and emotion.

In many cases, the attitudes of administrators toward student personnel work has been based upon some kind of policing conception and the overt recognition of this by any study may pose some problems. The student personnel worker who endorses greater freedom for students may find himself afoul of administration positions. This also carries over to the community and the general public. Student dress, student activism, and student morals have effectively antagonized large segments of the general public, and there are those in positions of power, within the institution and externally, who would like student personnel workers to provide more control.

One significant element in measuring the benefits of student personnel work is that implications may emerge for changing or eliminating some of the vested interests and career possibilities of student personnel workers. In fact, it is not evident that

student personnel work is a professional specialty. Much of
what is done by student personnel workers can be done by individuals with varied patterns of education and experience. Unlike
the academic on campus, there is no particular field which the
student personnel worker can claim on a high level of competency
and demonstrate this by his knowledge and his research output.
In his day-to-day activity, there is very little that is con-
vincing to others that special competencies and education are
required. And, in many cases, student personnel work jobs have
been assigned to people with limited qualifications. I once
suggested that counseling and student personnel work are a little
like kissing, in that everyone feels qualified to engage in
kissing, most everyone does, the results are diverse though not
necessarily intangible, it may establish a dependence relationship, and the act itself is so satisfying that there is no tendency to evaluate it otherwise.

Criteria

In evaluation, one tends to concentrate on the characteristics of the environment, on the characteristics of the processes
that go on, or on the attainment of outcomes. I wish to emphasize
the evaluation of outcomes since here reside the benefits. At
the same time, it seems important to note that the environment
itself can be studied by looking at its adaptations to individuals
and groups and at the processes and outcomes which are expected to
result from being in the environment. To a considerable extent,
the environment results from interaction of people and physical
facilities. In a large institution, there may be a number of
distinctive environments. The environment which emerges in any
segment of an institution is one which, on some comprise basis,
is acceptable to various factions there, or else there are continuing tensions or confrontations. The environment is changed;
the people change; the activities change; or some persons move to
another environment. For example, use of an open office pattern
for both faculty and clerical workers is likely to result in
faculty spending little time at their desks. The creation of a
situation in which students have direct access to faculty members
without some screening by clerical workers may effectively destroy any possibility of confidential counseling in one's office
or any scholarly activity.

The very processes that go on in student personnel work can
be, in some limited sense, evaluated by a number of quanitative
indices, such as the number of persons served, the kind of records
kept, and the extent to which they are used. The quality and
adequacy of coordination and of services provided inject more
subjective considerations. The evaluation of the extent to which
ethical practices are maintained is difficult indeed.

Turning to outcomes, I would suggest that there are five major ones: (1) the general satisfaction or dissatisfaction of the students, faculty, and administration with student personnel work; (2) an increase in retention rates due to better selection of programs and careers; (3) the knowledge and self-understanding generated in those students, faculty, and administrators who are served by the student personnel work program; (4) the development of skills and consequently of improved performance by students served by student personnel programs; (5) the general reputation and the demands placed upon the student personnel work staff. It will be noticed that some of these do not really measure benefits in any direct sense. Satisfaction with a program does not necessarily mean that it is educationally beneficial. On the other hand, dissatisfaction registered by students or faculty probably indicates that the program is, in some way, ineffective, and rather than facilitating the academic program of the campus, is interfering with it. The knowledge and self-understanding of students and the increased skills and improved performance are more tangible benefits, but it is likely that they accrue to a minority of the student body; hence, these direct effects may be less significant than some indirect ones. For example, modification of the environment or of regulations regarding behavior and use of the environment may ease tensions, meet certain student needs and demands, and increase the quality of academic performance of a large number of persons who are not directly contacted in any way by those who facilitate the change.

Measuring the Benefits

Returning to the basic questions regarding the precise benefits: to whom they accrue, the modes and costs of delivering the benefits, and the alternatives--both in benefits and delivery systems--it seems obvious that the ultimate question as to whether the benefits actually derived from student personnel work are worth the costs in comparison with other benefits foregone is, and is likely to remain, unanswerable. There are conflicts in values which prevent any resolution of these issues. The scriptural shepherd who endangered his own life and that of his flock by searching for one lost sheep depicts one aspect of the conflict. The president who requested admission of some 200 rejected applicants to his institution and remarked two years later, when told that only four were still in school, "Just as I thought, some of them can make it, if you let them in," depicts a slightly different, but related value orientation. An even more fundamental issue is the extent to which affective outcomes, including personal and group competency in self-determination of goals, are accepted as educational outcomes. Faculties and students are divided on this. To overgeneralize, science and humanities faculties emphasize mastery of content and analytic skills and (with few exceptions) have little interest (as scholars) in the yearnings of their students or the problems of society. The social scientists, I believe, are spread over a continuum from those who would like to view their disciplines as a science (and simultaneously as the modern substitute for a decadent humanities) and those who are themselves so disenchanted with their attempts to create disciplines that they turn their backs on scholarly endeavors and structures to bathe in the hot springs of human emotions. I suspect this experience of communal bathing is far more satisfying and therapeutic for those faculty members than for their students.

On the whole, I see the legislatures and the general public advocating higher education which develops useful competencies (with personal and social as well as economic implications) and dedication, not to our present society, but to its continuation and improvement. I hold this position myself. College is not like a winery--simply an aging and maturing process. I believe that, unlike bottles of wine, students must be shaken as well as pressured if they are to benefit from college. And, with students as with bottles of wine, some will go sour or even blow up under such ministrations. I do not trust faculty members generally to be either sufficiently sensitive, concerned, or knowledgeable to deal with such possibilities. Hence, I see the need for rein- forcing what I have called the informational and therapeutic role of student personnel work. And, as suggested earlier, I see the law and order responsibilities in their informational and educa- tional aspects as closely associated. The counselor surely cannot enforce rules, but he can point to their existence and their rationale. If he believes they are unjust, he should also say so and work to alter them.

Obviously, the full implications of this role for student personnel work (I would junk that terminology as tainted and useless today for the clearer and more restricted role that I am advocating) cannot be developed in a brief paper. Equally obviously, this role leaves out much that persons who now think of themselves as student personnel professionals are now doing. But I note that blacksmiths and buggy makers are also a rarity today because their role is almost irrelevant to a mechanical society.

In the limited role that I have prescribed, evaluation of the benefits of student personnel work would be most clearly defined; their costs and the alternative values foregone would be clear. I should expect that:

1. Student abilities, interests, and aspirations would become the basis for student programs rather than arbitrary departmental and college faculty requirements;

2. As a result of this, more students would find college a challenging experience, would complete their degrees, and find their education more relevant to life and work;

328

3.   By matching interest, abilities, and requirements, much wastage resulting from time-serving and irrelevant requirements could be eliminated;

4.   The clearer focus on competency would permit a larger proportion of education of motivated students to proceed off the campus with an increase in relevancy and a decrease in costs;

5.   Many of the dissatisfactions and affective concerns of students would be alleviated or would disappear because they were caught up in a more significant educational experience with definite ends of view.

Such benefits as these are measurable and they are important. The alternatives, which are to ignore individual characteristics and to continue to improve arbitrary and time-serving requirements, are eminently unsatisfactory in terms of a widely prevalent set of values in our society. Alternative delivery systems do not exist, for the disciplinary-oriented faculties have long since demonstrated that they value their own careers and disciplines more than they do the individual undergraduate or the needs of society. Finally, it is clear that the student would benefit by having a better and more relevant education; professors would benefit because the conflicts of interests between their careers and disciplines and their obligations to the student and society would be resolved. Others more oriented to student and societal concerns would have the responsibility of helping students select wisely from the smorgasbord of educational offerings or whip up their own dish. Finally, society would benefit because the product of the college would be better educated, more suited to social needs, and because educational costs now largely determined by faculty whims would be controlled by social and student needs and desires.

CHAPTER 36

RESEARCH IN COLLEGE STUDENT PERSONNEL SERVICES

George P. Robb

The word research generally seems to have a positive
connotation. Research is thought of as something that is
important and valuable--something worthwhile. But what is
research?

Mouly (1963, p. 4) describes research as

the process of arriving at dependable solutions to problems through the planned and systematic collection,
analysis and interpretation of data . . . we can define
educational research as the systematic and scholarly
application of scientific method; interpreted in its
broadest sense, to the solution of educational problems.

The key words in Mouly's definitions of research are planned
and systematic. Research must be thought through carefully
and deliberately and carried out in a thorough manner in
order to qualify as a sound study that the researcher and
others can rely upon.

There are many kinds of research, employing varying procedures, but in general all types of research serve one or
more of these functions:

1. To determine the status of phenomena (past and
    present);
2. To ascertain the nature, composition, and processes
    that characterize selected phenomena;
3. To trace growth, developmental history, change, and
    status of certain phenomena;
4. To study cause-and-effect relationships among and
    between certain phenomena (Turney and Robb, 1971,
    p. 2).

Students or professionals in the field of college personnel
work may be either consumers or producers of research, or

both. As consumers they are engaged in reading and utilizing
research reports or articles involving research studies, and
as producers they conduct their own research projects. Whether
one is a consumer or producer of research, an understanding of
the basic concepts and principles of research is essential.

Types of Research

Research may be classified or labeled in different ways.
For instance it can be classified as pure (basic) or applied
research. Fox (1969, pp. 93-94) differentiates the two types
of research as follows:

> At one end of the continuum is pure research which, in
> its extreme form is research motivated solely by intel-
> lectual interest and directed toward the acquisition of
> knowledge for knowledge's sake. In this extreme form,
> there is no known or intended practical application of
> the findings, even if the research is successfully com-
> pleted. In contrast, applied research in its extreme
> form would be directed toward solving a specific practi-
> cal problem, even though no new knowledge was acquired
> in the process.

An example of pure research would be a study to determine
whether there is a relationship between the official titles
of college student personnel offices and the functions of
the offices, if the researcher merely wants to satisfy an
"itch to know." A study designed to determine the efficiency
of operation of various organizational patterns of college
student personnel programs would be an applied research study
if the results were to be used to suggest changes in existing
programs in order to improve efficiency of operation. The
results of the study might have immediate, practical application. Sometimes, however, basic research will lead a
researcher or others into applied research at a latter time.

Another way to classify or categorize types of research
is according to the three areas of historical, descriptive,
and experimental research. Each type will be discussed
briefly.

331

Historical Research

As the term suggests, this type of research requires the collecting, organizing, and classifying of data pertaining to past events, conditions, situations, etc. An example is the tracing of the evolution of college student personnel programs from their origin to the present time. If properly carried out, this kind of research is just as sound and reliable as other kinds of research, but it may be difficult to carry out if the necessary data are non-existent, scarce or inacessible.

In conducting historical research, the investigator should attempt to utilize primary rather than secondary sources of information. Primary sources are original documents or accounts from actual eyewitnesses. Secondary sources are reproductions of original documents or reports from persons who interviewed actual eyewitnesses to events. Books, journal articles, monographs, and completed questionnaires are some examples of historical data.

The historical researcher is expected to exercise critical judgment in evaluating sources of information, looking for evidence of authenticity, accuracy, and completeness in documents that are to be used. Clues concerning the validity of historical data may be found in the dates reported, names, terms or events mentioned, and a comparison with other appropriate historical documents of the period being studied.

Descriptive Research

This type of research is designed to discover the status of people, conditions, institutions, etc. There are three different kinds of descriptive research that are so common that they deserve mention here: survey study, case study, and correlation study.

The survey study is conducted when there is a need to determine the nature of the present situation with respect to an institution, a community, or certain persons (with respect to such characteristics as attitudes, behaviors, needs, etc.) For example, a survey study could be made in order to gauge the opinion of college students toward the existing college counseling service.

The case study is limited to a single person, agency, or other unit, although a researcher could carry on several case studies at the same time. Terman's study of the gifted is an example, for this research required the gathering of intelligence scores and many other measures (mental, emotional, social and physical) for over 1,500 individual subjects.

Because the same subjects were studied over a period of several years (see Goleman, 1980), the Terman study is also classified as a longitudinal study, as contrasted with a cross sectional study that compares different persons or institutions at the same point in time. Some research combines the cross sectional and longitudinal comparisons to achieve he benefits that may result from both approaches. Cross sectional and longitudinal studies do not have to be of the case study type, but they are descriptive research studies.

A counselor in a college counseling service might wish to compare counseled and non-counseled students over a period of several years (during and after college attendance) on several variables, treating each client as a separate case. This would be an example of the use of the case study approach in research. A detailed comparison of two different community college financial-aid programs is another example, with each school being considered a "case."

A distinction should be made between the clinical case study and the empirical case study. The clinical case study of an individual generally will have an extensive case history of the client being studied, but it lacks precise measurement of the observations that are made. The empirical case study, on the other hand, definitely provides for systematic observation and measurement of client variables. In addition to focusing on the individual, the empirical case study typically provides for control of environment, careful and systematic observation of change in the subject, and use of response frequencies or degrees of response as measures of change.

A college counselor could use the empirical case study with individual clients to determine behavior change following the use of a particular treatment (such as a new reinforcement technique, stimulus, or other condition) that may be expected to produce some sort of client behavioral or attitudinal change. Schmidt (1974) advocates the use of the multiple baseline technique in research. This is a variation of the case study that involves the measurement of several behaviors over time. Behavior baselines are established for each behavior that is being studied, and then the procedure to be tested is applied to a behavior until a change is demonstrated. The procedure is applied to a second behavior, then a third, etc. If the behaviors are altered greatly at the point of introduction of the procedure, an inference of causal relationship can be made. The multiple baseline design not only can be applied across behaviors, but also across individuals and situations.

A correlation study involves the use of correlation techniques to determine the amount and nature of relationship between variables, such as test scores. Suppose that a researcher is interested in the possible relationship of the two variables of SAT scores and college grades for students at Euphoria University. The researcher could employ the Pearson product-moment correlation technique to find the degree of relationship between scholastic aptitude and grades at Euphoria University. With calculators and computers readily available, such data as test scores and grades can be processed quickly and accurately.

Experimental and Quasi-Experimental Research

This kind of research requires that a researcher vary a factor systematically in order to determine the effect that the varied factor has on some other factor or variable. The variable that is systematically manipulated is known as the independent variable, and the one that is affected by the independent variable is called the dependent variable. When there are other variables or conditions in the experiment that may influence the outcome of the experiment, they are referred to as the intervening variables. The researcher is supposed to control or carefully regulate the intervening variables in order to limit their effect. When the intervening variables are properly controlled, and the experiment is properly designed and carried out, the experimenter is justified in concluding that a change in the dependent variable resulted from change in the independent variable. Many studies of this type do not have an adequate control of all important variables, and such studies should be called quasi-experimental studies. If an experimental or quasi-experimental study is carried on in the field rather than a laboratory, the study is a field study.

An example of an experimental study would be a study in which college students who received group counseling (treatment group) were compared with students who did not receive counseling (control group) with respect to one or more variables, such as grade-point-average, anxiety, or self esteem.

Conducting Research

There are certain recommended steps in research that tend to insure that the research is well planned and executed, and that the study has an acceptable degree of validity. In other words, the research should be conducted in an orderly, systematic and scientific manner that permits drawing sound conclusions. The steps generally followed in acceptable research involve (1) defining a researchable problem, (2) formulating hypotheses or research questions, (3) review of the literature, (4) research design, (5) collection of data, (6) data analysis, and (7) drawing conclusions. These are the basic steps, but, of course, others can be included in certain unique studies.

Defining a Researchable Problem

The process of research begins with the selection of a problem that interests the researcher and is researchable. In determining whether the problem is researchable, several factors must be considered, such as the time required to complete the study, the expense involved, and the availability of subjects, facilities, research assistants (if needed), instruments, etc. Once a problem is judged to be worthy of research, and is researchable, it should be defined clearly. A clear, precise statement of the problem facilitates the structuring of a research design and the writing of the final report.

335

Formulating Hypotheses

Many research studies have one or more hypotheses that may serve the researcher by providing stimuli to research, suggesting methodology, providing criteria for evaluating research techniques, and providing organizing principles. In short, the hypotheses serve to guide and assist the researcher in the planning and conduct of a study. A hypothesis is a shrewd guess or inference concerning what the researcher may reasonably expect. The following statement is an example of a hypothesis: "At the conclusion of the study, the treatment group will exhibit greater assertiveness than the control group." Not all studies require the use of hypotheses, and some researchers prefer simply to use one or more research questions or statements of purpose in order to facilitate the planning and execution of the research. Some researchers believe that hypotheses may bias a researcher toward certain conclusions. In utilizing hypotheses, the researcher should not be blind to results in the study that may have relevance even though they do not relate directly to the stated hypotheses.

Review of Literature

A thorough survey of the literature that deals with the topic of the study chosen for research is an essential step in the completion of the study, for it helps the researcher in certain ways. For example, a review of material related to the research area can help in defining and limiting the problem. The review also may turn up new facts and ideas that can facilitate the planning and organizing of the research. When copious articles and books have been written in the chosen research area, the researcher is expected to be selective and to examine only those writings that are especially relevant, and then the most pertinent and useful sources of information can be used in the study.

Research Design

All studies have some sort of design, or framework, that the researcher has used. The better the design, the more likely that the researcher will be able to approach the problem

336

directly and test the hypotheses or answer the research questions. It goes without saying that the poorly designed study has doubtful, if any, validity. In the experimental or quasi-experimental studies, design is especially significant. The most important aspects of research design are sample selection, attitudes of subjects, measurement of variables, comparison of groups, and systematic bias.

Sample Selection

The method of choosing a sample for use in a study is important if one wishes to generalize the results of the study to a whole population, another sample, or another setting. A properly-selected sample will permit generalization of results to the population from which it is drawn. A sample is defined here as a subset of a population, which may be made up of people, animals, measurements, objects, etc. A sample may be as small as one, or a large as the whole population, but generally it is a fraction of the population.

The random sample is the basic type of sample for research, and it is defined as a sample that is drawn from the population in such a way that every individual in the population has the same chance of being selected for the sample. When one wants to be sure that all of the strata or subpopulations of the population are represented in the sample, one can draw individuals at random from each stratum, and thus have a stratified random sample. A random sample generally is drawn by the use of a table or random numbers. This simple procedure is explained in many statistics books.

Attitudes of Subjects

Studies in the field of college student personnel work often involve the use of human subjects as participants, and when this is the case the researcher must be cognizant of the importance of subject attitude. Whether the subjects are willing, unwilling, or indifferent may very well affect the outcome of a study. If volunteers are used, there may be a question of whether non-volunteers would respond in the same manner as the volunteers. Also, the researcher should guard against the well-known Hawthorne Effect, which means that a

337

mental set or attitude can occur when subjects in a study know that they are participants in the study. That is, they may perform better or act somewhat differently from what is normal for them when they realize that they are research participants. This attitudinal condition can become an intervening or confounding variable in a study, producing an unwanted effect on the outcome of the research.

In a survey that utilizes a questionnaire, the recipients of the questionnaire may not be willing to participate, so they may return incomplete or inaccurate questionnaires. If a high percentage of the returned forms are incomplete or if fewer than half of the questionnaires are returned, the researcher should seriously doubt the validity of the data, for the returned sample may be extremely biased.

Measurement of Variables

Most of the studies in the area of college student personnel work will involve the use of variables of some sort, and these must be measured or assessed some way. Even a simple survey of the use of student services on a campus will generally require collecting data and may involve the use of a standardized inventory. It is important to devise or select instruments that have the greatest possible validity and reliability. Validity refers to the instrument's ability to measure what it is purported to measure, while reliability pertains to the consistency of the device. Wide ranges of validity and reliability are found among the thousands of tests, inventories, questionnaires, check lists, rating scales, etc., that have been devised and used for research. When one is able to use existing tests or inventories for research, the instruments can be examined thoroughly by the researcher to judge their quality and usefulness. Books on psychometrics and Buros Mental Measurement Yearbooks can and should be consulted, too. When new instruments must be devised, the researcher should again refer to appropriate references for assistance in constructing the instruments. This point can not be over-emphasized, for one common weakness in behavioral-science research is poor instrumentation.

338

Comparison of Groups

As mentioned earlier, some studies involve the comparison of two or more groups with regard to some variable or variables. This might be done in various types of research, but it is most common in experimental or quasi-experimental studies. Regardless of the kind of research that one is considering, when groups are to be compared, certain conditions must be met before group differences can be properly assessed.

Suppose that Dean R. U. Schurr were trying to determine whether student academic achievement of Northeast Community College is higher than student achievement at Northwest Community College. The question might be, "Do students at Northeast tend to achieve better than do students at Northwest?" Because there are many factors that relate to achievement, such as scholastic aptitude, motivation, instruction, etc., Dean Schurr would not be able to answer this question by merely selecting a group of students from Northeast and one from Northwest, and then comparing their mean grade-point averages or achievement-test scores. A better approach would be to form two matched groups from the two colleges and then compare their mean grade-point average. The matching could be done on the basis of scholastic-aptitude test scores, reading-ability scores, sex, age, courses taken, etc., and thus the researcher would control several important intervening variables that might exert an influence on achievement. With adequate controls in his study, Dean Schurr would be able to draw sound inferences from his findings. If he found a difference in achievement, it would be necessary to test it for statistical significance. This will be discussed later.

As discussed previously, in experimental or quasi-experimental studies, two groups are generally compared with respect to some variable or variables. One group (the experimental or treatment group) gets the treatment that is to be studied for its effect, and the other group (control) gets no treatment. If there is a significant effect, the treatment is judged to be the cause of the effect.

When groups are compared on some variable, generally the mean scores of the two groups (there may be three or more

339

groups in some studies) are compared and tested for significance of a difference. Provided that the correct statistical test is made, the mean-score comparison is an appropriate procedure to use. A comparison of means, however, may obscure the individual changes that are made by the subjects in the study. That is to say, perhaps important change in behavior has occurred among some subjects, but the overall change is not statistically significant. Because of this possibility, researchers are urged to report (1) how many subjects in the groups gained or lost on the dependent measure, and (2) the magnitude of change for each subject. Thus, with both group means and a record of individual changes reported, the findings may have the maximum attainable value.

As an example, suppose that residence hall counselor, M. Pathee, has noticed that many college students in her dormitory have expressed concern about their test anxiety. Counselor Pathee might decide to do an experiment on test anxiety, using biofeedback as a treatment method for reducing anxiety. She could identify several test-anxious subjects for her populations, select two groups randomly from the population, treat one group (experimental) but not the other (control) and examine the results at the end of the study. She could compare mean anxiety scores for the two groups statistically to determine whether a significant reduction in test anxiety occurred in the experimental group, and she could examine scores of individuals to determine how many persons showed changes in anxiety level as well as the extent of change that occurred for each individual.

Systematic Bias

When two groups are formed in some manner other than random selection, the researcher should assume that the groups are not the same with respect to many of the variables that may be important in the study. In the study of test anxiety, random selection should eliminate or minimize the differences between the groups. When intact groups must be used for some reason, however, the researcher should assume that there is systematic bias present. This condition may occur because of the instruments to be used, as well as because of the way in which the groups were formed.

The problem of systematic bias can be dealt with in various ways. One method is through replication or repeating of the study to determine whether the same results are found when the same study is carried out in the same way again. Another method is to use the technique called balancing. When balancing is used in a study, the variables are permitted to vary, but they must vary the same way in the two groups. If sex is considered to be a variable that must be controlled, and can not be controlled, the groups can be balanced by having the same proportion of men and women in each group. Balancing might also be done for age, intelligence, reading ability, or other factors that are deemed important in the study. Analysis of covariance is a statistical technique that can be used to provide statistical control of variables when two intact groups are used rather than randomly-chosen groups.

Collection of Data

After a decision has been made concerning what kinds of data are needed to complete the study, the researcher must also decide how the data will be collected. If suitable instruments are available, these can be used; but, if not, the researcher may have to modify existing devices or develop new ones. As was mentioned earlier, close attention should be paid to evidence of validity and reliability or the instrument. Poor reliability will lower an instrument's validity, but high reliability (consistency) does not insure a high level of validity; thus, validity is the more important consideration. Good references and the assistance of persons with appropriate expertise should be sought when one is in doubt about data-collecting devices or techniques, and especially when a new procedure or instrument must be developed. Suggestions for the construction of questionnaires, check lists, rating scales, interviews, etc., can be found in books on psychometrics or research, such as Research in Education (Turney and Robb, 1971, pp. 129-160).

For some studies it is advisable to conduct a pilot-study before the major study is undertaken. The additional time that is required for a pilot study may be well spent because it may reveal weaknesses in the data-collecting procedures or instruments that could ruin the major study. Also,

341

a pilot study can provide evidence for the feasibility of the planned research project.

Once the data have been collected, they must be prepared for a data analysis. Careful planning with regard to the processing and analysis of data before the data collecting is done can save considerable time and effort later. It generally is wise for a researcher to look ahead at the time a study is designed to devise an efficient way to collect and record data in order to provide for efficient data processing and analysis later. For example, with some tests the researcher can have test answers recorded directly on computer cards by the participants in the study, thus eliminating the step of transferring data from answer sheets to the cards. Questionnaires and check lists also can be set up for efficient data processing.

Data Analysis

The method of analyzing the results of a study will necessarily have to fit the design of the study and kind of data collected. The findings of historical studies generally require subjective interpretations, the results of descriptive research may require both subjective analysis and statistical analysis of data, and the findings of experimental research will generally require extensive statistical analysis.

Statistical analyses help the researcher draw conclusions and make generalizations based upon the findings of research. An example may serve to illustrate this point. Suppose that Irma Helper, a counselor at Mountain View College, has conducted an experiment designed to determine whether regular attendance in a study skills seminar will boost student academic achievement. Suppose that the study has been well designed and has been carried out properly. If Ms. Helper finds a difference in grade-point average in favor of the study-skills group, should she conclude that the study-skills seminar is effective as a means of helping her college students achieve better? In attempting to answer this question she should use a statistical test that will indicate whether the difference in mean grade-point average for the study-

342

skills group is sufficiently larger than the mean grade-point average for the control group to rule out mere chance as the reason for the difference. This determination can be made in this instance by using a t-test for the significance of a difference between means. The researcher may set a level of significance (.05 or .01, commonly) and then see whether the t-value is large enough to meet the desired level of significance. If the .05 criterion level is used and met, the researcher is justified in assuming that such a difference is expected to occur by chance only five times out of 100 (hence the level of significance of .05). One time in 20, then, a difference as large as the one found will occur just by chance. A larger difference between means is required to meet the significance test at the .01 level.

This testing generally relates to a hypothesis of a study, and the testing is made on the basis of a null hypothesis. The null hypothesis, for example, might state, "There is no difference in achievement between the treatment group and control group." If the difference is significant, the null hypothesis is rejected in favor of the original stated hypothesis.

Several other tests may be employed to determine level of significance, such as analysis of variance, analysis of covariance, chi-square, Mann-Whitney U test, etc. Certain statistical tests are appropriate only for certain types of data and research designs. Selection of the appropriate statistical analysis should be based upon these considerations:

1. The level of the measure of the dependent variable (whether the data are nominal, ordinal, interval, or ratio);

2. The distribution of the dependent variable (whether the data are continuously distributed; whether the sampling distribution of the statistic closely approximates a normal distribution; whether the samples are drawn from populations having equal variances);

3. The number of samples (whether one, two, or more samples are used);

343

4. The methods of experimental or statistical control (whether controls are based upon matching, random selection of subjects for samples, or a statistical procedure).

The reader is urged to refer to statistics books, such as Fundamental Research Statistics for Behavioral Sciences, Roscoe, 1975), that treat the topic of analysis techniques in detail, or consult a statistician when assistance is needed in this area of research.

Statistical tests are not infallible, nor are research designs and procedures, so sometimes a researcher makes an error in rejecting a true null hypothesis (or concludes that an obtained difference is a true difference when it is not). This is called a Type I error. If the researcher accepts a false null hypothesis, or concludes that two groups are not different when they really are different, a Type II error is made.

Drawing Conclusions

This is an especially difficult, but extremely important, part of research. Too often people who read research reports that appear in journals are prone to accept the researcher's conclusions without question, and too often the conclusions are unwarranted. Unsound conclusions may occur when the researcher has used a faulty research design, selected inappropriate instruments or statistics, overgeneralized from the data, or has made some other serious error. Some investigators find it very difficult to report negative conclusions, so they find a way to draw inferences that are not valid. Perhaps they wish to avoid a sense of failure or perhaps they fear that a research article will not be published if it lacks positive or interesting conclusions. Whatever the reasons, examples of inappropriate conclusions are abundant in the literature.

When the findings of the study are known, the researcher ought to relate them to all aspects of the study, especially the previous research reported in the literature, the research design, the basic assumptions of the study, and the limitations of the study. The conclusions should not be mere statements of findings, such as "the difference between the mean grade-point average of the experimental and control group was 1.23 in favor of the experimental group." This statement is a statement of the results of the study. A conclusion would be an inference drawn from the results of the study, and (as an example) might be stated, "the study-skills program is an effective program for helping college students achieve." This statement is more than a statement of results or findings. It is an inference drawn from the findings of the study, and it should not go beyond what the findings and limitations of the study will permit. The writing of sound conclusions involves a combination of research knowledge, scientific attitudes, and some common sense.

Evaluation of Research

Producers and consumers of research should be able to evaluate research well enough to identify serious flaws as well as strengths in the research. The consumer should be able to discard or disregard those studies that are poorly designed or conducted. The producer should be able to plan, design, and execute studies that meet the criteria of good research and thus provide other people with a source of useful (hopefully relevant) information.

Strauss (1969) provides useful guidelines for the analysis of one's own research or the research reports in the literature. These guidelines cover twenty important areas: problem raised, previous work cited, objectives stated, hypotheses formulated, assumptions made, population studied, sample drawn, instruments used, designs examined, procedures followed, safeguards taken, observations recorded, findings assembled, statistics interpreted, interpretations discussed, conclusions reached, limitations recognized, further work projected, improvements suggested, and clarity of report.

Researchers should be able to apply the Strauss guidelines, or a similar set of criteria, to a research report and assess the value of the study described. Experience tells the author of this chapter that many research reports are woefully weak in one or more areas covered by the Strauss

344a

criteria. The reader is urged to read the Strauss article and consider its use in planning research or writing research reports.

Ethical Considerations

When research involves human subjects, certain ethical issues are raised. Foremost among these issues are deception, invasion of privacy, and informed consent.

In some experimental research in the past, subjects have been deceived regarding the purposes or procedures of a study in order to prevent a subject's knowledge of the study from influencing the results. Some studies, in fact, could not be carried out without some deception. It is obvious that deception can take many forms, from just being vague about the study to deliberately misleading the subject. The ethical "question" centers on deciding whether deception is justified and whether possible risks outweigh the possible gains that may result from the study. Debriefing, or the explanation of the study and its purposes to the participant in the study, may correct for some of the negative effects of deception. In a debriefing session, conducted soon after an experiment, the experimenter can explain the true nature of the study and the reasons for misleading the subject. Whether the debriefing is fully successful will depend upon many factors, but it is generally an essential part of a study in which some form of deception was utilized.

More than ever before, the American public is concerned about "invasion of privacy" or the action of acquiring information that is considered to be personal by an individual. One is likely to think of such matters as religious beliefs, political beliefs, sexual behavior, and income, when invasion of privacy is mentioned. Various questionnaires and personality inventories are subject to criticism because of questions that many people consider to be of a very personal nature. Many studies do not require asking a person to provide personal data, but for those that do, a person's right to privacy can be protected somewhat through anonymity and confidentiality.

344b

A researcher should be able, when necessary, to assure respondents that their responses are anonymous. The subjects may be told not to put their names on the questionnaire, answer sheet, etc., or they may be assured that the names will be removed after the data are collected. Code numbers, of course, can replace names and the code numbers are just as useful for organizing data. Confidentiality is another means of protecting the subject's right to privacy. Confidentiality, as used here, means that information of a confidential nature will not be disclosed to others unless the subject approved the release of information.

The term informed consent means that the subject understands the nature of the research (including the alternatives available and the possible benefits and risks) and agrees to participate. The agreement to participate should be without any type of coercion. Obviously, there may be many instances in research when the subject is not fully aware of all aspects of the research and has given consent with reluctance. The signing of a consent form, a procedure that is used to protect the researcher against complaints or charges of failure to inform a subject and receive consent, is a necessary step in many experiments, but it probably falls short of providing evidence that the subject really understands the research and has agreed to participate willingly.

The researcher who is using human subjects in research should follow acceptable ethical guidelines, such as the Ethical Principles in the Conduct of Research with Human Participants, published by the American Psychological Association in 1973. Researcher, subject, and society are likely to benefit when such guidelines are rigorously applied in research.

Concluding Comments

This discussion of research is meant to serve as an introduction to research for some readers and as a concise review for others. Research is a very broad area of study, and all of the aspects presented here could have been expanded considerably. For example, there are several different ways of analyzing research data. Space did not permit a

344c

more extensive coverage of the topics presented. The reader
is encouraged to go to appropriate research textbooks and to
journals or other sources for more complete treatment of
various aspects of research.

Research in counseling and student personnel services can
be an invaluable means of answering important questions, but
because it can require much time and the expenditure of a
considerable amount of money, researchers should be selective
when it comes to choosing research projects. Thoreson (1969,
p. 1) has said that most published research is a waste of
time and resources, and although he was referring mainly to
research in counseling, his criticisms may apply also to many
other areas in the behavioral sciences. Krumboltz (1967,
p. 191) suggests that research ought to meet a test of relevancy, which essentially asks, "What will counselors do differently if the results of this research come out one way
rather than another?" Granted that some nongeneralizable
research has heuristic value because it leads to an unexpected discovery or an idea for other research possibilities,
the person who has very limited funds or time generally
ought to keep the "test of relevancy" in mind and conduct
research that is promising. That is to say, the research
should have a high probability of eventuating in an outcome
that the researcher ultimately can use in some beneficial way.

References

Ad Hoc Committee on Ethical Standards in Psychological
Research. Ethical principles in the conduct of
research with human participants. Washington, D. C.:
American Psychological Association, 1973.

Anatasi, Anne. Psychological Testing. Riverside, N.J.:
Macmillan, 1976.

Baer, D. M. Perhaps it would be better not to know
everything. Journal of Applied Behavior Analysis,
10:167-172, 1977.

Bakan, D. The test of significance in psychological
research. Psychological Bulletin, 66:423-437, 1966.

Barber, T. X. Pitfalls in Human Research: Ten Pivotal Points. New York: Pergamon, 1976.

Beatty, W. W. How blind is blind: A simple procedure for estimating observer naivete. Psychological Bulletin, 78:70-71, 1972.

Bernstein, I. N., Bohrnstedt, G. W., & Borgatta, E. F. External validity and evaluation research: A codification of problems. Sociological Methods and Research, 4:101-128, 1975.

Bolgar, H. The case study method. In B. B. Wolman (Ed.), Handbook of Clinical Psychology. New York: McGraw-Hill, 1965.

Bracht, G. H., and Glass, G. V. The external validity of experiments. American Educational Research Journal, 5:437-474, 1968.

Brown, Clarence W., and Ghiselli, E. F. Scientific Method in Psychology. New York: McGraw-Hill, 1955.

Campbell, D. T., and Stanley, J. C. Experimental and Quasi-Experimental Design for Research. Chicago: Rand McNally and Company, 1963.

Carlsmith, J. M., Ellsworth, P. C., & Aronson, E. Methods of Research in Social Psychology. Reading, Mass.: Addison-Wesley, 1976.

Chassan, J. G. Research Design in Clinical Psychology and Psychiatry. New York: Appleton-Century-Crofts, 1967.

Cohen, J. The Statistical power of adnormal-social psychological research: A review. Journal of Abnormal and Social Psychology, 65:145-153, 1962.

Davitz, Joel R., & Davitz, L. G. A Guide for Evaluating Research Plans in Psychology and Education. New York: Teachers College Press, 1967.

344e

Dukes, W. E.   N = 1.   Psychological Bulletin, 64:74-79, 1965.

Edwards, Allen L.   Experimental Design in Psychological Research.   New York: Holt, 1962.

Fox, David J.   The Research Process in Education.   New York: Holt, 1969.

Goldman, Leo, Ed.   Research Methods for Counselors.   New York: John Wiley and Sons, 1978.

Goleman, David.   1,528 little genuises and how they grew. Psychology Today, February, 1980, 28-43.

Greenwald, A. G.   Consequences of prejudice against the null hypothesis.   Psychological Bulletin, 82:1-20, 1975.

Guilford, J. P.   Psychometric Methods, 2nd ed.   New York: McGraw-Hill, 1954.

Hillway, Tyrus.   Introduction to Research.   Boston: Houghton Mifflin, 1956.

Johnson, R. F. Q.   The experimenter attributes effect: A methodological analysis.   Psychological Record, 26:67-68, 1976.

Jones, R. R., Vaught, R. S., & Weinrott, M.   Time-series analysis in operant research.   Journal of Applied Behavioral Analysis, 10:151-166, 1977.

Kazdin, A. E., & Hartman, D. P.   The simultaneous-treat-ment design.   Behavior Therapy, 9:912-922, 1978.

_____, & Kopel, S. A.   On resolving ambiguities of the multiple-baseline design: Problems and recommendations.   Behavior Therapy, 6:601-608, 1975.

Kelman, H. C.   Human use of human subjects: The problem of deception in social psychological experiments. Psychological Bulletin, 67:1-11, 1967.

Kelman, H. C. The rights of the subject in social research: An analysis in terms of relative power and legitimacy. American Psychologist, 27:898-1016, 1972.

Kirk, R. E. Experimental Design: Procedures for the Behavioral Sciences. Belmont: Brooks/Cole, 1968.

Korchin, S. J. Modern Clinical Psychology. New York: Basic Books, 1976.

Krumboltz, John. Future directions in counseling research. In J. M. Whitely (Ed.) Research in Counseling. Columbus: Charles E. Merrill Co., 1967.

Lanyon, R. I., & Goodstein, L. C. Personality Assessment. New York: Wiley, 1971.

Lathrop, Richard G. Introduction to Psychological Research. New York: Harper, 1969.

Leitenberg, H. The use of single case methodology in psychotherapy research. Journal of Abnormal Psychology, 82:87-101, 1973.

Lindquist, E. F. Design and Analysis of Experiments in Psychology and Education. Boston: Houghton Mifflin, 1956.

Menges, R. J. Openness and honesty versus coercion and deception in psychological research. American Psychologist, 28:1030-1034, 1973.

Mischel, W. Personality and Assessment. New York: Wiley, 1968.

Mouly, G. J. The Science of Educational Research. New York: American Book Company, 1963.

Robb, G. P., and Williamson, A. Introduction to Individual Appraisal. Springfield: Charles C. Thomas, 1980.

Roscoe, John T. Fundamental Research Statistics for the Behavioral Sciences, 2nd ed. New York: Holt, 1975.

Rosenthal, D., & Frank, J. D. Psychotherapy and the placebo effect. Psychology Bulletin, 53:294-302, 1956.

Schmidt, J. A. Research techniques for counselors: the multiple baseline. Personnel and Guidance Journal, 53:(3):200-206, 1974.

Sellitz, Claire, et al. Research Methods in Social Relations. New York: Holt, 1967.

Shapiro, M. B. The single case in clinical-psychological research. Journal of Genetic Psychology, 74:3-23, 1966.

Sidman, M. Tactics of Scientific Research. New York: Basic Books, 1960.

Skinner, B. F. The experimental analysis of behavior. American Scientist, 45:343-371, 1957.

Solomon, R. L. An extension of control group design. Psychological Bulletin, 46:137-150, 1949.

Spence, Janet T., Underwood, Benton, Duncan, Carl, and John Cotton. Elementary Statistics, 2nd ed. New York: Appleton-Century, 1968.

Strauss, Samuel. Guidelines for analysis of research reports. Journal of Educational Research, 63:165-169, 1969.

Stricker, L. The true deceiver. Psychological Bulletin, 68:13-20, 1967.

Thoreson, C. E. Relevance and research in counseling. Review of Educational Research, 39(2):264-279, 1969.

Turney, B. L., and Robb, G. P. Research in Education. New York: Holt, Rinehart and Winston, 1971.

344h

Turney, B. L., and Robb, G. P. Statistical Methods and Behavioral Science. New York: Harper and Row, 1973.

Underwood, B. J., & Shaughnessy, J. J. Experimentation in Psychology. New York: Wiley, 1975.

Watson, R. I. The Clinical Method in Psychology. New York: Harper & Row, 1951.

Wiles, David K. Changing Perspectives in Educational Research. Worthington: Charles A. Jones Publishing Company, 1972.

West, S. G., & Gunn, S. P. Some issues of ethics and social psychology. American Psychologist, 33:30-38, 1978.

Wexler, D. B. Reflections on the legal regulation of behavior modification in institutional settings. Arizona Law Review, 17:132-134, 1975.

Winder, B. J. Statistical Principles in Experimental Design, 2nd ed. New York: McGraw-Hill, 1971.

Wood, Gordon. Fundamentals of Psychological Research. Boston: Little, Brown and Cole, 1974.

CHAPTER 37

RECENT RESEARCH ACCOMPLISHMENTS
IN COUNSELING AND GUIDANCE

Edwin L. Herr

Most fields within education have experienced a growing
body of research on which to base practice. The field of counseling and guidance is no exception. While many significant
research studies could be reported, three that represent major
programmatic research themes shaping counseling and guidance
perspectives and techniques will be examined here.

Counseling and guidance people have long been accused of
talking about what they do, not about results. Under the influence of accountability, however, counselors are being required
to identify their program goals, behavioral expectations for
students, and processes that will be used to achieve the behavioral changes sought. The seminal conceptualizations in this
area have occurred in behavioral counseling, particularly under
the leadership of Krumboltz and his colleagues at Stanford University (Krumboltz, 1966; and Sloane et al., 1975).

Since the early 1950s researchers have been investigating
types of attitudes, understandings, and skills that comprise
individual career development. The term career development encompasses such processes as exploratory vocational behavior,
decision-making behavior, interrelationships between career
development and personality development, educational choice and
achievement and work satisfaction, self-concepts, and views of
live alternatives (including careers). This line of research has
begun to identify the personal behaviors that need to be present
if career development is to proceed smoothly rather than be
impaired or delayed. It has further suggested that developmental
tasks occur at different life periods that can be anticipated and
can serve as the focus of developmental or preventative counseling and guidance activities as well as of career education
(Crites, 1974; and Super, 1969).

During the past two decades the components of the counseling
process and the relationship between a counselor and a client
have come under intense research scrutiny. In the past, research
on the counseling process and its outcomes has been generally
ambiguous. More recent research has shown that effective counselors tend to cancel out ineffective counselors and vice versa.

345

Thus the results obtained often do not strongly favor a counseling treatment over a competing treatment or a control group.
However, Carkhuff and his associates (1972) have extended the
earlier work of Carl Rogers in isolating the characteristics that
distinguish effective from ineffective counselors. This line of
research has shown that effective counselors do make a difference
and that counselors, teachers, or other helping persons can be
trained to be effective in the counseling relationship (Carkhuff,
1972). Major research bearing upon the systematic training of
counselors and other helping professionals would include Ivey
et al. (1968) and Wittmer and Lister (1972).

The research referenced above provides directions for improved educational practice by: (1) specification of objectives
that can be accomplished through counseling and guidance efforts,
(2) suggesting areas of content for the career development component of guidance programs, and (3) improving ability to discriminate between good and poor counseling.

References

> Carkhuff, R.R. "The Development of Systematic Human
> Resource Development Models." The Counseling
> Psychologist 3, 1972, 4-11.

> Carkhuff, R.R. "New Directions in Training for the Help-
> ing Professions: Toward a Technology for Human and
> Community Resource Development." The Counseling
> Psychologist 3, 1972, 12-30.

> Crites, J.O. "Career Development Processes: A Model
> of Vocational Maturity." Vocational Guidance
> and Human Development. Edited by E. L. Herr.
> Boston: Houghton Mifflin, 1974.

> Ivey, A.E., et al. "Microcounseling and Attending
> Behavior: An Approach to Prepracticum Counselor
> Learning." Journal of Counseling Psychology 12
> 1968, 1-12.

> Krumbolz, J.D. Revolution in Counseling: Implications
> of Behavioral Sciences. Boston: Houghton Mifflin,
> 1966.

> Sloane, R.B., et al. Psychotherapy Versus Behavior
> Therapy. Cambridge: Harvard University Press, 1975.

> Super, D.E. "Vocational Development Theory: Persons,
> Positions and Processes." The Counseling Psychologist,
> 1969.

References

Wittmer, J. and Lister, J. "Microcounseling and Microcounseling Consultation via Videotape." Counselor Education and Supervision 11, 1972, 238-240.

347

CHAPTER 38

MINORITY PERSON CONTRIBUTIONS TO COLLEGE STUDENT PERSONNEL

John Eddy

Introduction

The lack of coverage of minority contributions and minority
problems in the literature of college student personnel is
readily apparent as documented by Marshall (1976), Sue (1973),
Torres (1974), and Yasutake (1977). Moreover, of the few articles
and chapters in books that have appeared in print, the majority
dwell on minority problems rather than minority contributions
(Eddy, 1975). The neglect of minority staff and student treatment in the professional literature is an unfortunate situation.
Foreign students (Eddy, 1972) have been often given more attention in the profession. This is one of the many reasons for the
birth of the Association for Non-White Concerns in Personnel and
Guidance, as one of the thirteen Divisions of the American Personnel and Guidance Association, and its journal the ANWC Journal.
To correct the omissions of minorities over the centuries of
American higher education in a single narrative is not only impossible but presumptuous by the author who is himself a minority
member. However, the selected contributions of minorities will
be mentioned here in context to college student personnel work.
By minorities, the author specifically means here Americans who
are Black, Spanish Speaking, Asian, or Native Indian in their
ethnic heritage. It takes more than Title IX governmental laws
and their enforcement to rectify the discrimination of centuries
against minorities in this country and to take tangible steps
toward a color-blind America. However, this article will attempt
to bring some past and present contributions and suggest a relevant future study for the college student personnel profession
to recall past accomplishments of minority professionals.

It may seem strange to the non-minority person as to why
material like this should be necessary or why it is necessary
to recount the historical contributions of minority Americans and
the needs for integrated education in the field of college student
personnel. However, this reaction of not appreciating this historical recall is still common even among professionals in training who are non-minority persons (Eddy, 1975). This is the point
of the whole Minority Awareness Movement (MAM) within the profession. Since America's minorities have been neglected for so
long and have never been made to feel equal because of both overt

and covert discrimination, it takes an educational process such as this material itself represents, to be discussed within the profession as a learning experience. In 1974, Loyola University of Chicago recognized the contributions of minorities to its development and it published a brochure entitled, "Building Bridges: A Survey of Minorities Studies and Services at Loyola University of Chicago." It is easy for the non-minority person to feel these are not important matters for to have never have known the pains of prejudice is to have missed the evil side of humankind which is the opposite side of human goodness (brotherhood and sisterhood among humanity). To be a truly educated person, is to be a person who recognizes the past and present effects of minority discrimination and who can genuinely empathize with those who have and still suffer the consequences of human prejudice. For a person to fail to recognize and/or realize this phenomena of prejudice, is to identify a truly uneducated person. The student of human psychology should acknowledge by now that in order to have good mental health persons need to accept their physical and social background. However, if persons are not accepting the differences in human beings--as they often are not by research studies (Eddy, 1975)--then we have the problem of prejudice which is still evident in our society as well as world-wide. The book Roots by Alex Haley and the television production on Roots provides the depth understanding of the problem of prejudice and what it has done and still is doing to persons who are Black. Tracing our geneological roots is an exciting venture searching and it is a good exercise for appreciating the human experience (Eddy, 1978). One publishing house (Literary Guild) now has a program on how to do this--see reference list.

The material in this article is based on selected experiences of the author in: teaching at Rust College in Mississippi; serving in workcamps on American Indian Reservations in Minnesota; working at Central Mindanao Colleges in the Philippines and with Asian refugees from the Indo-China wars; and in counseling at New Mexico Tech in New Mexico. In addition, material comes from the results of pre-tests and post-tests on counselor cultural awareness from 1969-1977. Moreover, contributions are also drawn from the author's experiences in Mexico, Spain, India, Japan, Thailand, Hong Kong, China, Taiwan, Canada, and 48 of the 50 states of the U.S.A. as they relate to minority contributions described in the research mentioned here.

Historical Roots

Among the first American colleges where minorities became the largest majorities were:

First, Lincoln University (Black Americans), in Lincoln University, Pennsylvania, was founded in 1854.

Second, Navaho Community College (Native American Indians), in Tsaile, Arizona, was founded in 1968.

Third, New Mexico Highlands University (Spanish Speaking Americans), in Las Vegas, New Mexico, was founded in 1893.

Fourth, Harry S. Truman College, formerly Northeast College, (Asian Americans), in Chicago, Illinois, was renamed in 1976.

Among these colleges, came the first minority college student personnel workers for their respective ethnic group. However, in most universities and colleges beginning in the late 1960's more minority college student personnel became visible as an increasing larger number of minority students began attending more institutions of higher education across the nation for the first time since the founding of Harvard College in 1636 in Cambridge, Massachusetts. There is cultural shock--for some minority students who come from a high school where they were in the majority and they come to a college where they are now in the minority. This shock may come because of higher academic standards and distance from family and friends.

Minority Awareness Tests

Minority Awareness Tests (MAT) such as the Bitch Test (BT) by Robert Williams and the Cultural Awareness Test (CAT) by Robert Marshall have proven over the years that non-minority counselors have the following problems identified by these tests:

First, they fail to have acceptable vocabulary knowledge of various minority student clients.

Second, they fail to have acceptable cultural understanding of various minority students' backgrounds.

Consequently, lacking the vocabulary and background of minority students, is a tremendous disadvantage for any counselor to overcome in a counseling situation. Therefore, the effectiveness of a counselor with these deficiencies is greatly diminished.

When you study minority contributions you discover often yourself for we are all minorities in one area or another, by a broader definition than given here. As you discover in minority awareness of an ethnic people, you can rediscover your own humanity in accepting persons different than yourself.

Minority Awareness for Counselors

The author has been fortunate to have skilled bilingular and bi-cultural minority students who have been able to communicate minority awareness training. The book, Intergroup and

Minority Relations: An Experimental Handbook is an excellent
guidebook to use for exercises in groups to develop minority
awareness be actualized. Therefore, the author's classes over
the years have had units taught by specific minority counselors
on the following minorities:

1. American Blacks;

2. American Spanish Speaking;

3. American Native Indians; and

4. American Asians.

The results of these units have been the following based on
pre-tests and post-tests over an eight year period with hundreds
of students:

1. Some graduate students have been shown a greater appreciation of various minority cultural contributions than before;

2. Some graduate students have acknowledged their ignorance
in terms of vocabulary and cultural mores; and

3. Some graduate students have requested additional minority awareness exposure in their training program for college student personnel work.

Minority Job Demand

It is a strange irony that in the present employment picture
in this period of the 1970's in College Student Personnel History
that there is a strong demand for minority personnel. Whereas,
minority professionals were often passed over for promotion in
the past, there are many occasions in the present where different
racial minority persons have been actually pitted against each
other in competition for the same top positions in college student
affairs in urban settings. There is more hope for minority professionals to achieve their potentials and more help for minority
students who have more minority professionals available as models
in the colleges. Nevertheless, the need for even more minority
college student personnel workers is still evident.

Minority Firsts

It would make a unique study to discover the first employed
minority student personnel workers in every category from vice-
president for student affairs and dean of students to mention
everyone who was first employed in over 30 identifiable areas
within a large university student affairs division. Leonard
(1956) in her book, _Origins of the Personnel Services_, fails to

mention these minority firsts and her book is the single present
published historical work for the field. This new historical
study suggested would do two things:

First, it would show how long some minority persons have
been part of the tradition of American higher education.

Second, it would also demonstrate how long it has taken for
some minorities to have token representation in the employment
of college student personnel work. For example, the first Native
American Indian Dean of Students was at Navaho Community College
in 1969 and yet the Native American Indians have been on the land,
now called the United States of America, for thousands of years.
Because of the Native American Indians' bad treatment by immigrants to this continent, it took hundreds of years before Indians
trusted the educational system of the establishment enough to
serve it (1636-1969--333 years to be exact). The best philosophies of the Native American Indian are still needed in our country as a Blackfeet Chief wrote the following in a 19th Century
Treaty Council:

"Our land is more valuable than your money. It
will last forever. It will not even perish by flames
of fire. As long as the sun shines and the waters
flow, this land will be here to give life to man and
animals. We cannot sell the lives of men and animals;
therefore we cannot sell this land. It was put here
for us by the Great Spirit and we cannot sell it because it does not belong to us. You can count your
money and burn it within the nod of a buffalo's head,
but only the Great Spirit can count the grains of
sand and the blades of grass of these plains. As a
present to you, we will give you anything we have
that you can take with you; but the land, never."

References

Doane, G.H. Searching for Your Ancestors. New York:
Literary Guild, 1977.

Eddy, J.P. "Contributions of Native American Indians
to American Higher Education." Loyola University
of Chicago, Unpublished paper, 1975.

Eddy, J.P. "Dialogue One: Experience in Living, The
State of Vermont and New York City Cooperative Youth
Program at Johnson State College." The Quarterly
Review of Higher Education Among Negroes. October,
1968.

References

Eddy, J.P. "Ethnicity and the Counselor--A New Opportunity." Illinois Guidance and Personnel Association Quarterly. Fall, 1972.

Eddy, J.P. "Factors and Guidelines in Foreign Student Guidance." Journal of College Student Personnel, May, 1972.

Eddy, J.P. "Guidelines for Preparing Cultural Awareness Materials for Counselors." Illinois Guidance and Personnel Association Quarterly, Winter, 1976.

Eddy, J.P. "History of the Nurseries of Howard Lake: 1888-1976" The Eddy Family Association Bulletin. Vol. LXI, No. 1, May 1977.

Eddy, J.P. "The Problem of Standardized Tests." Council for College Attendance Journal, Winter, 1970-71.

Eddy, J.P. "The Return of the Last Mohicans (Mohegans)" Eddy Family Association Bulletin. Volume LVI, No. 2, May 1978, No. 66.

Eddy, J.P. and Kung, F. "Women's Contributions to World Peace." Peace Progress. Vol. 3, No. 3, 1977.

Eddy, J.P. "Women and World Order: International Women's Year of the United Nations." The Institute Report, Vol. 1, No. 2, Spring, 1976.

Fromkin, H.L. and Sherwood, J.J. Intergroup and Minority Relations: An Experiential Handbook. La Jolla, CA: University Associates, Inc. 1976.

Harper, F.D. Black Students: White Campus. Washington, D.C.: American Personnel and Guidance Association Press, 1975.

Haley, A. Roots. New York: Literary Guild, 1977.

Kimura, R. (Ed.) Mutual Understanding of Peoples and Minority Group Education. Hirosaki, Japan: Kahoku Shinppo Company, 1977.

Leonard, E. Origins of the Personnel Services. Minneapolis: University of Minnesota Press, 1956.

References

Marshall, R. "Contributions of Black Americans to American Higher Education." Loyola University of Chicago. Unpublished paper. 1976.

Palomares, U.H. (Ed.) "Culture as a Reason for Being." Personnel and Guidance Journal. October, 1971.

Sandler, B. "Project on the Status and Education of Women." Washington, D.C.: Association of American Colleges, 1977.

Sue, D.W. (Ed.) "Counseling the Culturally Different." Personnel and Guidance Journal. March, 1977.

Sue, D.W. and Sue, D. "Ethnic Minorities: Failures and Responsibilities of the Social Sciences." Journal of Non-White Concerns in Guidance. Spring, 1977.

Torres, M. "Contributions of Spanish Speaking Americans to American Higher Education." Loyola University of Chicago, Unpublished paper. 1974.

Yasutake, M. "Contributions of Asian Americans to American Higher Education." Loyola University of Chicago, Unpublished paper, 1977.

_____ Tracing Your Roots. New York: Literary Guild, 1977.

_____ "Building Bridges: A Survey of Minorities Studies and Services at Loyola University of Chicago." Chicago: brochure, 1974.

CHAPTER 39

COLLEGE STUDENT DIRECTED CAMPUS PROGRAMS:
DRUG EDUCATION

John Eddy and Mark Sohn

The U.S. Office of Education funded twenty student-administered drug education programs which were campus centered across
the country in 1972-74. From the study of these programs a
viable, college and community-oriented drug education model
emerged. The approach by the Federal government of entrusting
funds to college students initiated the first funding in the
history of American higher education. What college students did
with those projects is presented below in a unique study of the
funded projects by the authors. This program serves as an example of what college students can do in accomplishing campus sponsored and based activities.

Background

In March of 1971 the U.S. Office of Education, Drug Education
Branch, publicized a project prospectus for proposals under the
Drug Abuse Education Act of 1970 (P.L. 91-527). Distributed to
universities and colleges, the prospectus called for comprehensive
drug education programs designed and administered by students.
Of 820 proposals submitted, twenty were funded at the $20 -
$60,000 level.

In conducting this study, the authors reviewed the project
proposals and final reports from seventeen of the twenty funded
projects. In some cases, on-site visits and interviews were
possible.

Program Characteristics

The authors discuss here the significant areas of involvement common to all projects studied, unique aspects of several
projects, need for agency involvement, frequency of various types
of telephone requests, methods used in evaluation, effectiveness
of student leaders, future directions and the nature of professional support. Each of these is examined.

The areas of involvement common to all projects include
(1) preventive drug education, (2) crisis intervention, and (3)
drug alternatives. In all of the projects training is very

important. Students are trained for the responsibility they are to assume. In preventive drug education, for example, students approach the drug problem with the use of materials, programs and films for the public, assuming that, on the basis of information, a rational person would decide for himself not to use drugs.

A crucial element, common to all projects, is liaison with community agencies, since referrals to those agencies are a primary function of crisis intervention. The student coordinators maintain constant contact with the referral agencies to be assured of support, to continue developing rapport, and to ascertain what sort of service is delivered to the student referred.

One of the unique projects with an important focus is at Washington State College, Washington. This project focuses on the residence hall environment. Here the resident advisor, a student, is the key target. This student is highly trained in crisis intervention and conducts a self-study program, on his floor or in his section, the purpose of which is to identify the characteristics of the student and the environment which inclines students toward drug usage. He is then responsible to program for the results of his study.

Another unusual project was funded through the Burlington Valley University Consortium at the University of Vermont. This project emphasizes new approaches to expanding human consciousness. The designers believe that the array of approaches to personal growth and peak experiences without the use of drugs is theoretically limitless. They are, therefore, involved in such activities as Gestalt therapy, Zen-Buddhism, sleep and dream feedback control, hypno-drama, para-physics, diet control, telepathy, astroprojection, rhythmic chanting and many others.

Other unique projects focus on (1) minority sub-cultures, (2) hard narcotics, (3) counseling outreach, and (4) career development.

Since many of the programs include crisis intervention, the authors sought to determine the type and frequency of telephone contacts received. Project directors agreed that their calls were in the following areas: (1) parent-child problems, (2) male-female conflicts, (3) school adjustment, (4) marital problems, (5) drug overdoses, (6) questions about drugs, (7) pregnancy, (8) suicide related, (9) legal hassles, (10) general information and (11) prank calls. The authors hypothesize that newly established centers tend to get a high number of prank calls and that prank calls decrease as credibility is established. Further investigation of this inverse relationship is needed.

Projects such as the one at Ripon College in Wisconsin report that the number of parents calling to discuss their

356

children's drug "problems" increased over a period of time. It takes from six to twelve months for a project to develop support and credibility in the community it serves.

Methods of Program Evaluation

Measuring the effectiveness of the student-run programs was a difficult task for the authors and remains a difficult task for project leaders. Most projects measure their success in terms of input or programming. Here project personnel "count up" all the services performed either for volunteer staff or the target population. What is much more difficult to evaluate is output or if the projects actually lower the frequency of drug-related problems. This requires the use of instruments, pre- and post-measures, interviewing evaluation and long range follow-up studies.

A third level of evaluation employed gets at the feelings clients and staffers have toward each other and project goals. This form of evaluation can be carried out with group discussion, interviews, and observation.

The authors believe strongly in evaluation. The first and third methods are most appropriate where trained researchers are not available.

Interviewing project leaders revealed that most projects do feel their best results are in the area of community education. Communities admitted drug problems exist, which in itself was a major accomplishment. The most effective result of having college students operate the programs is the rapid increase in the number of young people approaching the center to solve personal problems.

The effect of having students carry such a responsibility was evaluated by the authors. Most of the projects state that students not only performed adequately but beyond expectations. Many of the students are good counselors. They often have had some experience with drugs and are less judgemental than some counselors may be.

In determining what the projects would do differently after several years of operation, most reported that they would emphasize drug alternatives. Project leaders stated that fear techniques did not work and emphasized clarification of values and building up a person's potential.

In most college communities where the projects are located the authors found that student personnel, other professionals and the department of education have been very supportive of student involvement. Students need the professionals and the professionals are very willing to have students work in the field, handle cases and make referrals.

357

Conclusion

All of the projects examined were refunded several years. Student interest has remained high. Students continue to train other students. Drug problems still exist, but the centers are reaching out and, hopefully, touching more drug abusers. One student describes such a hope in the project proposal:

> "The problem is drugs...availability of them; great increase in their use and abuse by all ages in this community and not enough programs, education and resources to deal with this problem...We are reaching our friends here on campus, our younger brothers and sisters ...We are bringing them here to the center for help, and then contributing this help by involving them in the center's program..."*

What is your institution doing in this critical area? According to a 1977 Gallup Poll Youth Survey, "Teen-agers consider the use and abuse of drugs the biggest problem facing their own generation."

---

*Campus-Community Involvement Center, East Los Angeles College, Los Angeles, California, The Project Proposal, April 14, 1974, pp. 5.

References

Eddy, J.P. "A DWI Education Program." Journal of Drug Education, Vol. 6, No. 4, Summer, 1976.

Eddy, J.P. "An Irony of Society; School Drug Problems— Est Counselors are Out," IGPA Fall Quarterly, Vol. 43, No. 4, Fall 1972.

Eddy, J.P. "Confidentiality and the Counselor." Illinois Guidance and Personnel Association Quarterly. March, 1973.

Eddy, J.P. and Sohn, M. "College and University Drug Program," NASPA Journal, Vol. 2 , No. 3, July 1973.

Eddy, J.P. and Sohn, M. "Common Elements of College and University Drug Programs," NASPA Journal, Vol. 11, No. 1, July 1973.

Eddy, J.P. "Counseling and Drug Education in the Schools." Chicago, IL: American Personnel and Guidance Association Cassette Tape, 1974.

References

Eddy, J.P. "Dealing with Student Behavior and Drug Abuse." South Holland, IL: Unpublished paper delivered at Thornton Community College, 1977.

Eddy, J.P. "Drug Use and Abuse." Grayslake, IL: Unpublished paper delivered at Lake County Community College, 1975.

Eddy, J.P. "Drugs" Science Activities. February, 1972.

Eddy, J.P. "Drugs and Disclosure." Personnel and Guidance Journal. November, 1969.

Eddy, J.P. "Drugs, Religious Groups and Educational Institutions." Higher Education--Christian Perspective, Vol. 2, No. 4. Fall, 1971.

Eddy, J.P. "Need for Laws to Protect Counselor and Client," Illinois Guidance and Personnel Association Quarterly. Winter, 1972.

Eddy, J.P. "Needs for School and College Drug Education" North Central Reporter, Annual Meeting of the North Central Association of Secondary Schools and Colleges, Chicago, IL. March 27, 1974.

Eddy, J.P. and Knoderer, B.M. "Need for College Drug Education Courses." Journal of Drug Education. Vol. 4, No. 4, Winter, 1974.

Eddy, J.P. "Questionnable Statistics and Drug Problems" Journal of Drug Education. March, 1972.

Eddy, J.P. "Resources for School Crisis Situations and Centers," Illinois Guidance and Personnel Association Quarterly, Fall, 1972.

Eddy, J.P. "The Breathing Rights of Persons." Journal of Durg Education, Vol. 6, No. 4, Winter, 1976.

Eddy, J.P. The Teacher and the Drug Scene. Bloomington, Indiana: Phi Delta Kappa Press, 1973.

Haggerty, D.J. and Zimmering, S. "Attitudes Toward Drugs and Drug Education." Journal of Drug Education, Vol. 2, No. 1, March 1972.

Knoderer, M.B. "An Investigation of High School Counselor Attitudes Toward Drug Problems as Related to Counselor

References

Knoderer (Cont'd)
Drug Knowledge." Doctoral dissertation, Loyola
University of Chicago, 1973.

Swanson, J.C. "Drug Education: Some impressions from
Experiences in Illinois." Journal of Drug Education.
Vol. 1, No. 2, June, 1971.

_____ "Driving While Intoxicated Facts."
Wheaton, Illinois: DuPage CLEC Staff, DuPage County,
Law Enforcement Commission, 1974.

CHAPTER 40

TRAINING STUDENTS FOR PRACTICUMS

Gerald L. Saddlemire

Student personnel professionals, both trainers and practitioners, are agreed that practical experience must be included in
preparation programs. The various statements of preparation standards issued by Associations representing the profession include
supervised experience as a necessary component. The nomenclature
may range from clinical, laboratory, practicum, internship, assistantship but the message is consistent. Supervised experience
must be included as a means of integrating and applying the knowledge and skills obtained from the academic coursework. The format
used by graduate institutions to provide learning experiences
varies substantially from program to program. A greater similarity
is apparent in academic coursework which comes together in a curriculum that has many common courses regardless of institution.

The practicum, however, is arranged within a looser framework.
It may have some of the characteristics of student teaching. It
sometimes is arranged as a field experience or it may be thought
of as an apprenticeship assignment. This chapter will describe and
discuss the approach to the practicum used by an established preparation program and show a technique for evaluation.

Past President, Anne Pruitt, recently (1977) surveyed the ACPA
leadership to ask their opinion about the importance of the supervised practicum experience. She reported that they were unanimous
in their support of this part of the curriculum and in some cases
suggested that it is the most important part of the preparation.[1]
Minetti, in reviewing the literature for his study, "Analytical
Description of the Relationship between the Academic Training and
Assistantship Experiences of Master's Degree Programs in Student
Personnel Administration," emphasizes the importance of the practical
component as part of the masters degree prepration program in student
personnel.[2] He studied the relationship between the formal training
process (academic courses) and the paid assistantship experiences of
masters degree candidates in college student personnel at Bowling
Green State University, Michigan State University, and the University of Vermont. He asked four populations, the graduate students
currently enrolled, the recent graduates of the program, the supervisors and the faculty where they thought the focus of preparation
should be for 43 competencies for entry level personnel work. All
but two of the competencies were seen as being acquired in both the

formal academic process and the paid assistantships. The subjects responses indicate that a competency is not truly acquired until theory and practice have been integrated.

Earlier studies conducted by Hoyt and Rhatigan substantiated the importance assigned to on-the-job training in preparation programs. Ostroth surveyed chief student personnel administrators and learned that 88.9% of them indicated that practical experiences were essential in a preparation program. Wallenfeldt and Bigelow studied the status of internships in student personnel training programs and rated on-the-job experience as more important than any coursework required of the students. Several researchers point out the need to establish the proper balance between academic and assistantship experiences. They must be integrated so that they help the student see each experience as the extension of the other. Each one alone is inadequate for training future student personnel workers.

The professional preparation program at Bowling Green State University requires that every entering masters degree student have a full year salaried practicum. The College Student Personnel Department has prepared a manual for graduate students and their supervisors that provides an orientation to the integration of academic course work and experiential learning. The following statements are taken from the department manual.

Graduate Assistantships
and Internship-Externship Assignments

Some of the offices at Bowling Green State University have opportunities for qualified persons who are interested in assignment to such functions as Residence Programs, Counseling Center, Student Activities, Admissions, Student Development, Sororities, Student Union. Minimum stipend is $2,450 for the academic year.

Arrangements have been made with colleges whereby graduate students in College Student Personnel are assigned to a staff position as a part of the degree program. The graduate student will be a fully admitted degree candidate who has had student personnel experience or one full quarter of course work before the practicum assignment. Compensation of approximately $4,200 will be paid by the cooperating college. This may include room and board.

The practicum experience required of all candidates if fulfilled by a three academic quarter paid internship at Bowling Green State University or at one of the cooperating/neighboring colleges. Each internship

362

proves the masters degree candidate with supervised professional experience in one or more higher education/student personnel functions. Faculty of the College Student Personnel Department coordinate the practicum assignments and work with the practicum supervisor to plan for appropriate areas of responsibility.

Each graduate student is enrolled in seminars that give them an opportunity to use the practicum experience as a frame of reference for analyzing higher education issues. The student is expected to develop insights about the institution and its strategies for responding to various issues.

The diversity of the job opportunity and the uniqueness of each individual's experience and background make it appropriate to individualize the program of study. Graduate students have many common learning experiences, but elective credits are used in the way which the student and the faculty advisor agree makes for maximum growth and takes into account the realities of the job market.

The department values the various practicum experiences which are available to graduate students on the Bowling Green campus and at cooperating colleges. Testimony from the graduate students and their supervisors supports the assumption made by the department that the practicum represents a very valuable learning experience for the graduate students.

Arrangements for graduate students to have assistantships are described below.

Bowling Green State University: College Student Personnel Department; Counseling Center, Residence Programs, Student Development, Student Activities, Admissions, Academic Advising.

The following colleges have made salaried positions available to the graduate students: The Defiance College, Lorain County Community College, Baldwin-Wallace, Findlay College, Firelands Campus of B.G.S.U., Urbana College, Heidelberg, Ashland College, Lima Tech, Bluffton, Westminster, Marion Tech, Northwest Tech.

The responsibilities assigned to the students have given them experience in: community service, fraternities-sororities, academic assistance, student development, minority student program, admissions-placement,

residence hall programs, counseling, and student
affairs.

The College Student Personnel Department found that it was
useful to spell out the role of the intern/extern and suggest
responsibilities of the on-site supervisor in the following section.

Learning Potential for the Practicum

Purpose. The degree candidate in College Student
Personnel has a practicum experience which will complement and balance his academic course work. This
practicum arrangement will assure the candidate an
opportunity to work under the supervision of an experienced student personnel practitioner.

Each graduate student is enrolled in seminars that
give an opportunity to use the practicum experience
as a frame of reference for analyzing higher education
issues. The student is expected to develop insights
about the institution and its strategies for responding
to various issues.

The department values the various practicum experiences which are available to graduate students
on the Bowling Green campus and at cooperating colleges. Testimony from the graduate students and
from their supervisors supports the assumption made
by the department that the practicum represents a very
valuable learning experience for the graduate student.

Status of the Graduate Assistant-Intern. The
graduate assistant should be considered a staff member.
He/she will conduct himself/herself as a professional.
At the same time, it must be recognized that the intern
is a graduate student who is expected to fulfill his
total obligations for all academic courses taken. This
requires a sensitivity on the part of the supervisor to
insure the proper merging of work responsibilities with
academic responsibilities.

The Role of Graduate Assistant-Intern. The internship is a very significant component of the Bowling
Green State University program in College Student Personnel. The coursework of the firt term prepares the
graduate assistant to assume limited responsibility
while working and reacting closely with a functioning
staff during his/her practicum assignment. The graduate
assistant will benefit to the extent to which he/she
participates in direct work with students and in the

364

deliberations, analysis, and planning by the students and staff. The graduate assistant will grow to the extent to which he/she can experiment and accept the responsibility for successes and failures. The value of the practicum experience lies in the gradual assumption of professional standards by the intern as he/she evaluates the program and is, in turn, evaluated in a constructive way.

Common Understandings. While the graduate assistant receives a stipend and can carry responsibility, he/she is not a full time faculty member and cannot expect to receive all the privileges thereof. At the same time, he/she is a professional trainee and should receive, wherever appropriate, privileges beyond those of under-graduate and even graduate students. He/she should be given his/her own specific responsibility other than pure routine procedures.

Determination of Campus Experience. The practicum supervisor will outline the general nature of the assignment. Description of this assignment will be shared with the College Student Personnel Department at the earliest possible time. The graduate student should be given a primary assignment which will continue for the academic year.

Supervision of the Intern. The campus supervisor will have the responsibility for immediate supervision and continuous evaluation of the student's performance.

Since the graduate student will also be taking courses concurrently, opportunities will exist for continuous communication between the College Student Personnel Department and the graduate student.

The campus supervisor will participate with the College Student Personnel Department in selecting the person to serve on the campus. Colleges are encouraged to consider more than one graduate student, if circumstances permit. The graduate student is expected to observe the calendar at the college to which he is assigned for the entire period of assignment.

Campus Supervisor-College Student Personnel Department Relationships. The College Student Personnel Department will bring the supervisors together on the Bowling Green State University campus regularly. The supervisors will be responsible for the seminar described in Section IX, will assist in regional meetings of graduate students and will participate in on-campus seminars when possible.

The College Student Personnel Department invites feedback from supervisors and graduate students at any time. In addition, the Department asks each supervisor to complete a written form at the end of three months (December) and again at the end of the spring quarter (May). The first evaluation includes the following questions:

1. Describe briefly the specific assignment(s) which the graduate student carried out.

2. Using the topics suggested below, evaluate the graduate student's development. The topics are intended to be suggestive only. Use illustrative anecdotes where possible.

    a. Personal qualities. Ability to express himself/herself verbally and in writing. Establishment of realistic goals for self. Extent of commitment to a career in higher education.

    b. Professional competency. Ability to handle demanding assignments. Skill in achieving student participation and productive involvement. Ability to deal with stress and conflict. Evidence of originality and initiative.

    c. Capacity for growth. Did the student continue to develop competencies and skills during the entire year? Was there conclusive evidence that the student is ready for a full time position in post-secondary institution?

The graduate student is asked to complete an evaluation on the same schedule. The questions include:

Description of Practical Experience

1. Describe briefly your primary responsibility (if you have not strayed from your job description, indicate that we can refer to that statement).

2. How much time (total per week) are you expected to spend "on duty", i.e., in activities directly related to your internship/externship?

3. Do you attend regular staff meetings. With which staff members are you most closely associated?

Evaluation of Internship/Externship Experience

1. General reaction to the experience.

   a. What are the good features or strengths of the
      experience?

   b. What seems to be the principle weaknesses or
      limitations of the experience?

   c. What activities or phases of the experience have
      been most meaningful to you?

   d. What are your reactions to the staff with which
      you are working?

2. What suggestions do you have for improvement of the
   experience afforded at your unit?

3. What steps could the Bowling Green State University
   College Student Personnel Department take to improve
   the experience?

   Both the supervisor and the graduate student are urged to
discuss their responses with each other before forwarding them to
the department.

   The department asks the supervisor of experiential learning
to meet weekly with the graduate student to discuss topics that
will help the graduate student understand the institutional context and policy determination.

   A. Orientation of the Graduate to the Institution

      1. Philosophy of the institution and its student
         personnel staff
      2. Administrative structure of the institution, the
         roles of the various departments and divisions,
         and the relationships between them
      3. Departmental structure and division of respon-
         sibility within student personnel staff
      4. Institution-wide regulations
      5. Resources in and relationships with the community

   B. Developing a Professional Philosophy

      1. The nature and purpose of a professional philosophy
      2. Its place in one's daily living
      3. Use of one's educational philosophy in interpreting
         the institution to students, parents, and the
         community

4. The legal and ethical considerations of student personnel work

C. Professional Development of Individuals and Staff

1. Utilization of staff talents, energies, and time, teamwork, communications
2. Principles of staff selection (applicable to both student counselors and professional staff)
3. Training programs--individual and group activities
4. Maintaining one's balance and perspective in student personnel work ("mental health")
5. The role of professional organizations

D. Principles and Practices of Administration

1. Purposes and use of records
2. Policy development and communication
3. Building management-maintenance and business functions

The graduate student meets regularly with the department faculty advisor to discuss practicum related issues. This gives the faculty advisor an opportunity to suggest professional literature related to the problem or issue under consideration.

A number of evaluation projects have provided feedback to the department and have been the basis for program modification. A masters thesis by Bonnie Betters-Reed (1974) and a doctoral dissertation by Robert Minetti provided perceptions about the experiential learning from supervisors, students, faculty and alumni.

A group of doctoral students and their instructor (Dr. Theodore Jenson) asked and received approval from the department to assess the learning potential in the practicum laboratory experience. They made the assumption that the College Student Personnel Department was concerned with how to make the practicum experience an effective and efficient learning experience in its program, how to relate theory and practice, how best to work with B.G.S.U. offices and cooperating institutions hosting the interns, how to identify specific objectives, how to measure attainment of objectives, how to affect better communication, and in general how to make the practicum experience more meaningful.

The instrumentation and approach used may be useful to other programs who are interested in evaluating themselves. The department made the following statement of aims and objectives to the doctoral seminar:

368

Aims and Objectives of the C.S.P. Internship

The rationale of the College Student Personnel program
is to aid the graduate student in his/her development
toward the role of a professional who can function in
higher education as an aggressive leader in planning and
implementing opportunities for student development in a
wide variety of collegiate settings. One of the major
components of the master's degree program is a nine-month
internship experience during which time the student will
function as a practitioner/learner in a supervised setting
with professional student development specialists.

The aims and purposes of the internship learning
experience are two-fold. The first area involves
professional enrichment for the field of student personnel and the second area involves the learning experience for the graduate student intern.

I.   The aims of the program are:

A. To professionalize the field of college student
    personnel through the structured internship
    program.

B. To construct significant learning experiences
    through the laboratory situation in which the
    student can function as a practitioner/learner.

C. To build a diversity of experiences and measure-
    ments so as to develop a program which will most
    significantly benefit the needs and interests of
    the graduate student intern.

D. To aid the student in defining his/her own
    career goals as they relate to the experiences
    received through the internship.

II. The aims for the graduate student are:

A. To develop an awareness of the need and method
    of integrating cognitive skills with actual
    practice.

B. To personalize the professional behavior role.

C. To develop an understanding of university decision-
    making process.

D. To develop basic human relations skills.

E. To become aware of individual differences and group commonalities.

III. The behavioral objectives for the program are:

A. To develop an awareness of and a sensitivity to various student subgroups within the collegiate setting, the intern will identify and assess student behavior through the development of a program dealing with a specific subgroup.

B. To increase the competency level of his/her human relation skills, the intern will establish an on-going helping relationship with an individual student.

C. To improve the competency level of his/her effectiveness in working with groups, the intern will develop a program dealing with growth awareness needs of the group.

D. To develop an understanding of the role of the student development specialist, the intern will periodically assess his/her own goals, values, and competencies.

E. To understand the faculty, administrative, and student political and social matrix of the campus, the intern will attend the appropriate faculty, staff, and student meetings, and campus functions and will demonstrate through action his/her understanding of these subcultures.

F. To improve the competency level of his/her decision-making skills, the intern will participate in relevant faculty and student meetings.

The doctoral students used the statement of goals and objectives to draw up a questionnaire for learning experience supervisors and for the graduate students. The supervisor assessment is shown below. The working was modified slightly to draw up another assessment form for use with the C.S.P. graduate students.

SUPERVISOR--ASSESSMENT OF THE LEARNING EXPERIENCE
BOWLING GREEN STATE UNIVERSITY

Your opinions and ideas--please.

Your assistance is requested in helping the Department of College Student Personnel in obtaining information and opinions on the learning potential of the practicum/internship portion of

370

the College Student Personnel degree program. Through your responses, the department hopes to improve its capability in producing a professional who can function in higher education as an aggressive leader in planning and implementing opportunities for student development in a wide variety of collegiate settings. All responses to this interview schedule will be treated as anonymous and confidential. Your help is very much appreciate.

DIRECTIONS: If you strongly agree, circle SA, if you agree with some reservations, circle A, if you disagree with reservations, circle D, and if you strongly disagree, circle SD.

1. The internship provides interns with an awareness of and a sensitivity to sub-groups within the student body.
   COMMENT: SA A D SD

2. Opportunities are provided in the internship experience for interns to generate and assume responsibilities for a specific subgroup program.
   COMMENT: SA A D SD

3. Ample opportunity is provided in the internship for interns to identify unique differences among subgroups.
   COMMENT: SA A D SD

4. The development of a subgroup program is an effective means for interns to identify and assess student behavior.
   COMMENT: SA A D SD

5. Experiences are provided in the internship for interns to develop meaningful helping relationships with individual college students.
   COMMENT: SA A D SD

6. Experiences are available for interns to improve their skills in working with groups.
   COMMENT: SA A D SD

7. The internship experience allows interns to develop a program dealing with growth awareness needs of a group.
   COMMENT: SA A D SD

371

8. The internship provides a basis for   SA A D SD
    interns to identify the role of the
    Student Development Specialist.
    COMMENT:

9. The internship experience aids interns   SA A D SD
    in defining their career goals.
    COMMENT:

10. Interns are provided opportunities for   SA A D SD
    the assessment of career competencies.
    COMMENT:

11. Experiences in the internship provide   SA A D SD
    interns with the opportunity of iden-
    tifying and developing their personal
    values.
    COMMENT:

12. The internship provides interns with   SA A D SD
    exposure to faculty, administrative,
    and student subcultures comprising the
    political and social matrix of the
    campus.
    COMMENT:

13. Opportunities in the internship enable   SA A D SD
    interns to interact with faculty, ad-
    ministrative, and student subcultures
    on the campus.
    COMMENT:

14. The internship provides interns with the   SA A D SD
    opportunity to demonstrate their under-
    standing of the socio-political nature
    of subcultures on the campus.
    COMMENT:

15. The internship provides opportunities for SA A D SD
    interns to participate in relevant campus
    meetings.
    COMMENT:

16. The experience of the internship helps   SA A D SD
    to improve the interns decision-making
    skills.
    COMMENT:

17. Interns are aware of the objectives and   SA A D SD
    purposes of the internship experience.
    COMMENT:

18. I think the internship experience could
    be improved by...

    The study provided useful findings for the College Student
Personnel Department. The entire report is available upon request.

Footnotes

[1]Pruitt, Anne. S. Preparation of Student Development
Specialists During the 1980's. Paper given at Summer
Colloquium on Preparation of Counselors and Student
Development Specialists During the 1980's. Southern
Illinois University, Carbondale, Illinois. June 23, 1977.

[2]Minetti, Robert H. An Analytical Description of the
Relationship Between the Academic Training and Assistant-
ship Experiences of Master's Degree Programs in Student
Personnel Administration. Unpublished Dissertation. A
study of the salaried assistantships at Bowling Green
State University, Michigan State University, and the
University of Vermont. 1977.

References

    American College Personnel Association. "The Role and
        Preparation of Student Personnel Workers in Institu-
        tions of Higher Learning." Journal of College Student
        Personnel. Vol. 8, No. 1, pp. 62–65, January 1977.

    American Personnel and Guidance Association. "Guidelines
        for Graduate Programs in the Preparation of Student
        Personnel Workers in Higher Education." Personnel
        and Guidance Journal. Vol. 47, pp. 493–498, 1969.

    Caple, R.B. "Molar Model for the Training of Student
        Personnel Workers." Counselor Education and Supervision.
        Vol. 12, pp. 31–41, September 1972.

    Cosby, B. "Professional Preparation for Student Personnel
        Work in Higher Education." Journal of the National
        Association of Women Deans, Administrators, and Counselors.
        Vol. 29, No. 1, pp. 14–18, Fall, 1965.

    Cottingham, J.F. "Roles, Functions and Training for
        College Personnel Workers." Personnel and Guidance
        Journal, Vol. 33, No. 9, pp. 534–438, 1955.

References

Council of Student Personnel Associations. 1967 and 1973
Statements (mimeographed).

Crookston, B.B. "Student Personnel--All Hail and Farewell!"
Personnel and Guidance Journal. Vol. 55, No. 1, pp. 26-29,
September 1976.

Fitzgerald, L.E.; Johnson, W., and Norris, W. (Eds.)
College Student Personnel: Readings and Bibliographies.
Boston: Houghton-Mifflin Company, 1970.

Hedlund, D. "Preparation for Student Personnel: Implica-
tions of Humanistic Education." Journal of College
Student Personnel, Vol. 12, No. 5, pp. 324-329,
September 1971.

Hill, G.E. and Green, D.A. "The Selection, Preparation
and Professionalization of Guidance and Personnel
Workers." Review of Educational Research, Vol. 30,
pp. 115-130, April 1960.

Houtz, P. "Internships in Student Personnel Programs."
From College Student Personnel: Readings and Bibliographies by L.E. Fitzgerald, W. Johnson, and W. Norris,
(Eds.), Boston: Houghton-Mifflin Company, 1970,
pp. 42-48.

Hoyt, D.P. and Rhatigan, J.J. "Professional Preparation
of Junior and Senior College Student Personnel Administrators." From College Student Personnel: Readings
and Bibliographies by Fitzgerald, L.E. (et. al.) (Eds.),
Boston: Houghton-Mifflin Company, 1970, pp. 35-38.

Kirkbride, V. "Practicum Experience in the Master's
Degree Program for Personnel Work." Journal of the
National Association of Women Deans, Administrators,
and Counselors, Vol. 34. pp. 80-84, Winter 1972.

Miller, T.D. "College Student Personnel Prepration:
Present Perspective and Future Directions." Journal
of the National Association of Student Personnel
Administrators, Vol. 4, No. 4, pp. 171-176, April 1967.

Mueller, K.H. "Educational Issues and the Training of
Student Personnel Workers." Journal of the National
Association of Student Personnel Administrators,
Vol. 4, No. 4, pp. 167-171, April 1967.

References

O'Banion, T. "Program Proposal for Preparing College Student Personnel Workers." _Journal of College Student Personnel_, Vol. 10, No. 3, pp. 249-253. January 1973.

Ostroth, D.D. "Master's Level Preparation for Student Personnel Work." _Journal of College Student Personnel_, Vol. 16, No. 4, pp. 319-322, July 1974.

_____. "Professional Preparation of Student Personnel Administrators as Perceived by Practitioners and Faculty." _Journal of College Student Personnel_, Vol. 9, No. 1, pp. 17-23, January 1968.

Trueblood, D.L. "The Educational Preparation of the College Student Personnel Leader of the Future." In Klopf, G.A. (ed.) _College Student Personnel Work in the Years Ahead_. ACPA Student Personnel Series No. 7, Washington, D.C., American Personnel and Guidance Association, 1966, pp. 77-84.

Wallenfeldt, E.C. and Bigelow, G.S. "Status of the Internship in Student Personnel Studies." _Journal of the National Association of Women Deans, Administrators, and Counselors_, Vol. 34, pp. 180-184, Summer 1971.

CHAPTER 41

A MODEL OF COUNSELING SUPERVISION

Peter Cimbolic

This chapter provides a model for the supervision of
counselors in training. The assumptions of the model, the
goals of supervision, the role of tension in the supervisory process, how one accomplishes supervisory objectives,
and the factors which impede the attainment of supervisory
goals are considered.

Assumptions

In choosing a supervisory model, research is not of much
assistance. Matarazzo, et al. (1966) in reviewing the literature, concluded that there has been essentially no
research about the teaching of psychotherapy (and counseling) or the process of supervision. Also, Garfield's
(1977) review on this topic found the current research lacking in substance and in the potential for utility.

Since research does not provide a helpful starting
point, the next consideration for supervisors would probably be their theoretical frame of reference in the development of a model of supervision. The goals of supervision
are contingent upon the goals of counseling, and the goals
of counseling will be a function of the theoretical model
employed (Garfield, 1977; Reisman, 1975).

The model presented in this chapter is predicated upon
an eclectic approach to counseling which is consistent with
the recent trend in the training of counselors (Garfield
and Kurtz, 1974).

An assumption of this supervisory model is that, in the
practicum or internship experience, the counselor comes to
the experience with a cognitive understanding of counseling
theory, but limited skill in translating theory into practice. This will be, of course, a primary goal of supervision.

Another critical assumption of this supervisory model is that the counselor is incompetent (particularly in the case of the beginning counselor). Counseling students often view the practicum experience as their chance to prove competence to their supervisors. While this may be the eventual goal, it is important for the supervisor to make it clear that the counselor-in-training is assumed to be less than competent initially. This may alleviate some of the pressure that student counselors experience; they are free to make mistakes, to try new approaches, and it relieves them from being defensive about what they do not know. It also may help minimize the constant comparisons that beginning counselors make between themselves and other counseling students in the training experience. It legitimizes the same starting point for all. The individual supervisor, however, must still be aware of and allow for individual supervisees' unique strengths and abilities.

The Goals of Supervision

One goal of supervision is the assistance to students in acquisition of those skills (interpersonal, theoretical, and technique oriented) which would allow counselors to be minimally competent to serve the public in their profession. The term "minimally" perhaps should be explained. The academic degree the individual is seeking is usually an entry level degree, which implies that individuals have completed a prescribed course of study. It is the public assurance of minimal competence.

A further objective is that counselors must become aware of themselves as factors in counseling, and determine how best to utilize themselves as therapeutic tools (Bordin, 1968; Harris, 1978). The supervisor must provide a climate in order for this self-awareness to develop. Coming to understand oneself not only implies knowing one's strengths, but also one's limitations. A goal of supervision, implicit in the knowledge of limitations, is for the supervisor to assist the counselor to recognize one's own limitations, and to know when to refer the client, that is, when the client's demands call for skills or personality characteristics which the counselor does not possess (Stamatakos, 1978).

377

Finally, the evaluation of a personal theory and approach to counseling, unique to the individual counselor, is another objective of supervision. At the end of the supervisory process, counselors should be able to articulate who they are as counselors, taking into consideration their personality, experiences, the client's personality, the problems experienced by the client, and the context in which the client's problem occurs.

To ensure the attainment of these goals, the supervisor must facilitate self-exploration on the part of the counselor-in-training. It is the author's firm belief that this is enhanced through the legitimization of open and direct communication in the supervisory process.

The Role of Tension in Supervision

Anyone who has ever participated in the supervisory process well remembers the feelings of tension associated around the supervisory hour. Tension cannot be avoided and some would argue that tension can be a facilitative phenomenon in supervision (Harris, 1972).

What contributes to this tension?

The practicum experience is often the terminal experience in the training program of counselors. They have completed the necessary course work, and at last are given the opportunity to function as counselors. Each supervisee must face the doubt as to whether he or she can be an effective counselor. Each may ask the question, "Can I do what, up until now, I have only read about?" In a sense they are putting themselves on the line. They have to prove to themselves and their supervisor that they have what it takes to be successful interventionists in the lives of others.

Supervisors may be uncomfortable with the duplicative nature of their functions. They must first be facilitators of the counselor's cognitive and affective learning, striving to be humanistic, and caring about the individual they are supervising. But they must also be evaluators, making the decision as to whether counselors will enter into their chosen profession.

Supervisors cannot deny that their ultimate commitment is to society. They serve as policemen of the profession in determining who will serve the public. Therefore, at times, they will be placed in the uncomfortable position of having to tell a counselor-in-training that he or she doesn't have what it takes, and will not be allowed to enter the public arena as an independent practitioner. This is often a painful decision for supervisors--causing personal pain to individuals in whom they have invested much of themselves. Supervisors, being humanists, may find the rejection of others contrary to their nature.

Therefore, the supervisory relationship is an intimate conditional one. Success for the counselors-in-training is conditional upon their performance during the practicum experience. Approval is conditional upon the demonstration of sound counseling practice on the part of the student. This presents a dilemma for the supervisors who, in their own counseling training, learned that unconditional positive regard was a valued position. There is a changing of ground rules on the part of the supervisor in shifting from a counseling to a supervisory role.

Counselors-in-training then are left in a quandry. Do they share their doubts, fears, and uncertainties, at the risk of potentially being perceived by the supervisor as incompetent, and ultimately being rejected as a counselor?

How can this dilemma be resolved for the counselors-in-training and their supervisors?

Supervisors must somehow be able to convey to the counselor that they, above all else, will be fair and consistent. In order to demonstrate fairness, supervisors must constantly convey their assessment of the counselor's performance throughout the supervisory process. Consequently, counselors will know where they stand at any given point with respect to the supervisor's assessment of their counseling skills. This avoids surprises, perhaps the most unfair of all potential consequences.

In order for tension in the relationship to be therapeutic, it is the supervisor's task to convey to the

379

counselors that disapproval of given elements of the counseling behavior of the trainee is not a rejection of the
counselor as an individual. This facilitates the hearing of
criticism by counselors and minimizes their defensive behavior.

How Does One Accomplish the Objectives of Supervision?

The critical first step toward the accomplishment of the
goals of supervision is that they be made explicit. Counselors bring into supervision certain assumptions as to what
will be expected of them during their practicum experience.
These expectations may, or may not, be consistent with those
of the supervisor. The extent to which expectations are
made explicit by both parties is the extent to which they
can be the subject of conversation and negotiation. It is
argued, at this point, that negotiation is legitimate, from
which will hopefully evolve mutually agreed upon expectations of the supervisory relationship (Harris, 1978).

One expectation that should be part of any supervisory
relationship is that the counselor come to the supervision
session with audio or video tapes of counseling sessions.
This is particularly important for the novice counselor.
The use of tapes in supervision is typical of most supervisory relationships, with perhaps the most sophisticated
and systematic approach being Kagan's (1973). What does
the use of tapes provide? Tapes provide actual data samples of the counseling interview. The data are not impres-
sionistic. In reviewing the tape of the most novice counselor, supervisors must attend initially to the counselor's
interpersonal skills and their application in the development of client rapport. It is the author's contention that
effective interpersonal skills are a prerequisite to any
successful counseling process. Supervisors cannot assume
that their students are adequate in this area. Truax and
Mitchell (1971) point out that "from existing data it would
appear that only one out of three people entering professional training have the requisite interpersonal skills to
prove helpful to patients."

The supervisor's use of tapes provides the opportunity
to assess the counselor's ability to be empathic, caring,

and active listeners, who are genuine and respectful of their clients as individuals. If the counselor does not possess the above characteristics, the author contends that the acquisition of these behaviors should be an early supervisory task. There is evidence that these behaviors can be taught (Elsenrath, et al., 1972; Ivey, 1974). Once these behaviors are acquired, counselors have reached the point where their behaviors won't prevent effective counseling.

The next major task for the supervisor is for the counselor to acquire the ability to translate theory into practice in the counseling process. This is the point in supervision where there is the need for intimacy. The supervisor must allow the counselor to translate theory through the counselor's self-system and then be in a position to evaluate the effect of this translation. Carkhuff and Berenson (1976) contend that if a theoretical approach makes the counselor less effective than he or she is as a human being, then that theoretical system is inappropriate for that counselor. Implicit in this position is that the supervisor must intimately know the supervisee. The supervisors must be able to say to the counselors, "That doesn't seem like you."

Further, the supervisor must encourage the counselor to "try on" as many approaches as possible. The supervisor must be willing to legitimize trial and error learning on the part of the counselor. Supervisors, in this phase of counseling, must realize that there will be mistakes. It is only through these mistakes that counselors can learn what will work for them and what will not.

To accomplish the above, supervisors must encourage counselors to take risks. This is often a difficult task in that, for fear of negative evaluation on the part of the supervisor, many beginning counselors are reluctant to take risks. The consequence to the counselor in not taking risks, however, is professional and personal stagnation. Counselors cannot grow and learn more about themselves and their potential as counselors. The position the author takes with his supervisees is that he will never admonish them for having tried something and failed, but he will for not having tried.

What is the basis for the decision as to whether a given approach has been successful? Too often, the appraisal of success or failure in judging a counseling intervention is the supervisor's evaluation of the intervention (Garfield, 1977; Beutler, 1972). Although this may be one measure of success, supervisors, it is argued, must evaluate counseling interventions as a function of the therapeutic outcome for the client. Do supervisors train students to please them, or is their training designed to insure that students are effective change agents? (These are not necessarily mutually exclusive.) It is the author's contention that supervisors have been somewhat remiss in not seeking client outcome measures as part of the supervisor's evaluation.

As previously mentioned, mistakes must be expected. However, what cannot be accepted by the supervisors is the lack of articulation on the part of counselors as to what they are doing, why they are doing it, and why it may or may not be appropriate.

This calls forth another supervisory task--treatment strategy formulation. An often surprise confronting the supervisor is that counselors-in-training articulate what they want to accomplish with a case and, if this is accomplished, the case has been a success. The question to the counselor, when this situation arises, is what does the client desire as the outcome of counseling. It is shocking how often supervisees have never asked this question of their clients. Just as the expectations of supervision must be mutually agreed upon and negotiated, so must the expectations of the counseling process be negotiated between the counselor and the client. This process is, of course, goal formulation. Without the mutually defined goals of counseling being explicitly negotiated, counseling can become no more than a wandering conversation. The counseling becomes confused and ambiguous, and ambiguity is not tolerated by most counselors (Lakovics, et al., 1976). Once the goals of the counseling process become explicit, the counselor has direction. The counselor knows what the counseling process is expected to accomplish. Explicit goals also provide a benchmark by which the counselor can assess how well the counseling is progressing.

The explicit agreement of goals also gives counselors the license to choose the treatment approach that they feel would be most likely to produce the desired outcome. It further allows counselors to explain their intervention strategies to the clients in the context of the goals. This helps the clients understand what will be taking place in counseling and why, thus minimizing confusion for clients, and hopefully helping them to be actively involved in their own counseling.

Goal formulation, however, does not preclude the changing of goals over time. Once a counseling goal has been achieved, the counselor and client often negotiate new ones. Another possibility is that the goals that had been negotiated become less critical then the resolution of newly evolved client problems. The counselor must be both flexible and sensitive enough to recognize when the contract must be renegotiated. But, this renegotiation should be explicit.

The supervisors' function with counselors, once the goals are explicitly negotiated, is to help the counselors determine a treatment strategy. Supervisors may share approaches that have worked with similar clients, experiencing similar problems. The danger here, however, is that often the supervisee will misinterpret the intent of this sharing, and assume that the manner the supervisor has dealt with similar cases is the way the counselor should approach this case. A point to be stressed with students is that what works for the supervisor may not be appropriate for the supervisee, and that there are many possible approaches for a given case. The critical variable in the selection of the treatment approach is that it be consistent with the counselor's personality. An example the author uses with his trainees is that, although he believes in many of the tenets of the Client Centered Approach, he cannot use this style since it is quite inconsistent with his personality.

A potential danger in developing treatment strategies is an overdependence on technique. Many students use supervision to "know what to do." They take what may have been discussed in supervision and bring it directly into the counseling session, independent of whether or not it may be appropriate at that moment for the client. Probably the most difficult task that confronts supervisors is to have counselors think on their feet--to be self-dependent and not technique-dependent. This is where the real creativity of counseling takes place. Somehow students need to learn that, although what took place in supervision may be helpful, the counselor in the session is in the best position to judge whether a given intervention strategy is appropriate at a given time. Supervisors need to nurture the confidence of counselors to trust their own judgment, and use it in the moment.

Role Modeling as a Supervisory Strategy

Hopefully, in the interaction with supervisees, supervisors are genuine, open, confrontive, and caring, and thus both parties can openly discuss their relationship. The supervisor may ask how the counselor can incorporate this learning into counseling relationships. Supervisors need to be aware of the inordinate influence they have over the counselors they train, as well as the impact they can have as individuals over students. If supervisors can own this "power," they may be more conscious of their own behavior in interacting with students, hopefully displaying behaviors that are consistent with effective counseling.

Since professors also serve as role models for their students, they have the responsibility to let students see their weaknesses as well as their strengths. Too often supervisors are seen by students as having all the answers. The author has found at times the most impactful answer to a question asked by a supervisee is, "I don't know."

How else can role modeling in supervision be used? It is very easy to critique someone else's tape of an interview and find what's "wrong" with it. This is a role that is comfortable for most supervisors, with very little personal risk. They are protected from having personal counseling weaknesses exposed since they are usually the possessors of the terminal degree, thus hiding behind their title. The author argues that they must be willing to expose themselves, by giving students the opportunity to critique tapes of the supervisor's counseling sessions. Or another way for the supervisor to reveal his counseling skill would be for the supervisor and trainee to carry cases together as co-therapists. A further possibility would be for supervisors to present a tape of one of their cases pointing out to the students where they were dissatisfied, and seek the counsel of the trainees as to points the supervisors may consider for the next client interview.

What is the consequence of such supervisory behavior? The student can come to recognize that even the most effective counselors have areas in which they, too, need to grow, and that a counselor's learning is never complete and is a lifelong process. It also allows the student the opportunity to see that supervisors also must grope, think, feel, and be uncertain before ultimately arriving at a treatment strategy.

The Role of Group Supervision

Up until now the focus of this chapter has been the interaction of individual counselors and their supervisors, which is the heart of any training program. However, an important adjunct to individual supervision is group supervision, preferably with two supervisors present.

What does this supervisory modality provide?

As stated earlier, most beginning counselors have many feelings of self-doubt, uncertainty and fears of incompetence. In group supervision there is the opportunity for these feelings to be shared so the counselors-in-training recognize that they are not alone with these feelings and that these feelings are merely a symptom of a stage of professional development. This can be very comforting to the neophyte counselor.

Another advantage group supervision provides is that counselors can be exposed to a wider range of cases than they experience individually. Also, they are able to listen to the cases of others with much less ego involvement. Since it would be expected that this would be less threatening, the counselor-in-training can think more objectively about how he or she would deal with the cases presented.

Still another advantage of group supervision, particularly when there are at least two supervisors, is that the student has the opportunity to see "experts" openly disagree as to how cases may be handled. This serves to heighten the awareness of the trainees that there is no one approach. Hopefully, this will stimulate critical thinking on the part of the trainees so that they might tease out the treatment elements of each of the supervisors which in the future they might want to try in their counseling.

Finally, group supervision is the first experience in the trainees' development as supervisors. They have the opportunity to witness the counseling of others, as well as to give their opinions about the cases presented.

Factors Impeding the Supervisory Process

The bases for selection in counseling training programs are usually academic, i.e., test scores on graduate admission batteries, previous scholastic achievement, etc. Letters of recommendation are usually only considered after the applicant has attained a minimal level on the first two criteria. While academic criteria are basic to the selection of individuals who hope to practice in an applied profession, Truax and Mitchell (1971), as well as the author, would argue that these criteria are not sufficient.

The consequence of this selection procedure is that in most cases the people selected as counseling graduate students were never evaluated on the most powerful tool they bring to the therapeutic process--themselves. Adding to this problem is that the practicum experience is usually the last experience in the training program. Practicums are usually reserved for those counseling students who have completed, or are completing, their course work. While success in course work is probably related to the admission criteria, success in the practicum is not. Thus, the most powerful therapeutic tool the student brings to counseling is the last to be assessed. While this is unfair to the student and the supervisor, it is the current reality.

What can the supervisor do, particularly in the case where the student counselor brings more problems to the practicum than the clients he or she is expected to serve?

The counselor-in-training, who is not interpersonally effective, must be recognized and assisted. Interpersonal effectiveness, or lack of it, can be recognized early through the evaluation of counseling tapes presented. (More than likely, supervisors probably have come to recognize the lack of interpersonal effectiveness in their own interaction with the student.) The use of the tapes allows supervisors the opportunity to point out the behaviors that are impeding interpersonal effectiveness. With most students, this is sufficient to allow them to shape their behavior so that the counseling impeding behaviors are quickly dropped. However, with some students their interpersonal ineffectiveness is merely suggestive of more serious personal problems.

What is the supervisor to do?

The writer is of the opinion that it is imperative that the supervisor be direct in addressing the problem. The supervisor may express a willingness for the supervisee to enter into a counseling relationship with the supervisor, or another counselor. This will, of course, vary from supervisor to supervisor. Some feel that they can not or should not formally counsel their supervisees, while others are not concerned by this approach. The point is that the supervisor must openly confront the behavioral difficulties of the trainee and the potential consequence for clients. And, further, the supervisor must point out that if these difficulties are not overcome, there will be little likelihood of success by the counselor during the practicum experience. The supervisor can only suggest counseling, not impose it upon the trainee, since this would constitute an intrusion into the student's privacy. The student might be more willing to accept the possibility of counseling if the supervisor would point out how prevalent the practice of

387

therapists receiving counseling is. Various studies have shown that as many as 65 per cent of surveyed therapists had undergone some form of counseling during their lives (Goldschmid, et al., 1969; Garfield and Kurtz, 1974; Lubin, 1962). However, in the event the student does not choose to enter counseling, and if his or her interpersonal behavior does not become effective, it is the supervisor's responsibility not to allow the student to continue to see clients. As mentioned earlier, the first commitment must be to the public served. The issues surrounding the discharge of a counselor from his training experience are complex (Redfering and Biasco, 1976; Bernard, 1975); nevertheless, they cannot be avoided.

Another factor that may impede the supervisory process is the supervisor-counselor match. The author contends that the counselor and the supervisor have the right to start their relationship without any negative preexisting history and with no "hidden agendas." The supervisory relationship is tense enough! In most instances, the counselor implicitly chooses his supervisor by the section of the practicum in which he or she enrolls; or in practicum settings where there is more than one supervisor, he or she may request that a given supervisor be assigned. But supervisors have their rights of selection, too! If the supervisor has had previous negative experiences with the counselor-in-training, the supervisor has the right to ask the counselor to seek out another supervisor in order that an unbiased supervisory relationship be established.

Other Factors to Be Considered in the Supervision of Counselors

A frequent topic of conversation in the area of supervision is the ideal supervision/client load ratio. Some traditional programs, particularly in clinical psychology, adhere to the model of one hour of supervision for every hour of client contact. This is an unrealistic expectation for the supervisor, unless the counselor sees very few clients. This approach exaggerates the importance of each phrase spoken in counseling, with the counselor-in-training feeling that "big brother" will be constantly observing or or listening. This might encumber the counselor in risk-taking behavior.

The other extreme might be where the counselor only gets to meet with the supervisor during group supervision on a weekly basis, where many counselors are competing for very little supervisory time. The approach is perhaps even more damaging to the trainee. The counselor does not have the opportunity to develop an intimate personal relationship with the supervisor, making it impossible for the supervisor to assess whether the treatment strategies being employed by the counselor are consistent with the counselor's personality. In this situation, supervision is sterile and impersonal and is much like a seminar.

It is the author's contention that the counselors most benefit from the practicum experience if they can see between eight to ten clients per week and receive at least one hour of individual supervision and two hours of group supervision per week. This approach allows each of the counselors to get the "feel" of being a counselor, in that each one has a number of cases, and can come to be more selective in recognizing those cases which are most in need of supervisory input.

A further consideration for the supervisor may be to supplement supervision with the use of didactic seminars. These are designed to address the universal technique needs which are a function of the kind of clients served in the practicum setting. For example, student counselors being trained in a university counseling center could benefit from familiarity with the Strong-Campbell Interest Inventory, since many of the clients in this setting seek vocational counseling. By teaching this or any other technique in a didactic seminar, all of the members of the practicum acquire a specific skill at the same time, while not tying up individual supervision time. The supervisors, if they consider the use of didactics, must first determine the specific techniques or skills being heavily called upon by the client population of the practicum. The more frequently skills are needed, the earlier a seminar on that topic would be presented.

387b

Another issue the supervisor may consider is whether there is a difference in the supervision of master's versus doctoral students. Certainly, one would expect the doctoral student to have a stronger academic preparation for the practicum experience, and also to have had at least one prior practicum experience; but it has been the author's experience that these differences may not be apparent in the counseling abilities between the two groups of students. The research around this question has produced conflicting results (Cimbolic, 1972; Ornston, Cicchetti, Leving, and Fierman, 1968; Caracena, 1965; Grigg, 1961; Fiske, Cartwright, and Kirtner, 1964; Bergin and Solomon, 1970).

Whether the student is at the master's or doctoral level, the supervisor must listen to the initial tapes of the counselors to be assured that the interpersonal behavior is not blocking the therapeutic process. Once it has been determined that the doctoral candidate is adequate interpersonally, the nature of the supervisory relationship may change, becoming almost colleagual.

Another function supervisors must exercise is to inform their trainees as to the generalizability of what they have learned to other client populations and/or settings. Whatever the field placement for the practicum, it is usually geared to a target population, i.e., school children with learning disorders, college students seeking service from a counseling center, or clients seeking assistance from a community mental health agency. Although each client is an individual, he or she possesses characteristics which are common to the target population that the agency was designed to serve. Therefore, some approaches would be more likely to be effective and consequently utilized more with that client population. Students must be able to assess the appropriateness of generalizing what they have learned in their practicum experience to other populations.

The last point of consideration in this chapter revolves around the end point of the supervisory process. Stamatakos (1978) argues for the need for life-long learning. Supervisors must impress upon their trainees that this is just the beginning of their life-long learning in their

387c

chosen profession. The author can vividly remember as a
graduate student wishing for his Ph.D. so at last he would
know everything, while in actuality the only thing his Ph.D.
taught him was how little he knew.

Although the need for life-long learning may be impres-
sed upon students, professors and supervisors may have to
assist them in determining the next starting point. This
process occurs at the end of the practicum experience. Here,
the supervisor, having come to know the relative strengths
and weaknesses of the student counselors, can give them
input concerning areas in which they should direct efforts
for personal and professional growth.

References

Bergin, A., and Solomon, S. Personality and performance
    correlates of empathic understanding in psycho-
    therapy. In Tomlinson, T., and Hart, J. (Eds.)
    New Directions in Client-Centered Therapy.
    Boston: Houghton-Mifflin, 1970.

Bernard, J. L. Due process in dropping the unsuitable
    clinical student. Professional Psychology, 1975,
    6(3), 275-278.

Beutler, L. E. Value and attitude change in psycho-
    therapy: A case for dyadic assessment. Psycho-
    therapy: Theory, Research, and Practice, 1972,
    9, 362-367.

Bordin, E. S. Psychological Counseling. New York:
    Appleton-Century-Crofts, 1968.

Caracena, P. Elicitation of dependency expressions in
    the initial stage of psychotherapy. Journal of
    Counseling Psychology, 1965, 12, 268-274.

Carkhuff, R. R., and Berenson, B. G. Beyond Counseling
    and Therapy. New York: Holt, Rinehart, and
    Winston, 1967.

Cimbolic, P. Counselor race and experience effects on black clients. Journal of Consulting and Clinical Psychology, 1972, 39, 328-332.

Elsenrath, D. E., Coker, D. L., and Martinson, W. D. Microteaching interviewing skills. Journal of Counseling Psychology, 1972, 19, 150-155.

Fiske, D., Cartwright, D., and Kirtner, W. Are psychotherapeutic changes predictable? Journal of Abnormal Psychology, 1964, 69, 418-426.

Garfield, S. L. Research on the training of professional psychotherapists. In Gurman, A. S., and Razin, A. M. (Eds.) Effective Psychotherapy: A Handbook of Research. New York: Pergamon Press, 1977.

Garfield, S. L., and Kurtz, R. A survey of clinical psychologists: Characteristics, activities, and orientations. The Clinical Psychologist, 1974, 28, 7-10.

Goldschmid, M. L., Stein, D. D., Weissman, H. N., and Sorrels, J. A survey of the training and practice of clinical psychologists. The Clinical Psychologist, 1969, 22, 89-107.

Grigg, A. Client response to counselors at different levels of experience. Journal of Counseling Psychology, 1961, 8, 217-233.

Harris, K. A. Developmental supervision: A model of contexts. In Eddy, J., College Student Personnel, Development, Administration, and Counseling. Washington, University Press, 1978.

Harris, S. J. The Authentic Person: Dealing with Dilemma. Niles, Ill.: Argus Communications, 1972.

Ivey, A. E. The clinician as teacher of interpersonal skills; let's give away what we've got. The Clinical Psychologist, 1974, 27, 6-9.

Kagan, N. Can technology help us toward reliability in influencing human interaction? Educational Technology, 1973, 13, 44-51.

Lakovics, M. Some problems in learning to do "good psychotherapy." American Journal of Psychiatry, 1976, 133(7), 834-837.

Lubin, B. Survey of psychotherapy training and activities of psychologists. Journal of Clinical Psychology, 1962, 18, 252-256.

Matarazzo, R. G., Weins, A. N., and Saslow, G. Experimentation in the teaching and learning of psychotherapy skills. In Gottschalk, L. K., and Auerbach, A. (Eds.) Methods of Research in Psychotherapy. New York: Appleton-Century-Crofts, 1966.

Ornston, P., Cicchetti, D., Levine, J., Fierman, L. Some parameters of verbal behavior that reliably differentiate novice from experienced psychotherapists. Journal of Abnormal Psychology, 1968, 73, 240-244.

Redfering, D. L., and Biasco, F. Selection and elimination of candidates in counselor education programs. Counselor Education and Supervision, 1976, 15(4), 298-304.

Reisman, J. M. Trends for training in treatment. Professional Psychology, 1975, 6(2), 187-192.

Stamatakos, L. C. Unsolicited advice to new professionals. Journal of College Student Personnel, 1978, 19(4), 325-330.

Truax, C. B., and Mitchell, K. M. Research on certain therapist interpersonal skills in relation to process and outcome. In Bergin, A. E., and Garfield, S. L. (Eds.) Handbook of Psychotherapy and Behavior Change. New York: Wiley, 1971.

CHAPTER 42

PRACTICUM EXPERIENCE IN THE MASTER'S
DEGREE PROGRAM FOR PERSONNEL WORK

Virginia Kirkbride

The Committee on Professional Development chose to focus its
convention session on practicum experience. Committee members
includes Mrs. Marian Bernhoft, Mary Evans, Ann Rednow, Ruth Renaud,
Mrs. Ann Redman, and Virginia Kirkbride, chairman.

Background

The committee of Professional Development of NAWDC was established as a standing committee in 1963, having been an ad hoc
committee since 1958. The committee was originally established
to supplement and support the work of the Inter-Association
Coordinating Committee, made up of representatives of ACPA, NASPA,
AACUHO, and NAWDC, on professional preparation and education of
student personnel workers. In 1962-63, LAACC was reorganized and
restructured as COSPA, Council of Student Personnel Associations,
consisting of various commissions, one of which was to be specifically concerned with professional development.

The NAWDC committee on Professional Development was established to work within the association to increase the competence
of personnel workers, with a focus on desired education and
training; to study criteria for evaluation of training programs;
and suggest long-range plans to upgrade the profession of educational personnel in counseling.

In 1967, on the recommendation of the chairman of the NAWDC
Research and Development, Publications, and Professional Development Committee, the Executive Board recommended a bylaws change
to establish the position of Vice-President to coordinate all
activities concerned with professional development. These activities were defined as (a) recruitment and selection, (b) placement, and (c) continuing education.

A vice-president for professional development was first
elected in 1968 to "promote and facilitate the development of
professional standards and growth" in the areas designated above.
At its first meeting in January 1970, the NAWDC Committee on
Professional Development agreed to define the term professional
development as "an ongoing process involving formal education,

in-service staff development, and individual study and assessment."
The general charge to the committee included:

1. To work in conjunction with the Vice-President of
    Professional Development and standing committees,
    such as the Workshop Committees, to arrange for
    summer programs for professional development, and
    the Research Committee to determine areas where
    assistance in professional development is most
    needed.

2. To communicate to the membership those items of
    professional interest that are occurring in the
    committee meetings and in other organizations
    where professional growth is concerned.

3. To encourage members who have ideas for professional
    development to communicate with the committee which
    in turn will act as a clearing house for material.

Practicum Description

Practicum is of concern to the entire membership of the
association: to the graduate students in master's programs who
are enrolled in practicum; to those who supervise practicum
students; to directors of training programs for preparation of
personnel educators; to members who will employ M.A. graduates in
personnel positions who have had no experience except the practicum; to those who have no time to train staff and yet require
experienced personnel. Current studies indicate that the majority of those entering the profession today are coming from graduate
training programs. What are the exceptions? What are the perceptions held?

Two studies provide additional background. In 1966, Commission XII of the American College Personnel Association authorized
a survey of and possible recommendations for the practical experience which should be included in the preparation of college
student personnel workers. Dr. N. T. Oppelt, Dr. June E. Stuckey,
and Dr. C. A. Quinlan of Colorado State College at Greeley prepared the report, which was published in April 1967. Responses
were received from 64 departments in colleges and universities,
of which 41 reported graduate training programs for college
personnel workers.

According to their report, various types of practical experiences are available to students majoring in college student personnel work. The practicum, which is available in 35 programs,
is generally described as a brief, introductory experience characterized by breadth rather than depth. At the same time, it
described as a closely supervised experience, often including

389

observation of a process as well as direct participation in it. Most programs include a seminar for the purpose of integrating practical and theoretical experiences of the students.

Some major strengths of the practical experience include real involvement in actual situations, a variety of experiences and a flexibility of experiences encountered, close contact with a specialist in the particular work area, autonomy under supervision, and the opportunity to test theoretical orientation against real circumstances. Frequently mentioned weaknesses are lack of properly trained supervisors, demands on supervisor's time and energy, short duration of the experience, failure to integrate theory with practice in the work situation, focus on getting the job done rather than on learning, poor quality of personnel services offered on campuses where the training programs exist.

A second study of consequence is that completed by Patricia Houtz in an unpublished dissertation from Michigan State. Reported in an article "Internships in Student Personnel Programs," published in the Journal of College Student Personnel (September 1967), her study sought to determine the kind of practical experiences that provide the greatest professional development for personnel workers. She found that graduate students and the professional panel of student personnel workers in top-level administrative positions were almost unanimous in agreeing that organized internship programs would be beneficial for workers in student personnel. The majority of both groups agreed that (a) practical experience and content courses should be concurrent; (b) practical experience with responsibility should be in only one or two areas of student personnel activity with orientation used as the method of training in other areas; (c) decision-making responsibility should be a part of both master's and doctoral level internships; (d) academic credit should be given for internships; and (e) internships should include time for professional reading and participation in professional activities, such as attendance at conventions.

Both the panel and recent graduates were asked to list other common or specialized experiences which they believed should be included in an internship. The panel of administrators listed the following:

1. There should be exposure to office work, such as keeping files; learning to give instructions to and work with secretaries; learning to handle office communications and to keep and report data for office use.

2. Orientation, leadership training, and cultural programs.

390

3.   Discussion of the role of women in a changing society, including ethics, goals, and philosophy.

Recent graduates included as suggestions:

1.   More experience in counseling; greater opportunity for constructive criticism, personal evaluation of work and discussion of mistakes by competent faculty, staff advisers, and supervisors.

2.   A detailed overview of the entire personnel area, in order to develop a perspective in the work.

3.   An opportunity to learn business functions.

4.   An opportunity to assume responsibility.

From her excellent study, Dr. Houtz concluded that:

1.   Professional workers generally agree that practical experience in the specialized areas of student personnel work should be an integral part of the education of a professional practitioner in this field.

2.   Institutions which do not have well-developed programs of practical experiences should develop programs which will enable future graduates to increase their professional skill and understanding of the total programs of student personnel services.

3.   Student personnel curricula should make provisions for internships and academic work to be taken concurrently.

4.   Internships should be developed as a method of providing an opportunity for organized and supervised practical experiences in one or two of the specialized areas for graduate students in student personnel curricula. Flexibility is essential.

NAWDC Committee Recommendations

1.   The primary purpose of the practicum experience should be to provide opportunities for the integration of knowledge and skills, theory and practice, and not to provide the overview or

introduction to the field.

2. The emphasis on the survey or the introduction to the field should be provided through seminars and laboratory experiences.

3. The practicum should be offered during the latter part of the formal training program or at the conclusion of the requirements.

4. The practicum should be of significant duration to offer extensive involvement of the student with the professional staff.

5. Greater emphasis should be placed on practicum students who work with generalists in the field rather than professionals in areas of specialization.

6. Teams of supervisors should be utilized to work with practicum students rather than assignment of students to individual supervisors.

7. Emphasis should be placed not on service as an end in itself but rather as it relates to student development and the development of the institutions.

Training for student personnel master's candidates may be viewed in the dimensions of the table on the next page.

	SURVEY-INTRODUCTION	INTEGRATION OF KNOWLEDGE & SKILLS THEORY-PRACTICE
TIME	Offered prior to formal course work or early in program	Made available toward completion of program or at its conclusion
	Several experiences of a duration	A few experiences of considerable length
SUPERVISORS	Less individualized approach	In-depth involvement
PROGRAM COORDINATORS	Responsibility to put isolated experiences into total overview of the field	Responsibility to assess integrative aspects of work experience and theory
NATURE OF EXPERIENCE	Little or no opportunity for direct involvement in decision making	Opportunity for actual involvement in operation and decision making process of office
EVALUATION	Severe limitations on means of evaluating experience	Responsibility to work with student on self-evaluation of the experience

CHAPTER 43

MYTH OF THE PROBLEM FREE PRACTICUM

John Eddy

A strange myth of some student counselors or college student personnel workers in-training is to desire a "problem free practicum" or to be uncomfortable with a practicum unless it is "problem free." Our American advertising world is always trying to get us to be problem free. We are bombarded by the mass media and our friends on getting an easy life. Of course, a practicum that has too many problems can paralyze persons--this is not a desirable situation. However, problems are inevitable in every practicum. Consequently, an unrealisitc goal is to not have problems. What is crucial is to have ways of solving problems in a practicum. A "problem free practicum" is a contradiction and a misconception.

Being a counselor or college student personnel worker does not eliminate one's problems. The fact that persons in the helping professions know how persons are supposed to act, think and feel does not mean counselors can always act, think or feel in a meaningful way themselves. This means that counselors sometimes need counselors to help them work through their problems. Recognizing you have problems to work out is a good value and a healthy approach to solving problems.

Many of our problems are created because we set unrealistic goals or set no goals at all. We need to establish a practical plan with short range and long range objectives. Next, we need to put limits on our objectives and goals by questioning such as:

1. Is it possible to accomplish it with your present abilities, time and resources?
2. Is it specific?
3. Is it measurable?
4. Is it acceptable?
5. Is it reasonable?
6. Is it the truth?

Finally, if you did not produce the result, you did not take the responsibility or you lacked the ability.

Flexibility and openness are good characteristics to have in all persons. However, the trainee student who demands these

394

characteristics of his supervisors and his clients, but not of himself, is indeed in trouble in preparing for a helping profession. Ask not what a practicum can do for you but what can you do in a practicum?

Some of the finest practicums students have had over the years were experiences that were extremely difficult. Of course, when the students were going through these practicums they didn't always grasp the significance of their working through these problems. Later, some students admitted that they learned more about their real life work by experiencing these problems in their practicum. A practicum that protects students from problems is an artificial and superficial practicum. There are some practicums that are literally "problem free." Later, students claim that their present job experiences is so different from their past practicum. Is it any wonder that some students complain that their practicums failed to produce on the job realities?

A good practicum helps the student not only practice knowledge and skills but also to learn of his or her personality limitations. Thus, a practicum that has its share of problems to test the student in training is a good practicum to experience.

The counseling and college student personnel profession is one that helps persons to help work through their problems. Without human problems to work on, there is little work for counselors. While this sounds so simple and reasonable, some students underestimate the problems that persons they deal with have from their supervisors to their clients. Sometimes the trainee student's personal problems in a practicum block their ability to help other persons who have problems. Taking responsibility for one's problems is the key to solving them and not blaming other persons.

Some examples of trainee students whose personal problems controlled them rather than in being control of their problems are:

1. The student who blamed his supervisor for being too hard on him for writing error free mimeos--this student was not taking responsibility for writing accurate mimeos that truly communicate desired results.

2. The student who blamed his clients for not being on time to their appointments--this student was not taking responsibility for telling his clients how his schedule needed on-time clients.

3. The student who blamed his or her video tape evaluator for not giving him feedback when he or she failed to stay for the entire feedback session--this student was not taking respon-

sibility for getting a thorough evaluation through the timed feedback process allowed.

4. The student who blamed her practicum coordinator for
lack of detailed orientation when she failed to read and understand the course syllabus--this student was not taking responsibility for her reading and understanding course regulations.

The "game of blame me" is a "copout" for taking responsibility.
Practicum students who play this game are in need of counseling
on how to take responsibility for their own lives and the assignments that are a regular part of an academic and/or work process.

The person's mental health, as suggested by the Wisconsin
Association for Mental Health, is essential to producing a good
life--and a practicum experience. For example, a student needs
a comfortable feeling about himself or herself so that the following is evident:

> You are not bowled over by your own emotions--by
> your fears, anger, love, jealousy, guilt or worries.
> You can take life's disappointments in stride. You
> have a tolerant, easy-going attitude toward yourself
> as well as others; you can laugh at yourself.

Again, the practicum student needs a right feeling about
others. For example, the following is evident:

> You are able to give love and to consider the
> interests of others. You have personal relationships
> that are satisfying and lasting. You expect to like
> and trust others, and take it for granted that others
> will like and trust you. You respect the many dif-
> ferences you find in persons.

Finally, the practicum student needs to meet the demands of
life. For example, the following is evident:

> You do something about your problems as they arise.
> You accept your responsibilities. You shape your
> environment whenever possible, you adjust to it
> wherever necessary. You plan ahead but do not fear
> the future.

References

Eddy, J.P. and Durst, G. Life and Management Respon-
    sibility. Albuquerque, New Mexico: The Training
    Company, 1976.

References

Ford, A.S. Directing the Student Experience: A Manual for Supervisors. Berea, KY: Berea College Press, 1976.

Giroux, R.F.; Biggs, D.A. and Pietrofesa, J.J. College Student Development: Programs, Issues, and Practices. Washington, D.C.: American Personnel and Guidance Association. Reprint Series Nine, 1977.

Kirkbride, V. "Practicum Experience in the Master's Degree Program for Personnel Work." National Association of Women's Deans and Counselors Journal, Winter, 1971.

Miller, T.K. and Prince, J.S. The Future of Student Affairs. San Francisco: Jossey-Bass, Inc., 1976.

Stadt, R.W.; Bittle, R.E.; Kenneke, L.L.; and Nystrom, D.C. Managing Career Education Programs. Englewood Cliffs, NJ: Prentice-Hall, Inc., 1973.

_____ "Consider the College Student Personnel Profession." Washington, D.C.: Commission on Professional Education of Student Personnel Workers in Higher Education of the American College Personnel Association, 1974.

_____ "Student Development Services in Higher Education," Washington, D.C.: American College Personnel Association Commission XII, 1975.

CHAPTER 44

EFFECTIVE PRACTICUM COMMUNICATION IS ESSENTIAL

John Eddy

It may seem strange to cover the subject of "Practicum Communication" when it is so basic and common to the training of College Student Personnel Workers and College Counselors. As Kirkbride suggests, more constructive criticism is needed. However, experience in teaching practicums for over eight years has taught the author that "Practicum Communication" is sometimes lacking between students and their supervisors.

The following information on "Practicum Communications" is based on interviews with over 120 former practicum students and over 40 practicum supervisors from training programs such as at Michigan State University, Indiana University, Columbia University, Purdue University, University of California at Berkeley, Southern Illinois University at Carbondale, University of Minnesota at Minneapolis, and Loyola University of Chicago from 1970-78.

"Practicum Communication" may be defined as follows: "Practicum Communication" is verbal and written communication that occurs between students and staff in a practicum situation.

"Inadequate Practicum Communication Elements" are identified as follows:

1. When the student fails to tell the supervisor frustrations that he or she faces in the practicum until the practicum is over or nearly over.

2. When the supervisor fails to set up or use meaningfully regular feedback sessions with the student to cover his or her accomplishments or disappointments.

3. When the supervisor knows the student is not doing a satisfactory job but fails to mention ways the student might improve his or her performance.

4. When the student and supervisor fail to correct problems in the practicum when both parties are aware of the difficulties.

It appears that these four previous statements identifying "Inadequate Practicum Communication Elements" seem to be common sense situations that everyone should be aware of and knowledgeable about in all practicums. However, one or more of these factors occur frequently with some students in practicums throughout the nation. The evidence for the previous statement comes from practicum students and supervisors who have graduated from some of the "so called finest or best known" university graduate programs in the country.

Why do practicum students avoid sharing their frustrations and fail to use feedback sessions? "Selected reasons why some practicum students fail to communicate" are the following:

1. The student fears that voicing his or her frustrations will be interpreted by the supervisor to mean he or she is not a "good candidate" for a position in this field and that the course grade will be affected.

2. The student fears that by discussing these frustrations that the supervisor will not accept him or her as a person.

3. The student fears that the supervisor will not write a good letter of recommendation for him or her that may lead to full-time employment.

4. The student fears "lack of peer acceptance" from other students in the practicum will interpret his or her problems to be a weakness on the part of the practicum student.

It is easier to identify the "Inadequate Practicum Communication Elements" and to provide "Selected Reasons Why Some Practicum Students Fail to Communicate" than to correct these kinds of situations. However, it is essential that both of the previous topics are known as regular problem areas. Perhaps, then, the communication between students and supervisors will begin to become more open and honest. Again, the practicum supervisor and student may use this chapter to break the barriers and begin to dialogue on their mutual frustrations, feelings, and failures. Hopefully, they will also mention the good growth experiences, the valuable helping relationships provided persons, and the constructive developmental opportunities in the entire process of the practicum.

It is apparent to the author that regularly scheduled feedback periods between the student and supervisor must include regular "frustration feedback" and not merely discussing what are the next activities (knowledge or skill competencies) to be practiced. Furthermore, strategies for dealing with the frustrations must be revised and worked into the Behavioral Objectives Contract. For example, let us take a common problem on many practicums.

The student is having difficulty in working in some valuable learning experiences during the practicum between his or her other classes, outside job, and personal living demands. In order to obtain these valuable learning experiences, adjustments on the part of the student need to be made which may include dropping a class that conflicts, making up time on his paying job to accommodate practicum experiences, and eliminating a social activity for the practicum term.

In conclusion, while the resolution of the illustration provided may sound rather ordinary and uncomplicated, it seems that decision making for effective communication is difficult for many students. The author recommends that every practicum, internship, and field work supervisor and every student assigned to a practicum, internship, and field work situation read and apply the principles in the book, Directing the Student Work Experience, mentioned in the reference list following this chapter.

Changing student personal, social, class, and work schedules to do a meaningful practicum is like the old saying--"It's easier said than done." Therefore, the more pre-practicum type experiences that a student has on communicative skills related to decision making and value clarification should help. Using the two books--It's Your Move: Working with Student Volunteers --A Manual for Community Organizations and Directing the Student Work Experience: A Manual for Supervisors is helpful.

The challenge areas of this chapter need to be faced daily and worked at in practicum if effective practicum communication is to happen.

As Ford (1976), points out, students in work supervision situations perform work assignments best when: "Job responsibilities are clearly defined by the supervisor (a set of behavioral objectives should be required at the beginning of every practicum, internship or field work assignment and they can be revised by supervisor and student according to the circumstances); mutual trust and respect are developed between supervisor and student; and evaluation and recognition of performance is constructive and continuous." Thus, in all of the supervision experience a priority is put daily on effective communication using the following supervisory checklist as a guide for human relations and work accomplishments.

The following checklist of supervisory functions (Ford, 1976) with prompting questions is included for quick reference:

1. In developing good relationships between yourself, the individual student and his job:

   .....How do you help a student feel comfortable working in your department?
   .....How do you work with different students in different ways and maintain impartiality?

2. To motivate the student to do the best job possible:

   .....In what ways do you identify the interests and expectations of each student?
   .....How do you inspire both quantity and quality work?

3. In encouraging each student to take responsibility and initiative:

   .....How do you know what the student is capable of accomplishing?
   .....In what ways do you achieve the greatest production or services and at the same time provide opportunity for expanded student responsibility and initiative?

4. To communicate department or area and college goals:

   .....How can the student best learn the importance of his work to the College and to your department or area?

5. In communicating work expectations to the student:

   .....What do you need to tell the student about the work?
   .....What ways are best to assure that the student understands what is expected of him?

6. To provide skill training:

   .....What skills must the student learn in order to do the job?
   .....How do you get the student trained for the skills needed?

7. In encouraging student opinions and suggestions:

   .....Do you take time to listen to student suggestions?
   .....In what ways do you try to use ideas students have suggested when possible, and explain to

401

7. (Cont'd)
   them why you can't when it isn't possible?

8. To teach by example good work habits and attitudes:

   .....Do you always feel comfortable that students
   might--and often do--copy the way you work
   and do things?

9. To provide constructive evaluation of the student's
   performance:

   .....How do you measure performance?
   .....How do you help students become aware of their
   strengths and weaknesses in their work?
   .....How do you assist students to overcome identified weaknesses?

10. In order to provide helpful counsel to the student:

    .....What do you need to know about the student?
    .....What are good ways to listen, ask questions
    and give advice?
    .....What situations and questions necessitate
    referring the student to another service or
    office?

11. To deal adequately with discipline problems:

    .....How do you deal with students who don't cooperate
    and don't try to meet expectations?
    .....How do you maintain morale and discipline at the
    same time?

12. In making the job an educational experience:

    .....How do you balance the student's needs with
    department needs?
    .....How do you help a student reflect on the learning
    that is taking place?
    .....In what ways do you provide more learning for
    the student that can also benefit production
    or services in the long run?

References

Ford, A.S. (Ed.) Directing the Student Work Experience:
A Manual for Supervisors. Berea, KY: Berea College
Press, 1976.

Hedling, D.E. "Preparation for Student Personnel: Im-
plications of Humanistic Education." Journal of
College Student Personnel. September, 1971. Vol. 12,
No. 5, 324-328.

Houtz, P. Internships in Student Personnel Programs.
Journal of College Student Personnel. September,
1967, Vol. 8, No. 5, 322-326.

Hurst, J.C. and Ivey, A.E. "Toward a Radicalization of
Student Personnel." Journal of College Student
Personnel. May, 1971, Vol. 12, No. 3, 165-168.

Kirkbride, V. "Practicum Experience in the Master's
Degree Program for Personnel Work." National
Association of Women Deans and Counselors Journal.
Winter, 1971.

Parker, C.A. The Place of Counseling in the Preparation
of Student Personnel Workers. Personnel and Guidance
Journal, November, 1966, Vol. 45, No. 3, 254-261.

_____ "It's Your Move: Working with Student
Volunteers -- A Manual for Community Organizations"
Washington, D.C.: U.S. Government Printing Office,
1976.

CHAPTER 45

COMPETENCY BASED PROGRAM FOR COLLEGE STUDENT PERSONNEL
DEVELOPMENT, COSPA FUNCTIONS, AND RESOURCES

John Eddy

Preface

This list is meant to be representative and not exhaustive
or complete.

TOPIC	SKILL
Career Education	* To know how to use, through practice, the Occupational Handbook* in the guidance of college students; * To know available postsecondary school opportunities and how to use selected guidance information on the same strengths and weaknesses of these educational institutions for future employment of graduates.
Self-Assessment	* To know how, through role playing, to use the American College Testing Forms* to do both academic and co-curricular advisement with students; * To experience the process of video-taping in developing counselors and administrators; * To know how to use the Task-Persons Inventory* in assessing some critical skills of a counselor and/or administrator in higher education; * To know how to use the Drug Survey* to discover personal problems that may lead to drug abuse, suicide and self harm;
Group Work	* To know about the different types of group work and to know how to use a student development approach to group work such as through the Human Potential Seminar*, Transactional Analysis*, and similar type exercises to help in the growth of a student's self worth and self concept;

404

Group Work (Cont'd)	* To know how to use a method of conflict resolution and problem solving for occupational applications;
College Student Personnel Models	* To recognize management by objectives in accountability as well as the different types of College Student Personnel models* such as "The Student Development Model," "The Student Services Model," "The Therapeutic Model," and "The Regulatory Model," through field trips, handouts, textbooks, and experience in class;
Confidentiality	* To recognize the need for confidentiality in developing trust and acceptance in counseling, administrative, and teaching higher education; * To be aware of protecting the client and counselor in confidential matters;
Referral Functions	* To realize the various types of referral possibilities* for college students with various interests and/or problems, such as suicide;
Job Placement	* To be aware of the kinds of positions open to paraprofessionals, masters graduates, and doctoral candidates in College Student Personnel as well as in related helping professions employing Student Personnel Work in Higher Education Graduates through vita kits*, professional meetings and job listings;
Testing and Self-Program Learning	* To know how to use Buros Mental Measurement* in evaluating prospective academic and personality instruments for college students; * To know how to use self program learning units in CSPW:
Minority Awareness	* To experience the BITCH test* or CAT test* as an illustration of a minority cultural awareness exercise, counseling tool, and screening device;
Professional Literature	* To discover the various ramifications of College Student Personnel through professional articles, books, reports, and other materials;

405

Administrative Role   * To find out what a dean of student's job
                        is through an interview and an on-campus
                        observation;

Crisis Awareness   * To be acquainted with resources for stu-
                        dents in crisis situations through class
                        exercises.

Professional Training and College Student Development

Introduction: The Council of Student Personnel Association's
(COSPA) Statement of 1975 is used as a professional guideline
for the training of College Student Personnel Workers following
the College Student Development Approach. In the following
Guidance courses and 16 sources, these ten functions of the COSPA
Statement are covered.

1.   Assessing behaviors that the student has already developed,
     Guidance 418 (Life and Management Responsibility and The
     Art of Helping).

2.   Formulating the student's behavioral objectives, Guidance
     418, 419 and 494 (Life and Management Responsibility, A
     Career Education Primer for Educators, College Student
     Personnel, Development, Counseling and Administration;

3.   Selecting college programs that build on existing behaviors
     to accomplish the student's objectives, Guidance 418 (Ca-
     reers In College and University Affairs and College Student
     Personnel Development, Counseling and Administration;

4.   Fostering student growth within the context of his or her
     own cultural background and encouraging his or her appre-
     ciation of the cultural backgrounds of the educational
     institution and of other students, Guidance 418-419
     College Student Personnel Development, Counseling, and
     Administration.

5.   Developing physical environments, human groups, institution-
     al organizations, and financial resources most conducive to
     the student's growth, Guidance 419 (Life and Management
     Responsibility and College and University Business Admini-
     stration; Guidance 427 (Higher Education in America).

6.   Integrating concurrent experiences outside the institution
     with the student's educational program as an aid in achiev-
     ing the student's objectives, Guidance 494, 466, 527, and
     528 Managing Career Education Programs, Directing the Stu-
     dent Work Experiences, and College Student Personnel Develop-
     ment, Counseling and Administration.

7. Modifying existing behaviors that block the further growth of the student, Guidance 418 (<u>Transactional Analysis, Social and Communication Training</u>) and Guidance 419 and 428 (<u>Human Potential Seminar Workbook.</u>)

8. Giving visibility to a value system that enables the student to judge the worth of behavior patterns, Guidance 418 and 436 (<u>Life and Management Responsibility</u>), <u>College Student Personnel Development, Counseling and Administration</u>; Guidance 427, (<u>Education and Ethical Inquiry, Value Clarification Exercises</u> and <u>Higher Education: Participants Confronted.</u>

9. Recording the student's progress as a means of facilitating his growth, Guidance 418, (<u>Life and Management Responsibility</u>), Guidance 419, (<u>Human Potential Seminar Workbook</u>).

10. Identifying appropriate environments for continued development before and after the student leaves his present educational setting, Guidance 418 and 427 <u>A Career Education Primer for Educators</u>, and <u>College Student Personnel Development, Counseling, and Administration.</u>

References

Carkhuff, R. <u>The Art of Helping III</u>. Amherst, MA: Human Resource Development Press, 1977.

Eddy, J.P. <u>College Student Personnel Development, Counseling, and Administration</u>. Washington, D.C.: University Press of America, 1978.

Eddy, J.P. <u>Education and Ethical Inquiry</u>. Johnson, VT: Johnson State College Press, 1968.

Eddy, J.P. and Durst, G. <u>Life and Management by Responsibility</u>. Albuquerque, New Mexico: The Training Company, 1976.

Dilley, J. <u>Higher Education: Participants Confronted</u>. Dubuque, Iowa: William Brown Company, 1970.

Ford, A.S. (Ed.) <u>Directing the Student Work Experience: A Manual for Supervisors</u>. Berea, KY: Berea College Press, 1976.

Henderson, A. and Henderson, H. <u>Higher Education in America</u>. San Francisco: Jossey-Bass, Inc. Publishers, 1974.

References

McHolland, J.D. and Trueblood, R.W. Human Potential Seminar. Evanston, IL: Kendall College Press, 1972.

Stadt, R.W.; Bittle, R.E.; Kenneke, L.L.; and Nystrom, D.C. Managing Career Education Programs. Englewood Cliffs, N.J.: Prentice-Hall, Inc., 1973.

Wernick, W.; Tiedeman, D.V.; Eddy, J.; and Bosdell, B.J. A Career Education Primer for Educators. Washington, D.C.: National Vocational Guidance Association - A Division of American Guidance and Personnel Association, 1977.

CHAPTER 46

PRACTICUM CHECKLIST FOR STUDENTS

Sheldon Siegel and John Eddy

The final report paper for the Practicum contains three
sections: (1) a diary of events, including number of hours
spent; (2) the behavioral contract (what you and the practicum
supervisor have agreed upon in terms of what you seek to ex-
tract form the experience); and (3) a critical analysis of the
experience.

Checklist for Practicum Students in the Field:

Can all these questions be answered adequately and satis-
factorily when preparing your final report paper and looking
objectively at the experience?

1. Is the involved area a bona fide student personnel function?

2. Were the hours and/or time segments agreed upon adequate in
   terms of a learning experience?

3. What kinds or types of activities either observed or worked
   in gave the best kind of experience?

4. Did the practicum relate to other student personnel work?

5. Was there license for you to operate freely within the
   office and to interact with all staff members.

6. Were questions asked and answered?

7. Were staff meetings attended?

8. Were some writing chores handled by you?

9. Were other individuals within the personnel division in
   other areas interviewed?

10. How did the office operate?

11. Did the supervisor use MBO, task-oriented, or other
    management procedures?

12. Did you have an opportunity to work in budgeting for his or her division?

13. What kind(s) of counseling approaches were used in dealing with students?

14. Was there a sense of a "student development" approach?

15. How well was this department respected among others?

16. Who prepared the salary schedules?

17. Were these people given faculty status?

18. What were the educational/experiencial backgrounds of the individuals at the management level?

19. Were paraprofessionals employed?

20. Were decisions made by staff members?

21. Was there adequate planning?

22. Was there a sense of "openness" and trust?

23. What recent studies in the literature related to the practicum which may be helpful to the supervisor and his staff?

24. Were there adequate supplies, staff, etc., for the operation for such a division?

25. What are some personal characteristics necessary for a person supervising this division? Did the person in charge exhibit these characteristics? Are these personal characteristics universal for all student personnel people at the managerial level?

26. Is the work the division doing important work? If so, how does it relate to the university and/or college as a whole?

27. Was group counseling used to help "growth" among staff members? If not, what kinds of "community-inspired exercises" are available so staff can relate to each other on a non-work basis? On a work basis?

28. How well did staff members handle themselves verbally?

29. Were letters written professionally?

30. How were telephone calls handled?

31. Were problems attended to immediately?

32. Did all staff members have a good sense as to the work of their division?

33. What was the general filing system in the office?

34. Will the experiences gained in the practicum relate to work in business and the non-educational realm?

35. Did your practicum supervisor enjoy having you "on his or her staff?"

36. Did students enjoy dealing with the people in this division?

37. Was there an informal or formal air in the office in the day-to-day operations?

38. Did people sometimes work beyond the 40 hour week?

39. In your opinion, was this a "respected" division within the student personnel division? Within the college or university?

40. Was the time spent in this practicum well worth the effort? Why? If not, why was the experience either a negative one or a waste of time? Be honest.

In your final report paper be sure to include evidence of the following:

1. The type of management scheme employed by the division;

2. A budget exercise;

3. A written document, memo, or letter that you did in relation to a job and/or exercise;

4. The line function or table of organization, indicating how the division relates to the student personnel division and the university or college as a whole;

5. An indication of verbal involvement by you in with interacting with students or staff by you in either interacting with students or staff. (This could be totally explained or presented in a tape);

6. One case study including problems facing the division, a staff member, etc.; and how they were solved.

7. At least one recent study in the literature relating to the work in the division;

8. A description of at least one staff meeting attended;

9. And the type of "student personnel model" exhibited by the division.

Material may be included in an appendix and referred to in the body of your paper.

CHAPTER 47

ASSESSMENT INSTRUMENT FOR PRACTICAL
EXPERIENCES IN ADMINISTRATION

Elizabeth A. Greenleaf

This instrument has been developed for the use in the assessment of practical experiences necessary in the preparation of student personnel administrators. Its utility is three-fold:

1. For the student: to identify tasks which may be performed or observed in an office; to assist in relating tasks performed to functions of administration; to assist in setting objectives for experiences; to assist in evaluation of learning.

2. For the supervisor: to stimulate ideas for experiences which may be provided for students; to be used in assisting the student in understanding the relationships of tasks performed to administrative functions; to assist in setting objectives for practical experiences.

3. For the coordinator: to counsel with students; to identify needed experiences and thus to assist in assignment of practical experiences; to identify the diverse experiences possible in various office settings; to assist in staff development of supervisors.

Since experiences vary from office to office and since students will have a variety of office assignments within a preparation program, it is best to have a cumulative record of the practical experiences. In using this instrument, it is possible to compile a master record by using a different color of ink for each experience. The instrument can also be a vehicle by which the supervisor, coordinator, and students relate experiences to administrative functions.

Proper use of the instrument suggests that the students assess experiences weekly by marking a "P" Performed or an "O" Observed in the first column. No one is expected to have exposure to all tasks in any one office. The student then analyzes the experience and checks in the proper column(s) the administrative function(s) being carried out. Example: Attending a meeting would be a "P"; the topics dealt with by the committee would determine the other areas checked, i.e., to change the requirement of attendance at summer orientation because of budget cuts

413

would be a check in policy formulation, budgeting, etc. Under policy formulation it is possible to further evaluate experience by indicating a "D" for policy decision, "IM" for policy implementation, or an "IN" for policy interpretation.

In the last column the student should indicate the nature of the task performed and evaluate the amount of personal learning: "E" Excellent, "G" Good, "P" Poor, "NL" No Learning. It is also possible to indicate type of experience.

Checklist Assessment Instrument for
Practical Experience in Administration

Preface

The following specific office operations which would be evaluated would be: (1) Policy Formulation; (2) Staff Selection; (3) Staff Supervision; (4) Budgeting; (5) Evaluation; and (6) Communication. The persons experience and degree of learning would be assessed against the following tasks:

I. Committee Participation

1.1 Making arrangements
1.2 Attending meeting
1.3 Participation in discussion
1.4 Taking minutes
1.5 Advising

II. Coordination (with):

2.1 Student groups
2.2 Administrative offices
2.3 Off-campus community
2.4 Faculty

III. Conference or Workshop

3.1 Scheduling space
3.2 Designing program
3.3 Securing leaders
3.4 Directing activities
3.5 Attending meetings

IV. Decision Making

4.1 Approval of action
4.2 Approval of effecting office
4.3 Identification of power structure
4.4 Issuing instructions

V. Diagnosing

5.1 Reviewing data
5.2 Administering tests
5.3 Recommending action
5.4 Imparting information

VI. Discipline

6.1 Identifying offender
6.2 Interviewing offender
6.3 Conducting hearing
6.4 Deciding action
6.5 Enforcing action

414

VII.	Faculty Interaction	VIII.	Fiscal Control

VII. Faculty Interaction

7.1 Securing involvement
7.2 Explaining office functions
7.3 Interaction on committees
7.4 For policy making

VIII. Fiscal Control

8.1 Setting objectives
8.2 Budget preparation
8.3 Approving expenditures
8.4 Securing funds
8.5 Reassessment, budget
8.6 Grant proposals

IX. Interacting w/Staff

9.1 Informal discussions
9.2 Attending staff mtgs.
9.3 Accepted as staff
9.4 Supervising staff

X. Preparation of Reports

10.1 Collecting data
10.2 Interpreting data
10.3 Written report
10.4 Oral report

XI. Office Operations

11.1 Sorting mail
11.2 Answering letters
11.3 Answering telephone
11.4 Serving as receptionist
11.5 Directing secretaries
11.6 Record keeping
11.7 Bulk mailing
11.8 Stapling papers
11.9 Determing office procedures
11.10 Developing data systems
11.11 Handling confidential information
11.12 Filing

XII. Orientation to Office

12.1 Interviewing staff
12.2 Reading assignments
12.3 Visits to other campuses
12.4 Seminars with supervisor
12.5 Prep. of reports

XIII. Preparing Publications

13.1 Gathering data
13.2 Designing
13.3 Writing copy
13.4 Editing copy
13.5 Revising publication

XIV. Programming

14.1 Designing activity
14.2 Advising leaders
14.3 Securing participation
14.4 Securing funds

XV. Public Relations

15.1 Explaining policy
15.2 Serving as representative
15.3 Preparing displays
15.4 Oral/written presentation

XVI. Research

16.1 Data collecting
16.2 Developing instrument
16.3 Computer programming
16.4 Office assessment

XVII. Staff development

17.1 Preparing job description
17.2 Staff hiring
17.3 Preparing staff manual
17.4 Orientation of staff
17.5 In-service seminars

XVIII. Student Interaction   XIX. Other Experiences

    18.1 Academic advising   19.1
    18.2 Activity advising   19.2
    18.3 Personal counseling   19.3
    18.4 Interviewing students   19.4
    18.5 Information giving   19.5
    18.6 Work with the "new   19.6
           student"

For each office experience the participant should list the following:

1. Most valuable experience;

2. Experiences you felt were available but not provided for you; and

3. Ways in which experiences could have been improved.

* The previous instrumental design was condensed and the original copyrighted instrument should be obtained from the author.

CHAPTER 48

COUNSELING VIDEO FEEDBACK GUIDELINES

John Eddy

Preface

Some guidelines for video work for counseling feedback for Guidance 494 practicum students are the following:

1. No feedback will be given without two or more personnel who are assigned to this course present.

2. No video work will be done unless time is available to do feedback for the video the day that it is filmed.

3. A personnel officer for Guidance 494 will be present in the studio for every video that is produced to insure quality control of production.

4. Each Guidance 494 student will make at least three video films per course and a complete evaluation of each film will be done by the staff assigned to this course.

5. Special arrangements will be made with Guidance 418, 419, and 427 and 428 client students to make all videos so that all of the above is done in a satisfactory manner with the 494 practicum student counselors.

6. Procedures for feedback are the following:

   First, the counselor trainee will evaluate himself or herself orally and using standard forms provided.
   Second, the client trainee will evaluate his or her feelings about the experience with the counselor orally and using standard forms provided.
   Third, the staff assigned to this course will give their comments orally and using standard forms provided.
   Fourth, the students present will add their comments.

7. A report of this video work will be given each term
    or semester to the Practicum Coordinator. This
    report will include the students participating and
    an evaluation of each student's work.

8. A copy of this set of procedures will be given to
    each student and to each staff member involved.

9. A short in-service prior to video work will be given
    to all students on how to participate effectively
    in video counseling experiences.

10. College student personnel type of experiences will
    be stressed in all video work. Examples of these
    kinds of experiences are found in the book, Higher
    Education: Participants Confronted, by Josiah Dilley
    published by the Wm. C. Brown Company Publishers,
    Dubuque, Iowa, 1970.

CHAPTER 49

PRACTICUM ACTION COMMUNICATION (PAC):
PRACTICUM FEEDBACK INSTRUMENT

John Eddy

Introduction

(The Graduate Student Supervisor will check this PAC System
regularly.) In order to help facilitate comprehensive communication between the supervisor and the student throughout the Practicum, the following system has been devised at the suggestion of
both students and supervisors. This system is called, Practicum
Action Communication (PAC). It operates as follows:

1. Time for use of PAC: It will be used at least once
per week after the last Practicum session for that particular
week.

2. Format for use of PAC: The supervisor will use the
following method with the student: First, "strength feedback
messages" will be given by the supervisor to the student. Second,
"weakness feedback messages" will be given by the supervisor to
the student. Third, "correction strategies" will be given with
the student setting priorities on correcting weaknesses.

3. Example for use of PAC: First, strength feedback
messages: "Your behavioral objectives and vita are satisfactory."
Second, weakness feedback messages: "Your late arriving and
early leaving this week was not appreciated. I know you told me
a few minutes in advance by phone you had this great opportunity
but it threw our schedule off here. We made a contract and we
want to stick by it. My time is as valuable as yours and I expect you to respect that commitment." Third, correction strategy:
Two priorities will be set up for next week. They are: the
student will arrive on time and stay for the entire contracted
period.

4. Other weakness examples of PAC: The list of weaknesses
would be a long one if we were to list all the things students
fail to do up to the supervisor's standards. However, the important thing is to get the student to work weekly on these weaknesses using the tools given to him or her through previous
courses. For example, Management By Objectives (MBO) might be
used to aid the student in working on weaknesses.

419

5.   Role of Graduate Student Supervisor in PAC: The Graduate Student Supervisor will review regularly with all supervisors
how the PAC System is working. In the beginning of each Practicum, the Graduate Student Supervisor will meet with each supervisor and student to explain how the PAC System works. Then,
throughout the Practicum term, the Graduate Student Supervisor
will check on the results. A regular periodic review will take
place. The Practicum Coordinator (Dr. John Eddy) will be informed
of each review and what steps are being taken to improve each and
every Practicum experience. At least three periodic reviews,
will be reported to Dr. Eddy at the quarter period--one fourth into
the Practicum; half way period--the Practicum is half over; and
the third quarter period--the Practicum is three fourths finished.
The Graduate Student Supervisor will also check that all students
are getting written reports on all their video taping after each
session from the video teaching team. Site visits will be made
by the Graduate Student Supervisor to check on all student efforts.
Results of site visitation will be reported to the Practicum Coordinator.

CHAPTER 50

SYSTEMS APPROACH TO PRACTICUM PLACEMENT:
MEETINGS TO MIMEOS

John Eddy

1. Practicum Statements: The
Student will formulate his
or her concise statement on
the area desired for a Prac-
ticum (such as for Career
Guidance Placement, Admis-
sions, Housing, Activities,
Foreign Students, Financial
Aids, Office of Dean of
Students and so forth);

1. Review of Practicum Statement: The Coordinator
will review this statement
for possible Practicum
opportunities and discuss
this with the Student;

2. Practicum Interviews: The
Student will be provided
opportunities to be interviewed by Practicum Supervisors approved by the
Coordinator and the Graduate Practicum Committee for
the Department of Guidance
and Counseling;

2. Practicum Interview Review
The Coordinator will con-
tact all interviewed Practicum Supervisors on their
assessment of the prospective Students;

3. Coordinator Notifies Student:
The Student will be contacted
by the Coordinator on the
results of the Practicum
Interviews; students are not
to contact the Supervisors
until after they are assigned
to a particular Practicum so
all parties are satisfied;
the Coordinator makes Supervisor Contacts and is the
liaison between all Students
and Supervisors.

3. Coordinator Notifies Student: in order to main-
tain good rapport with
the Chief Administrative
Officers and the Super-
visors at each college
and/or university the
described approach here
must be adhered to in each
Practicum Placement.

421

References

Eddy, J.P. "Communications Systems." UNISTAR: User
Network for Information Storage, Transfer, Acquisition,
and Retrieval. Huntsville, Alabama: National Aeronautics and Space Administration, 1970.

Ford, A.S. Directing the Student Work Experience: A
Manual for Supervisors. Berea, KY: Berea College
Press, 1976.

Systems Approach to Practicum Placement Form

Practicum 494; Field Work 527; and Internship 528 (each copy for supervisor, student and instructor above).

1. Supervisor's Name,
   Title, and College   _____

                                         _____

2. Student's Name, and   _____
   Work Assignment Area(s)
                                         _____

3. Student's signature releasing   _____
   the institutions involved
   from any personal liability
   during the experience   _____

4. Behavioral Contract Agreed
   On (Date)   _____

   Supervisor's Signature   _____

5. Supervisor's Rating Sheet
   Completed (Date)   _____
   And Practicum Paper Com-
   pleted (Date)   _____

6. Student's Final Grade   _____

7. Supervisor's Comments On
   Student's Performance   _____

Dear Practicum Student:

You have signed up to take a College Student Personnel Work Practicum in the term of _____. I am glad to work with you and welcome your cooperation. Here are a few things we need to do in order to help one another:

1. You need to meet with me as soon as possible to finalize your Practicum.

2. As soon as the area is agreed upon, I will contact the supervisor to clear it and to inform him or her you will call for an appointment to discuss it.

3. I have the Practicum syllabus done so you can take it with you to look over.

4. All Practicums are cleared first with me and then I have to discuss them with the Loyola University Committee before they are approved. Then, I make the direct contacts with the respective college personnel to check out the work. In no case does a student go ahead to arrange Practicum before my working the arrangements out with the Loyola University Committee and the respective officials of the institution of higher education where the Practicum will be taken.

5. The program at Loyola University is nationally accredited because we do take care in selecting the best possible Practicum Personnel who have qualifications and experience in the field. In all cases, these personnel have to be cleared by me with the chief administrative personnel office of each college and university involved. It is my job to do this and to work out the details of each Practicum with the Loyola University Committee.

6. All students are interviewed by a committee of college student personnel staff to hear the student needs. After this conference, the students will be notified by me of the decisions of the Committee.

7. The supervisor has the right to accept or reject a student in his or her Practicum area. One quarter way into the Practicum, if things are not working out well, the supervisor may terminate his or her Practicum.

8. When any change is made in a student's plan for a Practicum, the student should notify me immediately by letter, phone call or personal visit. Delay in notification only causes further problems for the Supervisor and the Coordinator. Difficulties are

424

sometimes created when students fail to leave
messages that include their phone numbers and
the time.
9. Please help me by being sure I get your communication.

I look forward to visiting with you. Best wishes to you.

Sincerely yours,

John Eddy
Professor of Guidance & Counseling

CHAPTER 51

A GUIDE FOR EDUCATIONAL ADMINISTRATORS,
COUNSELORS AND TEACHERS:
GLOSSARY OF ORGANIZATIONAL PLANNING AND PROGRAMMING TERMS

John Eddy

Introduction

This article provides a glossary of selected organizational planning and programming terms for educational personnel-administrators, counselors, and teachers. The need for a short glossary of terms covering organizational planning and programming for students preparing for careers in education has been apparent to the author for sometime.

The author is grateful for the Interagency Staff Task Force on Planning of the United Methodist Church for its contributions to many of the definitions provided here. The author modified some of their work and added additional terms specifically for education personnel.

Selected Terms

1. Alternative Futures—Ways an organization envisions new developments, considers desirable futures to work for, and possible actions that enable it to attain the ends it envisions.

2. Assumptions for Planning—That which we hold as true or take for granted about ourselves and the world. For planning, assumptions can be divided into two groups: (1) environmental (trends in our immediate community and the world of which that community is a part), and (2) operational (the way things work, the influences needed to get the desired ends accomplished). Assumptions in the planning process are those which pertain most directly to the decision to be made and which, if held, make a difference in the plan to be recommended. Listing assumptions helps to make explicit those things which we normally entertain only privately but which influence our opinion on where we ought to go and how we ought to get there.

3. Brainstorming—A device by which a quantity of ideas around a particular problem is solicited from the group and listed without comment. The purpose is to get quick intuitions and thoughts recorded, both to stimulate other thoughts within the

426

group and to yield some ideas which can be selected for closer examination and implementation at a later date. No value-judgment is given to ideas as they are listed. Value-judgments are made through later screening and selection.

4. CPM--Critical Path Method is a system for planning, scheduling and controlling operations necessary to complete a project. It shows basic decision points, actions and supplementary relationships.

5. Consensus--The agreement of the majority of a group for a course of action, while retaining the minority as a functioning part of the group.

6. Delphi Technique--A device for registering likely developments in the future by consulting individual experts in a field of investigation. Results from individual predictions are combined, leading to a cumulative judgment concerning what is likely to happen and by when. (For example, consulting 25 nuclear physicists on the probability of developing energy through nuclear fusion and the date by which that process is likely to be developed for practical application.)

7. Evaluation--Assessment or review of an area of work measuring achievement against stated goals. There are several stages of evaluation. The most general is purely descriptive, itemizing what is being done, with whom and utilizing what resources. A second general category of evaluation attempts to assess the effectiveness of a program, determining whether a program accomplished what it set out to accomplish.

8. Flow Chart--The representation of sequences of activities, decisions and resources outlining their interrelationships, timing and lines of responsibility. A flow chart often will indicate what activities are to be completed by when and by whom.

9. Force Field Analysis--A method of itemizing and making explicit the forces or agencies in a situation which are resisting the accomplishment of a desired state of affairs, or the forces which assist the accomplishment of this goal. Some rough estimate is made of the relative power of each of these forces by the relative size given to each of the forces in a diagram.

10. Forecasting--Deals with recognizing the future consequences of present decisions by analyzing the implications of assumptions, expectations, risks and alternative courses of action as they affect change, audience response or probable outcomes.

11. Goals or Action Goals--A statement of intention that specified ways by a specific time in the future, with observable

and measurable results.   (Who will do what? with whom? by when? with what results?)

12. Innovation--The introduction of that which represents a change of something new in the working of a group or in the environment within which it works.

13. Issue--A point around which there is contention concerning: alternatives to be adopted, values to be realized, groups who are to define the values to be realized, policies to be implemented. An issue may apply to the operations of a specific group, such as whether or not to adopt the four-day week, or may apply to contention on a wide-scale question of human survival, such as population control or the limits of growth.

14. MBO--Management-By-Objectives is a process and design where the officials of an organization identify an organization's goals, define each employee's assignments in terms of the results expected of the person, and uses these measures in operating the organizational unit as well as in determining the contribution of each person.

15. Model Building--A representation of a program or set of relationships showing the interconnections of its several parts and the way in which it utilizes incoming resources and produces effects or consequences. A model may be in the form of a picture, chart, scale replica, map, verbal description or some other representation.

16. Needs--That set of factors in a situation which may require strengthening or eliminating in an organization; or, a desired resource the absence of which blocks attaining goals.

17. Objectives--A general statement of intention for one aspect of the organization's purpose. Objectives are general statements of directions which convey identity to an organization.

18. Operations Analysis--A form of review or evaluation consisting of an itemization of means employed in rendering a service, such as persons to be served, kinds of services rendered. (For example, formal teaching sessions, interviews, surveys, consultations, counseling sessions and others.)

19. Operations Planning--Relates to the description of performance functions and the development of resources, services and leadership so that action goals may be attained.

20. Organizational Development--A method used to find the best ways to use human and material resources to solve institutional problems and strengthen operations by determining a meaningful system of operation, a commitment to long range goals, and

a core of high level administrators who plan and manage the work by focusing on interpersonal as well as group problems.

21. PPBS--Programming, Planning, and Budgeting system is a systems type approach that applies various cost accounting and cost estimate procedures to aid an organization in preparing its programming, planning, and budgeting.

22. Participative Planning Process--The process of designating objectives, action goals, programs, and strategies based on the identity of the group for which planning is done, a wide sampling of opinion about emerging needs and possibilities, priorities among these needs, appropriateness of goals and workability of plans. Participative planning is contrasted to planning conducted by a relatively small number of persons who designate goals for persons with whom tasks are to be conducted.

23. PERT Chart--Program Evaluation and Review Technique is a system of network diagraming which shows basic decisions and evaluation points in a scheduled network of activities and events.

24. Planning--A process of deciding upon ways to get to intended objectives. Planning is a process of "how to get from here to there." It implies having an idea of where the organization ought to be going, based on an understanding of the personnel and an analysis of the data concerning the situation which the organization serves and the future it envisions.

25. Possibilities--States of affairs which can be imagined in the future, visions or wishes outlining a situation which can be pictured and described. While incorporating trends and continuities between the present and the future, possibilities imply the emergence of novelty and change, the coming of the genuinely new.

26. Priority--An area of work, a program, or a concern which is given a high order of preference on the basis of its: (1) legitimate claim to a high proportion of resources available; (2) potential importance for the future; (3) timeliness or relationship to critical needs and opportunities; (4) connection with one or more of a group's mandated functions; and (5) indispensability for the effectiveness of the organization.

27. Program Budget--A program budget describes program activities and estimates the cost of each item so that persons may assess the cost and benefits of an activity as it is projected. It assumes that program should determine budget. It brings into question such positions as, "We must budget this item because we always have," and "Budget determines our program."

28. Program Evaluation--Provides for assessing the effectiveness of programs in the light of changing needs, action goals,
and priorities.

29. Purpose--A statement of purpose clarifies "why" an
organization does what it does. The statement sets forth "who
we are" and "what we ought to be doing".

30. Systems Approach--An identifiable collection of factors
that are interrelated and are assumed to function as an organizational entity in producing a product. A systems approach provides a technique for human decision making based on step-by-step
procedures, model development, evaluation, and information or
data that is accurate as well as meaningful.

31. Scenarios--An ordered way of thinking through sequences
of alternative futures and examining the consequences of present
decisions.

32. Strategic Planning--Relates to a process of making
basic decisions about what personnel and program should engage
the organization in the light of its potentials and the needs of
the constituency or consumers it seeks to serve.

33. Strategy--The way in which a group elects to achieve
its goals. The goals tell where a group is going, the strategy
outlines how it has chosen to get there.

34. Trends--Observable clusters of events which provide cues
for likely developments in the future. As clusters of events,
trends are interpretative categories by which to understand what
is happening in a situation and by which to think about the future.

CHAPTER 52

HUMAN BEHAVIOR, VALUES,
PROFESSIONAL EXPERIENCE AND LIFE DEVELOPMENT

John Eddy

Introduction

There are some things that need to be said that never seem to appear in print in the professional literature of the helping professions. Perhaps, some persons would judge these insights to be common sense or too practical for publication but the author believes that when dealing with human behavior it is a continuing learning process. Recently, the author came across some statements by Eppie Lederer, who has used the pen name and byline of Ann Landers for 22 years, that expresses some thoughts on human behavior, professional experience, and life development. In these comments, she mentions some valuable suggestions to students of human behavior and professionals who would deal with persons problems. In the following statements, she would advocate:

1. Get involved in a job that gives one an opportunity for meeting many types of persons for it gives one a "ringside seat to life."

2. Check with experienced and trained persons who have insight when you get a problem that you are not sure how to work out.

3. Do not be surprised at what humans will do under certain circumstances.

4. Do not trust one's education or credentials to be fully expressive of that person's capabilities or limitations.

5. Be ready for anything to happen to anyone.

6. Trust in the love and care that come from family and friends in tough times.

7. Trust in God in all of life and be responsible for your behavior.

8. Keep learning from living out one's life with others.

Some practical knowledge does not often appear in professional literature to aid beginning or entry level persons with the
insight of experienced persons. An example of this good advice
comes from Eppie Lederer who at 59 years of age has this insight
in 1977 to share about humanity after receiving thousands of
letters on problems persons face in life:

"My readers provided me with a ringside seat to life.
I learned from them what the real world was all about.
Dozens of good friends around the country, outstanding
authorities in medicine, psychiatry, dentistry, religion,
business, politics, and education were extremely generous
when I phoned them for help with difficult questions.
Without these professional consultants, I couldn't have
survived.

Before I became involved in this work, I was under the
impression that only a nut would write a newspaper about
a personal problem; but I was wrong. The cries for help
come from every segment of society, every social, economic and intellectual level...

One thing I know now that I didn't know before I started
to write the column is that an impressive family background
and sterling academic credentials offer no guarantee
against bad manners, shoddy standards or gross insensitivi-
ty to the needs and feelings of others. The true measure
of a human is how he (or she) treats his fellow man.
Integrity and compassion cannot be learned in college, nor
are these qualities inherited in the genes.

Man, it turns out, is the most unpredictable and complex,
the most noble and the most base of animals. I would
never toss a letter aside and label it a phony on the
grounds that "nobody would do such a thing"...

I've learned that all of us are capable of doing something completely out of character or totally irrational
when we're at a low point in our lives. Robert Louis
Stevenson proved to be an astute observer of the human
condition when he said, "We all have thoughts that would
shame hell"...

From my own life, I have learned that anything can
happen to anybody. So expect the unexpected and, when
it hits, hold your head up. Don't look back. Forward
march. You'll be surprised at how much strength you
have. And you'll be heartened by the outpouring of love
and caring from family and friends. Just remember that
the Good Lord never sends anyone more to trouble than
two of you can handle together. Eppie Lederer has learned
a lot from Ann Landers." (Landers, Ann. "What I Know
Now That I Didn't Know Then." Family Circle. Vol. 90,
No. 4, April 5, 1977, pp. 48, 50, 53 and 60.)

Certainly it is important to make some goals for one's life in developing into a more complete person. Some of the thoughts that still stretch personhood are some thoughts that might be called "Growth Goals." A few mentioned here are:

1. The mark of a genuine professional is that person who can take criticism without being defensive, can turn this criticism into positive improvement, and can tackle the next challenge that comes in life.

2. One of the greatest characteristics a counselor can posess is the ability to discover the other side or sides of a person's problems otherwise the counselor is captive to the client's bias which can be unfair, dishonest, and propaganda to all persons involved with the client's problems.

3. The ability of an administrator to find fault with every person or program is not a sign of strength but weakness unless he or the administrator can suggest how the fault can be turned into constructive change.

4. The college official who fails to praise his or her colleagues for their accomplishments in life is neglecting the personal joy of entering into their victories vicariously.

Taking Responsibility: Government, Students, and Staff

The nine year federally guaranteed student loan fund is more than $436 million in September, 1977 according to the General Accounting Office (GAO) of the national government. One student of every six who gets a loan is refusing to pay back the money. From 1968 to 1976, the government guaranteed over four million student loans worth $4.5 billion as it reimbursed banks, savings and loan associations, and credit unions for $297 million for the more than 280,000 recipients who defaulted. This problem is a combination of student irresponsibility, governement not enforcing repayment, banks not pursuing legal means to collect loans, and higher education institutions not doing more to educate students to be responsible.

It is unfortunate that many students' values are not developed morally to repay their debts and it is a clear example of the need for value education in higher education institutions. Again, it is deplorable that the government has not exercised its legal options at a greater level over this nine year period. Unless the government shows the consequences of bad behavior such as not repaying student loan funds, then, it too must take credit for irresponsible enforcement of its own laws.

Where the government has acted with its legal options such as in the San Francisco Regional Office of HEW, over $946,000 in defaulted student loans were collected in three months in 1977 because former students were taken to court for repayment. This helped encourage other former students to pay their back debts voluntarily. The San Francisco example was a record for collections. Former students should not be protected from their legal obligations by the government for this is continuing a In Loco Parentis Approach of having Big Daddy (Uncle Sam) bailing out the former students.

According the the government, some of the former students who will not pay their student loans are a pro basketball player making $85,000 a year and a psychiatrist admitting a $31,000 a year income. One wonders how the athlete and counselor—who both got their vocations because of their work in college and have top incomes for any citizen in this country in the 99 percentile—can rationalize out of their owing the government for their student loans. Perhaps this is another reason why the Department of Health, Education, and Welfare—with the biggest budget in the federal government in 1977 of $146 billion—should be separated to reduce the huge span of control so there are three separate departments— Education, Health, and Welfare—to insure fewer scandals such as this from happening. Again, what value system do these college graduates operate by in their present professional careers? These professionals are among the 17 percent who default their student loans annually and they help provide ammunition for public agitation to throw out the whole student loan program. Questions might be raised of these two professionals, such as: For the athlete: How can you be a part of the nonpaying graduates that would jeopardize the entire funding of this program for needy students who follow you? For the counselor: How can you be a party to the downfall of a program that would give possibilities to persons to fulfill their lives which is a fundamental thesis of the counseling profession?

Somehow the principles of some of our professionals are lacking and our colleges are failing to teach by personal example and teaching materials these ethical values. Taking a page from history, to assure the teaching of virtue and responsibility, a statute went into the Massachusetts General Laws in 1789 stating: "The President, professors, and tutors of the University of Cambridge and all teachers of academies shall exert their best endeavors to impress on the minds of youth the principles of piety and justice and a sacred regard for truth, love of their country, industry, and frugality, chastity, moderations and temperance, and those other virtues which are the ornament of human society and the basis upon which a republican constitution is founded... They will do this to secure the blessings of liberty as well as to promote their future happiness." While these words may sound strange to some persons, as this nation embarks in our third century, these are some of the principles that formed the foundation on which the American dream began.

Taking the defaulting of student loan funds in this nation's colleges and universities as an immoral example and the Massachusetts Laws of 1789 as a moral example for college and university staff into context, it seems we need to develop within Student Affairs Programs a regular values seminar that covers:

1. An honesty and openness in the dealings of persons with other persons and with institutions;
2. A sense of justice and fairness in dealing with persons and society;
3. A treatment of morality and the human standards of religions, governmental laws, and the United Nations' documents; and
4. A renewal of trust and confidence in persons and in their relationships with other persons.

Therefore, this example of a combined approach can help students develop morally. First, laws must be enforced so they have consequences when persons fail to live up to them. Second, colleges need to teach value education so that students are more aware of their options for decision making. Third, colleges need to have their students discover via case studies and gaming exercises the consequences of their not living up to the laws of the land.

Where to Begin Work on Human Rights

In 1961, the author had the opportunity, one year before her death, to visit with Eleanor Roosevelt, wife of former President Franklin D. Roosevelt, at a founding meeting of a United National Association of the United States Chapter in Mankato, Minnesota. Her dedication and hard work for human rights were apparent then as well as where we all can begin our witness for human rights and are well expressed in the book by Joseph P. Lash, Eleanor: The Years Alone from a letter as follows:

"Where, after all, do universal human rights begin? In small places, close to home--so close and so small that they cannot be seen on any maps of the world. Yet they are the world of the individual persons; the neighborhood he lives in; the school or colleges he attends; the factory, farm or office where he works. Such are the places where every man, woman and child seeks equal justice, equal opportunity, equal dignity without discrimination. Unless these rights have meaning there, they have little meaning anywhere. Without concerned citizen action to uphold them close to home, we shall look in vain for progress in the larger world."

435

References

Landers, Ann. "What I Know Now That I Didn't Know Then." *Family Circle*. April 5, 1977. Vol. 90, No. 4.

Lash, Joseph P. *Eleanor: The Years Alone*. New York: W. W. Norton & Company, Inc., 1972.

CHAPTER 53

THE LITERATURE OF COLLEGE STUDENT PERSONNEL--A SAMPLE

Robert R. Reilley and Ina A. Cauthen

There is a core of reference material that should be familiar
to persons in student personnel work. This is one attempt to
identify these basic sources. Areas included are general treatments of higher education, student characteristics and development,
administration and specific personnel services.

While it is probably true that college student personnel as
a profession suffers from being a loose confederation of diverse
disciplines (Penny 1969), a core of literature of general concern
to all professionals in the field is gradually gaining recognition.
Reference to these basic sources by writers and researchers prominent in the field is common. It is therefore, advantageous for any
serious professional in the area of college student personnel to
have a knowledge of this literature.

Any attempt to describe briefly the literature of a complex and
varied field is certain to encounter several difficulties: the need
to select and sample, the continuous appearance of new sources, and
differing professional opinions. Thus, it would be wise to consider
this article as offering a sample or a tentative selective listing,
rather than a definitive statement.

General Treatments Of Higher Education

Riegal and Bender (1972) have identified a group of books
recommended as basic reading by individuals teaching courses in the
field of higher education. Although no one source was suggested by
a majority of the 269 respondents in the study, the following 10
books were most frequently selected:

Blocker, C.E.; Plummer, R.H.; & Richardson, R.C. The Two-
Year College: A Social Synthesis (Prentice-Hall, 1965)
Brubacher, J.S., & Rudy, W. Higher Education in Transition:
A History of American Colleges and Universities, 1936-1968 (Harper
& Row, 1968)
Corson, J.J. Governance of Colleges and Universities (McGraw-
Hill, 1960)

Feldman, K.A. & Newcomb, T.M. The Impact of College on Students. 2 vols. (Jossey-Bass, 1969)

Hofstadter, R., & Metzger, W.P. Development of Academic Freedom in the United States (Columbia University Press, 1955)

Hofstadter, R., & Smith, W. (Eds.) American Higher Education: A Documentary History (University of Chicago Press, 1961)

Jencks, C., & Riesman, D. The Academic Revolution (Double-day, 1968)

Kerr, C. The Uses of the University (Harvard University, 1972)

Rudolph, F. The American College and University: A History (Knopf, 1962)

Sanford, N. (Ed.) The American College: A Psychological and Social Interpretation of Higher Learning (Wiley, 1962)

Among other texts on the Riegal and Bender list, the following discussions of higher education appear particularly appropriate for inclusion in this section:

Axelrod, J., et al. Search for Relevance: The Campus in Crisis (Jossey-Bass, 1969)

Barzun, J. The American University: How it Runs and Where It is Going (Harper & Row, 1970)

Caplow, T., & McGee, R.J., The Academic Marketplace (Double-day, 1965)

Eurich, A.C. (Ed.) Campus 1980: The Shape of the Future in American Higher Education (Celacorte, 1968)

Mayhew, L.B. Colleges Today and Tomorrow (Jossey-Bass, 1969)

Medsker, L.L. The Junior College: Progress and Prospect (McGraw-Hill, 1960)

Sanford, N. Where Colleges Fail: A Study of the Student as a Person (Wiley, 1962)

Trent, J.W., & Medsker, L.L. Beyond High School: A Psycho-sociological Study of 10,000 High School Graduates (Jossey-Bass, 1968)

A recent text by P. L. Dressel and L. B. Mayhew, Higher Education as a Field of Study: The Emergence of a Profession (Jossey-Bass, 1974), shows promise of joining these established sources.

Several journals relating to higher education can be identified: AAUP Bulletin, College Management, Educational Record, The Chronicle of Higher Education, and The Journal of Higher Education. Another journal which generally treats a narrower range of higher education topics is the Community and Junior College Journal.

Publications by the American Association for Higher Education, represent a major source of up-to-date information. An example would be the topic covered in the 1974 issue, "Life-long Learners--

A New Clientele for Higher Education." Under AAHE sponsorship,
L.B. Mayher regularly edits The Literature of Higher Education, a
concise overview and evaluation of books published each year dealing with higher education.

A number of other organizations have published series of
documents relating to higher education. Among the most prominent
of the contributors are the American College Testing Program, the
College Entrance Board, and the Carnegie Commission of Higher
Education. L.B. Mayher has published a summary evaluation of
50-some reports by the Carnegie Commission, The Carnegie Commission
on Higher Education: A Critical Analysis of the Reports and
Recommendations (Jossey-Bass, 1973).

Characteristics and Development of College Students

Several years ago, Chickering (1967) called for a new course
on the young adult in college personnel administration. He suggested a number of appropriate references for a course directed
at increasing one's understanding of college students and young
adults in general. Several of the texts he listed deal with the
characteristics and development of college students and are an
appropriate point of departure for this section:

Erickson, E.H. Childhood and Society (W.W. Northon, 1964)
Erickson, E.H. Challenge of Youth (Anchor, 1965)
Havinghurst, R.J. Human Development and Education
(Longmans, Green, 1953)
Heath, S.R. The Reasonable Adventurer: The Nature and
Development of Students in Higher Education (University of
Pittsburgh, 1964)
Kuhlen, R.G. The Psychology of Adolescent Development
(Harper, 1952)

Several additional items from the Riegal and Bender listed
are particularly appropriate to the college student and should
be included here. Certainly, the aforementioned Feldman and
Newcomb two-volume work, The Impact of College on Students, must
be noted. Others include:

Chickering, A.W. Education and Identity (Jossey-Bass, 1969)
Dennis, L., & Kauffman, J.F. (Eds.) The College and the
Student (American Council on Education, 1966)
Hazen Foundation, Committee on the Student in Higher Educa-
tion. The Student in Higher Education (Hazen Foundation, 1968)
Katz, J., et al. No Time for Youth: Growth and Constraint
in College Students (Jossey-Bass, 1968)
Yamamoto, K. (Ed.) The College Student and His Culture:
An Analysis (Houghton Mifflin, 1968)

Several additional texts should be included in this section, for example, Erick Erickson's Identity: Youth and Crisis (W.W. Norton, 1968). Another is an insightful text that developed out of many years experience in working with troubled college students: D.L. Farnsworth's Psychiatry, Education and the Young Adult (Charles C. Thomas, 1969). Others are:

Cross, K.P. Beyond the Open Door: New Students to Higher Education (Jossey-Bass, 1971)
Cross, K.P. The Junior College Student: A Research Description (Educational Testing Service, 1968)
Lloyd-Jones, E.M., & Estrin, H.A. The American Student and His College (Houghton Mifflin, 1967)
Moore, W., Jr. Against the Odds: The High Risk Student in the Community College (Jossey-Bass, 1970)
Newcomb, T.M. & Wilson, E.K. (Eds.) College Peer Groups: Problems and Prospects for Research (Aldine, 1966)

Three recent texts appear to be receiving considerable attention. F.B. Brawer's New Perspectives on Personality Development in College Students (Jossey-Bass, 1973) discusses the theory and application of a new concept in student assessment. Youth: Transition to Adulthood (University of Chicago, 1974), a report of the President's Science Advisory Committee, edited by J.S. Coleman provides a broad view of developing individuals and their relationships to college, work, and their own subculture; and A.L. Tollefson's New Approaches to College Student Development (Behavioral Publications, 1975) reports a variety of innovative student development programs and suggests emerging trends.

Characteristics of college students are discussed in numerous journals, both professional and popular. Frequent treatment of the topic is found in the Journal of College Student Personnel and the College Student Journal. Community and Junior College Journal is a common source for information regarding students in two-year institutions.

The American College Personnel Association's Student Personnel Monograph Series includes several titles relating directly to college students: for example, R.D. Brown, Student Development in Tomorrow's Higher Education: A Return to the Academy (ACPA, 1972); J.M. Whiteley (Ed.) Students in the University and Society (ACPA, 1970); and J.M. Whiteley and H. Sprandel (Eds.) The Growth and Development of College Students (ACPA, 1970).

Student Personnel Administration

In discussing the limited growth of student personnel work as a profession, Penney (1969) noted the serious lack of basic literature in the field. He listed only five sources that could be considered basic textbooks in student personnel. Of this list, only two have publication dates after 1960: K.H. Mueller, Student Personnel Work in Higher Education (Houghton Mifflin, 1961) and E.G. Williamson, Student Personnel Services in Colleges and Universities (McGraw-Hill, 1961).

In addition to these publications, which have been the major texts in college personnel courses for many years, four more recent works provide collections of readings generally relating to the area of student personnel administration: L.E. Fitzgerald, W.F. Johnson, and W. Norris (Eds.) College Student Personnel: Readings and Bibliographies (Houghton Mifflin, 1970); T.F. Harrington, Student Personnel Work in Urban Colleges (Intext, 1974); T. O'Banion and A. Thurston (Eds.) Student Development Programs in the Community Junior College (Prentice-Hall, 1972); and E.G. Williamson and D.A. Biggs, Student Personnel Work—A Program of Developmental Relationships (Wiley, 1975). The last-named text, Student Personnel Work, interprets considerable pertinent literature in delineating approaches to educational management consistent with the student development concept and provides a much needed modern textbook.

Another source bearing on student personnel administration is the 1965 report on a major evaluation of junior college student personnel programs in the United States, T.R. McConnell's Junior College Student Personnel Programs—Appraisal and Development (American Association of Junior Colleges, 1965).

The Student Personnel Monograph Series of the American College Personnel Association includes several works relating to student personnel administration, for example the following: D.L. Farnsworth College Health Services in the United States (ACPA, 1965); M.D. Hardee, Faculty Advising in Colleges and Universities (ACPA 1970); Programs (ACPA, 1971); and E.R. Oetting, A.E. Ivey, and R.G. Weigel, The College and University Counseling Center (ACPA, 1970).

The administration of student personnel services is well reported in professional journals. The Journal of College Student Personnel, the NASPA Journal (National Association of Student Personnel Administrators) and the National Association for Women Deans, Administrators and Counselors Journal, and, less frequently, the Personnel and Guidance Journal, carry pertinent articles.

Current thought regarding college student personnel administration is presented in a special section (pp. 354-375) of the September 1975 issue of the Journal of College Student Personnel. This section, "College Student Personnel: Two Alternatives for the Future," has an introduction by Marlin R. Schmidt and provides two contrasting models of societal change and human development by E.G. Williamson and Burns B. Crookston. It is likely to be

441

high on the list of required readings for future student personnel administrators.

Specialized Literature

Attempts to categorize the literature of college student personnel are quickly discouraged by the number of diverse specialized areas within the general field. Counseling, housing, activities, health services, and several other specializations each have developed their own literature.

Counseling has been suggested as the common denominator for student personnel workers since all personnel workers seem likely to need skills in counseling from time to time. Three publications in this area should be noted: E.R. Oetting, A.E. Ivey, and R.G. Weigel, The College and University Counseling Center; M. Siegel (Ed.), The Counseling of College Students (MacMillan, 1968); and D.F. Warnath, New Myths and Old Realities: College Counseling in Transition (Jossey-Bass, 1971). Warnath in New Directions for College Counselors: A Handbook for Redesigning Professional Roles (Jossey-Bass, 1973) provides a more current discussion of counseling on the college campus.

One of the more significant reports on the full range of professional psychotherapeutical services offered on college campuses is Mental Health on the Campus: A Field Study (APA & NAMH, 1973) by R. Glasscote and M.E. Fishman. It is an evaluation of the diverse procedures by which seven institutions delivered mental health services to students. Mental health was defined broadly and included counseling centers, psychological services, and related endeavors.

Another specialized area that seems destined to rival counseling in its universal relevance to personnel services is the legal aspect of student personnel work. A number of recent conferences and publications have been devoted to this topic. For example, R. Callis, The College and The Courts, Journal of College Student Personnel (1969, 10, 75-87); G.W. Holmes (Ed.), Law and Discipline on Campus (Institute of Continuing Legal Education, 1971); D.P. Young (Ed.), Higher Education, 1975.

In this constantly changing field perhaps the most practical approach to the problem of staying current would be that used in the handbook by Young and D.D. Gehring, The College Student and the Courts (College Administration Publication, 1973). This publication is a basic reference and guide to which quarterly supplements are added every year.

College residence hall programs appear to be a current area of concern, as shown by the recent publication of two important reports. Student Development and Education in College Residence

Halls (ACPA, 1974), edited by D.A. DeCoster and P. Mable, is a comprehensive presentation of research and theory. A.W. Chickering's Commuting versus Resident Students (Jossey-Bass, 1974) is a study of the inequities recently found in the education provided these two groups of students.

Over the years, the college environment has been a subject of considerable interest. Three of the basic works in this area are, A.W. Astin, The College Environment (American Council on Education, 1968); B.R. Clark and M. Trow, The Organizational Context, in T.M. Newcomb and E.K. Wilson (Eds.), and College Peer Groups (Aldine, 1966); and C.R. Pace and G.G. Stern, An Approach to the Measurement of Physiological Characteristics of College Environments, Journal of Educational Psychology (1958, 49, 269-277). More recent research on college climate appears regularly in current professional journals "The Practical Utility of Measures of College Environment" was the title of a 1974 article by L.L. Baird in the Review of Educational Research (1974, 55, 307-329).

The following publications of associations representing specialties in various aspects of student personnel work provide the major resources for articles: Journal of Counseling Psychology, Journal of the Association of College Admission Counselors, Journal of the American College Health Association, Journal of the National Association of Student Personnel Administrators, and National Association for Women Deans, Administrators, and Counselors Journal.

Additional Sources

With the number of articles and books in student personnel work now available, the role played by abstract and reference sources becomes more essential. Quick access to the literature dealing with specific topics is provided by a number of reference sources. Among the more useful aids are College Student Personnel Abstracts, published by the Claremont Institute of Administrative Studies, Claremont Graduate School, and "Student Personnel Abstract" included as a regular feature of the Journal of College Student Personnel. The July issues of this journal carry another valuable reference tool: a listing of dissertations completed in the field of college student personnel work during the previous year. Other valuable, though less specific, reference sources include Eric, the Review of Educational Research, and Psychological Abstracts.

Several sources provide the scholar with digests or summary statements regarding specific areas of student personnel. An example of this is K.A. Feldman's "Some Theoretical Approaches to the Study of Change and Stability of College Students: In the Review of Educational Research (1972,42,1-26), which represents a major attempt at the conceptualization of the assumptions underlying

443

the study of changes in college students. The article on the
utility of college environment data by L.L. Baird provides a
similar in-depth treatment.

Despite the difficulties inherent in a diverse discipline, a
literature of college student personnel is emerging. This body
of literature, originating from several fields, is varied and
changing, and those may well be characteristics of the profession's
development as a whole.

References

Chickering, A.W. The young adult, a new and needed
course for college personnel administrators.
National Association of Women Deans, Administrators,
and Counselors Journal, 1967, 30, 78-111.

Penney, J.F. Student personnel work: A profession
stillborn. Personnel and Guidance Journal, 1969,
47,958-962.

Riegal, P.S. and Bender, R.L. Basic readings in
higher education. Educational Record, Winter
1972, 85-89.

CHAPTER 54

LOOK AHEAD AND BEHIND--A MIRROR APPROACH

John Eddy

The final chapter of this book is not meant to be a "Catch 22" but it includes a number of elements such as facing the continuing unresolved problems within American higher education and the American society.

Planet Earth's Dilemma

For ages, college and university personnel have been accused of being in "ivy towers." This stereotyped tendency of higher education personnel to be impractical, unrealistic, naive and detached is unfortunate. Therefore, it would be hypocritical if this book failed to address itself to the hard problems facing the nation and the world. For example, the experts who make predictions of food and fuel shortages across the planet combined with the fears of nations that have these shortages and also nuclear weapons, will ultimately use them to start a war that will end us all. Therefore, college student personnel workers should not be like ostriches hiding our heads in the sand in social issues but as Carl Rogers has stated in another chapter of this book, we should be leaders, not laggers in this area. This is why "value education" must be taken seriously as a regular emphasis in our work and not as another fleeting fad of the profession. Too often colleges are guilty of being "trendy" rather than "trustworthy" to the real values we claim in our constitution and our religious heritage.

Youth Crisis In Cities

For too many years, minority youth from 18 to 24 years have been unemployed. Again, an undetermined percent of minority youth are also underemployed. The results of this social dynamite is evident. Two examples will be mentioned here. They illustrate figures and factors that show our society is in war with its own people.

First, in New York City's blackout in July 1977 due to the failure of power, over 3,000 persons were arrested for looting stores. Many of these persons were youth.

445

Second, over one-third of all the murders in Chicago in
1976-77 were committed by youth under 20 years of age. In a
city that has about 1,000 murders annually, this means about 333
persons are killed by youth.

Personnel employed in college student personnel work need to
be concerned about such problems. We need to make our higher
education institutions, our government, our cities'citizens and
other persons aware of these problems. Again, we need to find
ways to work out these problems for identification of problems is
only the first step.

The tragic unemployment and underemployment of the minority
youth in our cities is a great loss of talent. It takes only an
emergency for these forces to be let loose so persons who are in
this condition are tempted to commit crimes in order to gain food
and things they see other persons have on television.

Youth Crime

The youth crime rate in this nation is another tremendous
problem. For example, in 1963, one juvenile out of every 400
was arrested for a violent crime and by 1977 about one juvenile
out of every 140 committed murder, rape, robbery or aggravated
assault. About 30 percent of the crimes are solved among youth
under 18 years of age. At this period in our country's history,
we have a record number of persons in our jails and prisons--
over 530,000. New prisons are being built at $44,000 per bed
space and it takes over $17,000 a year to care for every person
the law officers lock up.

Therefore, the colleges and universities of the land have a
great opportunity to offer programs for prisoners. The author
has discussed these opportunities with officials of one of the
largest jails in the nation and plans are being made to begin a
new "college within the walls."

It is important that personnel in higher education speak out
on behalf of the poor, the oppressed, the repressed, the aged, the
prisoners, the hopeless, the helpless, the handicapped, the dis-
inherited, and the dispossesed in the world without the privileges
and advantages which college and university related persons take
for granted. No great changes for the betterment of people were
ever attained without concern, conflict, confrontation, and compassion. Higher education personnel need to be leaders in this
area of personal and social concern for persons.

Proposal for National Youth Employment (NYEP)

This is a national proposal for the employment of youth.
This nation is in one of its worst crisis periods with from

34 to 40 percent of its minority youth from 18 to 24 years of age unemployed so it calls for a new program to reach these youth. It is a proposal that includes a small cadre of full-time government staff members from already funded agencies to coordinate a group of volunteers, retired persons and others, who are financially independent from business, industry, labor and education. These volunteers will help coordinate a program in all 50 states and territories of the United States of America for employment of jobless youth. Volunteers will function in the capacities of administrators, teachers, counselors, and consultants. Cooperative private business, industry, labor and educational groups will obtain a tax deduction for their efforts in employing youth. Thus, this saves millions of dollars in cost sharing bureaucratic paper work. This program will, like the old National Youth Administration, Civilian Conservation Corps, and Job Corps, take a national approach to youth unemployment but it differs in being centered in the private sector of the economy in its administration, education and employment.

This national proposal, a combined cooperative educational work-study approach, has within its program a skill building approach that allows for educational credit in post-secondary institutions of higher education that prepares persons for a vocation or career. The financing of this program will come from the already existing state and federal funds available for student financial aids to higher education.

Volunteers from business, industry, labor and education as well as retired financially independent persons will provide at least one year of service as a governmental employee with an appropriate title according to their main function. For example, they might be called, such as, by their role: administrators--Program Administrator; teachers--Program Consultant; Program Instructor; counselors--Program Counselor; and consultants; A government title would be the reward for serving the country.

Volunteers would work out of the school districts and colleges-- many which have abundant office or residence hall space due to fewer students attending because of the lower birth rate. Office equipment from these schools and colleges would be used when necessary. In other cases, where certain business, religious, industry or labor groups have extra office room and equipment these volunteers would use these facilities.

The first phase of the proposal would be to bring together all known facts of past programs that have succeeded and have failed in employing youth. Then, the best elements of the most successful programs would be used where they have the finest opportunity to work in a particular setting.

Nationally known persons from the fields of sports, movies, and so forth would volunteer to hold conferences throughout the

447

nation where jobless youth are invited to attend half day (after-noon) programs to investigate entering one of the available pro-grams in their area. Youth would be bussed in using school district busses paid for by all-school fund drives in each com-munity.

Programs would be grouped, for example, in such categories as: Group I, Athletic Youth Employment Program; Group II, Ecology Youth Employment Program; Group III, National Defense Youth Em-ployment Program; Group IV, Agricultural Youth Employment Program; Group V, Business and Industry Youth Employment Program; and others.

Programs would work carefully and closely with all existing federal, state, and private agencies that have resources now available which are not fully utilized to aid the unemployed youth. State-wide conferences would be held in each state bring-ing together personnel from various public and private agencies to obtain their expertise and their resource support.

Any additional governmental employees that may be hired to help carry out the principles, policies, and programs of this proposal would all be at a reasonable salary to avoid high cost administration.

Additional details on this proposal and references document-ing this proposal are in the process of being completed.

A National Youth Employment Foundation, non-profit foundation, would be established that would work with all educational institu-tions, private social agencies, and government offices and that would obtain funds from private business, industry, and labor for youth employment programs as well as to do evaluations of youth employment programs. This Foundation would serve as a permanent organization around which to build future programs in the area of youth guidance for jobs and employment.

Perpetual Problems

The problems of higher education institutions are also the problems of College Student Affairs Divisions. Therefore, these problems are some of the "mutual monsters of the midway" or "campus circuses" that play their reoccuring themes. These selected problems have their roots from the beginning of colleges in this country. Thus, they have been with us a long time. Consequently, the cliche "nothing is permanent but change itself" is true but only in the context of these persistent problems. This is not to practice rational reductionism here so as to collapse all higher education problems to six selective--and not exhaustive problems--but only to try to be reasonable and man-ageable by giving representative samples within the colleges over the ages. Some large problems are not mentioned here, for example, inadequate and impersonal teaching has always been a problem.

Problems Ever Present In Higher Education

As one reviews the history of American higher education from 1636 (founding of privately controlled Harvard College) to 1978 (founding of another new public community college), history seems to repeat itself or at least never seems to change greatly on the big issues such as will be mentioned here. These issues are ones that College Student Personnel workers will need to deal with in the years ahead along with other college personnel (faculty, administrators, and support workers). Some selected issues are:

1. Financing of higher education: How much more can the cost of higher education be carried by the student (consumer), the state, and the federal government for the inflationary costs keep rising each year. With student enrollments decreasing due to the lower birth rates, financial contraints and other factors, institutions have been forced--as in the historical past--to made budget cutbacks in the Student Affairs Division as well as in the Academic Affairs. This affects all of the areas of the Office of Student Financial Aids as well as all of the Student Affairs Division.

2. Relevance of higher education curriculum: Since the curriculum traditionally seems to lag behind socio-economic trends, how to deal with the gap between available jobs and college academic majors continues to be a perpetual problem. The persistent liberal vs. vocational-technical or general vs. specialized education and efficiency and excellence problems will persist as but one example. Career counseling will continue to grow and develop to serve students.

3. Legal issues in higher education: With students and staff more aware of their legal rights, more laws protecting student and staff rights, and more legal advocates pushing for rights--legal issues have been growing annually on the campuses. This continued concern seems to be developing into a major challenge to authority and responsibility of the institution and its officials (individual vs. institutional control). More students and staff have discovered they can sue the college or university for any problem that stops their wish or need. The persistent problem of elitism vs. egalitarianism or quality vs. equality will keep us occupied until the end of the earth. As long as discrimination exists on the basis of sex, race, religion or ethnic origin, it will affect higher education so college Affirmative Action Services will also get more involved in these thorny difficulties along with College Legal Counsel Services. The question of where the responsibility, authority and autonomy of the college begins

and where it ends (and In Loco Parentis matters too) still persists
as a value question. The Ombudsperson role or function is still
an approach that could work through some of these cases that
could be settled better out of court for all parties to save
time, money, feelings, and frustrations.

4. Student discontent and unrest in higher education: The
discontent and unrest of students will be with us as long as there
will be colleges and institutions in society. Reasons for this
lie in academic curriculum, living conditions, individual freedom
for expression, problems of society, hunger, unemployment, underemployment, and so forth, and the list is endless. As students
become more self aware and assertative, they will find ways to
solve their needs. We must teach persons how best to live (value-
orientation to life) not just how to make a living. Of course,
student solutions will not always agree with those persons in
power positions within colleges and in communities. For example,
the Kent State University conflicts in 1970 over the National
Guard and student protest over the Indo-China Wars keeps going in
1978 with court battles over the building of a gym over the
property where four students were killed and nine students were
wounded in 1970. Consequently, the Student Affairs Division
staff members should recall these continuing problems students
remind society of in their protests and be skilled to use knowledge from "value education" and "peace education" to help students help themselves to reorder the priorities that perserve
our freedoms and our basic human rights. We have here the age
old problem of handling humanism vs. professionalism. Campus
religious personnel, when they work with students, can lead the
way in this area for they have training in the Judo-Christian
heritage and the world-wide religious traditions that laid a
basis for our United States Constitution and Bill of Rights. We
must consider the consequences of pursuing production and profit
values before people needs. Accountability for higher education
needs a "values checklist" not just a "how to graduate checklist."

5. Values in higher education: Institutions of higher
education must be concerned about their role in teaching about
values (from honesty to responsibility). We must try to define
our colleges' goals more on ethics than economics in dealing with
human equality needs. College professors and personnel must teach
values and this includes the value of intellectual curiosity as
well as social concern. Facing students with ethical questions
and illustrating to students ways to make responsible personal
and professional decisions is essential educational curriculum
content. As Dr. Theodore Hesburgh, C.S.C., President of Notre
Dame University has warned, "The university cannot afford to
ignore values that bear on global justice, professional values
and personal values like honesty, integrity, justice and compassion." In an increasingly more technological age where

machines not only do human work but even human decision making via computers, we must not turn our lives over to a "1984 Mentality." Perhaps, the "caring motif of the Good Samaritan story" is one of the greatest values to learn and to practice towards persons. Every college student personnel worker could do much by his or her modeling of the fundamental values mentioned here and by giving full support to student educational programs within the academic curriculum and in all extracurriculum that the Student Affairs Division has jurisdiction. Values by humans are not theory but practice as well as this poem illustrates:

You Tell On Yourself Values

You tell on yourself by the friends you seek,
By the manner in which you speak;
By the way you use your leisure time,
By the way you spend each dollar and dime.
You tell on yourself by the things you wear,
By the sort of things about which you care;
By the things that make you laugh;
By the records you play on your phonograph.
You tell what you are by the way you walk,
By the things of which you like to talk;
By the manner in which you take defeat,
And especially by the way you eat,
By the books you choose from the well-filled shelf,
In a thousand ways you tell on yourself.
So there really isn't a bit of sense in
   keeping up a false pretense.

(Anonymous)

6. <u>The power struggles with priorities in higher education</u>: The identification of power (political or personal) which is used to gain certain goals is fundamental. Priorities are paper promises without sufficient power to carry them out. College administration and some college Board of Trustees have long known how to do this, and recently Faculty Unions have been applying their power. Consequently, learning how to implement and actualize priorities is essential to solve the problems previously mentioned. Theory can only live when persons practice it. Too often, the best of professionals spend time formulating fine theories but neglect plans with behavioral objectives and adequate time to carry them (short range and long range goals) out.

American Higher Education: A Status Report

It seems appropriate that we cover some of the important accomplishments of American Higher Education since the founding of Harvard College in 1636. The author has traveled around the world and visited educational institutions in over 20 nations but never has read one article in the educational literature that treats all the elements mentioned here.

1.   The U.S. has the largest number of students attending post-secondary schools and colleges of any nation in the world. Over eleven million students are in various systems of higher education alone.

2.   The largest single business in the U.S is education--counting elementary, secondary, higher education, and continuing education.

3.   In 1976, was the all time high for total attendance for students in our schools and colleges--60.6 million attended with higher education still growing slightly with nursery school, elementary and secondary dropping.

4.   The U.S. has the widest variety of post-secondary schools and colleges of any nation in the world--vocational schools, two year colleges, four year colleges, multi-universities, post-graduate institutions, and continuing education institutions.

5.   The U.S. has the widest range of persons attending schools and colleges from the severely handicapped to senior citizens in their eighties.

6.   The U.S. has the most complex system of education ranging from total public to private that asks for no government aid due to their interpretation of the First Amendment on the Separation of Church and State.

7.   The U.S. has the most extensive educational counselor program and training programs for counseling for its schools and colleges of any nation on earth. In fact, school and college counseling was started in the U.S. The present membership in the world's largest educational counselors professional organization is over 44,000 in the American Personnel and Guidance Association that has over a dozen divisions. Counselors in higher education, that have membership in APGA, is over 12,000.

8.   The world's largest educational fraternity is Phi Delta Kappa and it is headquartered in Bloomington, Indiana.

9.   The world's largest combined labor unions in higher education include members of the National Education Association, the AFL-CIO Teachers Union, and the American Association of University Professors.

10.   The U.S. has the largest overseas educational program of any nation with the U.S. government alone managing over 250

schools, various religious groups having hundreds of schools and public state universities having many extension centers with the University of Maryland and Michigan State University among the largest.

After stating some selected facts about U.S. higher education, the author would also set forth some qualifying remarks such as:

1.   First, bigness or a quantity of a system does not mean excellence or quality is evident everywhere in a system. However, the U.S. also does have quality in its personnel, students, graduates, curriculum, facilities equipment and resources to match or surpass those in any nation today in specific situations. Of course, this means we can also improve our best.

2.   Second, the dual system of U.S. public and private education in this country is as well developed or supported as in any nations of the world. In fact, some nations have no private educational institutions at all and all education is under rigid and restrictive state regulation.

3.   Third, the U.S. is the most visited nation in the world when it comes to international educators coming to see our schools and colleges. Moreover, we have the largest body of foreign students studying here than of any nation in the world.

4.   Fourth, the world-wide brain drain continues with talented and educated persons from around the planet coming to settle here and still wanting to be U.S. citizens. Consequently, the U.S. is drawing some of the finest persons (educated) from overseas to benefit our educational institutions and the nation.

5.   Fifth, chief college student officers (vice-presidents for student affairs and/or deans of students) number 1,871 in this nation and have a mean salary of $22,524 according to the 1976-77 U.S. Department of Health, Education and Welfare statistics. So, the majority of the institutions of higher education have persons in this high position.

Future Factors to Consider

There are many accelerating changes occuring that are and will affect colleges and universities in the years ahead from college tuition costs predicted to double in the next ten years to many new types of jobs opening in the next decade. These factors mentioned here need to be considered in changing and adding Student Affairs programs and personnel. As the Student Affairs Divisions take into account these factors reported by the U.S. Census Bureau and Department of Labor in 1976, they will continue to develop--grow--and serve more students in post-secondary educational institutions.

1. In 1976, women made up 52 percent of the undergraduate student body outnumbering men by 200,000 and the trend for more women to attend post-secondary institutions is growing.

2. In 1977, a third of the college students are 25 and over, but predictions are that by 1980, 40 percent of the older students will compose the campus populations.

3. By the 1980's, one in five workers are predicted to be college educated as compared with one out of eight in 1978.

4. Changing job requirements seem to indicate that the average adult will have to develop new skills continuously.

5. Due to rapid changes in work, every person will remain a student most of his or her life.

6. More persons are retooling for newer and more suitable work every year so adults returning to post-secondary institutions for more education will be more common than uncommon.

7. Since 1970, the number of older students over 25 years, has more than doubled in attendance in colleges and universities.

8. Since 1966, the number of Black students have more than doubled from 4.6 percent to 10.7 percent in 1976 of the undergraduate student body of colleges.

For those Student Affairs Divisions that take into account such factors, it will mean at least some of the following:

1. Developing more career guidance and job placement positions;

2. Developing more programs for women;

3. Developing more minority student counseling positions;

4. Devloping more programs for older students' needs; and

5. Developing more programs for handicapped students.

Carl Rowan, at the Hamline University commencement of 1977, said that the greatest problem of our nation is the erosion of the family. He stated:

"We had just over 3 million single parents in 1970 and in 1977 we have 4.9 million. All but 500,000 of these families are headed by women, and those just happen to be the poorest families in the land because more

454

then half of the children in those families headed by
women live below the poverty line . . . . More than
11 million children under 18 live with only one parent
. . . . Those figures have something to do with the
crime statistics . . . and the teenage pregnancies that
are now epidemic in this society . . . . What can we
as a society do to give them the kind of opportunity
that will enable them to bring up families a lot more
stable than those in which they are growing up?"

Student Affairs personnel need to take into account these
factors, to respond in creative, proactive, and humanistic
ways. The time is short and planning should now be underway
for program implementation and personnel hiring.

New Areas for College Student Development

Some areas where college student personnel work might
move into in the near or in the distant future are the following:

1. Working with senior citizen retirement centers in
aiding senior citizens and in providing special extracurricular programs on the college campus for senior citizens
enrolled in college programs;

2. Working with students interested in developing more
meaningful marriages and families through special counseling
and educational types of projects;

3. Working with minority persons--in a sense we are all
minority persons in being different in our backgrounds and
human needs--on special self-concept and academic achievement
types of programs;

4. Working with meaningful programs for the handicapped
students who may be blind, disabled, and physically handicapped in some way to aid them in gaining their self-confidence and capacity to handle academic courses in responding
to the ideals of the Rehabilitation Act of 1973.

References

Brown, R. D. Student Development in Tomorrow's Higher Education--A Return to the Academy, Washington, D.C.: Student Personnel Series No. 15, American College Personnel Association, 1972.

Eddy, J. P. College Student Personnel Development, Counseling and Administration, Washington, D.C.: University Press of America, 1978.

Fitzgerald, L. E., Johnson, W. F., and Norris W. (Eds.) College Student Personnel: Readings and Bibliographies. Boston: Houghton Mifflin Company, 1970.

Giroux, R. F., Biggs, D. A., and Pietrofesa, J. J. (Eds.) College Student Development; Programs, Issures, and Practices. Washington, D.C.: American Personnel and Guidance Association Reprint Series Nine, 1977.

Harrington, T. F. Student Personnel Work in Urban Colleges. New York: Intext Education Publishers, 1974.

Herron, O. R. New Directions in Student Personnel Administration. New York: International Textbook Company, 1970.

Lloyd-Jones, E., and Smith, M. R. (Eds.) Student Personnel Work as Deeper Teaching. New York: Harper & Brothers, 1954.

Miller, T. K., and Prince, J. S. The Future of Student Affairs. San Francisco: Jossey-Bass, Inc., 1977.

Mueller, K. H. Student Personnel Work in Higher Education. Boston: Houghton-Mifflin Company, 1961.

References

O'Banion, T. and Thurston, A. (Eds.) Student Development Programs in the Community Junior College. New Jersey: Prentice-Hall, Inc., 1972.

Penney, J. F. Perspective and Challenge in College Personnel Work. Springfield: Charles C. Thomas Publishers- 1972.

Shaffer, R. H. and Martinson, W. D. Student Personnel Services in Higher Education. New York: The Center for Applied Research in Education, Inc., 1966.

Williamson, E. G. Student Personnel Services in Colleges and Universities. New York: McGraw-Hill Publishing Company, 1961.

Williamson E. G. and Biggs, D. A. Student Personnel Work: A Program of Development Relationships. New York: John Wiley and Sons, Inc., 1975.

BIBLIOGRAPHY

Preface

The bibliography for this book is divided into the subjects of each of the chapters. This system serves the reader well. First, the reader can turn to the table of contents and select the topic he or she is interested in. Second, the reader can turn to the list of references following each chapter and obtain additional resources to investigate this particular topic.

Hundreds of books and articles are listed in the manner just mentioned, following each chapter. This provides the reader with an abundant amount of resources.

Authors' Index

See page 466.

Subject Index

See Table of Contents, pages i through v.

APPENDIX A

COLLEGE STUDENT RETENTION STUDIES AND STRATEGIES

John Eddy, Judith Cochran, and Charles Haney

Introduction

In recent years, the educational literature has reflected a strong national concern for retaining students. Attempts to meet specific needs of various populations have included special types of arrangements made by colleges and universities; some have lowered admission requirements or initiated open admission policies, while others have provided special counseling and remedial programs. Times are becoming more difficult. The variety of strategies for addressing college student retention indicates trends for the future.

Some Current Strategies

Over 200 studies on college student retention have been identified (Eddy and Haney, 1980). Fawcett (1977) suggested the following as goals for all student retention plans: to increase student satisfaction and achievement at the university or college, and to reduce incidences of unnecessary dropping out and thereby increase student retention. Other recommendations by Fawcett include a marketing approach to student retention through the creation of an "office of student futures" whose principal function would be to provide a better quality of information to students about the institution's programs and services.

Cochran (1980) has categorized college student retention into three types--outreach, drop-in, and structured courses. The outreach program utilizes existing resources and does not alter the academic entrance requirements. A strategy in this approach would be to mail letters to entering high-risk students, who are identified by low high school grade point averages or low college entrance test scores, which would inform the students of appropriate campus counselors and existing support services.

459

The drop-in retention strategy would identify special counseling functions and services with the student initiating contact. Fawcett's (1977) "office of student futures" is an example of this approach. Other varieties of this theme range from Problem Intervention Teams in high student traffic areas, such as the student union, to 24-hour telephone assistance programs that provide short tapes on topics of concern to students.

The third retention format is the remedial course that has often been successful in reducing attrition. Titles of such courses reveal a variety of services, "Study Skills and Survival," "Students at Tech--Expand Your Potential," and "Vocabulary Development."

Whether outreach, drop-in, or course-structured retention strategies are implemented, the issue for many institutions is one of survival. When survival is at stake, attitudes do change and things get done (Eddy and Haney, 1980). In times of declining college-age populations (Astin, 1978), the importance of college retention is being recognized by both public and private institutions.

References

Astin, Alexander. "Observations on Higher Education," in NASPA Field Report, Volume III, Number 1, Fall, 1978.

Cochran, Judith A. "A National Profile of Student Retention Programs," unpublished paper given at Western College Reading Association, San Francisco, 1980.

Eddy, John, and Haney, Charles. "A Study of Student Retention Practices and Strategies among American Colleges and Universities." Denton, Texas; Division of Counselor Education, College of Education, North Texas State University, 1980.

Fawcett, Greg. Enrollment Decline, Parts One, Two and Three. Information Series C-77-1, 2, Office of Student Research, Vice Chancellor for Student Affairs, University of Missouri, Columbia, Missouri, February-March, 1977.

AN EXAMPLE OF HANDLING STUDENT CRISIS SITUATIONS:
CAMPUS CRISIS INTERVENTION SYSTEM

John Eddy, C. Alan Siebenthall, and Jackson Eng

Tarrant County Junior College, South Campus, in Fort
Worth, Texas, has a unique emergency network. Several counselors are equipped with an electronic device (pager) that
emits an audible signal plus a one-way voice communication
capability, which directs the counselors to a specific location or to the nearest campus phone for an emergency message.
This crisis counseling emergency network provides the college
with a service that meets student needs immediately.

The approach was first proven successful and useful by
medical personnel who needed to keep in contact with their
patients in need of care. Counselors have adopted the system, and they take turns in the emergency crisis approach.

This emergency system, which has been in use for three
years on the campus, has been beneficial to both staff and
students. The following results have been achieved with the
use of the emergency crisis approach: (1) experienced counselors have been utilized to deal more effectively with on-
campus emergencies; (2) students are served immediately when
an emergency situation arises; (3) Student Development Services has proven itself better able to serve the staff and
students; (4) Student Development Services has made its fundamental accountability known to its public through this crisis
system; (5) the Student Development Services area is keeping
more accurate records of student emergencies and outcomes,
which facilitates follow-up.

In addition to the instant call system, various college
counselors and their helping professionals make up a crisis
intervention team of referral personnel. Crises areas range
from drug abuse to marital difficulties. After the students
are given initial interviews, they are referred to college
counselors or community agencies who will deal specifically

with their particular problems. Thus, together, the paging system and the helping professional referral system provide a comprehensive college campus crisis intervention system. Over a three-year period, with an average of six emergency calls per week for counselors on duty, lives have been saved and hundreds have been helped significantly by this service to students at Tarrant County Junior College.

AFFIRMATION

Edward C. Bonk

An affirmation pertains to something that is true. This affirmation is divided into two parts - the profession and the professionals.

A profession is a vocation requiring knowledge in some specialized field of learning. This knowledge is gained from professionals in the field and from the printed word and this book's special purpose is to promote the development of college student personnel workers.

Colleges and universities have long recognized the value of attending to the needs of students. Some of the primary activities include articulation with and admission to the institution. From that point, we see a developmental program of activities pertaining to the life of the student until graduation. Universities do not complete their involvement with students at graduation but continue with such activities as placement and alumni affairs.

Students who study this book will not only gain an overview of student personnel work, but will also get a feel for the writings of professionals in the field.

Persons who work in assisting students in institutions of higher learning have a tremendous responsibility for helping students develop to their fullest potential. This is not only an obligation on the part of the student personnel worker but it is the right of the student that this be accomplished. Therefore, it behooves all of us to accept this responsibility and to carry it out to fruition. By doing this, we will help not only individuals, but all of society.

Having worked in institutions of higher education for nearly thirty years, I have seen the continued development of the student personnel field as well as a rise in the level of

professionalism. Underlying this growth of professional skills
is the recognition of individuals as people with needs - demonstrating a real caring for others. Unless we care for our
fellow human beings, our life and our work are very shallow and
have little meaning to ourselves and others. This is best
exemplified by Dr. C. Gilbert Wrenn in his care and concern
for all people. It is only when we care for others that their
best can be expected from them.

During the past four decades we have seen development in
many aspects of the field of counseling and student personnel
work. Counseling theories have grown and developed during
these years. It is also noteworthy that as "new" theories
have evolved that the "old" theorists have not stagnated but
have continued to grow in their professional development. For
example, let's examine the changes in views of such leaders
as E. G. Williamson, Carl R. Rogers and C. Gilbert Wrenn.
In the late 1930's, Williamson, working with John Darley at
the University of Minnesota, developed what, at that time,
was called directive counseling, which is often called trait
and factor counseling. During these early years, Williamson
was stereotyped as being directive - as one who "told" clients
what they should do. In reality, this really was not what
Williamson was like. I recall listening to him give a presentation at an APGA Convention, and the words and ideas he expressed reminded me of Carl Rogers' philosophy since he, too, was
concerned with the client's feelings and needs.

We can also see how Rogers' work in counseling has developed since he published Counseling and Psychotherapy in 1942.
During the past several years he has broadened his base by
working with groups and in family counseling. During the latter
years, we see him more active in the counseling process. Rogers
has been stereotyped as the passive, client-centered therapist
but that categorization is not fair as he has moved beyond
the client-centered classification.

G. Gilbert Wrenn developed in a unique way because he has
integrated many psychological theories into his philosophical
approach to counseling during his professional career. At one
point in his life, he stated he was an eclectic and chose what
was most appropriate in working with a client. I know him as
a professional and as a friend and can attest to his caring
for people. He is tuned in to the feelings of others which

is a natural outpouring of his being.

If each of us is to continue to grow personally and professionally, then we must be careful not to stereotype others but rather continue to read and share the works of the leaders in our profession as we grow with them. This is our challenge and our responsibility as professionals in the field of counseling and student personnel work.

AUTHORS' INDEX